Wissenschaftliche Untersuchungen
zum Neuen Testament · 2. Reihe

Herausgeber / Editor
Jörg Frey

Mitherausgeber / Associate Editors
Friedrich Avemarie · Judith Gundry-Volf
Martin Hengel · Otfried Hofius · Hans-Josef Klauck

213

Nicole Kelley

Knowledge and Religious Authority in the Pseudo-Clementines

Situating the *Recognitions* in Fourth Century Syria

Mohr Siebeck

NICOLE KELLEY, born 1975; 2003 Ph.D. in The Study of Religion, Harvard University; currently Assistant Professor of Religion at Florida State University.

BR
65
C55
R435
2006

ISBN 3-16-149036-3
ISBN-13 978-3-16-149036-1
ISSN 0340-9570 (Wissenschaftliche Untersuchungen zum Neuen Testament, 2. Reihe)

Die Deutsche Bibliothek lists this publication in the Deutsche Nationalbibliographie; detailed bibliographic data is available in the Internet at *http://dnb.ddb.de.*

The book was printed by Gulde-Druck in Tübingen on non-aging paper and bound by Buchbinderei Held in Rottenburg/N.

Printed in Germany.

For Henry

Preface

This book began in 2001 as a dissertation project at Harvard University, under the direction of François Bovon and Karen King. Up to that point I'd been interested primarily in questions of ancient Jewish and Christian identity, and issues revolving around Jewish-Christian relations in the ancient world. I had not worked on much of anything past the third century C.E. when François suggested that I consider Pseudo-Clementine literature as a dissertation topic. In many ways, this made perfect sense. The Pseudo-Clementines are perhaps the most famous example of "Jewish-Christian" texts that survive from antiquity, so what better way to study the construction and maintenance of religious identities than to look at the work of an author who finds himself betwixt and between Judaism and Christianity? These texts also had another very important thing going for them – one thing sought after by every prospective dissertation writer. They're neglected. Hardly anyone talks about the Pseudo-Clementines these days. This sounded like a potential contribution to scholarship.

Soon I began to meet people at conferences who, when they found out I'd decided to work on the Pseudo-Clementines, told me the story of someone else who had also written a dissertation on these texts at Harvard, and (as they told the story, anyway) the experience apparently did him in. After he finished the dissertation, he decided that the academic path wasn't for him. One day he loaded up all of his academic books and sold them out of the back of his vehicle, right in the parking lot in front of Andover Hall. The implication seemed to be that I, too, might find myself being driven away from an academic career by a set of late antique documents. I began to understand their concerns for my mental health as I became more familiar with modern scholarship on the Pseudo-Clementines. Much of it is at least one hundred years old, preoccupied with source-critical questions or arcane theological issues that hardly seem useful or even relevant today. The same might be said of the ancient texts themselves, which are long and repetitive and contain material that is not particularly original. Maybe this wasn't such a good dissertation idea after all.

As I began to write, however, I quickly realized that the Pseudo-Clementines were fascinating in ways that had not been addressed by modern scholars. For instance, there was plenty of literature on hypothetical first- and second-century sources that were thought to lie behind the texts, but remarkably little investigation of the fourth-century *Homilies* and *Recognitions*. Almost no one was looking at what these texts have to say, and how they fit into a broader understanding of early Christian history. Moreover, it seemed that people interested in the Pseudo-Clementines were not particularly curious about the fourth century, and very few people interested in the fourth century were concerned with the Pseudo-Clementines: most investivations of fourth-century Syria discuss the usual suspects such as Ephrem and Arianism and mention the Pseudo-Clementines briefly or skip them altogether. I started to wonder what might happen if these texts were brought into conversation with their fourth-century context. What do the Pseudo-Clementines tell us about fourth-century Syria, and how can fourth-century Syria help us to understand the Pseudo-Clementines? These are the initial questions that drove me to write this book.

As my research progressed, it became clear that the Pseudo-Clementines are important for understanding the history of how Christians constructed their own identities and orthodoxies and negotiated them in conversation with other groups. The *Recognitions* is particularly useful, because it gives us a window onto a rather complex religious, social and political situation that involved not only Jews and pagans but also a variety of Christian groups. The multifaceted rivalries reflected and embedded in the text, and the text's interests in authentic tradition and correct belief that lie behind its portrait of Peter, often have not been appreciated. This book seeks to bring some of these issues to light.

I am grateful to François Bovon for his gentle guidance and unfailing support, and his unparalleled knowledge of early Christian apocryphal literature, all of which have helped me tremendously. I thank Karen King too, for helping to shape the questions I ask of texts both ancient and modern, for being a great conversation partner, and for inspiring me – you make your students want to be as smart and talented as you are. I am grateful to those who have read the manuscript at various stages of its life and given me helpful feedback and criticism, especially Stanley Jones, Ellen Aitken, AnneMarie Luijendijk, Laura Beth Bugg, and Catherine Playoust.

Much of the writing of this book was made possible by a Graduate Society Dissertation Fellowship at Harvard University. The remainder of the project was completed in the company of several wonderfully supportive colleagues and friends in the Department of Religion at Florida State University, whose kind words of encouragement have meant a great deal to me. I am especially indebted to David Levenson, both for his friendship and for his generosity as a colleague. Two FSU graduate students also played essential roles in the production of this book. Jeff Petsis graciously helped with correction of my Latin translations, and Jason Staples worked tirelessly as a fact-checker and indexer. I am grateful to Jörg Frey and Henning Ziebritzki for their interest in the manuscript, and to Jana Trispel at Mohr Siebeck for her corrections and helpful suggestions. Finally, I thank Carol Birnbaum and Matt Day, for reasons they know.

Tallahassee, Florida, April 2006   *Nicole Kelley*

Table of Contents

Chapter 1

Studying the Pseudo-Clementines

Introduction

The historian Adolph von Harnack has said that "the Pseudo-Clementines contribute absolutely nothing to our knowledge of the origin of the Catholic Church and doctrine."[1] In his *History of Dogma*, von Harnack insists that the Pseudo-Clementines – a group of ancient Christian writings falsely attributed to Clement of Rome[2] which detail his travels with the apostle Peter, their ongoing disputes with Simon Magus, and Clement's eventual reunion with long-lost members of his family – are interesting only insofar as they contain remnants of earlier traditions about church origins. In von Harnack's estimation these texts do not preserve such ancient traditions about catholic Christianity, and as a result they are

---

[1] Adolph von Harnack, *History of Dogma*, vol. 1, transl. from the 3rd German edition by Neil Buchanan (Gloucester, MA: Peter Smith, 1974) 315. This view is affirmed by John Chapman, "Origen and the Date of Pseudo-Clement," *Journal of Theological Studies* 3 (1902) 441; and Hans Lietzmann, *The Beginnings of the Christian Church*, transl. Bertram Lee Woolf (rev. ed.; New York: Charles Scribner's Sons, 1949) 188. Cf. George Howard, "The Pseudo-Clementine Writings and Shem-Tob's Hebrew Matthew," *New Testament Studies* 40 (1994) 622: "It is doubtful that the Pseudo-Clementines contribute nothing to our knowledge of the origin of the Catholic Church. They have certainly influenced the study of early Jewish Christianity, and this can hardly be separated from the study of early Catholic Christianity." Portions of Chapter 1 appeared in an earlier publication: Nicole Kelley, "Problems of Knowledge and Authority in the Pseudo-Clementine Romance of Recognitions," *JECS* 13.3 (2005) 315-348.

[2] For a discussion of the relation between the "Clement" of the Pseudo-Clementines, Clement the bishop of Rome, and Flavius Clemens, see Bernard Pouderon, "Clément de Rome, Flavius Clemens et le Clément Juif," *Studi su Clemente Romano: Atti degli Incontri di Roma, 29 marzo e 22 novembre 2001*, ed. Philippe Luisier (Orientalia Christiana Analecta 268; Rome: Pontificio Istituto Orientale, 2003) 197-218; idem, "Flavius Clemens et le proto-Clément juif du roman pseudo-clémentin," *Apocrypha* 7 (1996) 63-79, esp. 66; F. Stanley Jones, "Clement of Rome and the *Pseudo-Clementines:* History and/or Fiction," *Studi su Clemente Romano*, 139-61; Meinolf Vielberg, *Klemens in den pseudoklementinischen Rekognitionen: Studien zur literarischen Form des spätantiken Romans* (TU 145; Berlin: Akademie Verlag, 2000); and Georges Ory, "Réflexions sur les écrits clémentins: Qui était Clément?" *Cahiers du Cercle Ernest-Renan* 32 (1984) 33-38.

altogether unremarkable.[3] Most authors have disagreed with von Harnack's assessment of the *historical* value of the traditions preserved in these texts, arguing instead that the Pseudo-Clementines do contain traditions that can be traced to the formative period of the church.[4] However, by focusing largely on these older traditions that lie behind the Pseudo-Clementines, they have upheld one of von Harnack's *theological* presuppositions: these texts are valuable if and only if they are repositories of earlier Christian materials.[5] Because they are thought to preserve more ancient sources, these texts have been mined by contemporary scholars who hope to shed light on Christian origins.[6] As recently as 2003, for example, F. Lapham introduced his treatment of the Pseudo-Clementines by saying that "the value of such purportedly historical works lies...in their ability to throw into relief the traditions that lie behind their sources."[7] As a result of this perspective, the *Homilies* and *Recognitions* – the two major works of

---

[3] Von Harnack's argument rests on two observations. The first is doctrinal: Jewish Christianity, defined by its nationalistic and legalistic proclivities, had very little influence on the rest of Christianity, which was universalistic in scope (*History of Dogma*, 1.289-90). The "immediate sources" of the Pseudo-Clementines reveal "a Jewish Christianity strongly influenced by Catholicism and Hellenism" (1.315). Because of his assumption about the mutual incompatibility of Jewish and catholic Christianity, von Harnack doubts that this kind of accommodating Jewish Christianity exists; he suggests that it may be a "Catholic literary product" (1.314-315). The second is chronological: even if the Pseudo-Clementines may be used "to determine the tendencies and inner history of syncretistic Jewish Christianity" – not catholic Christianity – "[i]t cannot be made out with certainty, how far back the first sources of the Pseudo-Clementines date" (1.315).

[4] To give but one example, the Pseudo-Clementines have been studied as part of the search for the historical Jesus; see Leslie L. Kline, *The Sayings of Jesus in the Pseudo-Clementine Homilies* (SBLDS 14; Missoula, MT: Scholars, 1975).

[5] This has been noted as well by Annette Yoshiko Reed, "'Jewish Christianity' after the 'Parting of the Ways,'" in *The Ways that Never Parted: Jews and Christians in Late Antiquity and the Early Middle Ages*, ed. Adam H. Becker and Annette Yoshiko Reed (Tübingen: Mohr Siebeck, 2003) 199-201, 218 n. 91.

[6] In particular, they have been used by F. C. Baur and the Tübingen school as evidence of conflict between two competing doctrinal trajectories in earliest Christianity: Petrine "Jewish" Christianity and Pauline Christianity. The classic formulation of this thesis is F. C. Baur, "Die Christuspartei in der korinthischen Gemeinde, der Gegensatz des petrinischen und paulinischen Christenthums in der ältesten Kirche, der Apostel Petrus in Rom," *Tübinger Zeitschrift für Theologie* 5 (1831) 61-206. In this context one might also mention the elusive search for the *Kerygmata Petrou* – thought to be an early source with gnosticizing Jewish-Christian tendencies that was used by the author of the *Grundschrift* – undertaken by Georg Strecker and others. G. Strecker, *Das Judenchristentum in den Pseudoklementinen* (TU 70; 2nd ed. rev.; Berlin: Akademie-Verlag, 1981) 92-96.

[7] F. Lapham, *Peter: The Myth, the Man and the Writings. A Study of Early Petrine Text and Tradition* (JSNTSS 239; London: Sheffield Academic Press, 2003) 83.

Pseudo-Clementine literature – have often been reduced to textual husks to be discarded in the search for historical or dogmatic kernels of earliest Christianity.

The narratives of the Pseudo-Clementine writings have been neglected even when the project of Christian origins is not so clearly at stake. This disregard seems to be a product of what might be termed "the lousy book factor." Richard Pervo says of the *Recognitions* and its treatment of Paul *qua* Simon Magus, "This is a smear-piece no less dreadful than it is tedious."[8] Pervo's wry comment hints at one frequent criticism of the *Recognitions*: it seems to be poorly edited, a series of juxtaposed and inadequately integrated sources rather than a coherent narrative. M. J. Edwards makes a typical assessment of the author's editorial prowess: "The editor of the *Recognitions* (one whom it would be equally uncritical and unkind to style the author) convicts himself of incompetence when he recapitulates a series of homilies as though they occurred in the novel, though in fact he has retailed the plan and content of a rather different work (3.85 [*sic*])."[9]

To be sure, many ancient novels have been criticized repeatedly, in antiquity and in modern scholarship, for their stylistic and literary faults. For example, Brigitte Egger has noted the frosty reception of the ancient novel in general and Chariton's *Callirhoe* in particular: "Scholarly opinions of the genre as a whole have tended to be low since nineteenth-century philologists dismissed it as popular and trivial, and *Callirhoe* was seen as a simple book aimed at 'the poor in spirit'."[10] Other works are held in even less esteem. David Konstan notes that Xenophon of Ephesus' *Ephesian Tale* is "universally regarded as the worst of the lot."[11] But the *Recognitions* arguably stands out even in such illustrious company, because it is long, boring, repetitive, and full of chronological and theological difficulties. To give an example of a chronological

---

[8] Richard I. Pervo, "The Ancient Novel Becomes Christian," in G. Schmeling, ed., *The Novel in the Ancient World* (Leiden: E. J. Brill, 1996) 707.

[9] M. J. Edwards, "The *Clementina*: A Christian Response to the Pagan Novel," *Classical Quarterly* 42 (1992) 461. Edwards, who is not particularly interested in the traditions behind the *Recognitions* or the text's relationship to the larger Pseudo-Clementine corpus, seems to misunderstand the function of the "table of contents" given in *Rec* 3.75.1-12.

[10] Brigitte Egger, "Looking at Chariton's *Callirhoe*," in *Greek Fiction: The Greek Novel in Context*, ed. J. R. Morgan and Richard Stoneman (London and New York: Routledge, 1994) 31, quoting B. E. Perry, *The Ancient Romances* (Berkeley and Los Angeles: University of California, 1967) 177.

[11] David Konstan, "Xenophon of Ephesus: Eros and narrative in the novel," in *Greek Fiction: The Greek Novel in Context*, 49.

inconsistency, *Rec* 1.27-71,[12] which has been identified as the *Anabathmoi Jakobou* mentioned by Epiphanius in *Haer.* 30.16,[13] contains a chronology that differs from the rest of the *Recognitions*. *Rec* 1.7.3 leads the reader to believe that Jesus is still alive when Clement arrives in Caesarea, but *Rec* 1.43.3 says that seven years have already passed since Jesus' death.[14] This same source also makes it difficult to reconstruct the *Recognitions'* position on astrological knowledge. *Rec* 1.32.3 indicates that astrology led Abraham to knowledge of God,[15] but *Rec* 9.17ff (which itself belongs to another source layer) is an extended discourse against the possibility of astrological knowledge. At points like these, the *Recognitions'* willingness to place different sources side by side,[16] with seemingly little concern for the chronological and theological contradictions created in the process, suggests its author's lack of interest in the editorial process. This would seem to confirm Stanley Jones' observation that "R [the author of the *Recognitions*] is generally viewed as a redactor whose tendency can be broadly determined but whose system of thought does not merit extensive discussion."[17] On this reading, the *Recognitions* is hardly a book at all, but merely a vessel for the sources it contains.

Critiques of the Pseudo-Clementines' editorial finesse are also criticisms of their originality. These charges of unoriginality begin not

---

[12] There has been a great deal of debate on the extent of this source and its precise identification, but there exists little doubt that this section of the *Recognitions* comes from a separate source. On this question see Robert E. van Voorst, *The Ascents of James: History and Theology of a Jewish-Christian Community* (SBLDS 112; Atlanta: Scholars, 1989) 1-46.

[13] The *Recognitions* uses this source by virtue of its inclusion in the *Grundschrift*. While van Voorst supports the identification of *Rec* 1.33-71 with the *Anabathmoi Jakobou* (van Voorst, *Ascents of James*, 43-46), Stanley Jones argues against this connection (F. S. Jones, *An Ancient Jewish Christian Source on the History of Christianity: Pseudo-Clementine Recognitions 1.27-71* [Atlanta: Scholars, 1995], 146-48).

[14] F. S. Jones, "The Pseudo-Clementines: A History of Research Part I," *The Second Century* 2 (1982) 24 n. 177. As Jones notes, this chronological inconsistency was first observed by G. Uhlhorn, *Die Homilien und Recognitionen des Clemens Romanus nach ihrem Ursprung und Inhalt dargestellt* (Göttingen: Dieterische Buchhandlung, 1854) 314-315.

[15] This was a common trope in ancient literature, probably owing to the mention of Abraham's Chaldaean heritage in Genesis 11.27. On this see J. L. Kugel, *Traditions of the Bible: A Guide to the Bible As It Was at the Start of the Common Era* (Cambridge, MA: Harvard University Press, 1998) 249-51.

[16] Although in many cases the *Grundschrift* originally combined the various sources in question, there are also a number of instances (e.g. the two astrology passages just listed) where the *Recognitions* appears to be responsible for the juxtaposition.

[17] F. Stanley Jones, "The Pseudo-Clementines: A History of Research Part II," *The Second Century* 2 (1982) 77.

with the *Recognitions*, but with the *Grundschrift*, the hypothetical common source for the *Recognitions* and the *Homilies*.[18] Bernhard Rehm, Hans Joachim Schoeps, and Georg Strecker each have argued that the author of the *Grundschrift* was not really an author, but a compiler who contributed almost nothing original. In Rehm's words, "Die Grundschrift ist nur zum geringsten Teil ein originales Werk."[19] Rehm goes on to show that virtually all of the *Grundschrift*'s ideas may be traced to other sources. This criticism of the *Grundschrift*'s originality applies to the *Homilies* and *Recognitions* as well, since these extant texts seem to be little more than tendentious copies of their predecessor. Because none of these authors added much that was new, source criticism does not really ignore the narratives by looking *behind* the texts – after all, the narratives themselves have nothing to offer but a mishmash of sources. In this model, source criticism produces most of (if not all) the information anyone could want to know about the Pseudo-Clementines, and is consequently more worthwhile than other modes of analysis.[20]

These criticisms might lead one to wonder if the Pseudo-Clementines are worth reading, or if they contribute anything new to our knowledge of the ancient world. To my way of thinking, however, such criticisms of the Pseudo-Clementines' editing and originality have never addressed one of the fundamental questions they raise: Why would anyone go to the trouble of creating a text that included all of these sources in the first place?[21] Why

---

[18] The *Grundschrift* is much like Q in the Two-Source Hypothesis of the New Testament Synoptic Problem.

[19] B. Rehm, "Zur Entstehung der pseudoclementinischen Schriften," *Zeitschrift für die Neutestamentliche Wissenschaft* 37 (1938) 157. See also H. J. Schoeps, *Theologie und Geschichte des Judenchristentums* (Tübingen: J.C.B. Mohr [Paul Siebeck], 1949) 38-42; and Strecker, *Judenchristentum*, 256, 259.

[20] A quick read of Stanley Jones' important review of the history of Pseudo-Clementine scholarship suggests that this view has prevailed throughout much of the history of scholarship on the Pseudo-Clementines; virtually all of the discussion centers around source critical issues.

[21] As Kate Cooper notes, although "the literary art of the *Recognitions* is by no means breath-taking," it remains important to understand how the *Recognitions* uses sources and generic conventions in support of its apologetic agenda. Kate Cooper, "Matthidia's Wish: Division, Reunion, and the Early Christian Family in the Pseudo-Clementine *Recognitions*," in *Narrativity in Biblical and Related Texts/La narrativité dans la Bible et les textes apparentés*, ed. G. J. Brooke and J.-D. Kaestli (Leuven: Leuven University Press, 2000) 244-45. Indeed, as is the case with other areas of research, this shift toward redaction-critical and narrative-critical studies of the Pseudo-Clementines is characteristic of more recent scholarship; see e.g. Reed, "'Jewish Christianity,'" 203; Frédéric Amsler, "Les *Reconnaissances* du Pseudo-Clément comme catéchèse romanesque," in *La Bible en récits: l'exégèse biblique à l'heure du lecteur*, ed. D. Marguerat (Geneva: Labor et Fides, 2003) 443; Dominique Côté, *Le thème de l'opposition entre Pierre et Simon dans les Pseudo-Clémentines* (Études Augustiniennes,

produce and reproduce a text in which practically every idea is derivative, either because it has been adopted from another specific source or because it is a commonplace in ancient thought? More specifically, why would someone be interested in placing a philosophical treatise alongside an astrological one, and why should these two sets of material belong with a story about Jesus and the apostles or a romance of recognitions? Might such juxtapositions reveal something about the Pseudo-Clementines' socio-historical and theological context? This book seeks to answer precisely these kinds of questions.

It would be impossible, however, to ask these questions of the entire Pseudo-Clementine corpus in a single study. I have chosen to focus on the *Recognitions* rather than the *Homilies* or the *Grundschrift* for three main reasons.[22] First, the *Recognitions* generally has been given less attention than its sister text, probably because it lacks the very qualities that have made the *Homilies* interesting (specifically, its preoccupation with Arianism as well as its "Jewish Christian" elements, which define correct religious belief and practice in the language of late antique, possibly rabbinic,[23] Judaism). This makes the *Recognitions* an ideal prospect for a new study. Second, the *Recognitions* (more so than the *Homilies*) places special emphasis on the romance of recognitions and the astrological materials, which I regard as intimately connected with its larger epistemological concerns. This emphasis allows me to make a stronger case for the sources' integral connection to the author's main ideas about knowledge. Third, the *Recognitions'* interest in establishing and maintaining a particular vision of orthodoxy[24] allows me to connect my

---

Série Antiquités 167; Paris: Institut d'Études Augustiniennes, 2001) 3; idem, "La fonction littéraire de Simon le Magicien dans les Pseudo-Clémentines," *Laval théologique et philosophique* 57 (2001) 513-23; and William Robins, "Romance and Renunciation at the Turn of the Fifth Century," *JECS* 8 (2000) 531-57.

[22] My treatment of the *Homilies* is in most cases limited to citations of parallels it shares with the *Recognitions*.

[23] On this see Albert Baumgarten, "Literary Evidence for Jewish Christianity in the Galilee," in *The Galilee in Late Antiquity*, ed. L. Levine (New York, 1992) 41-47.

[24] For example, the *Recognitions* eliminates many of the Jewish Christian and anti-Pauline elements of the Grundschrift, even though these have been preserved to some degree; it downplays the syzygy principle and the doctrine of false pericopes. See F. J. A. Hort, *Notes Introductory to the Study of the Clementine Recognitions: A Course of Lectures* (London and New York: Macmillan, 1901) 120; G. Strecker, "The Pseudo-Clementines: Introduction," in *New Testament Apocrypha, Volume Two: Writings Related to the Apostles; Apocalypses and Related Subjects*, rev. ed., ed. E. Hennecke and W. Schneemelcher and trans. R. McL. Wilson (Tübingen: Mohr Siebeck, 1989) 485; and Rehm, "Zur Entstehung," 161-63. I use the term "orthodoxy" advisedly here: my intention is not to suggest that one set of beliefs was universally accepted by fourth-century Christians, but rather to indicate that many Christians of this era – whatever specific set of beliefs they may have held – were interested in the project of constructing

argument about knowledge to the text's claims about its own authority. By arguing that the author of the *Recognitions* uses diverse materials in the service of a coherent narrative agenda about knowledge and authority, I hope to use the *Recognitions* as a case in point to demonstrate why the Pseudo-Clementines should no longer be neglected, but rather should be considered as a valuable resource for the study of ancient Christianity. In order to begin this process of looking at the narrative of the *Recognitions* in its own right, we must first become more familiar with the entire corpus of Pseudo-Clementine literature.

Overview of Pseudo-Clementine Literature

The Pseudo-Clementines consist primarily of two lengthy works of approximately the same size: the *Recognitions*, which is divided into ten books, and the *Homilies*, which consists of twenty "sermons." Both works claim to be written by Clement of Rome, and include first-person accounts of his conversion, his adventures with Peter, and his separation and eventual reunion with long-lost members of his family. The subplot of Clement losing and later finding his family members belongs to a specific genre known as the *romance of recognitions*, of which the Pseudo-Clementines are the first extant Christian example.[25] The title of the *Recognitions* reflects this generic categorization, while the *Homilies* are so called because they consist mainly of addresses given by Peter.

In addition to the *Recognitions* and the *Homilies*, there are two epistles that claim to be written by Peter and Clement, both addressed to James. These are called the *Epistula Petri* and the *Epistula Clementis*, respectively. At the end of the *Epistula Petri* there is a brief appendix,

---

an orthodoxy. This desire to bring ideas, texts and the like in line with beliefs perceived to be correct is clearly behind the Recognitionist's appropriation and modification of its predecessor the *Grundschrift*.

[25] F. Stanley Jones, "Clementines, Pseudo-," *The Anchor Bible Dictionary*, ed. David N. Freedman (New York: Doubleday, 1992) 1.1061. There has been extensive scholarly discussion of the relationship between the romance of recognitions and the pagan novel. See e.g. Wilhelm Bousset, "Die Wiedererkennungs-Fabel in den pseudoklementinischen Schriften, den Menächmen des Plautus und Shakespeares Komödie der Irrungen," *Zeitschrift für die neutestamentliche Wissenschaft* 5 (1904) 21; Hans Waitz, *Die Pseudoklementinen Homilien und Rekognitionen: Eine Quellenkritische Untersuchung* (TU 10.4; Leipzig: J. Hinrichs, 1904) 250-51; Werner Heintze, *Der Klemensroman und seine griechischen Quellen* (TU 40.2; Leipzig: J. C. Hinrichs, 1914) 114-38; cf. Erwin Rohde, *Der griechische Roman und seine Vorläufer* (5th ed.; Hildesheim and New York: Georg Olms, 1974) 507, and Karl Kerényi, *Die griechisch-orientalische Romanliteratur in religionsgeschichtlicher Beleuchtung: Ein Versuch mit Nachbetrachtungen* (Darmstadt: Wissenschaftliche Buchgesellschaft, 1962) 77.

usually called the *Contestatio,* in which James instructs his hearers about the transmission of the books of Peter's preaching. In the manuscript tradition the letters typically are attached to the beginning of the *Homilies.* There is also a translator's preface to the Latin edition of the *Recognitions* that was written by Rufinus of Aquileia.

The Pseudo-Clementine Narrative

Before we examine the Pseudo-Clementine texts' individual tendencies and characteristics, we need to take a closer look at the narrative outline they all share.[26] The *Recognitions,* which presents itself as an autobiographical account written by Clement and addressed to James, begins with Clement's recollection of his concerns about philosophical and religious problems during his boyhood in Rome.[27] He continues to be vexed because philosophical reasoning provides no definitive answers to his questions, until one day he hears rumors that a Judean is preaching the kingdom of the invisible God and promising eternal life to his disciples. This rumor is confirmed when Barnabas preaches in Rome, where he is inhospitably received by the populace and finds refuge with Clement.

Barnabas returns to Judea for a feast; Clement is detained momentarily but soon follows Barnabas and is introduced to Peter. Peter teaches Clement about the True Prophet, who will bring an end to all the uncertainty troubling Clement. The narrative then says that Clement wrote down Peter's teaching and sent the book to James. Peter and Simon, a magician from Samaria, are scheduled to dispute with one another soon after Clement arrives in Judea, but Simon postpones the debate. This allows Peter an opportunity to tell Clement about God's actions from the beginning of the world until the present day. Peter's account includes a story about a disputation on the temple steps between the apostles and members of various Jewish groups (priests, Sadducees, Samaritans, scribes and Pharisees, and disciples of John the Baptist). The apostles are just about to prevail when the disputation is interrupted by a ruckus – the instigator is unnamed but obviously Saul/Paul – during which James is thrown down the temple steps and the crowd is dispersed. The disciples flee to Jericho, and the nameless enemy goes to Damascus in pursuit of

---

[26] In choosing which materials to include here, I consulted the summaries of C. Bigg, "The Clementine Homilies," in *Studia Biblica et Ecclesiastica: Essays Chiefly in Biblical and Patristic Criticism* (Oxford: Clarendon, 1890) 2.158-60; G. Salmon, "Clementine Literature," in *A Dictionary of Christian Biography, Literature, Sects and Doctrines* (Boston: Little, Brown and Company, 1877) 568-70; and J. A. Fitzmyer, "The Qumran Scrolls, the Ebionites and their Literature," *Theological Studies* 16 (1955) 346.

[27] Clement's search for knowledge is, of course, one example of a common literary trope. See e.g. Justin, *dial.* 1-8; Plutarch, *Moralia* 410a-b, 421a-b; Josephus, *BJ* 2.8.14; *AJ* 13.5.9; 18.1.3; Lucian, *Pisc.* 11-12; Philostratus, *VA* 1.7; 6.11.

Peter and intent on causing havoc. In Jericho, James is informed by Zacchaeus that Simon is causing trouble at Caesarea. James then sends Peter to Caesarea to refute Simon, and Peter is instructed by James to report his activities every year.

The *Recognitions* then introduces two disciples of Peter, Niceta and Aquila, who are former associates of Simon. They tell Peter about Simon's activities and magical powers, noting that Simon believed his powers to have come from the soul of a murdered boy whose image was preserved in Simon's bedroom.[28] Peter then begins a three-day-long dispute with Simon that centers around problems of theodicy – namely, does the presence of evil in the world necessitate belief in a God different than the Creator? – and the question of the soul's immortality. Peter, knowing the skeletons in Simon's closet, offers to settle the debate by interrogating the soul of the murdered boy. Simon realizes his secret is out and humbles himself, but recants when he learns that Peter came by this knowledge through his associates rather than through prophetic ability. By this time the audience is indignant and Simon is driven away; Simon explains to his followers that he must leave because divine honors await him in Rome. Peter decides to follow Simon among the gentiles in order to expose his corruption. He sets out for Tripolis (the center of Simon's activity) after remaining in Caesarea for three months, having worked to further establish the church and having ordained Zacchaeus as its bishop. At this point the narrative says that Clement sent to James an account of Peter's discourses in ten books, giving a brief summary of each of these books.

When Peter arrives in Tripolis, he learns that Simon has again evaded him by fleeing to Syria. Peter then takes the opportunity to instruct the folks in Tripolis. These discourses, which contain a lengthy polemic against paganism, continue over the course of the next three books of the *Recognitions*. Book six ends with the baptism of Clement and the ordination of a bishop at Tripolis. Peter leaves for Antioch after these events, having spent three months in Tripolis.

Book seven begins the story of Clement's "recognition" of his family. Through a series of miraculous incidents, Clement is reunited with his mother and brothers. In books eight and nine Peter, Clement, Niceta and Aquila (the latter two turn out to be Clement's long-lost brothers) are involved in a disputation against one Faustinianus, who says that prayer is useless, that God and providence do not exist, and that everything is governed by astrological fate. Together with his brothers, Clement argues on behalf of providence and discusses the evidence for astrology. As a rejoinder, the man tells the story of his astrologically-determined and

---

[28] This may be compared to Lycomedes' portrait of John in *A. Jo.* 26. I am grateful to François Bovon for bringing this to my attention.

tragic separation from his entire family. Peter then recognizes this story as the same sad tale mentioned by Clement's family, and is able to simultaneously reunite Clement's father with his family and win the dispute by showing the complete falsification of Faustinianus' astrological prediction. Book ten contains discourses that are designed to bring about Faustinianus' conversion to Christianity.

At this point in the story, Simon comes back into the picture. While in Antioch, he succeeds in performing wondrous deeds and stirring up the people's hatred of Peter. One of Peter's friends, however, has devised a plan to get rid of Simon. This friend tells Cornelius the centurion to say that Cornelius had been sent by the emperor to destroy Simon and other sorcerers in the area. A Christian spy, pretending to be Simon's friend, informs Simon of this development. Simon retreats to Laodicea, where he meets Faustinianus, who had come to visit their mutual friends Appion and Anubion. The devious Simon then uses his magical powers to make Faustinianus look just like him, so that the sorcerer-hunter might arrest Faustinianus instead of Simon himself. Peter uses this device to his advantage, however, by sending Faustinianus *qua* Simon to Antioch, where he pretends to be Simon and makes a public confession of both his own imposture and the divine inspiration of Peter's mission. When the real Simon arrives back in Antioch and desires an audience, he's driven away in disgrace. The *Recognitions* ends with Peter being received honorably in Antioch and baptizing Faustinianus.

The *Homilies* tells largely the same story, with a few major differences. Here Clement meets Barnabas in Alexandria instead of Rome.[29] Peter's initial instructions to Clement are different, as is Peter's disputation with Simon at Caesarea, because both include an almost Marcionite outlook on the corruption of scripture. Peter, anticipating the scriptural problems Simon is likely to address in the debate, teaches to Clement a secret doctrine that should not be discussed in public. Peter tells Clement that Simon will probably bring forward texts that seem to speak of many gods, or indicate that God is imperfect and mutable, or accuse the patriarchs of sinning. While it would be unwise to publicly question the authority of these passages, Peter tells Clement the secret truth: these scriptures have been corrupted. Every text that speaks against God or questions the righteousness of the patriarchs is to be rejected as a spurious addition. Though this doctrine is initially presented as esoteric, Peter goes on to repeat it in the public disputation with Simon that follows his instructions to Clement.

---

[29] For a discussion of this geographical discrepancy see Jones, "Clement of Rome and the *Pseudo-Clementines*," 146-47 n. 16, 148.

The disputation itself is shorter than its counterpart in the *Recognitions*. Simon flees to Tyre in defeat. Niceta, Aquila and Clement are then sent ahead by Peter to Tyre, where they meet Appion. Clement and Appion face off in a public disputation about such matters as the existence of evil, astrology, free will, polytheism, and mythology. Soon Peter arrives in Tyre, only to find that Simon has fled to Tripolis. When Peter reaches Tripolis, he seizes the opportunity to give a discourse to the pagans in that city, but realizes that Simon has once again run away to Syria. Before Peter finally catches up with Simon, the narrative tells the story of Clement's discovery of his long-lost family (similar to that of the *Recognitions* but with differences of detail). Peter and Simon finally meet in a disputation held at Laodicea, where Clement's father (here named Faustus rather than Faustinianus) acts as a judge. The last homily contains a series of explanations given by Peter to his companions after Simon leaves the scene yet again, and concludes with the account of the transformation of Clement's father, as in the *Recognitions*.

The Grundschrift

In order to understand the extant Pseudo-Clementine texts, we must begin with the hypothetical *Grundschrift*. As is the case with the Gospels of Matthew and Luke in the New Testament Synoptic Problem, the *Homilies* and *Recognitions* share so much material in common that some sort of literary relationship must exist between them. The current consensus about this relationship is that a *Grundschrift* or Basic Writing must have been the source for both the *Homilies* and *Recognitions*. Most scholars would date the *Grundschrift* to between 220 and 260 CE[30] and locate it somewhere in Syria, though there is still considerable disagreement on its exact location.[31] According to Strecker, who has been followed by Jones on this point, the major elements of the romance of recognitions (described below)

---

[30] The *Grundschrift*'s use of Bardaisan establishes the *terminus post quem* of 220 CE. The date 260 CE is sometimes chosen because it lies halfway between 220 and 300 CE (the *Grundschrift* is widely considered to be a product of the third century, which places the latest possible date at 300). For an extensive discussion of the dating and characterization of the *Grundschrift*, see Jones, "The Pseudo-Clementines," 8-14. Jones, who sees no reason to date the *BLC* after Bardaisan's death in 220, argues for a date of circa 220 CE for the *Grundschrift*. Jones, "Clement of Rome and the *Pseudo-Clementines*," 144-45.

[31] The Transjordan and Rome have also been proposed as possible locations. For the former view, see Carl Schmidt, *Studien zu den Pseudo-Clementinen* (TU 46.1; Leipzig: J. C. Hinrichs, 1929) 313; and Oscar Cullmann, *Le Problème littéraire et historique du roman pseudo-clémentin. Étude sur le Rapport entre le Gnosticisme et le Judéo-Christianisme* (Paris: Librairie Félix Alcan, 1930) 156-57. For the latter view, see Waitz, *Pseudoklementinen*, 74-75, 366.

are already present in the *Grundschrift*.[32] It reflects the "age of the apologists" in its insistence that righteous behavior – that is, a life lived in accordance with rationality – ensures one's endurance of the final judgment.[33] Although his assessment is surely correct, Strecker seems to base his characterization of the *Grundschrift* on its stark differences with other Christian writings, especially those by Paul: "Belief plays only a subordinate role; the death of Jesus has no religious significance; the Christological problem scarcely exists."[34] The most prominent figure in the *Grundschrift* is the True Prophet, who is the source of the prescriptions for the practical religious life and whose teachings are authenticated by the truth of his prophetic predictions.[35]

It is generally agreed that the *Grundschrift* makes use of a number of different source documents, and much of the modern academic discussion of the Pseudo-Clementines has focused on the identification and isolation of these sources. I will say more about three of these sources in the "History of Scholarship" section below, because they each have important bearing on my analysis of the *Recognitions*.[36] It is important to note that

---

[32] Strecker, "Introduction," 485.

[33] Strecker, "Introduction," 485.

[34] Strecker, "Introduction," 485.

[35] Strecker, "Introduction," 485. Within Pseudo-Clementine literature, "True Prophet" is the primary Christological title of Jesus. H. J. W. Drijvers offers an excellent and convincing analysis of the True Prophet motif in the *Grundschrift* in his "Adam and the True Prophet in the Pseudo-Clementines," *Loyalitätskonflikte in der Religionsgeschichte: Festschrift für Carsten Colpe*, ed. Christoph Elsas and Hans G. Kippenberg (Würzburg: Königshausen & Neumann, 1990) 314-23. Charles A. Gieschen analyzes the relationship of the True Prophet to other figures, such as Adam and Moses, who are characterized by the Pseudo-Clementines as prophets, in his "The Seven Pillars of the World: Ideal Figure Lists in the Christology of the Pseudo-Clementines," *Journal for the Study of the Pseudepigrapha* 12 (1994) 47-82. See also L. Cerfaux, "Le vrai prophète des Clémentines," *Recherches de Science Religieuse* 18 (1928) 143-63; and G. Strecker, *Das Judenchristentum*, 145-53.

[36] The most famous source behind the *Grundschrift* is the so-called *Kerygmata Petrou* (KP). It is generally characterized by its Ebionite (or Jewish-Christian), anti-Pauline flavor. According to Strecker, the *Grundschrift*'s polemic against Simon Magus was originally directed against Paul in the KP. The figure of the True Prophet belongs to the level of the KP, and the divinely revealed knowledge he possesses is equivalent to the Mosaic law. In addition, the KP also contains the doctrines of syzygies and false pericopes, as well as instruction about baptism and good works. However, the contents and even the existence of the KP are widely contested; the elements Strecker assigns to the KP may well belong to the level of the *Grundschrift*. Georg Strecker, "Appendix I: On the Problem of Jewish Christianity," in Walter Bauer, *Orthodoxy and Heresy in Earliest Christianity*, 2nd German edition with added appendices by Georg Strecker; translated by a team from the Philadelphia Seminar on Christian Origins; ed. Robert A. Kraft and Gerhard Krodel (Mifflintown, PA: Sigler Press, 1996) 257-71. The KP is

most of the "sources" mentioned in this book are not generally thought to have been employed directly by the author of the *Recognitions*. Rather, they were used by the *Grundschrift*, which was in turn used by the *Recognitions*. (In some instances, however, it is unclear whether a particular source has been used by the *Grundschrift* or the *Recognitions*.[37]) Whatever the precise delineation of the sources behind the *Grundschrift* may be, this document provides a substantial common foundation for the two major surviving works of Pseudo-Clementine literature, to which we now turn.

The Homilies

Both the *Homilies* and *Recognitions* were originally written in Greek, but each has been preserved differently. The Greek of the *Homilies* survives in two medieval manuscripts, the eleventh- or twelfth-century *Parisinus Graecus* 930 (P) and the fourteenth century *Vaticanus Ottobonianus* 443 (O).[38] The text of the *Homilies* is known to be quite a bit older, however, because there are Syriac fragments of the *Homilies* in British Museum Add. 12150, a manuscript written in Edessa and dated to 411 CE.[39] The

---

usually thought to be distinct from the *Kerygma Petrou* mentioned by Clement of Alexandria. On the *Kerygma Petrou*, see now the impressive edition by M. Cambe, ed., *Kerygma Petri* (CCSA 15; Louvain: Brepols, 2003); and idem, "La *Prédication de Pierre* (ou: Le *Kérygme de Pierre*)," *Apocrypha* 4 (1993) 177-95.

[37] For example, this is the case with some of the astrological materials. For example, Rendel Harris, "Notes on the Clementine Romances," JBL 40 (1921) 132-33 has argued that the *Recognitions* is dependent on the *Book of the Laws of the Countries*, while others such as Han J. W. Drijvers have concluded that the *Grundschrift* borrowed from the *Book of the Laws of the Countries* (or a text closely related to it). H. J. W. Drijvers, *Bardaisan of Edessa* (SSN 6; Assen: van Gorcum & Co., 1966) 74.

[38] Bernhard Rehm, *Die Pseudoklementinen I: Homilien* (3d ed., rev.; Die griechischen christlichen Schriftsteller der ersten Jahrhunderte 42; Berlin: Akademie Verlag, 1992) ix. There are also two Greek epitomes which are dated to the Middle Ages. See Franz Xaver Risch, "Was tut ein Epitomator? Zur Methode des Epitomierens am Beispiel der pseudoclementinischen *epitome prior*." *Das Altertum* 48 (2003) 241-55. A history of research on the epitomes can be found in Franz Paschke, *Die beiden griechischen Klementinen-Neuausgabe der Texte* (TU 90; Berlin: Akademie-Verlag, 1966) 13-28. The epitomes exist in Arabic, Georgian, and Armenian versions, as well as a Slavonic fragment and a number of later witnesses. On this see F. S. Jones, "Pseudo-Clementines," 6-7.

[39] Rehm, *Homilien*, xvi-xx. For a recent study of this manuscript, see F. Stanley Jones, "Early Syriac Pointing in and behind British Museum Additional Manuscript 12,150," in *Symposium Syriacum VII: Uppsala University, Department of Asian and African Languages, 1-14 August 1996*, ed. René Lavenant (Orientalia Christiana Analecta 256; Rome: Pontificio Istituto Orientale, 1998) 429-44. The critical edition of the Syriac text (for both *Homilies* and *Recognitions*) is Wilhelm Frankenberg, *Die syrischen Clementinen mit griechischem Paralleltext: Eine Vorarbeit zu dem literargeschichtlichen*

Syriac version includes *Homilies* 10.1-26; 11.1-36; 12.1-24; 13.1-21; 14.1-12 (that is, all of *Homilies* 10, 11, 13, and 14, and most of *Homily* 12). The current consensus is that the date of the Syriac manuscript and the *Homilies'* Arian tendencies place this text in mid-fourth century Syria.[40]

With regard to its redactional tendencies, the *Homilies* is generally considered to reproduce the content of the *Grundschrift* more closely than the *Recognitions*.[41] For example, the doctrines of the syzygies and the false pericopes are featured much more prominently in the *Homilies* than in the *Recognitions*.[42] Because the *Homilies* is probably closer to the *Grundschrift* than the *Recognitions*, it makes sense to work with the hypothesis that differences between the *Homilies* and *Recognitions* are more likely to be a result of the *Recognitions'* editorial activity. Although the Homilist may be a more faithful scribe than the Recognitionist, the *Homilies* has several noteworthy theological and doctrinal proclivities.

The academic discussion of these interests is marked by disagreement over the dogmatic categories to which they can be assigned. In particular, the *Homilies'* emphasis on a single creator god and its seeming lack of interest in (or denial of) Jesus' divinity has suggested a range of possibilities. For example, F. C. Baur described the *Homilies'* doctrine as Christian gnosticism developed in conflict with Marcion. According to Baur, belief in the one creator God was fundamental to the *Homilies*, although this framework easily accommodated gnostic ideas as well: Baur saw both "Jewish ethical" and "gnostic metaphysical" conceptions of God at work in the *Homilies*.[43]

However, Baur differed from most subsequent commentators because he did not relate the *Homilies* to the Trinitarian controversies of the fourth

---

Problem der Sammlung (TU 48.3; Leipzig: J. C. Hinrichs, 1937). Frankenberg makes use of both the fifth and ninth century manuscripts in his creation of the critical text.

[40] Bigg, "Clementine Homilies," 167, 191-92; Waitz, *Pseudoklementinen*, 368-69; Strecker, *Judenchristentum*, 268; Rehm, "Entstehung," 160.

[41] This has been argued by Hort, *Notes Introductory*, 120; and Strecker, "Introduction," 485. However, this is not always the case; see e.g. the argument in Jones, "Clement of Rome and the *Pseudo-Clementines*," 146 n. 16.

[42] The syzygy principle is the notion that God has "distinguished all things into pairs and opposites," one of which is true/good/male and the other false/evil/female; this applies to prophecy and certain individuals, e.g. Cain and Abel, Aaron and Moses, Simon Magus and Peter, and so on; see e.g. *Hom* 2.15.1; 3.49.1 – 3.57. The doctrine of false pericopes, which stems from the syzygy principle, holds that some prophecies and passages of scripture are true and others false. One of the primary tasks of the True Prophet is to teach people to distinguish between true and false passages, and thereby achieve not only correct interpretations of scripture, but also a proper understanding of God's action in and governance of the world (*Hom* 2.15.1-5; 3.32.1-2; 3.33.1).

[43] F. C. Baur, *Die christliche Gnosis oder die christliche Religions-Philosophie in ihrer geschichtlichen Entwicklung* (Tübingen: C. F. Osiander, 1835) 313, 326-27.

century. Charles Bigg, for example, argued successfully that the *Homilies* participates in the *homoousian* debates associated with the so-called Arian controversy.[44] Waitz, together with Chapman, Harnack, and others, followed Bigg in characterizing the Homilist as an Arian whose theology was combined with "Jewish Christian" Gnostic views.[45] Schmidt and Cullmann, however, returned to Baur's approach in suggesting that the so-called Arian passages could more easily be explained as Jewish-Christian.[46] Despite this resurrection of the Baur approach, it is now generally agreed that the *Homilies* stands in some relation to Arianism. Now that we have some sense of the *Homilies'* characteristics as they have been understood in modern scholarship, let's move on to the *Recognitions*.

The Recognitions

This book analyzes the *Recognitions* as it appears in a Latin translation made by Rufinus of Aquileia around the year 406 CE,[47] which has been transmitted in a large number of manuscripts dating from the fifth to fifteenth centuries.[48] The original Greek text has been lost altogether except for very small fragments preserved by patristic writers such as Eusebius.[49] The *Recognitions* is partially preserved in a Syriac version found in two manuscripts, the early fifth-century Edessene manuscript mentioned above[50] and the ninth-century British Museum Add. 14609.[51] Although the Syriac and the Latin are often considered to be of equal text-

---

[44] Bigg, "Clementine Homilies," 167, 191-92.

[45] Waitz, *Pseudoklementinen*, 368-69.

[46] Schmidt, *Studien zu den Pseudo-Clementinen*, 301 n. 2; Cullmann, *Problème littéraire*, 161.

[47] On this period of Rufinus' life see C. P. Hammond, "The Last Ten Years of Rufinus' Life and the Date of his Move South from Aquileia," *Journal of Theological Studies* n.s. 28 (1977) 372-429.

[48] Because *Rec* 3.2-11 was not translated by Rufinus, it will be excluded from consideration here. The *Recognitions* probably circulated more widely than the *Homilies* because of its more "orthodox" tendencies (which are either due to the Recognitionist or to the editorial activity of Rufinus, or both). J. Neville Birdsall, "Problems of the Clementine Literature," in *Jews and Christians: The Parting of the Ways A.D. 70 to 135*, ed. J. D. G. Dunn (Grand Rapids, MI: Eerdmans, 1992) 347, 352. For an exhaustive survey of the manuscript tradition of the *Recognitions*, see B. Rehm, *Die Pseudoklementinen II: Rekognitionen in Rufins Übersetzung* (2d ed., rev.; Die griechischen christlichen Schriftsteller der ersten Jahrhunderte 51; Berlin: Akademie, 1994) xvii-cxi.

[49] On these Greek fragments see Rehm, *Rekognitionen*, c-cv.

[50] BM Add. 12150 contains *Recognitions* 1-4.1. Although the *Recognitions* and the *Homilies* are transmitted together in this manuscript, they were recorded by different hands. Frankenberg, *Syrischen Clementinen*, viii-ix.

[51] For a discussion of the manuscripts see the introduction in Frankenberg, vii-xxii.

critical value,[52] it should be noted that on the whole, the Syriac has been largely ignored in critical editions and translations.[53] Because of the early fifth century date of the first Syriac manuscript, and because there are identifiable traces of the Arian debate in the *Recognitions*, it is usually dated to the mid-fourth century and located in Syria.[54]

The redactional tendencies of the *Recognitions* differ somewhat from those of the *Homilies*. While the *Homilies* apparently remains faithful to the *Grundschrift*, this is not the case with the *Recognitions*. In the first place, the *Recognitions* abbreviates the *Grundschrift*; Waitz considered this the main contribution of the *Recognitions* to the Pseudo-Clementine corpus.[55] Many have argued that the author of the *Recognitions* eliminated anything in the *Grundschrift* he found to be heretical; this included the Jewish Christian and anti-Pauline elements of the *Grundschrift*, even though these have been preserved to some degree.[56] For example, it appears that the *Recognitions* uses Gospel citations that are more in line with the canonical New Testament Gospels than those found in the *Homilies*.[57] It also downplays the importance of the syzygy principle and the doctrine of false pericopes. According to Waitz, the author of the *Recognitions* is particularly interested in archaic material and matters of practical piety.[58] Like the *Homilies*, the *Recognitions* emphasizes the oneness of God and the importance of righteous actions. It is worth observing that any determination of the *Recognitions'* redactional tendencies is complicated considerably by two other factors. The first is Rufinus' translation activity, which likely involved the omission and alteration of material he regarded as unacceptable.[59] The second is the

---

[52] For a comparison of the relative text-critical value of the Syriac and Latin versions, see F. Stanley Jones, "Evaluating the Latin and Syriac Translations of the Pseudo-Clementine *Recognitions*," *Apocrypha* 3 (1992) 237-57. While Jones concludes that both translators try to fairly represent the Greek, he does note the pro-Nicene editorial tendencies of Rufinus. Others like Frankenberg have contrasted the Syriac with what they believe to be the weaknesses in Rufinus' work (Frankenberg, ix-xii).

[53] This is true in the work of both Bernard Rehm and Georg Strecker, for example.

[54] Although fourth-century Syria seems to be the current consensus on the provenance of the *Recognitions* and *Homilies*, there has been considerable debate on this issue over the years. For a summary of other proposed dates and locations see Jones, "Pseudo-Clementines," 69-79.

[55] Waitz, *Pseudoklementinen*, 370.

[56] Strecker, "Introduction," 485.

[57] A. Schliemann, *Die Clementinen nebst den verwandten Schriften und der Ebionitismus* (Hamburg: Friedrich Perthes, 1844), 325.

[58] Waitz, *Pseudoklementinen*, 370.

[59] F. S. Jones notes that Rufinus has modified *Rec* 1.69.6-7, which appears to be a Eunomian interpolation (*Ancient Jewish Christian Source*, 48-49). Rufinus suggests as much in sections 10-11 of the prologue, though shortly thereafter he emphasizes the

probable presence of interpolated passages that were inserted at a later date than the *Recognitions'* initial composition; this is most likely the case, for example, with the Eunomian material in *Rec* 3.2-11.[60]

History of Scholarship

F. Stanley Jones has already performed the difficult task of constructing a general history of scholarship on the Pseudo-Clementines, and I will not duplicate his efforts here.[61] Instead, this section is a targeted history of scholarship written with two purposes in mind. First, because this book is primarily concerned with the philosophical and astrological materials in the *Recognitions*, it is important to survey the existing scholarship on these parts of the narrative. This should give the reader a more concrete sense of how the present work intersects with and contributes to the existing conversation. Second, a bit later in this chapter I will use these two fairly limited scholarly discussions of the philosophical and astrological materials to suggest that source criticism, while a valuable and informative mode of analysis, actually serves to *obscure* the *Recognitions'* rhetorical and discursive aims.[62]

Before source criticism came to dominate the academic discussion of the Pseudo-Clementines, it was not unusual to consider the *Homilies* and *Recognitions* as narrative unities. Here it will suffice to give three brief examples. In 1844, Adolph Schliemann attempted to present the *Homilies*

---

literalness of his translation of the *Recognitions* (in contrast to other, freer translations he has made in the past). On the introduction see Ernst Bammel, "Rufins Einleitung zu den Klemens zugeschriebenen Wiedererkennungen," in *Storia ed esegesi in Rufino di Concordia* (Udine: Arti grafiche friulane, 1992) 151-63. On Rufinus' translation practices generally, see E. C. Brooks, "The Translation Techniques of Rufinus of Aquileia," in *Studia Patristica 17: Papers presented at the Eighth International Conference on Patristic Studies, Oxford, Sept. 3-8, 1979*, ed. Elizabeth A. Livingstone (3 vols.; Elmsford, NY: Pergamon Press, 1982) I.357-364; and M. M. Wagner, *Rufinus, The Translator. A Study of his Theory and his Practice as illustrated in his Version of the Apologetica of St. Gregory Nazianzen* (Patristic Studies 73; Washington: The Catholic University of America, 1945).

[60] On the considerable discussion surrounding this passage, see Jones, "Pseudo-Clementines," 76-79. Because my analysis deals only with Rufinus' Latin translation of the *Recognitions*, *Rec* 3.2-11 has been excluded from consideration.

[61] Jones, "Pseudo-Clementines," 1-33, 63-96. See also the more recent survey of scholarship by Pierre Geoltrain, "Le Roman pseudo-clémentin depuis les recherches d'Oscar Cullmann," in *Le judéo-christianisme dans tous ses états: Actes du colloque de Jérusalem, 6-10 juillet 1998*, ed. Simon C. Mimouni and F. Stanley Jones (Paris: Éditions du Cerf, 2001) 31-38.

[62] I am grateful to Karen King for her help in formulating this idea.

and *Recognitions* as two unitary texts, but he was castigated by later scholars for organizing his analysis around modern theological categories.[63] Shortly after Schliemann's publication, Adolph Hilgenfeld investigated the *Lehrbegriff* of the *Homilies*. He made the important step of differentiating between sources and redactional material in the *Homilies*, although his pursuit of the Pseudo-Clementines' *Lehrbegriff* did not extend to the *Recognitions*.[64] Gerhard Uhlhorn acknowledged Hilgenfeld's differentiation of redactional and source material in the *Homilies*, but suggested that both sets of material nevertheless reflected the views of the *Homilies'* final redactor.[65] Regarding the *Recognitions*, Uhlhorn did offer a reconstruction of its *Lehrbegriff* based on both practical and doctrinal elements.[66] These early attempts at analysis of the Pseudo-Clementines' narratives were dismissed as naïve and pre-critical by later source critics.[67]

Even after the advent of source criticism, there has been some resistance to the source critical project. Some scholars have suggested that the putative sources are merely a fiction, a result of strategic composition on the part of the author.[68] For example, A. C. Headlam concluded that the Pseudo-Clementines "are all products of one design and plan, coming from one writer or group of writers, and we have no need to inquire about older sources, which in all probability did not exist."[69] Other scholars, such as J. Chapman and E. Schwartz, have voiced similar hesitation about the existence of sources and the utility of scholarly pursuit of them.[70] The problem with this skepticism, however, is hard to overlook: in some cases we have (direct or indirect) access to such sources, and there is no denying that some sort of literary relationship exists among these texts. For better or worse, we are stuck with the problem of sources. This is the view of the

---

[63] Schliemann, *Clementinen,* 130-251.

[64] Adolph Hilgenfeld, *Die clementinischen Recognitionen und Homilien nach ihrem Ursprung und Inhalt dargestellt* (Jena: J.B. Schreiber – Leipzig: Chr. E. Kollmann, 1848) 281.

[65] Uhlhorn, *Homilien und Recognitionen,* 153.

[66] Uhlhorn, *Homilien und Recognitionen,* 233-34, 259-62.

[67] This seems to be Stanley Jones' opinion; see his comments on Uhlhorn in "Pseudo-Clementines," 72.

[68] This paragraph partially follows the summary provided by van Voorst, *Ascents of James,* 17-18.

[69] A. C. Headlam, "The Clementine Literature," *Journal of Theological Studies* 3 (1902) 49-50.

[70] J. Chapman, "On the Date of the Clementines," *ZNW* 9 (1908) 21-34, 147-59; E. Schwartz, "Unzeitgemäße Beobachtungen zu den Clementinen," *ZNW* 31 (1932) 151-99. Chapman on *Rec* 3.75, which was central to theories of a *Kerygma(ta) Petrou*: "It is surely obvious that the whole chapter is merely a part of the gigantic fraud; it is calculated to assist the verisimilitude which the writer is so anxious to introduce and maintain!" Chapman, "Date," 148.

majority of Pseudo-Clementine specialists, myself included. As I have already indicated, much of the modern work on these texts embraces the source critical pursuit, so that source analyses tend to overshadow other kinds of inquiry. It should come as no surprise, then, that the *Recognitions*' philosophical and astrological materials have been discussed primarily as source critical concerns.[71]

The Dispute with Appion and the Philosophical Source are two putative sources of the *Grundschrift* that reflect philosophical ideas. The astrological materials of the *Recognitions* can be attributed to the *Grundschrift*'s use of the *Book of the Laws of the Countries*, which reflects Bardesanite views but was probably written by Bardaisan's disciple Philippus rather than by Bardaisan himself.[72] Of all the sources used by the *Grundschrift* and subsequently appropriated by the *Recognitions*, I have chosen to examine these three – and the topics of astrology and philosophy – for two reasons. First, because my major argument (see below) is about knowledge, philosophy and astrology are particularly relevant in that each represents an institutionalized discipline that transmits specialized and often esoteric knowledge. Second, using a small selection of sources and topics enables me to show how source criticism has obscured the way they work together within the *Recognitions*, by demonstrating in detail that these sources and topics are used to accomplish very similar goals but in separate epistemic arenas.

For this reason I have excluded the material that deals with idolatry, since the debates over idolatry cannot really be said to concern knowledge. There is a significant amount of material in the *Recognitions* that deals with magic which I have also chosen to exclude. This is not because magic is unconnected with knowledge/expertise, since a significant amount of magical practices require expert and esoteric knowledge that has been transmitted in institutionalized settings. However, as it appears in the *Recognitions*, magic has much more to do with displays of power than with knowledge *per se*.[73] Whereas the astrological and philosophical

---

[71] Primarily, but not exclusively; see the recent scholarship mentioned in n. 20 above. See William Adler, "Apion's 'Encomium of Adultery': A Jewish Satire of Greek Paideia in the Pseudo-Clementine *Homilies*," *HUCA* 64 (1993) 15-49, for a very learned analysis of *Homilies* 4-6 against the background of a Hellenistic Syriac romance. Similarly, F. Stanley Jones' "Eros and Astrology in the *Periodoi Petrou*: The Sense of the Pseudo-Clementine Novel," *Apocrypha* 12 (2001) 53-78 represents a move away from the source critical paradigm.

[72] Stanley Jones disagrees with the common view that the *BLC* was written after Bardaisan's death in 220 CE, saying "there is no evidence that clearly supports this view." Jones, "Clement of Rome and the *Pseudo-Clementines*," 144.

[73] Of course, long ago Michel Foucault showed that knowledge and power are intimately connected. See e.g. his *The Archaeology of Knowledge* (trans. A. M. Sheridan

discussions center around questions of knowledge, the magical materials are concerned with Simon's and Peter's ability to perform miracles and amazing feats. Moreover, it quickly became clear to me that the philosophical and astrological materials are so extensive that they preclude any discussion of the sections on magic, which are largely separate from the astrological and philosophical materials. In addition, the magical materials – while related to astrological practices in a certain sense by the *Recognitions*, because both magic and astrology are the work of demons and are traced back to the same source – are not concerned with providence, fate, and human free will, whereas the philosophical and astrological discussions are primarily concerned with these issues and hence they overlap substantially.

The Dispute with Appion and the Philosophical Source[74]

Scholars have identified at least two major blocks of philosophical material that may be attributable to sources prior to the Pseudo-Clementine *Grundschrift*: Niceta's speech on providence in *Rec* 8.9.1 - 8.34.8 and Peter's dispute with Appion[75] in *Hom* 4.7.1 – 6.25.2 (~*Rec* 10.17.1 – 10.51.6).[76] The history of scholarship on these passages begins with the research of Adolph Hilgenfeld. He suggested that the dialogues of Peter and Appion mentioned by Eusebius (*Hist. Eccl.* 3.38.5) had been used by the *Homilies* and *Recognitions* as a source for *Hom* 4.7.1 – 6.25.2 and *Rec* 10.17.1 – 10.51.6.[77]

Hans Waitz agreed with Hilgenfeld on the existence of a source behind the dispute with Appion. First, in his estimation, the quotations in this section were all taken from gentile writings rather than from the Bible.

Smith; New York: Pantheon Books, 1972), esp. 178-95. However, I am interested in the way knowledge produces power within the text (as is the case with astrology and philosophy), rather than the ways in which power is displayed (as is the case with magic).

[74] The following section is partially dependent on the summary of Jones, "Pseudo-Clementines," 30-31.

[75] In the *Recognitions*, this section is a discussion among the protagonists (particularly Niceta and Aquila), rather than a dispute between Peter and Appion. I have chosen to refer to the *Homilies*' version simply because that is how it has been discussed in source critical circles. On the figures of Ap(p)ion and An(n)oubion in the Pseudo-Clementines and elsewhere, see Jan N. Bremmer, "Foolish Egyptians: Apion and Anoubion in the *Pseudo-Clementines*," in *The Wisdom of Egypt: Jewish, Early Christian, and Gnostic Essays in Honour of Gerard P. Luttikhuizen*, ed. Anthony Hilhorst and George H. van Kooten (Leiden: Brill, 2005) 311-29.

[76] Werner Heintze has also analyzed *Rec* 9.19-28 in connection with *Rec* 8.10-20. Heintze, *Klemensroman*, 90-110. Because the material in *Rec* 9.19-28 is more closely connected to the astrological debates, however, it will be discussed in Chapter 3.

[77] Hilgenfeld, *Clementinischen Recognitionen und Homilien*, 224.

Second, he proposed that no theological element of this episode could be identified as Jewish Christian or Christian. (Note that Waitz's genealogical logic presumes a rather discrete division of Jewish, Gentile, and Christian theological ideas.[78] While the Pseudo-Clementines do make use of divisions between Jews and Gentiles,[79] it is fair to say that the theological compartmentalization posited by Waitz and others is not a helpful way of describing the narrative workings of the texts.) Finally, Waitz observed that the language of this section differed from the rest of the *Homilies* and *Recognitions*. He suggested that Eusebius had referred to the *Grundschrift* rather than some other source used independently by the *Homilies* and *Recognitions*. The *Grundschrift*, in turn, had relied on a source for this dispute, but Waitz thought it impossible to say anything definitive about this source.[80]

Werner Heintze, however, believed that he could say more about the source used by the *Grundschrift*. He proposed that a Jewish book of disputations, written around the year 200 C.E., was the source for both Peter's dispute with Appion as well as the disputes about philosophy and astrology.[81] For example, Heintze recognized that other Pseudo-Clementine passages on philosophy resembled material found in pagan philosophical texts.[82] In particular, he found strong correspondences between *Rec* 8.11-12, 20-33 and Cicero's *De natura deorum* 2.17, 19; 75-150.[83] Heintze concluded that both Cicero and the *Grundschrift* must have used the Jewish book of disputations as their common source for this material.[84]

Heintze's thesis proved to be quite persuasive and was subsequently adopted by Schmidt, Cullmann, Schoeps, and Waitz.[85] Others, however,

---

[78] I owe this point to Karen King.

[79] The author of the *Recognitions*, for example, never uses designations such as "Jewish Christian" or "Christian," nor does he refer to "Judaism." All three of these terms are commonly employed in secondary literature on the Pseudo-Clementines. Jones briefly mentions this terminological issue as it pertains to *Rec* 1.27-71 in his *Ancient Jewish Christian Source*, 159-60.

[80] Waitz, *Pseudoklementinen*, 30-32, 251-56.

[81] Heintze, *Klemensroman*, 48-50, 108-9, 112. Heintze further suggested that this Jewish book of disputations was dependent on the Pseudo-Aristotelian *Peplos* for the dispute with Appion.

[82] Heintze, *Klemensroman*, 51-107.

[83] Heintze, *Klemensroman*, 76-86.

[84] Once again, Heintze suggested that the book of disputations was dependent on yet another earlier source – Posidonius' *Peri Theōn* – for the discussion of divine providence. Heintze, *Klemensroman*, 86.

[85] Each of these made slight modifications to Heintze's thesis. Schmidt, Cullmann, and Schoeps thought that the date of this Jewish book of disputations must be before 135 CE. Waitz suggested that the Jewish book of disputations was redacted by a Christian

were not convinced.[86] Schwartz, for example, thought that Peter's dispute with Appion in *Rec* 10 could be more easily explained with reference to fourth-century philosophy.[87] Strecker disagreed with Heintze on two critical points: he believed (1) that the *Grundschrift* used pagan philosophical sources directly;[88] and (2) that the dispute with Appion in the *Homilies* should be attributed to the Homilist.[89] Bernhard Rehm said that Heintze's hypothesis is simply "zu kompliziert."[90] Recent scholars like Drijvers have also expressed serious doubts about Heintze's source reconstruction.[91]

Bardaisan's (or Philippus') Book of the Laws of the Countries

As Stanley Jones has noted, "The astrological material in [the Pseudo-Clementines] has yet to be systematically sorted with respect to the various redactional layers."[92] It is clear that the *Grundschrift* has some sort of literary relationship to – indeed, probably used – the *Book of the Laws of the Countries* written by a follower of Bardaisan, as well as the *Book of Elchasai,* which contains some astrological teachings. Although the *Homilies* generally stays closer to the *Grundschrift* in its redaction, in this case the *Homilies* lacks longer parallels to the extended discussion on astrology that occurs in *Recognitions* 9.1.1 – 10.12.7. Hence the astrological materials have been given a far more prominent place in the

---

before it reached the *Grundschrift* author. Schmidt, *Studien zu den Pseudo-Clementinen*, 125-59; Cullmann, *Problème littéraire*, 116-31; Schoeps, *Theologie und Geschichte*, 42-43; Waitz, "Die Pseudoklementinen und ihre Quellenschriften," *Zeitschrift für die neutestamentliche Wissenschaft und die Kunde der älteren Kirche* 28 (1929) 268-69. This discussion is noted by Jones, "Pseudo-Clementines," 30-31.

[86] As Jones notes, some were content to ignore Heintze altogether. Jones, "Pseudo-Clementines," 30. Harris, who made no reference to Heintze's work (apparently because he was unaware of it), suggested that *Rec* 8.9-35 was taken from a Stoic treatise on providence written sometime between Seneca and the Antonines. He also suggested that the dispute with Appion in *Rec* 10.17ff was from "a Greek defence of the ancient mythology" by Metrodorus the Epicurean. R. Harris, "Notes on the Clementine Romances," *Journal of Biblical Literature* 40 (1921) 134-35, 141-42.

[87] Schwartz, "Unzeitgemäße Beobachtungen," 186 n. 2.

[88] Strecker, *Judenchristentum*, 256.

[89] Strecker, *Judenchristentum*, 81-84.

[90] Rehm, "Entstehung," 128 n. 152.

[91] Drijvers, *Bardaisan of Edessa*, 73: "The existence of a Jewish Apology or a "jüdisches Disputationsbuch" is purely hypothetical; we know nothing of such a work. Moreover, this hypothesis complicates the relationships while ignoring the facts given above."

[92] F. Stanley Jones, "The Astrological Trajectory in Ancient Syriac-Speaking Christianity (Elchasai, Bardaisan, and Mani)," in L. Cirillo and A. van Tongerloo, eds., *Atti del Terzo Congresso Internazionale di Studi "Manicheismo e Oriente Cristiano Antico"* (Louvain: Brepols, 1997) 199 n. 66.

Recognitions than in the *Homilies*, even if it is clear that the interest in astrology originated with the *Grundschrift*.

Jones has argued – correctly, in my view – that astrology is the key to the narrative of the *Grundschrift*. Jones suggests that the *Grundschrift* adopted Bardaisan's belief that astrology could be used theologically to explain why events happened in people's lives. He also notes that both the *Homilies* and *Recognitions* have obscured this idea. For example, the *Recognitions* seems to have omitted the passage in *Hom* 19.23.5 which states that events happen to human beings by lot. *Rec* 9.25.8 likewise leaves out a passage from the *Book of the Laws of the Countries* that contains the same idea. Hence the author of the *Recognitions*, while in a certain sense placing a greater emphasis on astrology by including a long discussion of astrological doctrines, has also attempted to undermine any acceptance of astrological tenets contained in the *Grundschrift*.

Scholarship on the astrological materials within the Pseudo-Clementines has been concerned primarily with determining the relationships among three texts. The first text is *Recognitions* 9.19.1 - 9.29.2, where Clement provides a series of examples of laws and customs in other countries that challenge ideas associated with astrally-determined fate, or *genesis*. This lengthy passage is preserved in the *Recognitions*, but is usually considered to be derived from the *Grundschrift*. The second text is Bardaisan's *Dialogue on Fate*, which is twice mentioned by Eusebius.[93] The third text is the *Book of the Laws of the Countries* (or *BLC*).[94] The question about these three texts is simple: who borrowed what from whom? The answer to this question, however, is anything but simple.[95] Let's take a brief look at a few of the possibilities.[96]

---

[93] Eusebius, *Hist. Eccl.* 4.30 and *Praep. Ev.* 6.9-10.

[94] The standard edition of the *BLC* is Bardesanes, *Liber legum regionum*, ed. F. Nau (Patrologia Syriaca 1.2; Paris: Didot, 1907) col. 536-611.

[95] With regard to this particular discussion, it is easy to agree with Rehm's opinion: "Die Frage ist schon fast zum Überdruß erörtert worden, und kaum eine theoretisch mögliche Kombination ist unversucht geblieben." B. Rehm, "Bardesanes in den Pseudoclementinen," *Philologus* 93 (1938) 222.

[96] Jones has covered the history of scholarship on Bardaisan's *Book of the Laws of the Countries* more extensively than is possible here. See his "Pseudo-Clementines," 20-24. This section is partially dependent on his summary. Drijvers also has written a more extensive summary of this complex of issues; see his *Bardaisan of Edessa*, 60-76.

One group of scholars (notably A. Merx,[97] F. J. A. Hort,[98] A. Schliemann,[99] J. Langen,[100] G. Uhlhorn,[101] and R. Harris[102]) has suggested that the *Recognitions* is directly dependent on a Greek version of the *BLC*. For Hort and Harris, Eusebius was also dependent on the *BLC*.[103] For Merx, although the *Recognitions* was dependent on the *BLC*, the passages in the *Recognitions* that were drawn from the *BLC* were written into the *Recognitions* not by its initial author, but by the hand of a later interpolator.[104] Merx pointed out that there are other places in the *Recognitions* that appear to be dependent on Bardaisan's thought as well.[105]

Another group of scholars (beginning with A. Hilgenfeld,[106] who was followed by P. Wendland[107] and F. Boll[108]) has suggested that the *BLC* borrowed from the Pseudo-Clementines, while Eusebius was dependent on the Greek version of the *BLC*. For Hilgenfeld, *Recognitions* 9.17, 19-27 was borrowed from yet another earlier work against astrology.[109] Werner Heintze also argued that the *Grundschrift* was used indirectly by Eusebius and the *BLC*, although he posited an intermediary source in the form of a dialogue of Philippus.[110] Whereas Hilgenfeld had suggested that *Recognitions* 9.17, 19-27 was dependent on an earlier anti-astrology document, Heintze suggested that this material was drawn from the same book of Jewish disputations that was the source of the philosophical

---

[97] A. Merx, *Bardesanes von Edessa, nebst einer Untersuchung über das Verhältnis der clementinischen Recognitionen zu dem Buche der Gesetze der Länder* (Halle: C.E.W. Pfeffer, 1863) 88-114.

[98] F. J. A. Hort, "Bardaisan," in *A Dictionary of Christian Biography, Literature, Sects and Doctrines*, vol. 1, ed. W. Smith and H. Wace (London: J. Murray, 1877-1887) 250-60.

[99] Schliemann, *Clementinen*, 269 n. 10.

[100] J. Langen, *Die Klemensromane: Ihre Entstehung und ihre Tendenzen aufs neue untersucht* (Gotha: Friedrich Andreas Perthes, 1890) 147-50.

[101] Uhlhorn, *Homilien und Recognitionen*, 368-69.

[102] Harris, "Notes on the Clementine Romances," 132-33.

[103] Hort, "Bardaisan," 258; R. Harris, "Notes on the Clementine Romances," 132-33.

[104] Merx, *Bardesanes*, 112-13.

[105] Merx, *Bardesanes*, 88ff.

[106] A. Hilgenfeld, *Bardesanes, der letzte Gnostiker* (Leipzig: T.O. Weigel, 1864) 74ff.

[107] P. Wendland, *Philos Schrift über die Vorsehung: Ein Beitrag zur Geschichte der nacharistotelischen Philosophie* (Berlin: R. Gaertners Verlagsbuchhandlung, 1892) 27-33.

[108] F. Boll, "Studien über Claudius Ptolemäus: Ein Beitrag zur Geschichte der griechischen Philosophie und Astrologie," *Jahrbücher für classische Philologie* 21, supplementary vol. (Leipzig, 1894) 181.

[109] Hilgenfeld, *Bardesanes*, 148.

[110] Heintze, *Klemensroman*, 105.

material.[111] Heintze's view was then adopted by Schmidt,[112] Cullmann,[113] Schoeps,[114] and Waitz.[115]

Finally, a third possibility was advanced by Bernhard Rehm[116] and followed by Georg Strecker.[117] Rehm argued that the *Grundschrift* was directly dependent on Bardaisan's *Dialogue on Fate*. Eusebius and the *BLC* were also indirectly dependent on this dialogue of Bardaisan's, but their immediate source was another dialogue by Philippus.

These are only three among many suggestions that have been made about the relationship of these texts to one another. Although I have not given a complete picture of the source critical discussion that centers around the philosophical and astrological materials, even a brief sketch clearly demonstrates that these complicated discussions are concerned more with intertextual relationships than with the function of the philosophical and astrological passages within the *Recognitions* itself.

Recently, F. Stanley Jones has moved away from this kind of source-critical myopia by exploring the role of astrology in the *Grundschrift* itself.[118] Other scholars such as William Adler and Dominique Côté have made a similar transition away from exclusively source critical work and toward other forms of analysis on the *Homilies*.[119] My work, which focuses on the relatively ignored narrative of the *Recognitions*, is a continuation of this emergent trend. I would like to suggest that future scholarship might profitably continue this trend toward redaction, narrative, and rhetorical analysis of the Pseudo-Clementines.

---

[111] Heintze, *Klemensroman*, 106f.

[112] Schmidt, *Studien zu den Pseudo-Clementinen*, 155-57.

[113] Cullmann, *Problème littéraire*, 35.

[114] H. J. Schoeps, "Astrologisches im pseudoklementinischen Roman," *Vigiliae Christianae* 5 (1951) 88-89.

[115] Waitz, "Pseudoklementinen," 269. Waitz, however, believed that the Jewish book of disputations was the common source for both Bardaisan and the *Grundschrift*.

[116] Rehm, "Bardesanes," 233-35.

[117] Strecker, *Judenchristentum*, 256.

[118] Jones, "Eros and Astrology," 53-78. At the heart of Jones' essay is an argument about the parameters and nature of the *Grundschrift*, and to this extent Jones is operating as a source critic. However, the article provides a very helpful analysis of the role of astrological and erotic motifs in the narrative of the *Grundschrift*, which represents more than the delineation of a source. I will say more about how my own research intersects with Jones' work on astrology in Chapter 3.

[119] Adler, "Apion's 'Encomium of Adultery'," 15-49. Although Adler's larger argument is source critical in nature, his analysis of *Homilies* 4-6 clearly demonstrates how the *Homilies* has employed a source in the service of a larger agenda. See also Dominique Côté, *Le thème de l'opposition entre Pierre et Simon dans les Pseudo-Clémentines* (Études Augustiniennes, Série Antiquités 167; Paris : Institut d'Études Augustiniennes, 2001).

Students of New Testament literature may be puzzled by this seemingly anachronistic suggestion; after all, New Testament studies made just such a shift over half a century ago. In 1919, Martin Dibelius could state that "[t]he literary understanding of the synoptics begins with the recognition that they are collections of material. The composers are only to the smallest extent authors. They are principally collectors, vehicles of tradition, editors."[120] This characterization of the synoptics, which sounds much like the prevailing consensus about the Pseudo-Clementines, set the agenda for New Testament scholarship: "Our primary task is to arrive at *the tradition* which lay before the collector, and thus to reconstruct a narrative in its original, isolated condition, a speech in the form which gives it its point."[121] Hence New Testament scholarship in the first half of the twentieth century regarded the evangelists as collectors, and as a result the primary scholarly task was form criticism: the isolation and reconstruction of individual units of tradition collected by these editors.

Although redaction criticism existed before Günther Bornkamm's "The Stilling of the Storm in Matthew," this seminal essay marked a watershed moment in New Testament studies because it shifted the scholarly focus onto the editorial activity of the evangelists and its theological importance.[122] Bornkamm's work was followed by other redaction critical studies of the Gospels,[123] with the result that redaction criticism is now a widespread and influential method of analysis for the entire New Testament.

In my view, this same transition should be taking place among Pseudo-Clementine specialists. While it is virtually impossible to deny that there are sources behind the Pseudo-Clementines, and it would be remiss to ignore the differences between sources and redaction in these texts, it is vitally important that we return to Gerhard Uhlhorn's 1854 suggestion that the Pseudo-Clementine authors employed source materials *in the service of*

---

[120] Martin Dibelius, *From Tradition to Gospel*, trans. Bertram Lee Woolf (German original, 1919; New York: Charles Scribner's Sons, 1935) 3.

[121] Martin Dibelius, "Zur Formgeschichte der Evangelien," *Theologische Rundschau*, Neue Folge 1 (1929) 210, quoted in English translation in Willi Marxsen, *Mark the Evangelist: Studies on the Redaction History of the Gospel* (German original, 1956; Nashville and New York: Abingdon, 1969) 20.

[122] Günther Bornkamm, "The Stilling of the Storm in Matthew," in *Tradition and Interpretation in Matthew*, ed. Günther Bornkamm, Gerhard Barth, and Heinz Joachim Held (Philadelphia: Westminster, 1963) 52-57. I am grateful to François Bovon for suggesting that I mention the connection between this project and redaction criticism of the New Testament.

[123] Of particular importance are Willi Marxsen's *Mark the Evangelist* and Hans Conzelmann's *The Theology of St. Luke*, transl. G. Buswell (New York: Harper & Brothers, 1960).

their own distinctive theological agendas. Recent publications by Dominique Côté and Meinolf Vielberg reveal that this shift in perspective can result in a more complete understanding of Pseudo-Clementine literature. Further reconsideration of the *Recognitions* from a redactional and narrative perspective, such as that offered in this book, should continue to open new windows onto the text and its socio-historical context.

Argument and Chapter Outline

A moment ago I suggested that source critical divisions work to obscure the *Recognitions'* rhetorical and discursive aims. Rather than reinscribing these divisions, my work attempts to show how, in Rufinus' early fifth-century Latin translation of the *Recognitions*, philosophical and astrological materials that often have been artificially separated by source criticism are used together in a single discourse about *true knowledge*.

In antiquity, philosophy and astrology were different pursuits with a common goal: attaining knowledge. Philostratus, for example, sees such a connection between philosophy and astrology: "the 'Method of the philosophers resembles the prophetic art which is controlled by man and was organized by the Egyptians and Chaldeans and, before them, by the Indians, who used to conjecture the truth by the aid of countless stars: the sophistic method resembles the prophetic art of soothsayers and oracles.'"[124] As they appear in the *Recognitions*, both claim to provide knowledge of how the world began, how the world works, and how the world will someday end. Because this is precisely the kind of knowledge the protagonists in the *Recognitions* claim to possess, philosophers and astrologers like Faustinianus are ideal rivals for Peter, Clement, Niceta and Aquila.

The *Recognitions* is essentially an extended series of debates about knowledge waged by the individuals who fall into one of these two opposing groups. These debates about philosophy and astrology are used for two distinct but interrelated purposes. In the first place, such discussions are intended to demonstrate the protagonists' expertise in both areas. Clement, Niceta and Aquila are skilled in philosophy and astrology not only because of their innate talent and intelligence, but also because they have received specialized training. Clement, for example, has been

---

[124] Translation from Anitra Bingham Kolenkow, "A Problem of Power: How Miracle Doers Counter Charges of Magic in the Hellenistic World," in *Society of Biblical Literature Seminar Papers* 10, ed. G. MacRae (Missoula, MT: Scholars Press, 1976) 106.

instructed by both Platonists and Aristotelians, and he is intimately familiar with the particulars of astral determinism. On my reading, these claims to expertise are designed to show that the protagonists are well-acquainted with – indeed, masters of – every possible form of knowledge. Such mastery suggests that the protagonists' own knowledge is learned and cosmopolitan, the result of an intensive quest along every possible path, rather than a consequence of ignorance or provincialism.

The text also suggests that Peter, though an uneducated and rustic man, has both expertise and rhetorical skills. However, the *Recognitions* treats this as a gift from God rather than the result of specialized training. Peter's divinely-given knowledge of philosophy and astrology is connected with another seemingly contradictory tendency in the *Recognitions*. Despite its insistence on its heroes' expertise in the different paths to knowledge, the text also suggests that philosophy and astrology cannot really provide the access to true knowledge which they claim.[125] What philosophers and astrologers call "knowledge" is mere conjecture and opinion, which is at best the product of fallible human reason and at worst the result of demonic powers.[126] As it happens, the *Recognitions* has a peculiar epistemological requirement that is articulated by means of these discussions about philosophy and astrology: true knowledge comes only from prophets. While the *Recognitions* believes it is possible for human beings to know things with certainty, such certain knowledge can only be handed down directly from a prophet. Chapters 2 and 3 will explore how the *Recognitions* uses the materials on philosophy and astrology in order to make these claims.

Of course, it should come as no surprise that the knowledge Peter, Clement and their companions claim to possess is precisely this kind of prophetic knowledge. The text not only insists that its heroes have prophetic knowledge, but also goes to great lengths to describe how they acquired it. It continually emphasizes Peter's historical association with Jesus, the "True Prophet,"[127] along with Peter's accurate transmission of

---

[125] Although these competing claims may point to the *Recognitions'* use of different sources, I prefer to think of them as complementary elements in a defensive strategy that attempts to cover every possible objection – much like the old joke about the lawyer who simultaneously insists that his client "wasn't even there" *and* "had a good reason to steal the cash."

[126] Cf. *Hom* 19.24.1-2, where Simon claims that his views represent knowledge rather than conjecture.

[127] Within Pseudo-Clementine literature, "True Prophet" is the primary Christological title of Jesus. Not only is Jesus a prophet who possesses the kind of true knowledge sought in the *Recognitions*, he is also the most important and most knowledgeable of all the prophets. On True Prophet as a Christological title see e.g. Charles A. Gieschen,

Jesus' message. According to the *Recognitions*, Peter is a personal acquaintance and faithful disciple of Jesus who speaks only what he has learned directly from his master. Moreover, both Peter and Clement have remarkable capacities for memorization of these divine truths. These unique qualifications give Peter and Clement unrivaled access to knowledge that can be obtained only from Jesus, the True Prophet. In other words, prophetic knowledge is the only true knowledge, and this kind of understanding comes only through a direct and tangible relationship to Jesus himself. Chapter 4 analyzes in some detail these arguments about the authority of Peter and the authenticity of his knowledge.

When the *Recognitions* is read this way, it is possible to see that the text's interest in knowledge – and the transmission of that knowledge from Jesus to Peter and then to Clement – is really an argument about the authority of the *Recognitions* itself. Because Peter reproduces Jesus' words exactly, and because Clement writes a verbatim account of Peter's words, the *Recognitions* is a complete and reliable collection of the words of the True Prophet himself. Because of the text's broader program to defend this prophetic knowledge against the other major claimants to knowledge in antiquity, it is clear that the *Recognitions* has in mind not only Paul or Marcion in its polemical stance, but a range of imagined competitors. When seen in this light, the *Recognitions* contains not just a jumble of mismatched sources, but an elaborate and far-reaching argument that sets out to claim an authoritative status for the text itself.

Chapter 5 attempts to situate these observations about the *Recognitions* within the larger social, religious, and historical framework of fourth-century Syria. This chapter provides an overview of the political, cultural, and religious histories of late antique Antioch and Edessa. It explores the dynamics of religious competition among Jewish and Christian groups such as Marcionites and Arians, but it also goes beyond these internecine squabbles to examine how non-Jewish and non-Christian truth-claims also functioned as epistemic competition in the religious marketplace of these two cities. By taking a broader view of the perspectives that may have been in competition with the *Recognitions*' own views, we can gain a better understanding of the text and its functioning within a specific historical context.

Theoretical Framework

I would like to conclude this chapter by highlighting the larger theoretical issues at play in this discussion of the *Recognitions*. More explicitly, I want to discuss Pierre Bourdieu's notion of *field*, because it is the most

---

Angelomorphic Christology: Antecedents and Early Evidence (Leiden: Brill, 1998) 201-13.

central theoretical element of my project.[128] Bourdieu is perhaps best known for his idea of *habitus*, which may be described as "the coordination of plans and purposes in a regular pattern 'without in any way being the product of rules ... [and] without presupposing a conscious aim or an express mastery of the operations necessary to attain them.'"[129] Put another way, *habitus* is a set of deep dispositions that enable people to act and react in certain ways, to behave appropriately in a number of different situations, without even thinking about it. *Habitus* is not a state of mind but a state of the body, because these dispositions are located within the body itself. The body has a specific memory just as the mind does, and it's this memory that allows people to act in regular and fairly predictable ways, without their making recourse to a set of rules in their heads. *Habitus* gives people a "practical sense" of how to behave.[130]

For Bourdieu, particular practices are the product of the relationship between *habitus* and particular *fields*, or specific social contexts.[131] It is a given of modern anthropological and historical scholarship that individuals always act in particular contexts, in particular settings.[132] Bourdieu takes this simple idea and retools it, characterizing *field* as "an area, a playing field, a field of objective relations among individuals or institutions competing for the same stakes."[133] He has taken our conventional idea of context – not to mention Wittgenstein's reflections on (language) games – and added something new: a field, as opposed to a social or historical

---

128 It is difficult to isolate a single *locus classicus* for Bourdieu's ideas about field, but a clear exposition of the concept can be found in "Haute Couture and Haute Culture," in idem, *Sociology in Question* (Transl. R. Nice; London: Sage Publications, 1993) 132-38.

129 James Bohman, *New Philosophy of Social Science: Problems of Indeterminacy* (Cambridge, MA: The MIT Press, 1991) 160, quoting Pierre Bourdieu, *An Outline of a Theory of Practice* (Cambridge: Cambridge University Press, 1977) 72.

130 Bourdieu has been criticized by Theodore Schatzki because he suggests that habitus is responsible for all individual actions, which effectively "denies to thought the capacity to determine action. ... Thought, in other words, is a mere accessory to behavior." T. Schatzki, "Overdue Analysis of Bourdieu's Theory of Practice," *Inquiry* 30 (1986) 133.

131 John B. Thompson, "Editor's Introduction," in P. Bourdieu, *Language and Symbolic Power* (Cambridge, MA: Harvard University Press, 1991) 14.

132 One well-known expression of this idea is Clifford Geertz's *The Interpretation of Cultures* (New York: Basic Books, 1973) 6-10, which details the ethnographic ideal of *thick description*.

133 Bourdieu, "Haute Couture," 133. Loïc Wacquant provides a similar definition: "field consists of a set of objective, historical relations between positions anchored in certain forms of power (or capital)." P. Bourdieu and L. Wacquant, *An Invitation to Reflexive Sociology* (Chicago: University of Chicago Press, 1992) 16.

context, is a necessarily competitive space where the competitors have a shared sense of what is at stake.

These stakes, often called *capital*, are always scarce; as a rule there is never enough capital to go around. This is true whether such stakes are monetary (*economic capital*) or something altogether different like prestige, ingenuity, style, or salvation (*symbolic capital*). Bourdieu's ideas about symbolic and cultural capital are an expansion and reworking of Karl Marx's vocabulary of economic capital. For example, Bourdieu criticizes the Marxist class theory for "reducing the social world to the economic field alone," which thereby condemns it "to define social position with reference solely to the position within the relations of economic production."[134] Bourdieu's quasi-Marxist premise of limited resources brings into play other aspects of field.

In Bourdieu's assessment, the competition over the stakes in any given field is based on a single structural principle – some players are dominant and some players are dominated. Those in dominant positions oppose the introduction of new competitors through "conservation strategies,"[135] while newcomers conversely employ "subversion strategies."[136] The dominant are trying to keep what they've got, and the newcomers are trying to get what the dominant already have. There's more to this picture of endless warfare, however: these newcomers' strategies are designed[137] to "overthrow the very principles of the game – but always in the name of the game, the spirit of the game. Their strategies of returning to the sources consist in turning against the dominant figures the very principles in the

---

[134] Bourdieu, *Language and Symbolic Power*, 244. In another sense, Bourdieu's idea of field is an imaginative application of Weber's proposed correction to Marx. According to Weber, society consists of a number of distinct, quasi-autonomous spheres – political, aesthetic, religious, and so on – that are governed by their own internal logic rather than determined by economic considerations. Max Weber, "Religious Rejections of the World and Their Directions," in *From Max Weber: Essays in Sociology*, ed. H. H. Gerth and C. Wright Mills (New York: Oxford, 1946) 323-59.

[135] That is, strategies "aimed at deriving profit from progressively accumulated capital." Bourdieu, "Haute Couture," 133. Those in dominant positions have slowly acquired a great deal of capital over time, and their strategies are designed to retain this existing capital.

[136] "The newcomers have *subversion strategies,* oriented towards an accumulation of specific capital which presupposes a more or less radical reversal of the table of values, a more or less revolutionary subversion of the principles of production and appreciation of the products and, by the same token, a devaluation of the capital of the established figures." Bourdieu, "Haute Couture," 133.

[137] Designed, that is, by the unconscious workings of *habitus*. The players themselves need not be consciously aware that they are positioned within a field, acting strategically, or interested in a particular form of capital.

name of which they justify their domination."[138] The game itself is not destroyed in this process, but the hierarchy of its players may change.[139] In other words, players can only win the game if they play by the rules. Imagine a day at Fenway where somebody hits a stand-up double and decides to run straight to second base, skipping first base altogether – the game just doesn't *play* that way. When a competitor ignores the rules, sanctions may be imposed, but the game isn't destroyed. In the above example baseball itself wouldn't be eradicated but, to use Bourdieu's vocabulary, the batter would be "removed" from play or lose his place in the "hierarchy" of the batting order. Put another way, he'd be out, and he'd probably get benched.

Another way of parsing this issue is to say that all the people or institutions in a given field, regardless of their standing, share certain basic presuppositions by virtue of their connection to the field. "The very existence and persistence of the game or field presupposes a total and unconditional 'investment', a practical and unquestioning belief, in the game and its stakes. Hence the conduct of struggle with a field ... always presupposes a fundamental accord or complicity on the part of those who participate in the struggle."[140] In order for the game to work, players must submit to the principles and believe in the value of the game – just as participants must play by the rules.

At this point you might wonder what any of this has to do with events in the *Recognitions*. In my view, Bourdieu's notion of field makes it possible to move away from conventional source critical divisions of the text, by bringing to our attention patterns that these divisions have obscured. When we use field as an interpretive lens, what once seemed like unimportant "noise" suddenly becomes relevant *data*.[141] For instance, if we think of the *Recognitions* as describing or participating in a field, we begin to get a clearer picture of the players involved. It does not classify these contestants as orthodox Christians, Gnostics, Arians, and Jewish Christians, as source critics have often divided the text. Within the field as the *Recognitions* depicts it, there are only two sides, with players grouped according to the *source of their knowledge*. Those with prophetic (and therefore certain) knowledge find themselves on the side of Peter and

---

138 Bourdieu, "Haute Couture," 134.

139 Bourdieu, "Haute Couture," 134.

140 Thompson, "Editor's Introduction," 14.

141 P. Feyerabend, *Against Method* (New York and London: Verso, 1993) 27; and idem, *Realism, Rationalism, and Scientific Method: Philosophical Papers*, vol. 1 (Cambridge: Cambridge University Press, 1981) 72.

Clement, while those with other, more fallible claims to knowledge are their opponents.[142]

Moreover, if we posit that the protagonists are the relative newcomers to the field, while astrologers and philosophers are more established contenders, we can begin to understand why the text's argument about knowledge unfolds in particular ways. Specifically, the text's wholesale appropriation of well-known philosophical and astrological ideas makes sense when we consider that newcomers in a field must employ subversion strategies to gain access to capital already possessed by others. The newcomers strategically invoke philosophical and astrological vocabularies to demonstrate their mastery of established epistemological paths. This appropriation, however, is really a subversion, since the protagonists adopt these competing vocabularies in order to show that such knowledge is fundamentally flawed or requires supplementation.

In addition, Bourdieu's concept of field allows us to see clearly that the interests of both individuals and institutions are at play – and in conflict – within the *Recognitions*. In other words, we are dealing not just with the persons of Peter and Clement, but with the institution of the apostolate. Likewise, Faustinianus serves as a representative of astrology, whose

---

[142] Bourdieu's idea of *religious specialists* is a more precise way of articulating the identity of the players in the field, especially the protagonists, in terms of salvific capital. They are individuals who are "socially recognized as the exclusive holders of the specific competence necessary for the production or reproduction of a *deliberately organized corpus* of secret (and therefore rare) knowledge." Pierre Bourdieu, "Genesis and Structure of the Religious Field," *Comparative Social Research* 13 (1991) 9. (Italics in original.) This description is remarkably resonant with the *Recognitions*' description of Peter and his followers that is reviewed in Chapter 4. They are the exclusive possessors of Jesus' words; they know precisely how to faithfully transmit and reproduce this message in its proper order; and they characterize this knowledge as both rare and secret. As a result, they control access to the "goods of salvation" and thereby maintain their authority over and against other specialists. Likewise, philosophers and astrologers constitute two rival groups of experts who have their own claims to secret or rare knowledge. Bourdieu's language of *delegation* is yet another way to describe the protagonists' claims to authority. According to Bourdieu, a "delegate...is a person who has a mandate, a commission or a power of proxy, to represent – an extraordinarily polysemic word – in other words, to show and throw into relief the interests of a person or a group." (Bourdieu, *Language and Symbolic Power*, 203.) As Bourdieu says, "the authorized spokesperson is only able to use words to act on other agents and, through their action, on things themselves, because his speech concentrates within it the accumulated symbolic capital of the group which has delegated him and of which he is the *authorized representative*." (Bourdieu, *Language and Symbolic Power*, 109-10. Italics in original.) In this case, however, Peter is the delegate not of a *group* but of a *person*. While a United States senator might be authorized by his constituents to represent the interests of the group, Peter is said to be authorized by Jesus to represent him and his message.

practitioners were politically powerful (even dangerous) and highly influential. We also see philosophical schools as an important institution within the field; they are represented not just by Faustinianus, but by the arguments of the protagonists as well.

Finally, using the idea of field enables us to see what is at stake in this contest. On one level, the cultural capital in question is truth, or true knowledge. All the competitors desire exclusive access to this knowledge, which grants them the ability to make conclusive pronouncements about the way the world is. This, in turn, is essentially the power to say how people should behave, and to determine who has status and authority.[143] And since knowledge is the key to salvation for the *Recognitions*, this claim to true knowledge also means control over salvation and the fate of the soul. As we shall see, this competition revolving around knowledge and salvation is an important key for understanding not only what takes places within the narrative, but also how the *Recognitions'* author understood his place in the religiously competitive milieu of fourth-century Syria.

Taking a New Look at the Pseudo-Clementines

Readers already familiar with scholarship on the Pseudo-Clementines will have noticed that this book does not address in any detail those issues with which the texts are most often associated, namely "Jewish Christianity" and its accompanying doctrinal and theological peculiarities. In the next several chapters, topics such as the syzygy principle, the doctrine of false scriptural passages, the polemic against the Jerusalem temple and its sacrificial system, and the insistence on the unity of God – characteristic features of the *Grundschrift* and the *Homilies* that are often taken to be the *sine qua non* of the Pseudo-Clementines – take a back seat to issues that are more important for the *Recognitions* but less often considered in connection with these texts.

There are, I believe, at least two good reasons for this shift in focus. In the first place, the "Jewish Christianity" of the Pseudo-Clementines already has received a good deal of attention, both in the history of scholarship and in current academic analyses. For many interpreters the *Homilies'* assignment of equal weight (and equal salvation-historical

---

[143] Although Geertz is not terribly popular these days, I find it helpful in this instance to think about the connection he makes between *ethos* ("the moral (and aesthetic) aspects of a given culture") and *worldview* ("the cognitive, existential aspects"). As Geertz argues, "the ethos is made intellectually reasonable by being shown to represent a way of life implied by the actual state of affairs which the world view describes, and the world view is made emotionally acceptable by being presented as an image of an actual state of affairs of which such a way of life is an authentic expression." Clifford Geertz, *The Interpretation of Cultures*, 126-7.

priority) to the teachings of Moses and Jesus is precisely what makes the Pseudo-Clementine corpus valuable for the study of ancient Judaism and Christianity. My aim is not to deny the importance of this issue, but to suggest that we can broaden our perspective on the Pseudo-Clementines. This brings me to my second reason for momentarily shifting the focus away from the Pseudo-Clementines' Jewish-Christian elements. Many modern scholars since the time of von Harnack have analyzed these texts – our main firsthand literary sources for "Jewish Christianity" – in relative isolation from other branches of Christianity and Judaism. The *Homilies* and *Recognitions* often are not placed in conversation with other late antique Syrian Jewish and Christian texts, and it is even less common to see these works used as evidence in scholarship which traces theological, political and social developments in fourth-century Syrian Christianity. This book seeks to bring the *Recognitions* into some of these conversations about late ancient Christianity and Judaism, by focusing on the text's engagement with some of the more pressing epistemological issues of its time.

Chapter 2

Philosophers and the Quest for Philosophical Truth

Introduction

The traditional interpretation of the Pseudo-Clementines, as articulated most systematically by F. C. Baur, argues that these texts – at least in their earliest layers – chronicle a conflict over authority that pits the apostles Peter and Paul against one another.[1] On this reading, Paul is the primary target of the Pseudo-Clementines' campaign to establish Peter's preëminence. Other scholars have understood these writings primarily as polemics against Marcion or Simon Magus.[2] All three readings of the opponents inscribed within the text are arguably correct, since the historical referents differ according to the source layer in question. Georg Strecker, for example, maintained that the very early *Kerygmata Petrou* contained a polemic against Paul alone, but that other textual layers have included additional polemics against opponents like Simon and Marcion.[3]

---

[1] There have been several studies of the Pseudo-Clementines' anti-Pauline tendencies since Baur. Five recent examples are: Jürgen Wehnert, "Petrus *versus* Paulus in den pseudoklementinischen Homilien 17," in *Christians as a Religious Minority in a Multicultural City: Modes of Interaction and Identity Formation in Early Imperial Rome. Studies on the Basis of a Seminar at the Second Conference of the European Association for Biblical Studies (EABS) from July 8-12, 2001, in Rome*, ed. Jürgen Zangenberg and Michael Labahn (Journal for the Study of the New Testament Supplement Series 243; London and New York: T & T Clark, 2004) 175-85; Luigi Cirillo, "L'antipaolinismo nelle Pseudoclementine. Un riesame della questione," in G. Filoramo and C. Gianotto, eds., *Verus Israel: Nuove prospettive sul giudeocristianesimo* (Brescia: Paideia Editrice, 2001) 280-303; Simon Légasse, "La polémique antipaulinienne dans le judéo-christianisme hétérodoxe," *Bulletin de Littérature Ecclésiastique* 90 (1989) 5-22, 85-100; idem, *L'antipaulinisme sectaire au temps des pères de l'église* (Cahiers de la Revue Biblique, no. 47. Paris: J. Gabalda, 2000); and Côté, *Le thème de l'opposition.* I am grateful to Ellen Aitken and François Bovon for bringing these to my attention.

[2] For example, see A. Salles, "Simon le Magicien ou Marcion?" *Vigiliae Christianae* 12 (1958) 197-224. Cf. Côté, *Le thème de l'opposition*, 95: "Simon est avant tout un μάγος." On pp. 110-23, Côté analyzes the various late antique correspondences between philosophers and magicians, which are crucial for understanding the relation between Peter and Simon in the Pseudo-Clementines.

[3] Strecker, *Judenchristentum*, 154 n. 1, 187ff. The question of Simon Magus' symbolic importance in the Pseudo-Clementines is distinct from the question of Simon's

M. J. Edwards makes an observation along the same lines: "[T]he novels are intended to annihilate many foes with a single weapon."[4] My project, however, attempts to understand why the final redactor of the *Recognitions* might have juxtaposed and layered multiple polemics aimed not only at Paul or Marcion, but at other groups with competing philosophical and astrological views as well.[5] Unlike many previous analyses, this chapter will not focus on the question of the historical figures who have been targeted by the Pseudo-Clementines. To my way of thinking, this kind of search misses an important quality of the *Recognitions*' defense of Peter's message: it is not only directed against a select group of historical figures, but more generally takes aim at *all* epistemic competition that might challenge Peter's claim to knowledge of the truth. Chapters 2 and 3 attempt to look closely at two neglected groups of "epistemic rivals" inscribed within the text: philosophers and astrologers.

Why, you might ask, are philosophical views targeted by the *Recognitions*? On the one hand, it may be tempting to conclude that philosophy is present in the *Recognitions* by virtue of the *Grundschrift*'s philosophical source(s), and leave it at that. On the other hand, when we look closely at the narrative of the *Recognitions*, we find that the philosophical materials cannot be dismissed as carelessly repeated sources,

---

identity as an historical figure. On Simon Magus see e.g. R. McL. Wilson, "Simon, Dositheus and the Dead Sea Scrolls," *Zeitschrift für Religions und Geistesgeschichte* 9 (1957) 21-30; Karlmann Beyschlag, "Zur Simon-Magus-Frage," *Zeitschrift für Theologie und Kirche* 68.4 (1971) 395-426; Gerd Lüdemann, "The Acts of the Apostles and the Beginnings of Simonian Gnosis," *New Testament Studies* 33 (1987) 420-26; Alberto Ferreiro, "Simon Magus: The Patristic-Medieval Traditions and Historiography," *Apocrypha* 7 (1996) 147-65; M. J. Edwards, "Simon Magus, the Bad Samaritan," in *Portraits: Biographical Representation in the Greek and Latin Literature of the Roman Empire*, ed. M. J. Edwards and S. Swain (Oxford: Clarendon, 1997) 69-91; T. Adamik, "The Image of Simon Magus in the Christian Tradition," in *The Apocryphal Acts of Peter: Magic, Miracles, and Gnosticism*, ed. Jan N. Bremmer (Leuven: Peeters, 1998) 52-64; and A. Tuzlak, "The Magician and the Heretic: The Case of Simon Magus," in *Magic and Ritual in the Ancient World*, ed. P. Mirecki and M. Meyer (Leiden: Brill, 2002) 416-26.

[4] Edwards, "Clementina," 462 n. 8. Edwards argues that Simon Magus and Marcion are not mutually exclusive choices for the texts' polemic, because Simon was considered "the father of all heresies" (Irenaeus, *haer.* 1.23.2); Edwards does not consider philosophers and astrologers in his treatment.

[5] Luigi Cirillo rightly points this out when he says, "Ce débat [i.e., the protagonists' debate with Faustinianus in *Rec* 8.1-10.52] a pour l'auteur la même importance (voire peut-être une importance plus grande) que la polémique de Césarée contre Simon le magicien." Cirillo goes on to say that there is no exact parallel to this discourse in the *Homilies*; he concludes that "la matière traitée est en grande partie propre aux *Reconnaissances*." Luigi Cirillo and André Schneider, *Les* Reconnaissances *du pseudo Clément: Roman chrétien des premiers siècles* (Turnhout: Brepols, 1999) 55.

because they are critically important for the text's epistemological agenda. Robert Wilken points us toward an explanation of philosophy's significance in the *Recognitions* when he writes:

The philosophical schools achieved great popularity in the Greco-Roman world because they could offer a compelling and credible way of life as well as an intelligible explanation of man, the gods, and the world. In short they gave men the certainty they were seeking.... The schools offered, writes Nock, "intelligible explanations of phenomena.... [and] a life with a scheme. One of the terms for a school of philosophy, whatever its kind, is *agoge*, which means way of teaching and way of living."[6]

In other words, philosophers were widely recognized both for the way of life they practiced and for their understanding of things divine and human.[7] Suddenly the presence of unnamed philosophers in our text begins to make sense, because the heroes of the *Recognitions* wish to be recognized and emulated for precisely the same things: their way of living and their knowledge of God and the world. It is well-known that ancient Christian authors such as Justin and Origen regularly presented Christianity as a philosophical way of life, and the *Recognitions* is no exception, at least in the sense that it employs philosophical language and ideas in articulating its vision of the Christian life.[8]

Pierre Bourdieu's concept of *field* may help to clarify this idea about the *Recognitions'* multi-level defense against competing truth-claims. Recall that Bourdieu defines *field* as "an area, a playing field, a field of objective relations among individuals or institutions competing for the same stakes."[9] If this idea is to be used to understand the inner workings of the

---

[6] Robert L. Wilken, "Collegia, Philosophical Schools, and Theology," in *The Catacombs and the Colosseum: The Roman Empire as the Setting of Primitive Christianity*, ed. Stephen Benko and John J. O'Rourke (Valley Forge, PA: Judson Press, 1971) 273; quoting A. D. Nock, *Conversion: The Old and the New in Religion from Alexander the Great to Augustine of Hippo* (Oxford: Clarendon Press, 1933) 167.

[7] Pierre Courcelle provides a survey of the characterization of philosophers by various Latin writers in antiquity, in his "La figure du philosophe d'après écrivains latins de l'Antiquité," *Journal des Savants* (1980) 85-101.

[8] Côté, *Le thème de l'opposition*, 124; Pierre Hadot, *Philosophy as a Way of Life: Spiritual Exercises from Socrates to Foucault* (transl. Michael Chase; Oxford: Blackwell, 1995) 128-30; G. Bardy, "'Philosophie' et 'philosophe' dans le vocabulaire chrétien des premiers siècles," *Revue d'Ascétique et de Mystique* 25 (1949) 97-108. Note, however, the important qualification by Côté that will be explored in great detail in Chapter 4: "les rares passages où il est fait mention de φιλοσοφία et de φιλόσοφος servent plutôt à démontrer la différence radicale qui existe entre la philosophie et la vérité du *Verus Propheta*." *Le thème de l'opposition*, 125.

[9] Bourdieu, "Haute Couture," 133. Loïc Wacquant provides a similar definition: "A field consists of a set of objective, historical relations between positions anchored in certain forms of power (or capital)." Bourdieu and Wacquant, *Invitation to Reflexive Sociology*, 16.

Recognitions, several things must be spelled out: the identity of the competitors, their particular arrangement within the field, what exactly is being contested, and what is at stake in the competition. For the sake of discussion, let's say that the field in question can be called Knowledge/Salvation. This field is described by the text, and has a narrative life of its own, even though it may correspond in various ways with sociological realities – "real life" – that exists outside the text (on this see Chapter 5). There are seven named individuals who are major players within this field: Peter, Barnabas, Clement, Niceta, Aquila, Faustinianus, and Simon Magus. These participants fall into one of two groups, depending upon the source of their knowledge. On one side are Peter, Barnabas, Clement, Niceta, and Aquila, who all have access to the prophetic knowledge provided by Jesus. On the other side is Faustinianus, whose knowledge comes from his training and expertise as a philosopher. Simon Magus, to the extent that he is present during the philosophical debates, is also a philosophical rival of Peter and his followers.[10] Whereas Faustinianus is characterized as a friendly and open-minded opponent, Simon is deceitful and unrelentingly antagonistic: in the end Faustinianus shifts his allegiance to the protagonists and their way of thinking, whereas Simon does not. In addition, there are individuals in the crowds who participate in the discussions; they are present both as supporters and antagonists of Peter and his companions, although their antagonistic role is both more prominent and more important for our purposes. These unnamed interlocutors often provide the occasion for a negative valuation of philosophical and sophistical expertise, as we shall see below.

This characterization of the philosophical rivals in the field becomes more precise if we allow that they are what Bourdieu (and Weber before him) called *religious specialists*: individuals who are "socially recognized as the exclusive holders of the specific competence necessary for the production or reproduction of a *deliberately organized corpus* of secret

---

[10] Simon is described by Aquila in *Rec* 2.7.1 as *arte magus, Graecis tamen litteris liberalibus adprime eruditus* ("by trade a magician, yet especially learned in the Greek liberal education"). Niceta (*Rec* 2.5.4) describes him in this way: *super haec autem omnia et ipse Simon vehementissimus est orator, in arte dialectica et syllogismorum tendiculis enutritus, quod autem est omnibus gravius, et in arte magica valde exercitatus* ("But besides all these things, also Simon himself is a very passionate orator, brought up in the dialectic art, and in the snares of syllogisms; but what is more troublesome than everything, he is greatly experienced in the magic art"). Simon, as the primary named opponent of Peter and his followers, wears many masks – philosopher, magician, idolater – in the *Recognitions*. Nevertheless, his philosophical skills take a back seat to his magical and idolatrous activities, which are far more prominent. Note, however, the correspondences between philosophy and magic observed by Côté, *Le thème de l'opposition*, 96-123.

(and therefore rare) knowledge."[11] This description fits well with the institutionalized transmission of organized and often esoteric knowledge that occurred in ancient philosophical schools.[12] Since both sides of the debate are represented by experts who claim to have been trained in various schools of philosophy, it makes sense to describe their debates as a competition among specialists.

However, the two groups of specialists in question are not on equal footing. Recall that for Bourdieu, competition in a field requires that some players are dominant and other players are dominated. Put another way, this means that every field has established players as well as newcomers to the competition. While the established players attempt to maintain their authority through "conservation strategies," the newcomers try to topple the established players using "subversion strategies" that devalue their opponents' capital. Such an idea fits well with what we know of Christianity in Syria: "In contrast to Judaism and paganism, Christianity was a newcomer on the religious scene with revolutionary ideas and deviant behaviour..."[13] It also fits well with the situation depicted in the *Recognitions*. In the philosophical debates, Faustinianus is the primary representative of the establishment because he defends the propositions of ancient philosophical schools. Peter and his companions are the newcomers because they claim to derive their epistemic authority from a relatively new source: the prophet Jesus, who has only recently died and never received any formal education, let alone advanced philosophical training.

Once we have established the relative position of the competitors within the field, we can see conservation and subversion strategies at work in their disagreements about what constitutes the knowledge that they possess. Both sides agree that such knowledge consists of answers to a

---

[11] Pierre Bourdieu, "Genesis and Structure of the Religious Field," 9. Italics in original. It may seem inappropriate to include philosophers under the category of "religious specialists," particularly since Bourdieu and Weber had in mind the modern Roman Catholic priesthood in their creation of this concept. Although at first blush it may seem that I am imposing a concept about modern religion on ancient philosophy, my use of this category makes sense if one considers the commonly held view that philosophical practices are the closest analogue in antiquity to modern religious life. This is suggested by Jean Leclercq's observation that "...in Antiquity, *philosophia* did not designate a theory of a means of knowledge, but a lived, experienced wisdom, and a way of living according to reason." J. Leclercq, "Pour l'histoire de l'expression 'philosophie chrétienne'," *Mélanges de Science Religeuise* 9 (1952) 221, cited by Hadot, *Philosophy as a Way of Life*, 130.

[12] We will see in Chapter 4 that the protagonists fit the definition of religious specialists in yet another way, as a result of Peter's personal connection to Jesus.

[13] Han J. W. Drijvers, "Jews and Christians at Edessa," *JJS* 36 (1985) 89.

specific set of questions: how the world came into being, how the world is governed, how individuals should act in the world, and how the world will end (if at all). The debates over these issues form the substance of the competition within the field. However, in voicing their divergent answers to such questions, the two sides reveal a deeper disagreement about the *source* of this knowledge. On the one hand, the opposition believes that such knowledge comes from philosophical expertise, which is an attempt to reinforce and retain the capital already possessed by established philosophers represented by Faustinianus (and, to some extent, Simon). The protagonists, on the other hand – despite their own philosophical expertise – believe that only prophetic knowledge handed down from Jesus really counts as knowledge. Hence while they claim to possess just as much specialized training as their opponents, they also subvert their rivals' claim to capital by appealing to prophetic knowledge as the only path to epistemological certainty. This sketch of what is being contested suggests that the symbolic capital at stake within the field is epistemic authority (or, put differently, the possession of "true knowledge"). This in turn implies other forms of capital such as prestige and power, since such knowledge gives one authority to say how the world works, as well as prescribe people's behavior within the world. Now that we have an overall sense of the parameters of the field, let's take a closer look at what the *Recognitions* has to say about the material in question.

The philosophical debates appear primarily in books 1, 2, 8, and 10 of the *Recognitions*, with some references in book 3 as well. My reading of this material suggests that it can be organized into two major analytic sections. (This arrangement reflects my own understanding of the argument's logic; the text itself has not positioned the material into these two discrete units.) The first half of my chapter, entitled "What Does it Mean to be a Philosopher?" considers the strategies used by the *Recognitions* to differentiate between philosophical expertise and real knowledge. Particular attention is given to the use of Plato's denunciation of eristic to create difference between the two opposing sides of the debate. While the text's use of Plato establishes the philosophical legitimacy of Clement, Niceta, and Aquila over and against other philosophers, its employment of the twin criteria of simplicity and brevity are used simultaneously to undermine the importance of philosophical skill.

The second half of my chapter, which is called "The Quest for Philosophical Truth," will deal with the major issues that are contested in the philosophical debates. Here we will survey what the *Recognitions* considers to be the constituent elements of the search for philosophical truth: questions about divine providence, creation, and judgment. The text presents its heroes' teaching as the only certain answer to this quest.

Moreover, it uses the two groups' positions on providence, creation and judgment to divide the world into two sides: those who agree with the protagonists' message and those who do not. The conclusion of this chapter points forward to Chapter 4's examination of the *Recognitions'* epistemological conviction that prophets are the only source of real knowledge. The philosophers may seem wise because of their sophistical expertise, but their reliance on opinion necessarily means that they have no true knowledge. Peter and his followers, however, have privileged access to knowledge because of their direct connection to the True Prophet. As we shall see toward the end of the book, this distinction between the two groups, based on the source of their knowledge, is an ingenious strategy designed to bolster the *Recognitions'* claim that all who disagree with its contents are essentially rejecting the single source of epistemological certainty.

What Does it Mean to Be a Philosopher?

Even a brief look at the writings of ancient authors such as Justin Martyr, Clement of Alexandria, Origen, or the Cappadocian Fathers reveals that philosophical skill was essential to their understanding and presentation of Christianity.[14] The second-century apologists in particular relied on their own eloquence and familiarity with philosophical terminology to present Christianity as a – often *the only* – philosophy. Hence it can be argued that the *Recognitions* participates in a well-established tradition when it makes a point of showing that Clement, Niceta and Aquila, who are charged with defending Jesus' and Peter's message against philosophical opponents, are themselves properly trained in philosophical matters. This stress on the importance of philosophical training shows that the field of philosophy is indeed a contest waged by experts.

Moreover, the text's emphasis on the protagonists' skills can be read as an attempt to gain more of the symbolic capital at stake in the field, since it challenges the idea that their philosophical opponents have exclusive possession of this capital by virtue of their own expertise in well-established philosophical traditions. However, it is significant that the *Recognitions* does not go so far as to suggest that the protagonists are themselves philosophers. Rather than challenging their credibility, this

---

[14] See e.g. Justin, *dial.* 8.1; Origen, *Cels.* 1.9. This is true even when such authors denigrate philosophical paths other than Christianity (e.g. Justin, *2 apol.* 5-6). On these writings see Chadwick, *Early Christian Thought*; Anne Marie Malingrey, *"Philosophia." Étude d'un groupe de mots dans la littérature grecque, des Présocratiques au IVᵉ siècle après J.-C.* (Paris: C. Klincksieck, 1961).

allows the text to demonstrate how these men live out philosophical ideals without falling into the institutional trappings of the philosophical establishment. Now that we have some idea of the import of these statements, let's took a closer look at what the *Recognitions* has to say about its heroes' training.

Philosophical Training: Clement, Niceta, and Aquila

At the very beginning of the *Recognitions* (1.1.1-5), the reader learns that Clement sought the answers to philosophical questions early in life.[15] This led him to study in an unspecified number of philosophical schools, which he mentions briefly in *Rec* 1.3.1. Moreover, he demonstrates his experience with philosophical interpretations of Greek literature in *Rec* 10.30.1-2:

Omnis sermo apud Graecos, qui de antiquitatis origine conscribitur, cum alios multos, tum duos praecipuos auctores habet, Orfeum et Hesiodum. horum ergo scripta in duas partes intellegentiae dividuntur, id est, secundum litteram et secundum allegoriam; et ad ea quidem quae secundum litteram sunt, ignobilis vulgi turba confluxit, ea vero quae secundum allegoriam constant, omnis philosophorum et eruditorum loquacitas admirata est.

Every discourse among the Greeks that is written on the origin of antiquity has not only two principal authors, Orpheus and Hesiod, but also many others. Now the writings of these [men] are divided into two parts of knowledge, that is, literal and allegorical; and the mob of low-born rabble flocked to the literal, but the philosophers and learned ones, in all of their loquaciousness, have lent their admiration to the allegorical.[16]

Clement's easy familiarity with these subjects suggests that he has received a good education. This is confirmed in *Rec* 8.7.6 by his brother Niceta, who says Clement was trained in the schools of the Platonists and Aristotelians.[17] Moreover, when Faustinianus wishes to discuss the issue of

---

[15] Cf. *Hom* 1.1.1 – 1.4.7. All references are to Clement as a character in the narrative of the *Recognitions* rather than as an historical figure. For an analysis of the historical basis of the person of Clement in the *Recognitions*, see Bernard Pouderon, "Flavius Clemens et le proto-Clément juif," 63-79.

[16] Cf. *Hom* 6.3.3-6.6.4, where Appion discusses Hesiod and Orpheus (and *Hom* 6.11.2-6.25.2, where Clement responds with his own expertise on matters of Greek mythology). The provenance of this material has been discussed by J. van Amersfoort, "Traces of an Alexandrian Orphic Theogony in the Pseudo-Clementines," in *Studies in Gnosticism and Hellenistic Religions presented to Gilles Quispel on the Occasion of his 65th Birthday*, ed. R. van den Broek and M. J. Vermaseren (Leiden: Brill, 1981) 13-30. Citations of the Latin text are taken from the Rehm/Strecker *GCS* edition. All translations of the Latin are my own unless otherwise noted. The only English translation of the Pseudo-Clementines available at this time is in the dated and somewhat unreliable *Ante-Nicene Fathers* series.

[17] As John Townsend notes, "The study of philosophy generally presupposed a secondary education…." John Townsend, "Education," in David Noel Freedman, ed., *The*

the existence of good and evil as it is raised by Greek philosophy, he asks to discuss this matter with Clement. This is probably because he considers Clement to be a worthy partner in debate (*Rec* 10.6.4).[18]

Much like their brother, Niceta and Aquila also have received extensive philosophical training. In *Rec* 8.7.5-6, for example, Niceta specifically mentions the philosophical schools where he and his brother were trained: *...ego non sum ignarus quae sint definitiones philosophorum...maxime quia prae ceteris philosophis Epicuri scholas frequentavi. frater autem meus Aquila magis Pyr<r>onios secutus est...itaque cum eruditis tibi auditoribus sermo est* ("I am not inexperienced with the propositions of the philosophers...particularly because I have often attended the schools of Epicurus in preference to the other philosophers. But my brother Aquila has followed Pyrrho more...therefore your discussion is with learned hearers").

We are given a fuller picture of their philosophical training when Niceta mentions his childhood with his brother Aquila in *Rec* 7.32.2-4:

vendiderunt nos cuidam Iudaeae,[19] honestae admodum feminae, Iustae nomine; quae cum emisset, habituit loco filiorum, ita ut etiam Graecis nos litteris liberalibus adtentissime erudiret. ubi autem adolevimus, etiam philosophorum studiis operam dedimus, quo possemus religionis divinae dogmata philosophicis disputationibus adserentes confutare gentiles.

...they sold us to a certain Jewess, a quite respectable woman, named Justa, who when she emancipated [us], treated us as sons, so that she very carefully instructed us in Greek liberal education. And when we grew up, we also gave our attention to studies of philosophers, so that we might be able to silence the Gentiles, by defending the teachings of the divine religion by philosophical disputations.

It seems, then, that each brother has received a solid secondary education as well as advanced training in at least one of the philosophical schools. Taken together as a group, they seem to have mastered almost the entire gamut of ancient philosophy. Such training gives each of them an opportunity to display his specialized expertise in answering various questions posed by Faustinianus, Simon or the anonymous crowds: each

---

Anchor Bible Dictionary, vol. 2 (New York: Doubleday, 1992) 315. On ancient education in general see the classic work of H. I. Marrou, *Histoire de l'éducation dans l'antiquité*, 7th ed., (Paris: Éditions du Seuil, 1971).

[18] If this were Simon choosing an opponent, we might assume he preferred Clement because he considered him to be a weak partner in debate. Faustinianus, however, is presented as eager to be converted to Clement's way of thinking. In *Rec* 8.40.5, he states: *non enim erubescam discere, si audiero quod verum est, et recte dicenti adquiescere* ("I would not be ashamed to learn, if I hear what is true, and to assent to the one speaking rightly").

[19] Other manuscripts have *iudae, iudueae,* and *viduae* in place of *Iudaeae* here (B. Rehm, *Rekognitionen*, 212). Cf. this account with *Hom* 13.7.4.

brother contributes a particular skill to the discussion. Moreover, an even stronger argument can be made based on their collective claim to knowledge of the entire philosophical canon: because Clement, Niceta and Aquila together appear to possess virtually all philosophical knowledge, this eliminates the possibility that their arguments are in any way compromised by ignorance of philosophical matters.[20] Although the brothers nowhere refer to themselves as philosophers, their expertise is not in doubt: as partners in debate, they are the equals of professional philosophers.

Although Clement, Niceta and Aquila have acquired their philosophical skills through specialized instruction, there is another way in which the protagonists can acquire such expertise: they obtain it directly from the spirit of God. This idea emerges when the reader learns that even Peter is not excluded from the realm of expertise – he, too, is someone *quem ne Graeca quidem latet eruditio, quia spiritu dei repletus est quem nihil latet* ("to whom not even Greek learning remains unknown, because he is filled with the spirit of God, to whom nothing remains unknown"; *Rec* 8.5.4). The *Recognitions* nowhere suggests that Peter has been formally trained – in fact, it emphasizes precisely the opposite (see below) – but his knowledge of Greek learning, which is divinely given, is at least equal to that possessed by his companions.

Returning to Bourdieu's vocabulary for a moment, the asserted expertise of the protagonists challenges the established players' exclusive claim to capital in two ways. In the first place, it does so by suggesting that, by virtue of their specialized training, these newcomers to the field have the same kind of expertise as their philosophical opponents. In the second place, at least one of the newcomers possesses such expertise because it has been divinely given to him; this again challenges the established players' exclusive possession of capital, but it also undermines the field itself by suggesting that expertise may be acquired from an authority higher than the institutions of the field. By now it should be clear that the *Recognitions* claims that its heroes possess philosophical expertise in one form or another. Up to this point, however, the equivalence between

---

[20] For an example of this kind of critique, see Origen, *Cels.* 1.10: "What man who is urged to study philosophy and throws himself at random into some school of philosophers, comes to do so for any reason except either that he has come across a particular teacher or that he believes some one school to be better than the rest? He does not wait to hear the arguments of all the philosophers and of the different schools, and the refutation of one and the proof of another, when in this way he chooses to be a Stoic, or a Platonist, or a Peripatetic, or an Epicurean, or a follower of some such philosophical school." Unless otherwise noted, all translations of Origen's *Contra Celsum* are taken from H. Chadwick, *Origen: Contra Celsum* (Cambridge: At the University Press, 1965). Cf. Galen, *de Ordine Libr. Suor.* 1.

philosophical expertise and knowledge has gone virtually unchallenged. We shall see in the next few pages that a differentiation between expertise and knowledge is at the heart of the *Recognitions'* philosophical program.

Ornate Speech: The Philosophical Opponents

At the same time the text insists that its heroes are experts in philosophy, it maintains that philosophers – or at least most philosophers – are little more than sophists.[21] Consider Clement's evaluation of his time spent in the philosophical schools (*Rec* 1.3.1, 3; cf. *Hom* 1.3.1-4):

ubi nihil aliud quam dogmatum adsertiones et inpugnationes videbam ac sine fine certamina, artes syllogismorum conclusionumque [agitari] versutias. ... sed hoc tantum intellegebam, quod sententiae ac definitions rerum, non pro natura sui ac veritate causarum, sed pro ingeniis defendentium, falsae imaginarentur aut verae....

There I saw nothing other than doctrines being asserted and attacked, and a contest without end, and the arts of syllogisms and the subtleties of conclusions being discussed.... But I understood only this, namely that opinions and definitions of things were imagined to be true or false, not in accordance with their nature and the truth of the matter, but in proportion to the cleverness of those who supported them.[22]

Clement is troubled that the practice of philosophy – which he assumed would provide answers to his questions about creation, divine providence, and the afterlife – doesn't seem to be concerned with answers at all! Instead, the point of philosophy appears to be an endless debate where an assertion and its exact opposite might be made with equal conviction by the same person. Clement's conclusion is that truth and falsehood in this context are not important at all. The appearance of truth is only a matter of opinion, and based largely upon the argumentative skill of the partners in debate. This is confirmed by Faustinianus in 10.5.1 (cf. Appion's assertion in *Hom* 5.10.3): *Est quidam sermo apud Graecorum philosophos vehemens valde, qui dicit, in vita hominum re ipsa neque bonum esse aliquid neque malum; sed quae videntur hominibus usu et consuetudine praeventis,*[23]

---

[21] In the *Recognitions*, sophistry is understood to be the use of ornamental language in order to win arguments, usually at the expense of the truth of a matter.

[22] Cf. Arnobius, *Adv. nationes* 2.10, as well as the view expressed centuries earlier by Plato's rival Isocrates, *Helen* 1: "There are some who are much pleased with themselves if, after setting up an absurd and self-contradictory subject, they succeed in discussing it in tolerable fashion; and men have grown old, some asserting that it is impossible to say, or to gainsay, what is false, or to speak on both sides of the same questions, others maintaining that courage and wisdom and justice are identical, and that we possess none of these as natural qualities, but that there is one sort of knowledge concerned with them all; and still others waste their time in captious disputations that are not only entirely useless, but are sure to make trouble for their disciples." Translation by George Norlin, *Isocrates* (LCL; Cambridge, MA: Harvard University Press, 1980).

[23] Here I am following the reading chosen by Rehm, which admittedly produces a rather awkward translation. The manuscript tradition reflects this judgment as well;

haec aut mala dicunt aut bona ("There is an exceedingly vigorous discussion among the Greek philosophers, which says that there is no such thing as good or evil in the life of a human; but that they call things good or evil as they are seen by men, hindered by the experience and custom of life"). For the *Recognitions*, then, philosophical argumentation (1) is more interested in arguments than answers, and (2) shows no concern for the truth.

This point is reiterated many times throughout the text. For example, in *Rec* 1.9.7 (cf. *Hom* 1.11.3-7) Clement scolds the unnamed philosophers who are taunting the apostle Barnabas: *qui veritatem non in simplicibus verbis, sed in versutis et callidis creditis habitare, et innumera milia verborum profertis, unius verbi nequaquam pretio pensitanda* ("You think that truth dwells not in simple, but in ingenious and subtle words, and produce countless thousands of words which are in no way equal to the value of even one word"). In other words, the philosophers mistake their long-winded and clever arguments for the pursuit of the truth, when in fact they are worthless in such a quest.[24] As Clement says in 1.8.2, syllogisms are *deliramenta* ("nonsense").[25] Elsewhere, in *Rec* 1.17.7, Peter says to Clement that sophistic discourse *non veritatem continens, sed imaginem veritatis* ("does not contain truth, but a semblance of truth") and depends on *specie et ornatu* ("display and ornament") for its persuasiveness. Once again, philosophy may look like the search for truth, but in reality it is nothing more than smoke and mirrors.

Peter's declaration in *Rec* 8.61.1, 4-6 adds yet another dimension to the *Recognitions'* take on philosophy:

nam quia philosophi introduxerunt verba subtilia quaedam et difficilia, ita ut ne ipsa quidem vocabula sermonum nota esse omnibus possent et intelligibilia, deus eos qui sibi artifices verborum videbantur, per omnia imperitos esse erga agnitionem veritatis ostendit. ... cetera omnia aestimatione tractantur, in quibus firmum esse nihil potest. quis enim sermo est, qui non recipiat contradictionem? et quae argumentatio est, quae non possit alia argumentatione subverti? et inde est quod ad nullum finem scientiae et

---

Rehm lists four alternatives to *praeventis* offered by different manuscripts (B. Rehm, *Rekognitionen*, 327). In any case, the sense seems to be that human beings are predisposed to consider certain things good or evil based upon their own habits and customs.

[24] Cf. *Hom* 1.14.1, where Clement offers to "embellish" (κοσμήσας) Barnabas' words with his own.

[25] The Latin *syllogismus* can denote "a form of reasoning in which a conclusion is drawn from two premises." Charlton T. Lewis and Charles Short, *A Latin Dictionary* (Cambridge, UK: Oxford University Press, 1956), s.v. *syllogismus*. The *Recognitions*, however (along with writers such as Aulus Gellius, *Noctes Atticae* 1.2.4; 5.11.8), seems to understand this term to refer to "fallacious arguments or sophisms." P. G. W. Glare, *Oxford Latin Dictionary* (Oxford: Clarendon, 2005) s.v. *syllogismus*.

agnitionis per huiusmodi disputationem pervenire homines possunt priusque finem vitae inveniunt quam quaestionum.

For because the philosophers have introduced certain subtle and difficult words, so that not even certain terms of the discussions could be known and understood by everyone, God reveals that those who considered themselves masters of words are through all things unskillful regarding the knowledge of the truth. ... All other things are conducted by estimation, in which there can be nothing firm. For instance, what discourse is there which does not receive an objection? And what argument is there that cannot be overturned by another argument? And hence it is, that by such disputation of this sort men can reach no end of knowledge and understanding, and reach the end of life sooner than they discover [the end of their] questions.

In the second half of this excerpt, Peter observes that the philosophers' arguments do not lead to definite answers. This is similar to the passages already listed above, but in this case Peter offers a slightly different explanation for the problem of uncertainty. Whereas other parts of the text stated that the philosophers showed little concern for the truth, this passage goes further than this by suggesting that they *cannot* reach the truth because they rely on opinion.

I would like to suggest that it is useful to think about these criticisms of professional philosophers in light of Plato's denunciations of sophistry. Why, you might ask, is it useful to frame our discussion of the *Recognitions* in terms of the views of a philosopher who died long before the fourth century began? To begin with, the *Recognitions* knows something of Plato's writing because he is mentioned three times in *Rec* 8.[26] Despite this relatively short list of direct references, the question remains: Why not seek to locate such ideas in more contemporary conversations?[27] Although this approach has its merits, my choice of Plato instead of fourth-century philosophical conversations reflects the overall aim of the project. Using Plato to frame this part of the analysis enables us to isolate the *Recognitions'* appeal to authority, and to address the problem of the *Recognitions'* banality.

Let me elaborate on this a bit. In the first place, the influence of Plato's thought in antiquity is unparalleled by virtually any other thinker; this is particularly true of his attacks on sophistry and eristic being considered here. As G. B. Kerferd notes, Plato's views on sophistry more or less

---

[26] For example, in *Rec* 8.20.2 the *Timaeus* is mentioned by name. Even if these references in *Rec* 8 are present by virtue of the *Grundschrift* and its philosophical sources, it remains true that the *Recognitions* is at least indirectly aware of Plato's writings.

[27] This has been done by E. Schwartz, who suggested that the philosophical material common to *Hom* 4-6 and *Rec* 10 need not be explained with reference to the use of earlier source materials; he attempted to explain this material solely on the basis of fourth-century philosophy. Schwartz, "Unzeitgemäße Beobachtungen," 186 n. 2.

"remained the standard view for the next two thousand years."[28] Hence using the great philosopher's ideas meant appealing to a recognized – indeed perhaps the highest – authority in the philosophical realm. The power of association with Plato's ideas would have given the *Recognitions'* assertions an air of authority and legitimacy.

In the second place, Plato's ideas were so widely disseminated in the ancient world – either because he established frameworks for future philosophical discussions, or because he made significant contributions to age-old conversations – that they could legitimately be said to be "in the air." In particular, Plato's views on sophistry were so well known that the *Recognitions* could invoke them and expect them to be widely recognized, even by individuals who had never read Plato for themselves: they were a common trope in antiquity. This means that the author could invoke Plato's ideas and expect them to be widely recognized as "philosophy," even by non-philosophers. Hence Plato's criticisms of sophistry had not only authoritative but also representative powers; as such they were an ideal tool the *Recognitions* could use to create a distinction between legitimate and illegitimate philosophy. Now that we have established why the text might have appealed to views on sophistry put forth by Plato as an authoritative and recognizable philosophical tool, let's take a look at the material in question.

In *Phaedrus* 267a6-b9, Socrates mentions Tisias and his pupil Gorgias, who "realised that probabilities deserve more respect than things that are true, and further made small things seem large and large things seem small by the power of language."[29] Elsewhere, in his *Euthydemus* 272a7-b1, Plato says that the brothers Euthydemus and Dionysodorus "have become so very skilled in fighting in arguments and in refuting whatever may be said, no matter whether it be true or false." Perhaps his most eloquent statement of this problem is found in the *Phaedo* 89d1-90c7:

And above all those who spend their time dealing with antinomies [*logoi antilogikoi*] end as you well know by thinking that they have become the wisest of men and that they are the only ones who have come to understand that there is nothing sound or secure at all

---

[28] G. B. Kerferd, *The Sophistic Movement* (Cambridge: Cambridge University Press, 1981) 5. Note, however, Alexander Nehamas' observation that "in the fourth century B.C. terms like 'philosophy,' 'dialectic,' and 'sophistry' do not seem to have had a widely agreed-upon application," even though "in the long run, of course, Plato...emerged victorious." Nehamas, "Eristic, Antilogic, Sophistic, Dialectic: Plato's Demarcation of Philosophy from Sophistry," *History of Philosophy Quarterly* 7.1 (1990) 5.

[29] Translation by Kerferd, *Sophistic Movement,* 32. On the rather widespread assertion that sophists were relativists, see Richard Bett, "The Sophists and Relativism," *Phronesis* 34.2 (1989) 139-69. I thank Russ Dancy for his bibliographic advice about Plato's attacks on sophistry.

either in facts or in arguments, but that all things that are, are simply carried up and down like the [tidal flow in the] Euripus and never stay at any point for any duration of time.[30]

In these passages, Plato takes issue with *antilogic* and *eristic* as they are used in philosophical discourse. Antilogic, as Plato uses it, is the practice of "opposing one logos to another logos, or…discovering or drawing attention to the presence of such an opposition in an argument or in a thing or state of affairs."[31] Unlike eristic, according to Kerferd, it is a specific technique: "proceeding from a given logos, say the position adopted by an opponent, to the establishment of a contrary or contradictory logos in such a way that the opponent must either accept both logoi, or at least abandon his first position."[32]

Eristic, on the other hand, derives from ἔρις, which is defined as "strife, quarrel, contention, disputation."[33] As Plato uses the term, it means "'seeking victory in argument,' and the art which cultivates and provides appropriate means and devices for so doing."[34] Eristic is not necessarily concerned with truth, because truth is not essential for winning arguments. According to Kerferd, "fallacies of any kind, verbal ambiguities, long and irrelevant monologues may all on occasion succeed in reducing an opponent to silence and so be appropriate tools of eristic."[35] Plato was completely against eristic practices, and regarded antilogic as a technique that, while in itself neither good nor bad, could be used in the service of eristic.[36] In sum, Plato objected to sophistic techniques of argumentation insofar as they were designed to ensure victory in argument at the expense of the truth. This is precisely the objection voiced by the protagonists of the *Recognitions*, as we have seen. Since Plato's negative valuation of sophistry and eristic were widely disseminated and adopted, it is reasonable to assume that the *Recognitions* is making use of these ideas as

---

[30] Translation by Kerferd, *Sophistic Movement*, 66.

[31] Kerferd, *Sophistic Movement*, 63. Cf. James Stuart Murray, "Interpreting Plato on Sophistic Claims and the Provenance of the 'Socratic Method'," *Phoenix* 48 (1992) 130-1, who agrees with Kerferd's assessment about "Plato's ambivalent attitude toward ἀντιλογική"; and Nehamas, "Eristic, Antilogic, Sophistic, Dialectic," 6-10, who takes issue with some aspects of Kerferd's characterization of Plato on antilogic and dialectic.

[32] Kerferd, *Sophistic Movement*, 63. For example, the technique of antilogic might involve arguments that a given practice is both just and unjust. Nehamas disagrees with Kerferd's argument that antilogic is a method, preferring instead to characterize antilogic as "the use of dialectic for the purpose of generating (or avoiding) a contradiction." Nehamas, "Eristic, Antilogic, Sophistic, Dialectic," 9.

[33] H. G. Liddell, R. Scott, and H. S. Jones, *A Greek-English Lexicon* (Oxford: Clarendon Press, 1996) s.v. ἔρις.

[34] Kerferd, *Sophistic Movement*, 62.

[35] Kerferd, *Sophistic Movement*, 63.

[36] Kerferd, *Sophistic Movement*, 65.

a common trope of philosophical discourse. The *Recognitions'* use of this trope enables it to divide philosophers into two groups: professionals who are more interested in arguments than true knowledge, and the protagonists, who – whether professionally trained or not – are searching for the true answers to philosophical questions. While the latter group is engaged in a legitimate and praiseworthy pursuit, the former group is little more than a gaggle of sophists.

Although the previous paragraphs might suggest otherwise, the *Recognitions'* denigration of sophistical maneuverings does not necessarily mean that it disdains or devalues polished language. For example, a statement made by Clement in *Rec* 1.25.2 shows that the *Recognitions* values eloquence: *qua si utamur in antiquitatis erroribus, in perniciem vitae verborum decore ac suavitate decidimus; si vero ad adserendam veritatem eruditionem sermonis et gratiam conferamus, puto ex hoc non parum utilitatis adquiri* ("And if we use [learning in asserting] the errors of antiquity, we ruin ourselves by gracefulness and pleasantness of language; if, on the other hand, we apply learning and grace of language to the assertion of the truth, I think that not a little advantage is gained from this"). Eloquence can be advantageous, but only if it is used to speak the truth; as we have seen, the *Recognitions* has little tolerance for graceful speech that upholds "the errors of antiquity." While eloquence is appreciated, simplicity and brevity in speaking are also desirable. Let's take a closer look at this new idea to see if it makes sense in conjunction with what we have learned thus far.

Simple and Brief Speech: Barnabas and Peter

Although the *Recognitions* may have been able to make philosophical experts of Clement and his brothers, its characterization of Peter and Barnabas is quite another matter. After all, it was a well-established tradition – in the New Testament Gospels, the book of Acts, and other early Christian texts – that Jesus' disciples generally were not well-educated people.[37] Acts 4.13 is particularly important in this regard, because it is somewhat similar to what we find in the *Recognitions*. It says that the rulers, elders, and scribes were amazed when they saw the boldness (παρρησίαν) of Peter and John and realized that they were uneducated (ἀγράμματοι) and ordinary people (ἰδιῶται).[38] Since the

---

[37] The Gospels' characterization of the apostles is relevant because the *Recognitions* uses at least two of them (Matthew and Luke) as sources. My references to Barnabas and Peter are as characters in the *Recognitions* rather than historical persons.

[38] The western text D, however, does not contain the reference to Peter and John as ἰδιῶται. A similar sentiment is expressed in John 7.15, where Jesus is described by "the Jews" as never having been taught (μὴ μεμαθηκώς). It is important to note that in these contexts, Jesus and the disciples' lack of education was probably not a reference to

Grundschrift's sources (and hence the *Recognitions*) seem to be directly dependent on Acts in certain places,[39] and since this characterization of the disciples was relatively common in any case, we can assume that the author of the *Recognitions* was familiar with it. How, then, could these famous figures who were widely recognized as ordinary, uneducated men fit into the portrait of philosophical expertise that has been sketched thus far? How could Barnabas and Peter, as characters in the *Recognitions*, hold their own against professional philosophers? Moreover, given their lack of education, how could they possibly claim to have specialized knowledge that was unavailable to their interlocutors? The *Recognitions* solves this problem in an ingenious way. Rather than attempt to portray Barnabas and Peter as skilled philosophers,[40] the narrative suggests that their *lack of expertise* gives them more direct access to philosophical truth.[41] Such a strategy effectively means that the text now has two rather different ways of asserting the protagonists' philosophical legitimacy. We have already seen the argument that Clement, Niceta and Aquila have an equally valid claim to philosophical expertise, which challenges the established philosophers' exclusive claim to capital. We have also witnessed the text's assertion that philosophical expertise is not necessarily concerned with true knowledge, which undermines the field of philosophy itself. At this point, we arrive at a third argument designed to suggest that the protagonists have more direct access to truth precisely because they *lack* the trappings of the philosophers. Simplicity and brevity now become the markers of philosophical truth, and emerge as the first step in a campaign to take over the newly compromised field of philosophy.[42]

---

institutionalized philosophical training. The *Recognitions*, however, appropriates these references and uses them to refer to the disciples' lack of philosophical expertise.

[39] On the question of the relationship between Acts and the *Grundschrift*, see F. Stanley Jones, "A Jewish Christian Reads Luke's Acts of the Apostles: The Use of the Canonical Acts in the Ancient Jewish Christian Source behind Pseudo-Clementine *Recognitions* 1.27-71" (SBLSP 34; Atlanta: Scholars Press, 1995); and idem, "An Ancient Jewish Christian Rejoinder to Luke's Acts of the Apostles: Pseudo-Clementine Recognitions 1.27-71," *Semeia* 80 (1997) 223-45.

[40] In several places the *Recognitions* states that Peter and the other apostles are "unlearned" (*imperitus*) and "rustic" (*rusticus*); see *Rec* 1.62.2-7 and 1.63.1, for example.

[41] As I mentioned above, the exception to this is *Rec* 8.5.4, which suggests that Peter has acquired *Graeca...eruditio* ("Greek learning") directly from the spirit of God. Although it would be easy to understand *Rec* 8.5.4 as contradicting the text's emphasis on Peter and Barnabas' simple speech, I believe it makes more sense to regard these as two complementary rhetorical strategies at work. On this reading, the text can simultaneously assert that (1) Peter is a formidable foe for his philosophically-trained opponents and (2) Peter and Barnabas are more honest and knowledgeable than their rivals.

[42] Origen makes a similar argument in *Cels.* 1.62: "For it was not any power of speaking, or any orderly arrangement of their message, according to the arts of Greek

According to the *Recognitions*, simplicity in speaking is a sign of true knowledge in several respects. In the first place, plain speech is an indication of honesty. This is shown clearly by an episode that takes place in *Rec* 1.7.14 (cf. *Hom* 1.9.2; 1.10.1-2). There Clement, fresh from his stint with the philosophical schools and weary of their posturing, finds the apostle Barnabas a refreshing change: *intellegebam sane quod nihil dialecticae artis esset in homine, sed simpliciter et absque ullo dicendi fuco, quae audisset a filio dei vel vidisset, exponeret* ("Truly I understood that there was nothing of dialectical artifice in the man, but speaking simply without any pretense, he explained what he heard from the Son of God, and what he saw"). It is important to note that a correspondence is set up between skillful speech and deception on the one hand, and simple speech and honesty on the other hand.[43] Barnabas' straightforward and plain style of exposition shows that he is an honest man. As we have seen, honesty is not a prominent characteristic of the philosophers – they are willing to do everything in their power, including telling lies, to win arguments.

Second, Barnabas' and Peter's plain speaking shows that they want their message to reach the widest possible audience. This is precisely the opposite of the professional philosophers' goal, according to the *Recognitions*. Consider Clement's defense of Barnabas' simple preaching

---

dialectics or rhetoric, which was in [the apostles] the effective cause of converting their hearers. No, I am of the opinion that if Jesus had selected some individuals who were wise according to the apprehension of the multitude, and who were fitted both to think and speak so as to please them, and had used such as the ministers of his doctrine, he would most justly have been suspected of employing artifices, like those philosophers who are the leaders of certain sects, and consequently the promise respecting the divinity of his doctrine would not have manifested itself; for had the doctrine and the preaching consisted in the persuasive utterance and arrangement of words, then faith also, like that of the philosophers of the world in their opinions, would have been through the wisdom of men, and not through the power of God." Cf. Minucius Felix, *Octavius* 16, which argues that "the more unskilled the discourse, the more evident the reasoning, since it is not colored by the pomp of eloquence and grace; but as it is, it is sustained by the rule of right"; and Theophilus of Antioch, *Autol.* II.35, which characterizes the Hebrew prophets as ἀγράμματοι καὶ ποιμένες καὶ ἰδιῶται ("illiterate, and shepherds, and uneducated"). Translations of Minucius Felix and Theophilus of Antioch are from A. Roberts and J. Donaldson, *The Ante-Nicene Fathers* (10 vols.; Grand Rapids, MI: Eerdmans, 1975).

[43] Cf. Athenagoras, *leg.* 11: "[philosophers] ever persist in delving into the evil mysteries of their sophistry, ever desirous of working some harm, making skill in oratory rather than proof by deeds their business. With us, on the contrary, you will find unlettered people, tradesmen and old women, who, though unable to express in words the advantages of our teaching, demonstrate by acts the value of their principles. For they do not rehearse speeches, but evidence good deeds." Translation by Cyril F. Richardson, *Early Christian Fathers* (New York: Collier, 1970) 310.

in 1.9.4-5 (here he is condemning the philosophers who taunt Barnabas; cf.
Hom 1.11.4):

*nam cum videatis praedicatores voluntatis dei advenisse, quia nullam sermo eorum
grammaticae artis scientiam profitetur, sed simplicibus et inpolitis sermonibus perferunt
ad vos divina mandata, ita ut omnes qui audiunt, sequi possint et intellegere quae
dicuntur; ridetis salutis vestrae ministros et nuntios, ignorantes quia vestra, qui vobis
periti et eloquentes videmini, condemnatio est, quod apud agrestes et barbaros habetur
veritatis agnitio.*

For when you see that preachers of the will of God have come, because their language
makes no show of knowledge of grammatical skill, but in plain and unrefined speeches
they announce to you the divine commands, so that all who hear may be able to follow
and to understand the things that are spoken, you ridicule the servants and messengers of
your salvation, not knowing that it is the condemnation of you who think yourselves
skillful and eloquent, that knowledge of the truth is had by rustic and uncivilized men.

While the philosophers' complicated maneuverings have greatly restricted
access to knowledge of the truth (*Rec* 8.61.1), Peter and Barnabas want to
make such knowledge available to the widest possible audience. By
speaking in a straightforward manner, the protagonists ensure that
everyone who seeks after the truth will find it: no one will be excluded
because he lacks skill in philosophical matters.

If we return to Clement's portrait of Barnabas in *Rec* 1.7.14, we find a
third way in which simple speech is a sign of true knowledge: in this
passage, his unadorned language is evidence of his personal connection to
the True Prophet, or – put another way – his direct access to the truth.
Peter makes a similar assertion in *Rec* 8.61.2 (cf. *Hom* 1.19.2-4): *simplex
enim est et manifesta ac brevis rerum scientia, quae per verum prophetam
traditur, quam isti per devia incedentes et scrupeas verborum difficultates,
tota ignoraverunt via* ("For the knowledge of things that is handed down
by the True Prophet is simple, and plain, and brief; these [philosophers],
moving through indirect ways and through the rough difficulties of words,
are completely unaware of such [knowledge]").[44] The text has turned the
meaning of straightforward speech on its head: instead of being a sign of
ignorance or lack of education, it becomes a mark of direct access to the
certain knowledge provided by the True Prophet. The philosophers, who
are known for their eloquence, become those who are ignorant of the
correct path to knowledge. This appeal to directness is underscored by the
use of *devia* here, which connotes something out of the way, or "off the
beaten path."

Fourth, Peter's statement to Clement in *Rec* 1.17.7 (cf. *Hom* 1.20.7), on
the eve of the former's disputation with Simon, adds two other dimensions
to this part of the discussion. Here Peter expresses his hope that the

---

[44] I am grateful to François Bovon for his help with this translation.

audience at the disputation will be able to recognize *qui sermo ex arte sofistica veniat, non veritatem continens, sed imaginem veritatis, et qui [sit qui] simpliciter ac sine fuco prolatus, omnem vim non in specie et ornatu, sed in veritate et ratione possideat* ("the sort of speech which comes from sophistical skill, not containing truth, but an image of truth; and what, advanced simply and without pretense, has all its power not in display and ornament, but in truth and reason"). Here there is a differentiation between appearance and reality: overblown language and sophisticated techniques of argumentation might *look* like truth, but their power lies only in "display and ornament." Plain speech like that in Peter's preaching is not dependent on rhetorical pyrotechnics for its effectiveness. Instead, his message is powerful because it draws on truth and reason. There is a parallel example in *Rec* 2.67.2, where Peter's message is regarded as powerful because it draws on the (Pentateuchal) law. Here in *Rec* 1.17.7, reason is not opposed to faith, but essential for reinforcing what is received by faith. In other words, at this moment the *Recognitions* is appropriating a core tenet of philosophy in order to beat philosophers at their own game. Just as philosophers (particularly Stoics) in this era made appeals to reason in their philosophical arguments, the *Recognitions* makes its own appeal to reason in order to suggest that Peter's preaching is the most reasonable philosophy of all.

In this section, we have seen that the *Recognitions'* emphasis on the simplicity of Barnabas' and Peter's speech serves several purposes. It suggests that they are honest men, and that they want their message to be understood by everyone who hears it. Their plain speech shows that they are passing on the words of the True Prophet, whose message is always simple and direct.[45] Moreover, their unadorned language has a power that comes from reason and from the workings of God, rather than from the bells and whistles of their own philosophical ingenuity. In all these ways, Peter and Barnabas' simple speech demonstrates their possession of real knowledge rather than a mere appearance of knowledge. As a result of this maneuvering, the *Recognitions* can claim that its protagonists possess the knowledge that counts as symbolic capital in the newly reconstituted field of Knowledge/Salvation. Philosophical expertise initially appeared to be identical to knowledge, but together these textual strategies have worked to take over the field of philosophy by suggesting that philosophical expertise is not necessarily knowledge after all. The philosophical opponents' expertise may now count against them in this reconfigured field, since such skill may actually be a hindrance to the acquisition of true knowledge.

Thus far we have explored the multiple implications of the *simplicity* of Barnabas' and Peter's words. In addition to emphasizing their unadorned

---

[45] This idea will be developed in greater detail in Chapter 4.

language, the text also refers to the *brevity* of the protagonists' speech on a number of occasions.[46] For instance, when Clement asks Peter to answer his philosophical questions about the origin of the world, Peter replies in *Rec* 1.14.5: *Breviter, inquit, tibi, o Clemens, rerum scientiam tradam* ("I shall briefly transmit to you the knowledge of these things, O Clement"). The brevity and concision of Peter's answer is underscored a few paragraphs later in *Rec* 1.25.4-5, when Clement recites this knowledge he has learned from Peter:

Unus est deus, cuius opus mundus est, quique quia iustus est omnimodis, unicuique pro actibus suis reddet. et post haec addidisti, dicens: Pro cuius dogmatis adsertione innumera verborum milia movebuntur; sed his, quibus veri prophetae concessa scientia est, omnis ista verborum silva succisa est.

There is one God, whose work the world is, and who, because he is wholly just, renders to everyone according to his deeds. And after this you [i.e. Peter] added, saying: For the assertion of this dogma countless thousands of words will be occasioned; but for these, to whom knowledge of the True Prophet is granted, all this forest of words is cut down.[47]

This passage tells us several things. First, the content of this knowledge has only four elements: there is only one God; God made the world; God is righteous; God will reward and punish individuals based on their deeds. Second, knowledge of the True Prophet makes it possible for Peter and his followers to clearly and briefly articulate this message. Third, those who do not know the True Prophet display their lack of knowledge by speaking at great length. Brevity, then, becomes the mark of true knowledge and evidence of one's connection to the True Prophet. This conclusion is spelled out explicitly by Peter in *Rec* 8.61.2: *simplex enim est et manifesta ac brevis rerum scientia, quae per verum prophetam traditur* ("For the knowledge of things that is handed down by the True Prophet is simple, and plain, and brief").

Characters in other philosophical texts share the *Recognitions'* preference for brevity in speaking (βραχυλογία). In several of Plato's

---

[46] This valuation of brevity seems supremely ironic in light of the overwhelming length of the *Recognitions*, much of which consists of long-winded speeches given by its various characters.

[47] Peter, speaking to Simon, makes a nearly identical statement in *Rec* 2.36.4-5: *cupio enim quod salutare et utile est omnibus adduci in notitiam, et ideo proferre quam brevissime non morabor. unus est deus, idemque conditor mundi, iustus iudex et unicuique pro actibus suis quandoque restituens. iam vero pro adsertione horum scio innumera posse verborum milia commoveri* ("Indeed I wish that what is beneficial and useful be brought together in the acquaintance of all; and therefore I shall not delay to mention it as briefly as possible. There is one God; and he is the founder of the world, a just judge, rendering to everyone at one time or other according to his deeds. But now for the assertion of these things I know that countless thousands of words can be produced.")

dialogues, Socrates' sophistic interlocutors make claims to βραχυλογία.[48] In Plato's *Gorgias* 449b10-c3, for example, Gorgias tells Socrates that he will "try to be as brief as possible; for indeed it is one of my claims that no one could express the same thing in briefer terms than myself."[49] This same predilection is often expressed by the Platonic Socrates; he repeatedly objects to long speeches and demands brief answers to his questions.[50] He tells Protagoras: "For you say yourself, and it is said about you, that you are able to speak in a company both at great length and with extreme brevity – for you are a wise man...."[51] The sophistic *Dissoi Logoi* (8.1; 8.13), according to Kerferd, leads to the conclusion that speaking briefly is "the mark of the man who knows the truth about things."[52] Returning to the *Recognitions*, we can say that its emphasis on the brevity of Peter's speech suggests that the apostle knows exactly what he is talking about. Once again, the protagonists appear to be the ones holding all the capital within the field of Knowledge/Salvation. Now that we have a sense of how the text positions its characters within this field, let's take a closer look at what is being contested within the field.

The Quest for Philosophical Truth

Thus far we have seen that all the major characters are portrayed in terms of their philosophical skills (or lack thereof). It should come as no surprise,

---

[48] Murray, "Interpreting Plato on Sophistic Claims," 118-19.

[49] Translation by W. R. M. Lamb, *Plato: Lysis, Symposium, Gorgias* (LCL; Cambridge, MA: Harvard University Press, 1961) 267.

[50] See, for example, *Prt.* 329b1-5, 334e4-335a3; *Grg.* 449c4-6, 461d6-462a2. Kerferd, *Sophistic Movement*, 32. There has been some discussion about whether *brevity* refers to a method of inquiry or a terse style of speaking. E. R. Dodds, for example, has suggested that in *Grg.* 449c2, "Plato's language seems to imply that the συντομία of Protagoras and Gorgias was simply a laconic style, 'putting a thing in the fewest possible words', not a technique of investigation." E. R. Dodds, *Plato, Gorgias: A Revised Text with Introduction and Commentary* (Oxford: Clarendon Press, 1959) 195. Kerferd, who thinks it implausible that any sophist would want to speak briefly about anything, believes that brevity was "a technique of argument and of teaching." Kerferd, *Sophistic Movement*, 33. Cf. Murray, "Interpreting Plato on Sophistic Claims," 118-19, 128-30; and the classic article of H. Sidgwick, "The Sophists," *Journal of Philology* 4 (1872) 288-307.

[51] *Prt.* 335b7-10. Translation is from Murray, "Interpreting Plato on Sophistic Claims," 119. It should be noted, however, that such brevity on the part of the sophists is not necessarily taken as a mark of true understanding in Plato's Socratic dialogues; see e.g. Socrates' sarcastic comment in *Grg.* 449d1-4. Murray, "Interpreting Plato on Sophistic Claims," 126.

[52] H. Diels and W. Kranz, *Die Fragmente der Vorsokratiker* vol. 2 (6th ed.; Zürich: Weidmann, 1985) 90. Quote is from Kerferd, *Sophistic Movement*, 32.

then, that the *Recognitions* presents itself as a text that deals primarily with philosophical matters. Such is the case at the very beginning of the *Recognitions*, where we find Clement's summary of his early life. As a young man growing up in the city of Rome, Clement was preoccupied with questions about the beginning of the world and the afterlife. His desire to find the answers to such questions led him to schools of philosophy, as *Rec* 1.3.1 reports (cf. *Hom* 1.1.2 – 1.4.7). Readers will probably recognize this canonical pattern of the philosophical search from Justin Martyr's *Dialogue with Trypho*, Josephus' *War* and *Antiquities*, and Philostratus' *Life of Apollonius*.[53] The satirist Lucian of Samosata uses this trope as well. In his *Piscator*, he parodies the pattern with an unexpected outcome: *his* quest for philosophical truth leads him to a prostitute![54] Although Clement does not end up in circumstances as interesting as these, Lucian's satire suggests that this kind of quest would have been easily recognized by ancient readers – it was so familiar, in fact, that it could be parodied. The *Recognitions*, then, has made use of a well-known narrative device to let its readers know from the very beginning that it is concerned with philosophical matters.

Moreover, the opening storyline tells the readers something else: the *Recognitions'* own message constitutes the knowledge that is the true answer to the philosophical quest narrated within its pages. As Clement says in *Rec* 1.2.3 (cf. *Hom* 1.17.1-4), *haec me animi intentio ad inquisitionem veritatis et agnitionem verae lucis adduxit* ("this exertion of intellect led me to the search for truth, and the acknowledgement of the true light"). Specifically, Clement's search will provide him with answers to his questions about humanity's place in the world, as well as the world's beginning and end; the correct understanding of these topics constitutes the "truth" as the *Recognitions* sees it. In this section of Chapter 2, we will look at three subjects closely related to Clement's questions: providence, creation, and judgment. These issues form the substance of the debates between the two groups of competitors studied earlier in the chapter. In addition, each issue is used to reinforce the dividing line between the two

---

[53] Justin, *dial.* 2; Josephus, *BJ* 2.8.14 (162-63, 66); *AJ* 13.5.9 (172); 18.1.3 (12-15); Plutarch, *Moralia* 410a-b, 421a-b; Philostratus, *VA* 1.7; 6.11. Justin writes a more detailed account of the time he spent with individual philosophical schools than is found in the *Recognitions*. Josephus is speaking of Jewish sects rather than philosophical schools *per se*. As has often been noted, however, he presents the Pharisees, Sadducees, and Essenes as philosophical schools rather than religious sectarian groups. For other examples of the quest trope see Ian Moyer, "Thessalos of Tralles and Cultural Exchange," in *Prayer, Magic, and the Stars in the Ancient and Late Antique World*, ed. Scott Noegel, Joel Walker, and Brannon Wheeler (University Park, PA: Pennsylvania State University Press, 2003) 41 n. 9.

[54] Lucian, *Pisc.* 11-12.

groups, with the result that the protagonists are on the side of God, pious human beings, and the truth, while their opponents side with false prophets, idolaters, and the like.

Providence

Although Stoics are perhaps best known for such ideas, discussions of fate and divine providence occupied a prominent place in many philosophical circles in antiquity.[55] The ubiquity and importance of these conversations help us to understand how providence functions in the *Recognitions*. Generally speaking, the text maintains three things about providence: (1) it "rules and governs" the world; (2) it always works for good; and (3) it cannot always be understood by human beings. At this point one might wonder if we should even bother to discuss these ideas in any detail. After all, it is immediately obvious that such views are commonplace in antiquity, just as the critiques of sophistry covered earlier in this chapter are rather ordinary. Rather than dismiss the significance of these views for the *Recognitions* simply because they are pedestrian, I would like to suggest that such ideas may have been chosen *precisely because* they were ordinary and easily recognizable. In other words, the author values not originality but familiarity: the presence of these notions of providence in both philosophical and biblical materials indicates that they will be widely understood and accepted by the *Recognitions'* readers.[56] Moreover, although these topics can be located in many other ancient texts, this tells us little about what such ideas accomplish for the *Recognitions* itself. Understanding how these seemingly humdrum topics work *within the text* remains a vital task. In the following paragraphs, we will pay special attention to the three characteristics of providence as they appear in the

---

[55] Origen in particular offers a close parallel to the *Recognitions'* ideas on fate and providence. For Origen, fate annuls free will, as well as responsibility and merit for one's actions. On this point, and for a general survey of ideas on fate, free will, and providence, see D. Amand, *Fatalisme et liberté dans l'antiquité grecque: Recherches sur la survivance de l'argumentation morale antifataliste de Carnéade chez les philosophes grecs et les théologiens chrétiens des quatre premiers siècles* (Université de Louvain, Recueil de travaux d'histoire et de philologie, 3rd series, fasc. 19, 1945; reprinted Amsterdam: Adolf M. Hakkert, 1973). To cite another example, Harold Attridge has argued convincingly about Josephus' preoccupation with God's providential design in his *Antiquities*; see Harold W. Attridge, *The Interpretation of Biblical History in the Antiquitates Judaicae of Flavius Josephus* (Harvard Dissertations in Religion 7; Missoula, MT: Scholars Press, 1976). One need hardly mention the Stoic preoccupation with nature, which designates "the rational order which presides over the evolution of the visible world." Hadot, *Philosophy as a Way of Life*, 283.

[56] Both philosophical and biblical materials are understood by the author as authoritative; both are appealed to during the debates. As we shall see, the author sees providential design behind a number of the biblical stories.

major philosophical passages on the subject: a discourse by Niceta in *Rec* 8[57] and the romance of recognitions that is scattered throughout the *Recognitions*.[58]

There are three ways the *Recognitions* works to establish God's providential governance of the world.[59] First, the protagonists offer interpretations of events from the biblical past that demonstrate the workings of providence. The *Recognitions'* use of these biblical texts[60] tells us that the author and his readers probably agree on their authoritative status, since it is presupposed rather than questioned. However, the protagonists' providentially-centered rereading of these stories sometimes eclipses their original contents. Consider Peter's description of the "fall" of humanity in *Rec* 4.10.3:

hinc proficiunt in deterius, ut neque providentia dei mundum regi crederent neque virtutibus esse aliquem locum, quandoquidem semetipsos scirent nullis prius bonis operibus adsignatis otii ac deliciarum summam tenere et amicos dei absque ullis laboribus haberi.

For this reason they become worse and worse, when they believe neither that the providence of God governs the world, nor that there is any place for virtues, inasmuch as they realized that they themselves, having been assigned no good works before, possessed the greatest of leisure and delights, and without any labors were considered friends of God.

Here *vexationis iter ac tribulationis* ("the way of distress and tribulation"; *Rec* 4.11.5) for humanity has its roots in privileging *rerum sorte* ("the chance of things"; *Rec* 4.10.1) over God's providential ordering of the world. It appears that the denial of providence (rather than eating from the tree of the knowledge of good and evil as reported in Genesis) is the cause of the "fall" of humanity, which is characterized by *Rec* 4.11.2 as *deliciarum et amoenitatis exclusi sunt loco* (exclusion "from the place of delights and charm"). Elsewhere, in *Rec* 1.29.4, Peter attributes the Genesis flood to *iusta dei providentia* ("the righteous providence of God"). In *Rec* 1.32.3, he praises the patriarch Abraham for recognizing the

---

[57] Recall that this material is most likely a separate source originally used by the *Grundschrift* and adopted by the *Recognitions* (as well as the *Homilies*).

[58] This may also be a separate source used by the *Grundschrift*, although Rehm and Strecker have expressed doubts. For a summary of this discussion see Jones, "Pseudo-Clementines," 31-33.

[59] Readers may notice that this survey of the text's treatment of providence does not really deal with *debates* on providence at all. The discussion of providence in this chapter is intended to lay the foundation for the actual debates about astral determinism and providence that will be covered in Chapter 3.

[60] Most examples are drawn from the Pentateuch, although some refer to New Testament Gospel episodes as well.

workings of providence from the arrangement of the stars.[61] In *Rec* 1.38.3, divine providence helps the Israelites conquer their enemies. Providence is even credited with the spread of the gospel (i.e. belief in Jesus as the messiah) to Jews (*Rec* 1.43.1) and gentiles (*Rec* 5.12.1).

These interpretations of biblical history along providential lines serve several interrelated purposes. They make the important point that biblical texts can be appealed to as historical evidence of God's providential design, and hence can be used in the context of philosophical debates. This essentially means that biblical texts are recognized as containing philosophical knowledge. Moreover, these rereadings – which, like the biblical texts themselves, are accepted by narrator and implied audience alike – affirm the protagonists' status as authoritative interpreters of philosophical texts and ideas. In particular, since the audience knows that he is correct, Peter's understanding of these biblical stories establishes him as an authoritative interpreter of events. This lays the foundation for the rest of Peter's interpretive agenda.

In addition to their interpretation of the biblical past, the protagonists also argue that the events happening around them – that is, in the "now" of the narrative – should be understood in light of providential design. The "ever-present" nature of providence is prominent in the *Recognitions*, especially because the protagonists (most notably Peter) interpret many events as providential design unfolding before their eyes. For example, in *Rec* 1.21.4 (cf. *Hom* 2.36.1-2) Peter tells Clement not to worry about the delay in his dispute with Simon: *Qui credit summi dei providentia dispensari mundum, non debet, o amice Clemens, de singulis quae quoquo modo accidunt, aspernanter accipere, certus quod iustitia dei etiam ea, quae superflua videntur aut contraria, in unoquoque negotio oportuno exitu conpetentique dispensat* ("He who believes that the world is managed by the providence of the Most High God should not, O Clement my friend, receive contemptuously the manner in which these things happen individually, because [it is] certain [that] the righteousness of God manages even these things, which seem superfluous and conflicting in every single situation, to an advantageous and suitable end"). He assures Clement that the postponement is the result of providence, rather than a hindrance to the apostolic mission.

Yet, Peter is not the only one who knows about providence. In *Rec* 2.6.8, Aquila tells Peter that his former involvement with Simon was the result of providence: *unde et arbitror opus fuisse divinae providentiae, ut nos primo familiares eius effecti notitiam caperemus, quomodo vel quali arte prodigia quae facere videtur efficiat* ("And for this reason I think that

---

[61] This idea is found in a number of texts from antiquity; see Kugel, *Traditions of the Bible*, 259-61. Abraham's astronomical/astrological skills will be discussed in Chapter 3.

it was the work of divine providence, that we, first having been made his companions, should get to know what way or by what art he produces the marvels which he seems to perform"). In fact, all of the protagonists seem to understand that whatever occurs may be safely understood to be part of God's plan. In *Rec* 7.3.1 (cf. *Hom* 12.3.1), Peter's followers tell him that they are not saddened by their impending separation from him, because they know providence has called on Peter to make such a decision: *Non valde nos contristat hoc agere quia a te iubemur, qui omnia et bene agere et bene consulere per Christi providentiam electus es* ("It does not greatly sadden us to do this, because we are appointed by you, who have been chosen by the providence of Christ to do well and to advise well in all things"). Clement also looks to divine providence as a guiding force. In *Rec* 7.7.6 (cf. *Hom* 12.7.6), he says to Peter that he is grateful to God's providence, *quod parentum loco habere te merui* ("because I have deserved to have you instead of parents"). Clement believes that providence has brought him to Peter; he is able to see the divine purpose even in the face of losing his own parents. Of course, there is irony of Clement's statement: providence is already at work restoring his biological parents (and siblings) to him.

Although most of the protagonists are cognizant of these providential designs, Peter is careful to remind anyone who might be uninformed or forgetful. Indeed, as M. J. Edwards has noted, Peter "plays that character whose role in ancient novels is to discern the laws that lie behind the superficial play of incident."[62] While the other characters in the narrative fret about the course of events, Peter is the one who understands such moments as the unfolding of providential design. In *Rec* 10.52.4 (cf. *Hom* 20.11.4), Peter tells Faustinianus that he may visit his friends Appion and Anubion, who are staying with Simon: *verumtamen considera, quomodo per providentiam dei omnia tibi ex sententia concurrunt: ecce enim non solum affectio tibi propria, deo praestante, reparata est, sed et amicorum praesentia procuratur* ("However, consider how all things coincide for you according to [your] liking by the providence of God; for look, not only has personal affection been restored to you by the eminent God, but also the presence of your friends is arranged for you"). All of Peter's followers, then, are aware that providence is the force driving most events in their lives.[63] The providential interest in these characters also underscores their importance in the divine plan, inasmuch as they receive as much attention from God as Abraham or the Israelites. Hence providence's guidance of

---

[62] Edwards, "*Clementina*," 471.

[63] At this very late point in the narrative, Faustinianus has almost completed his task as friendly interlocutor and will be baptized twenty chapters later at the end of the *Recognitions*.

events on two literary-historical levels – the biblical past and the narrative present – underscores its pervasive influence in human history.

Thus far we have seen that the protagonists offer providentially-centered *interpretations* of certain events from the past and present. In addition, the theme of providential design appears in a slightly different context: the subplot called the "romance of recognitions." A great deal of ink has been spilled about this romance of recognitions, particularly by those who have been involved in debates about the source of this storyline in the Pseudo-Clementines.[64] While one line of thought holds that the story is irrelevant to the Pseudo-Clementines' didactic material, having been added only to make their lengthy and repetitive speeches more palatable,[65] another line of reasoning argues persuasively that the romance of recognitions is integrally related to the theological message of the texts as a whole. The majority who regard the storyline as an essential component of the Pseudo-Clementines' theology can be further divided into two groups based on source critical considerations. Some interpreters believe that the Pseudo-Clementines have used a lost (Greek or Hellenistic Jewish) novel as the basis of their story.[66] Others, however, argue that the Pseudo-Clementine romance of recognitions is a Christian novel in its own right, and not merely a Christianized reworking of another tale.[67]

In an article about this romance, Edwards has argued that the *Recognitions* is an interesting counterpart to pagan novels because it "den[ies] that divine activity is capricious."[68] His point is that in pagan

---

[64] For a detailed summary of the scholarly discussion, see Jones, "Eros and Astrology," 65-74.

[65] For this view, see Perry, *Ancient Romances*, 291; Sophie Trenkner, *The Greek Novella in the Classical Period* (Cambridge: Cambridge University Press, 1958) 101; and (to a lesser extent) Tomas Hägg, *The Novel in Antiquity* (Oxford: Blackwell, 1983) 163.

[66] Bousset, "Wiedererkennungs-Fabel," 21; idem, "Die Geschichte eines Wiedererkennungsmärchens," *Nachrichten von der königlichen Gesellschaft der Wissenschaften zu Göttingen, philologisch-historische Klasse* (1916) 533; Waitz, *Pseudoklementinen*, 250-51; Heintze, *Klemensroman*, 114-38. Bernard Pouderon, "Aux origines du Roman clémentin. Prototype païen, refonte judéo-hellénistique, remaniement chrétien," in *Le judéo-christianisme dans tous ses états*, 231-56, argues that the Pseudo-Clementine storyline originates from a Jewish novel that was in turn derived from a pagan recognition tale.

[67] On this point, see Rohde, *Griechische Roman*, 507. Kerényi, *Griechisch-orientalische Romanliteratur*, 77, and Jones, "Eros and Astrology," 75, follow Rohde's view insofar as they argue that the Pseudo-Clementine novel draws motifs from the Greek novels but is not itself a careful reworking of a single story.

[68] Edwards, "*Clementina*," 466. This substitution of providence for fortune is one of many features shared by the *Recognitions* and the book of Acts. The *Recognitions'* interest in providence is a reflection of the *Grundschrift*, which uses the providentially-centered romance of recognitions as well as the book of Acts among its many sources.

novels fortune is always fickle; it may be malicious or benevolent, but never predictably so.[69] These novels typically feature lovers who are improbably separated from each other by acts of fortune in order to advance the plot. The *Recognitions*, however, substitutes divine providence for fortune.[70] Whereas Fortune is the unseen and inescapable force that governs the narrative events in pagan novels, divine providence is the driving force behind the occurrences of the *Recognitions*. Clement's family is providentially separated, so that each relative in turn comes to accept Peter's teaching about Jesus. When they are reunited at the end of the narrative, everyone understands that God intended the separation to accomplish this purpose. Hence for the *Recognitions*, providence – unlike fortune – works in a purposeful way to lead the characters to "a knowledge of the truth."[71] Not only does providence lead these individuals to an understanding of truth, but it also happens to be one of the constitutive

---

On the *Recognitions*' use of Acts see Jones, "Ancient Jewish Christian Rejoinder," 223-45. For a discussion of the apologists' preoccupation with the use of *controversiae* (rhetorical exercises in which students argue one of both sides of a case) concerning providence, see e.g. G. W. Clarke, "The Literary Setting of the Octavius of Minucius Felix," *Journal of Religious History* 3 (1965): 195-211, esp. 203-4; and Simon Price, "Latin Christian Apologetics: Minucius Felix, Tertullian, and Cyprian," in *Apologetics in the Roman Empire: Pagans, Jews, and Christians*, ed. M. Edwards, M. Goodman, and S. Price (Oxford and New York: Oxford University Press, 1999), 105-29, esp. 117-18. Ancient references to the *controversiae* include Quintilian, *Inst.* 3.5.6; 5.7.35; 7.2.2; Aelius Theon, *Prog.* 12; Hermogenes *Prog.* 11.

[69] Apuleius' *Metamorphoses* 11.15, however, has a conception of fate that is neither changeable nor fickle. In this section the priest of Isis interprets the meaning of the tale as follows: "For hostile fate has no power over those whose lives have been claimed by the majesty of our goddess. ... Now you have been received into the protection of a Fortune who is not blind, but sees, and who illumines the other gods too with the radiance of her light. ... [Lucius] has been freed from his former sufferings and, rejoicing in the providence of mighty Isis, he is victorious over his Fortune." Translation from Apuleius, *The Isis-Book (Metamorphoses Book XI)*, trans. J. Gwyn Griffiths (Leiden: Brill, 1975) 87-89. On this see Alan F. Segal, "Hellenistic Magic: Some Questions of Definition," in *Studies in Gnosticism and Hellenistic Religions*, 349-75, esp. 362-70. I thank Eldon Epp for this reference.

[70] Christian texts are not alone in substituting the power of providence for fate. Several texts associated with Mithras and especially Isis assert that the god is in control of the cosmos and human destiny: see e.g. Apuleius, *Met.*, 11.15. For other references see Nicola Denzey, "A New Star on the Horizon: Astral Christologies and Stellar Debates in Early Christian Discourse," in *Prayer, Magic, and the Stars*, 213-15.

[71] Edwards, "*Clementina*," 466-7. Based on these observations, Edwards argues persuasively that the romance of recognitions was created in order to illustrate the religious views espoused in Peter's preaching. Edwards does not comment on precisely *who* he thinks constructed the romance of recognitions – he makes no mention of a *Grundschrift* – although he seems to regard it as earlier than either the *Homilies* or *Recognitions*.

elements of that truth: providence leads the characters to acknowledge, among other things, the reality of providence.

I propose that the romance of recognitions accomplishes several tasks for the larger philosophical discussion in question. In the first place, the romance is used to demonstrate the workings of providence in the lives of the *Recognitions'* characters. It is particularly significant because this part of the narrative appears *not* to have been put forth by one side of the philosophical debate – rather, the romance of recognitions presents itself as "what really happened" within the text. Because it stands outside of the debates, the providential separation and reunion of Clement's family appear to be uninterpreted events that confirm the truth of the protagonists' arguments about providence. Second, because the storyline of the romance is remarkably similar to a number of contemporary novels that were in circulation, the audience likely understood from the very beginning that Clement's family would be eventually reunited.[72] This is important because it suggests that the audience knows ahead of time that Peter and his companions are right all along about God's guidance of events. The heroes' accuracy of interpretation is never in doubt, thanks to the romance of recognitions: providence does indeed govern the world.

If providence governs the world, this necessarily means that divine providence always works toward a greater good. Fate or chance may be changeable and indifferent, but this is not the case with providence. The examples above already demonstrate how providential design turns out well in the end: the delay in Peter's dispute with Simon may have been disappointing for Clement, but it allows Peter to give him a robust explanation of true knowledge. Aquila and Niceta may have been risking eternal damnation when they were followers of Simon, but their intimate knowledge of his tricks helps Peter convince the crowds that Simon should not be trusted. Whatever occurs must be the result of providence, the text insists, and whatever is providential must be for the greater good.

This conviction is implicit in *Rec* 9.7.2, where Clement tells Faustinianus that inequality among human beings is unavoidable, but *hanc inaequalitatem quae mortalium vitam necessario subsecuta est, divina providentia in occasionem iustitiae, misericordiae humanitatisque convertit* ("this inequality, which necessarily is adhered to the life of mortals, divine providence has turned into an occasion of justice, mercy, and compassion"). According to Clement, there will always be masters and

---

[72] In the case of the *Recognitions*, the audience is helped along by a number of obvious foreshadowings. For example, Clement, Niceta and Aquila refer to Faustinianus with the honorary term "Father" during their debates, just as Faustinianus often says "my son" in return.

servants, but providence has acted for good by allowing the former an opportunity to act humanely to their subjects.[73]

Elsewhere, Peter is even more explicit about the goodness of providential design (*Rec* 10.39.1-2):

> *Certus esto, dulcissime Aquila, quia omnia per bonam dei providentiam gesta sunt, ut non solum infirma et fragilis, verum et turpis esset causa quae futura erat contraria veritati. si enim validior et verisimilior fuisset erroris adsertio, haud facile quisquam qui in eo deceptus esset, ad iter veritatis rediret.*

> Be certain, dearest Aquila, because all things happen by the good providence of God, that not only trivial and weak, but even shameless, was the cause which was to be contrary to the truth. For if the defense of error had been stronger and more realistic, anyone who had been deceived by it would not readily return to the way of truth.

Shortly before this aside, Aquila is troubled by the "base and shameful observances" (*dedecorosis et turpibus observantiis*; *Rec* 10.35.2) of pagan religious practices. Peter's answer suggests that even these reprehensible acts are within God's providential design – if they were closer to the truth, it would be far more difficult to persuade people to abandon such practices. Providence always acts for the greater good, even if that good is not immediately obvious.

In fact, this conviction that providence works for the greater good seems to be at the very heart of Peter's preaching. In *Rec* 4.8.1, as he begins to address the crowds, he says: *Incipienti de vero dei cultu facere sermonem necessarium mihi videtur, eos qui nondum de hoc aliquid scientiae consecuti sunt, primo omnium docere, per omnia inculpabilem ponendam esse divinam providentiam, per quam mundus regitur et gubernatur* ("When beginning a speech about the true worship of God, it seems to me necessary first of all to teach those who have not yet acquired any knowledge of this, that through all things the divine providence be assumed to be blameless, by which the world is ruled and governed").[74] It is fair to say, then, that for the *Recognitions* one cannot properly understand the workings of providence unless one realizes that everything happens for a good reason. This idea accomplishes an important task by reinforcing the reader's perception that Peter is an authoritative interpreter of events. After all, he is able to make sense of events that seem contrary to God's purposes by pointing out how these incidents fit into a larger – and ultimately good – plan for humanity. In making these interpretive

---

[73] This same idea occurs in *Hom* 19.23.1-5. Origen often talks about the problem posed by "inequalities of life" in debates on providence. For example, after discussing the matter in *Cels.* 3.38, he concludes that "[p]robably the causes of these inequalities lie entirely in the sphere of providence, and it is not easy for men to come upon their explanation."

[74] Cf. *Hom* 8.9.1, where Peter refers to God rather than divine providence.

moves, Peter suggests that he has a more comprehensive view of the workings of providence than the other characters in the narrative: his conviction that providence works for the greater good allows him to "tap into" God's purposes, so to speak. Toward the end of the chapter we will see that Peter's connection to God is no accident, just as his understanding of providence is not simply a matter of his own good judgment.

If we return briefly to Peter's conversation with Aquila in *Rec* 10.39.5, we find yet another feature of the *Recognitions*' conception of providence. Peter states: *sed et cetera omnia simili modo conpetenter et commode dispensat divina providentia, licet nobis ignorantibus rerum causas bonae et optimae dispensationis divinae non liqueat ratio* ("But in a similar manner divine providence also manages all other things properly and advantageously, even if the reasonableness of the good and excellent divine management is not clear to us who do not know the causes of things"). Peter again suggests that divine providence always works for good, but this time around he adds something: human beings – even individuals like Peter who are very close to the True Prophet – cannot always understand providential governance. However, Peter also says that human beings *can* understand the workings of providence if they know the causes of things. But is such knowledge of "the causes of things" available to everyone? A declaration made by Niceta in *Rec* 8.27.1 answers this question. There he says:

> *sed et in hoc admiranda est divina providentia, quod videre nos quidem et agnoscere fecit quae fiunt, quomodo autem et qualiter fiant, in secreto posuit et in occulto, ut non indignis ad agnitionem subiaceant, sed dignis et fidelibus, cum meruerint, patefiant.*

> But in this also divine providence is admirable, because it has caused us to see and know the things that happen, but the way and manner in which they are done it has placed in secrecy and concealment, so that they may not lie close to the knowledge of the unworthy, but may be made accessible to the worthy and faithful, when they have earned it.

This excerpt makes it clear that God does not allow just anyone to recognize his providential design. Such understanding is not open to those who are *indignus* ("unworthy"). Rather, it is restricted to those who are *dignus* ("worthy") and *fidelis* ("faithful"). Niceta's statement works rhetorically to exclude those who do not understand providence, by labeling them as unworthy (and, by implication, unfaithful) in God's eyes. Up to this point, it has seemed that God's providence was an intellectual matter to be discussed in learned circles. Now, however, it becomes clear that to deny the existence of providence is to declare oneself "unworthy." Nevertheless, the precise meaning of *worthy* and *unworthy* remains uncertain. A short while later (*Rec* 8.34.5-6), Niceta clarifies this with a more specific statement. After anticipating questions about the timing and design of the created world, he says:

est apud illum profecto certa ratio, sunt evidentes causae, cur et quando et qualiter fecerit mundum, quas hominibus, quibus haec quae ante oculos posita sunt et de eius providentia contestantur, inquirere et intellegere pigrum fuit, aperiri utique non oportuit; quae enim in occulto habentur et intra sapientiae sensus velut intra regios thesauros recondita sunt, nemini patent nisi his qui ab illo didicerint, apud quem signata sunt haec et reposita. deus ergo est qui fecit omnia, et ipse a nemine factus est.

In his view, there is certainly a specific reason, and there are evident causes why, and when, and how he has made the world; but undoubtedly it was not right to reveal these things to human beings who are slow to examine and understand these things which are placed before their eyes and attest to his providence. For those things which are kept in secret, and are hidden within the senses of wisdom, just as within a royal treasury, are open to no one except those who have learned from that one, by whom these things are sealed and preserved. Therefore, it is God who has made all things, and he himself has been made by no one.

This passage, like the one above, suggests that providential design cannot be understood by everyone. God has his reasons for doing things, but he is unwilling to share them with just anyone. Here Niceta has replaced the vocabulary of *worthy* and *unworthy* with a slightly different one: the secrets of God's providential design are available only to *those who are eager to understand the things that testify to divine providence*, and *those who have learned of him*. Put another way, providential design can only be understood by those with a proper understanding of the origins of the world. The key to unlocking the mystery of providential design – and, by implication, the path to faithfulness and worthiness in God's eyes – is found in the story of creation. The text's exclusionary rhetoric, which is alluded to here in its treatment of providence, will become clearer as it deals with different theories of creation. Before we can begin the next section on creation, however, let's return to Bourdieu's idea of field for a moment.

At this point it might not seem obvious that providence plays an important role in determining the position of the competitors within the field of Knowledge/Salvation. After all, the above discussion was less a series of debates about providence than a summary of the protagonists' – and hence the text's – views on the subject. However, when we return to the debates about astral determinism in Chapter 3, the import of this initial treatment of providence will become clearer. For the moment, since we have established what the text regards as the "correct" understanding of providence, we can begin to understand the importance of such views for situating the competitors in the field of Knowledge/Salvation. Consider Aquila's statement of the syzygy principle in *Rec* 8.53.1, 3: *igitur in omnibus mundi rebus habetur ista divisio, et sicut sunt pii, ita et impii, ut*

*sunt prophetae, ita et falsi prophetae ... et inde est unde apud philosophos
alii adserunt providentiam, alii negant* ("Therefore this division is retained
in all the things of the world; and just as there are pious people, so there
are also impious people; as there are prophets, so also there are false
prophets ... And hence it is that among the philosophers some assert
providence, others deny it"). Here philosophers are divided into two
groups: those who believe in providence and those who deny that it exists.
This is significant first because philosophers are defined by their positions
on the issue of providence – not by their physics, ethics, or anything else
that may have been commonly used to distinguish philosophical schools in
antiquity. Providence is the decisive issue for this text, like a threshing tool
used to separate the philosophical wheat from the chaff. All philosophers
who accept providential design are aligned with the protagonists, while
those philosophers who accept fate or some other mechanism side with
their opponents. Second, the text's use of providence implies a division not
just between philosophers, but also between pious and impious people, true
and false prophets, and the like, so that the entire world is then divided into
two halves:

Peter, Clement, Niceta, Aquila	Simon, unnamed people, sophists
Philosophers who accept providence	Philosophers who deny providence
Pious people	Impious people
True prophets	False prophets

In the next two chapters we will see that a number of other groups are also
sorted according to this dualistic scheme; as a rhetorical device this is
extremely important for understanding how the text organizes the multiple
groups of rivals inscribed within it. For the moment, however, let's move
on to the philosophical debates about creation.

Creation

If we return to Clement's quest narrated at the outset of the *Recognitions*,
we find that it adds yet another dimension to our understanding of the
quest for philosophical truth. Among other things, Clement wants to find
out *quando factus sit mundus aut si omnino factus sit, vel antequam fieret,
quid erat, an vero semper fuerit. nam certum videbatur, quod si esset
factus, esset profecto solvendus, et si solvatur, quid iterum erit?* ("when
the world was made, or if it was made altogether, or perhaps what was
before it was made, or in fact if it had been always. For it seemed certain,
that if it had been made, it was surely going to be destroyed; and if it is
destroyed, what will it be for the second time?" *Rec* 1.1.4-5; cf. *Hom* 1.1.4-

5). The quest for philosophical truth, then, is fundamentally a search for certainty about the origins of the world.[75] As a result, the *Recognitions'* delineation of the creation – and the philosophical arguments about competing cosmogonies – are central to its presentation of the philosophical materials. In order to understand how the creation debates work in the text, we have to start at the very beginning.

In *Rec* 1.27.1 – 1.28.4, Peter gives an account of the world's creation that is the standard by which all others must be measured: it is *the* authorized version. The content of this report, which is quite similar to the first chapter of Genesis,[76] is less important for our purposes than the work it does within the *Recognitions'* philosophical materials. According to the text, those who commit Peter's creation account to memory can "move toward the friendship of the Creator" (*ut tendamus ad amicitiam conditoris*; *Rec* 1.26.3). Hence this story of the world's origin is divinely approved by the Creator himself.[77] Because Peter's creation narrative is presented as so authoritative, it serves as a litmus test to determine who has certain knowledge of the world's origins.[78] That is, only those who

---

[75] As Walter H. Wagner notes, "Questions about creator and creation deal with more than how time and space started. Accounts about origins reflect a community's understanding and experience of life's beginning and purpose." W. H. Wagner, *After the Apostles: Christianity in the Second Century* (Minneapolis: Fortress Press, 1994) 67. Of course, the *Recognitions'* interest in creation also reflects its dialogue with Marcionite and so-called "gnostic" theories of creation, although it is presented more as a philosophical debate with Platonists, Epicureans, and Stoics than anything else. Clement's questions correspond to the topics of natural philosophy mentioned in Philostratus, *VA* 3.34; 6.22. Ulrich Berner, "The Image of the Philosopher in Late Antiquity and in Early Christianity," in *Concepts of Person in Religion and Thought*, ed. Hans G. Kippenberg, Yme B. Kuiper, and Andy F. Sanders (Religion and Reason 37; Berlin: de Gruyter, 1990) 128.

[76] The source behind *Rec* 1.27-71 is likewise dependent on the Book of Jubilees; see James M. Scott, *Geography in Early Judaism and Christianity* (Society for New Testament Studies Monograph Series 113; Cambridge, UK: Cambridge University Press, 2002) 97-125; and F. Stanley Jones, "Jewish-Christian Chiliastic Restoration in Pseudo-Clementine *Recognitions* 1.27-71," in *Restoration: Old Testament, Jewish, and Christian Perspectives*, ed. James M. Scott (Leiden: Brill, 2001) 529-47.

[77] This divine authorization is established on three levels. First, the account is very similar to Genesis 1, which is understood as scripture by the author and his readers. Second, the statement in *Rec* 1.26.3 asserts explicitly that memorization of this material will ensure God's friendship. Third, as we shall see in Chapter 4, Peter says and does only the things Jesus taught; hence this creation account can be understood as having come from the mouth of Jesus himself, the True Prophet.

[78] The authority of the Genesis creation narrative is not in doubt within the *Recognitions*, but it was certainly questioned in contemporary philosophical debates about the origins of the world. Origen, for instance, goes to great lengths to defend the Genesis account against the accusations of Celsus, who argued that "Moses and the

agree that there is one righteous God who created the world can be said to have such knowledge. This knowledge about creation, in turn, becomes a constitutive element of philosophical truth. Hence those whose account of the creation agrees with Peter's are said to possess true knowledge, while those whose creation account differs from Peter's are said to rely on human opinion and conjecture. Creation, much like providence, serves as a tool to distinguish philosophers (and everyone else) into two groups: those who rely on knowledge, and those who rely on opinion.

At this point we need to look closely at the major philosophical discussion of creation, which takes place in *Rec* 8.[79] It is a debate between Niceta, who accepts Peter's retelling of Genesis, and Faustinianus, who represents opposing accounts of creation.[80] Niceta states his position clearly in *Rec* 8.6.6-7: *dico providentia dei gubernari mundum, in his dumtaxat quae gubernatione eius indigent. unus est enim omnia tenens qui et mundum fecit, iustus deus, unicuique secundum gesta sua quandoque redditurus* ("I say that the world is governed by the providence of God, at least in those things that need his government. For he alone is master of all things, who also made the world; the just God, who shall at some time render to everyone according to his deeds"). This statement about creation, providence and judgment is a succinct summary of what Peter has said, and is the main argument defended in the ensuing debate. (*Debate* is probably a misnomer, since Niceta speaks uninterrupted for most of the discussion. He even anticipates the arguments of Faustinianus – he raises and answers his objections in the same breath. For the most part, Faustinianus speaks only to praise the skill of Niceta.) Since there really is not a two-sided debate to speak of, I suggest that we look closely at how Niceta defends his philosophical position; this analysis should demonstrate that the *Recognitions* considers the question of the world's origins – much like the issue of providence – to be a source of a fundamental division between two kinds of philosophers.

Everything Niceta says is designed to show that he is the consummate philosopher. For example, the very method he uses to present his case is modeled, at least indirectly, on Plato's ideal of *dialectic* (see below). Niceta's argument about creation depends on the assent of his opponent at various points. After declaring his philosophical credentials in 8.7.5, Niceta begins the discussion along the lines of a Socratic *elenchus*: he

---

prophets who left our books had no idea what the nature of the world and of mankind really is, and put together utter trash." Origen, *Cels.* 4.49ff.

[79] Recall that this was one of two episodes attributed to a separate philosophical source; see the History of Scholarship section in Chapter 1.

[80] "Opposing accounts" is intentionally plural here, since Faustinianus represents not one coherent competing idea about creation, but several rival hypotheses.

starts with the most basic divisions, establishing *logoi* about which both he and his opponent can agree.[81] Niceta's first division is this: *Omne quod est, aut simplex est aut compositum* ("Everything that is, is either simple or compound"; *Rec* 8.9.1). He goes on to explain that what is simple must be infinite and without an author – this is the creator. What is compound, on the other hand, must have been put together by someone. Since the world is composed of four elements, it must have been made by a creator. Faustinianus agrees with this assessment: *Optime, inquit, et doctissime dicis, fili* ("He says, 'You speak very well and learnedly, my son'"; *Rec* 8.9.3).

Niceta builds on this agreement when he moves on to the question of the world's creation in *Rec* 8.10.1-2:

De mundi nunc ergo ratione prosequendum est, cuius prima quaestio in duas partes dividitur. quaeritur enim utrum factus sit an non; et si quidem non est factus, ipse erit illud ingenitum, ex quo omnia. si vero factus est, de hoc rursus quaestio in duas partes scinditur, utrumnam ex se ipso factus est an ab alio.

Now then, what follows will concern the account of the world, of which the first inquiry is divided into two parts. For it is asked whether it has been made or not; and if in fact it has not been made, [the world] itself will be that unbegotten from which all things [are]. If, however, it has been made, concerning this again the question is divided into two parts, for instance whether it has been made by itself, or another.

Since Niceta has already noted that the world is compound, it follows that the world must have been made. He immediately dismisses the notion that the world was made by itself, because this would exclude the possibility of providence. But providence cannot be excluded, because *si providentia non recipitur, frustra animus ad virtutem provocatur, frustra iustitia custoditur, quippe si non est qui iusto pro meritis aliquando restituat* ("if providence is not accepted, the mind is called to virtue for nothing, justice is maintained for nothing, obviously, if there is no one to render to the just person at some time according to [his] merits"; *Rec* 8.10.3). So there must be providence, he concludes, and this providence must have created the world. This conclusion raises yet another set of questions about how providence works. Does it act "(a) generally towards the whole,[82] or specially towards the parts, or (b) generally also towards the parts, or (c)

---

81 On the Socratic elenchus, see Murray, "Interpreting Plato on Sophistic Claims," 115-34, esp. 119-26. On p. 123 he writes, "Whereas the sophist's display invites any and every question, the conduct of the interrogator within the elenchus is limited to questions assuming premises to which the interlocutor agrees."

82 Celsus (as reported by Origen in *Cels.* 4.99) seems to make this kind of argument: "But God does not take care, as Celsus imagines, only of the universe as a whole, but in addition to that he takes care of every rational being. And providence will never abandon the universe."

both generally towards the whole, and specially towards the parts?" (*Rec* 8.11.1).[83] According to Niceta, the correct answer is (c) – God made everything in the beginning, *et usque ad finem per singulos quosque providentiam gerat, ut unicuique reddat pro actibus suis* ("and regulates providence over each individual all the way to the end, and renders to everyone according to his deeds"; *Rec* 8.11.4). Here Niceta agrees with Peter (see above) when he says that God made the world, governs it providentially, and will judge humanity by its actions.

The *Recognitions'* understanding of providential governance is intimately connected with these ideas of future judgment and the importance of good works. If someone were to argue for (a) or (b), as Faustinianus does against Clement in *Rec* 10, this would mean that *ab initio deus fecerit omnia et cursu atque ordine rebus inposito de reliquo nihil ad se revocet* ("God made all things in the beginning, and having imposed a course and order upon things, he does not apply himself to the rest"; *Rec* 8.12.1), and that *secundum genesim geri cuncta* ("all things are conducted according to fate"; *Rec* 8.12.1). On Faustinianus' reading, God made the world but then left it in the hands of unchangeable fate. Niceta says this cannot be the case, because fate would make virtuous practices and worship of the divine meaningless. If everything that happens could not have happened any other way, why would anyone bother to be good, or to petition the gods?

Even this small excerpt of the "creation debate" should be enough to demonstrate how Niceta, in standard philosophical fashion, starts with a set of propositions on which he and his interlocutor agree and proceeds to construct his argument through a series of intermediate conclusions. In short, Niceta's argumentation might be said to be a classic (albeit modified) example of *dialectic*, which David N. Sedley defines as "the science of conducting a philosophical dialogue...by exploring the consequences of premises asserted or conceded by an interlocutor."[84] Moreover, Niceta seems to be following Plato's particular understanding of dialectic as a "co-operative investigation based on agreed premises, in contrast to the essentially obstructive method of 'eristic.'"[85] This Platonic quality is especially evident given that his argument proceeds "on the basis

---

[83] *utrum generaliter erga omnia an specialiter erga partes an et generaliter erga omnia et specialiter erga partes.*

[84] 'Modified' because Niceta's interlocutor, Faustinianus, does not speak quite as much as Socrates' conversation partners usually do. Simon Hornblower and Antony Spawforth, eds., *The Oxford Classical Dictionary* (3d ed.; Oxford: Oxford University Press, 1996) s.v. "dialectic."

[85] Hornblower and Spawforth, *Oxford Classical Dictionary*, s.v. "dialectic." Eristic will be discussed later in Chapter 2.

of Division of things by Kinds,"[86] rather than relying on verbal contradictions. Niceta's argument about creation, then, shows that he is an ideal philosopher:[87] he is interested in leading his opponent toward a true understanding of creation, rather than confusing or silencing his opponent through a demonstration of rhetorical skill.

Niceta's dialectical argument also evidences the *Recognitions'* dialogue with – not to mention his own expertise in – the major schools of Hellenistic philosophy. He uses the testimony of other unnamed philosophers to support his arguments: *nunc...quia factus sit mundus iste visibilis, testantur etiam philosophorum plurimi sapientes viri* ("Now...that this visible world has been made certainly very many wise men among the philosophers testify"; *Rec* 8.13.1). It is critical to note that, although Niceta suggests that other philosophers agree with his vision of creation, he simultaneously asserts that he does not need to rely on them to make his case. For example, immediately following the sentence just quoted, he insists that he relies only on the logical underpinnings of their thought, rather than the authority of the philosophers themselves. This does not prevent him from citing other philosophers' arguments in support of his case, however. In *Rec* 8.14.1-2, he states, *et quidem plures philosophorum hoc magis sensisse scio, quod ex uno corpore, quam illi materiam vocant, divisiones ac discretiones conditor fecerit deus, quod tamen ex quattuor simplicibus et in unum temperamento quodam divinae providentiae admixtis constaret elementis* ("And in fact I know that the majority of the philosophers thought this, that God the creator made divisions and distinctions from one body, which they call matter, which nevertheless is composed of four elements mixed into one by a certain measure of divine providence"). He adds that while he agrees with this understanding of creation, he disagrees with those philosophers who have suggested that the body of the world is simple (that is, composed of only one element, and indivisible). As the *Recognitions* portrays him, Niceta is clearly familiar with a range of philosophical opinions about the origins of the world, and can situate his own understanding – which the text presents as the only correct one – within these conversations.

Niceta's philosophical prowess becomes even more explicit in *Rec* 8.15.1-5, where he displays his familiarity with the full range of creation theories from Pythagoras to Zeno to Epicurus.[88] He breezes through this

---

[86] Kerferd, *Sophistic Movement*, 63-4. According to Kerferd, division of things by kinds is the essential feature of Platonic dialectic.

[87] Ideal, that is, in the sense of Plato's *Sph.* 253e, where dialectic and true philosophy are equated.

[88] There are close correspondences between Niceta's list of Greek philosophical creation theories in *Rec* 8.15.1-4 and a scholion on Basil the Great's *Homiliae in*

catalogue of philosophical heavy hitters, only to conclude that in their disagreement they all point to one incontrovertible fact: *omni ex parte, qui plura in unum collegerit et rursus collecta in diversas species duxerit, ostenditur deus, et probatur per haec non potuisse machinam mundi sine opifice et provisore constare* ("from every part God is revealed, who has assembled many into one, and again when they were collected, he has formed [them] into separate species; and by this it is demonstrated that the fabric of the world could not have stood firm without a maker and a provider"; *Rec* 8.15.5). All the philosophers, then, attest to the reality of a providential God.

This particular section of the *Recognitions* accomplishes three things. First, it shows that Niceta knows every major theory of creation put forth by other philosophers. Such wide-ranging expertise indicates that his own views are the result of a careful examination of all possible points of view. Second, Niceta professes belief in the biblical creation account, which effectively situates the story in Genesis 1 within the canon of philosophical theories about creation. Third, it suggests that the philosophers mentioned by Niceta – either wittingly or unwittingly – attest to his belief in a providential creator. In other words, not only is the Genesis story *superior* to all other philosophical creation theories, it also is *authenticated* by these rival theories.

If everyone's arguments point to this providential creator, Niceta asks, *qui erit Epicuro locus introducendi atomos et adserendi quod ex corpusculis insensibilibus non solum sensibilia corpora, sed et mentes intellectuales ac rationabiles fiant?* ("what room will there be for Epicurus to introduce atoms and to claim that not only bodies that can be perceived by the senses, but also intelligent and rational minds, are made from insensible atoms?" *Rec* 8.16.5). The paragraphs that follow this question are an indictment of Epicurean physics, complete with answers for anticipated objections to this analysis.[89] In *Rec* 8.19.6 Niceta concludes

---

Hexaemeron I.2 (PG 29b, 8A 13/14); for details see Rehm, *Rekognitionen*, 225. This suggests that Niceta's words may have been drawn from an existing catalog of creation theories, which could have been recognizable to readers and hearers of the *Recognitions*. If this is the case, it reinforces the point I'm trying to make: Niceta's philosophical inventory demonstrates his familiarity with existing theories of creation.

[89] For example, in *Rec* 8.17.1 Niceta says to Faustinianus: *sed dices, ut Epicuro visum est* ("But you will say, according to the vision of Epicurus ..."). Faustinianus is not even given a chance to voice his objections. Niceta knows the counter-arguments so well that he is able to anticipate and diffuse them before they are made by Faustinianus. On the Jewish and Christian suspicion of Epicureans see F. Niewöhner, "Epikureer sind Atheisten: Zur Geschichte des Wortes apikuros in der jüdischen Philosophie," in *Atheismus im Mittelalter und in der Renaissance*, ed. F. Niewöhner and O. Pluta (Wiesbaden: Harrassowitz, 1999) 11-22.

that the collision of atoms cannot possibly account for the careful formation of bodies; this could only come from *opus rationis...quam rationem ego verbum et deum appello* ("the work of reason, which I call the Word, and God"). This last bit identifies Niceta's providential God with the philosophical idea of the *logos* that governs the world. Perhaps the names are different, but Niceta asserts that the philosophers are really talking about his creator God when they speak about *logos: de nomine controversia est* ("the controversy is about a name"; *Rec* 8.20.1).

In *Rec* 8.20.1-2 Niceta moves from Epicurus to Plato, but his point is essentially the same. Plato testifies that the world was made, because it is visible and corporeal; and if it has been made, it must also have a maker.[90] Although Plato and the other philosophers do not say much about the creator of the world, no one can deny that this creator exists. The next several chapters of the *Recognitions* are taken up with an extended argument from design, including a discussion of astronomical movements (8.22.1-4), climates (8.23.1-7), rivers and seas (8.24.1-4), plants and animals (8.25.1-6), the germination of seeds (8.26.1-7), the weight of water (8.27.1-5), and the human body (8.28.1-8.32.4). Niceta concludes his long speech by arguing that God must have had a good reason for creating the world when he did – his timing was not arbitrary, but *quibus haec quae ante oculos posita sunt et de eius providentia contestantur, inquirere et intellegere pigrum fuit, aperiri utique non oportuit* ("undoubtedly it was not right to reveal these things to those who are slow to examine and understand these things, which are placed before their eyes and attest to his providence"; *Rec* 8.34.5).

To sum up, the *Recognitions'* major discussion of creation demonstrates that Peter's creation account is the foundation of true knowledge about the origin of the world. This account is repeatedly vetted in the vocabulary of every major philosophical school by Niceta. Not only is Niceta's knowledge the result of his expertise and intimate familiarity with the entire range of philosophical discussions, but even more important, Niceta is able to use his expertise to demonstrate that all other philosophers attest to the truth of his own propositions – which are a direct reflection of Peter's creation narrative – even if they are unaware of it. Once again, the rival philosophers find their own expertise used against them, with the result that any philosophy opposed to the protagonists' propositions is intellectually and morally compromised. This will become clear in the next section on judgment, which looks in some detail at the ethical implications of the philosophical life.

---

[90] Origen too pits the authority of the Genesis creation account against Plato; see *Cels.* 1.19.

Judgment

Up to this point we have passed over the multiple references to judgment found alongside statements about creation and providence. Moreover, until now our discussion has been concerned primarily with the philosophers' debates over intellectual matters that involve a certain amount of technical expertise. In the *Recognitions'* remarks on judgment, however, we find that a distinction between *lived philosophy* and *philosophical discourse*,[91] which has been lurking in the background all along, comes to the fore. Recall that in a number of places, the *Recognitions'* protagonists distinguish between philosophical expertise and true knowledge. This epistemological differentiation also has implications for one's personal conduct. Consider Diogenes Laertius' citation of Polemon:[92]

> we should exercise ourselves with realities, not with dialectical speculations, like a man who has devoured some textbook on harmonics, but has never put his knowledge into practice. Likewise, we must not be like those who can astonish their onlookers by their skill in syllogistic argumentation, but who, when it comes to their own lives, contradict their own teachings.[93]

Here Polemon is talking about the difference between philosophy as a matter of technical expertise and philosophy as a lived experience. It is one thing to master philosophical argumentation, but quite another matter to live one's life in accordance with philosophical ideals. Rather than a technical discipline limited to those with specialized credentials, Pierre Hadot argues that "[p]hilosophy thus took on the form of an exercise of the thought, will, and the totality of one's being... [it] was a method of spiritual progress which demanded a radical conversion and transformation of the individual's way of being."[94] In other words, living as a philosopher

---

[91] By "philosophical discourse" I mean philosophical conversations about technical and intellectual matters, which are often divided into logic, ethics, and physics. This distinction between lived philosophy and philosophical discourse is maintained by Hadot (*Philosophy as a Way of Life*, 266-67).

[92] Polemon of Athens (314/313-270/269 BCE) was one of the heads of the Academy. He was known for "dismiss[ing] the purely theoretical side of philosophy as sterile." Hornblower and Spawforth, *Oxford Classical Dictionary*, s.v "Polemon (2)."

[93] Diogenes Laertius, *Lives of the Philosophers* 4.18, as quoted in Hadot, *Philosophy as a Way of Life*, 267.

[94] Hadot, *Philosophy as a Way of Life*, 265. Elsewhere he states: "To be a philosopher was not to have received a theoretical philosophical education, or to be a professor of philosophy. Rather, it was to profess, as a result of a conversion which caused a radical change of life-style, a way of life different from that of other people." Pierre Hadot, *The Inner Citadel: The* Meditations *of Marcus Aurelius*, transl. Michael Chase (Cambridge, MA: Harvard University Press, 1998) 5. My acceptance of Hadot's characterization of philosophy may seem to contradict my earlier application of Bourdieu's (or Weber's) notion of religious specialists to ancient philosophy. I agree with Hadot that philosophy

involved more than intellectual assent to a set of doctrines – the philosophical life meant a complete reorientation of the individual within the world, including (as Polemon observes) demands on one's life practices. The Neoplatonist Damaskios affirms this idea when he writes, "I have myself encountered people who were brilliant as far as the externals of philosophy were concerned, and who impressed me with memories laden with a multitude of theories, with the sudden forcefulness of endless syllogisms and with an unending faculty for superhuman perceptions, but who were inwardly barren of soul and lacking in true knowledge."[95] True knowledge, then, is not memorization of philosophical doctrines, but rather lived philosophical practices that had profound effects on one's soul.

In *Rec* 10.47.4-5, Peter gives a synopsis of his teaching that is quite similar to the formulations that have been cited already:

qui dicit honorandum esse deum et patrem omnium conditorem eiusque filium...solus enim est lex et legislator et iudex iustus, cuius lex decernit honorandum esse deum et dominum omnium per vitam sobriam, castam, iustam, misericordem, et in ipso solo omnem collocandam spem.

[Our preaching] says that God the father, the author of all things, and his son should be honored... for he alone is the law and the lawgiver, and the just judge, whose law decrees that God, the Lord of all things, should be honored by a temperate, chaste, just, and merciful life, and that all hope should be placed in him alone.

Belief in God the creator and his son, then, requires both intellectual assent and a regulation of behavior; among other things, one must live "a sober, chaste, just, and merciful life."[96] Peter goes on in *Rec* 10.48.1-4 to differentiate his own way of life from that of the philosophers:

sed dicet aliquis, etiam a philosophis huiusmodi praecepta dari. nihil est simile; nam de iustitia quidem ab eis et sobrietate mandatur, sed remuneratorem deum gestorum bonorum malorumque non norunt, et ideo leges et praecepta eorum accusatorem tantummodo publicum vitant, conscientiam vero purificare non possunt. quid enim timeat in occulto peccare, qui occultorum esse arbitrum et iudicem nescit? ... aiunt autem et illud philosophi, deum non irasci, nescientes quid dicant.

---

in antiquity was first of all a set of lived practices, but hold that *as it is characterized by the Recognitions*, philosophy is primarily the realm of experts. In some sense, the *Recognitions* supports Hadot's claim when it emphasizes how individuals not trained in the technical specifics of philosophy nevertheless live up to philosophical ideals.

[95] Damaskios, *Isid.* 17 (*Epitoma Photiana*), quoted by Garth Fowden, "The Pagan Holy Man in Late Antique Society," *Journal of Hellenic Studies* 102 (1982) 36.

[96] The Pseudo-Clementines, of course, are known for their "Jewish" or "Jewish Christian" conviction that human beings as individuals are judged by God, and accordingly rewarded or punished, based on their actions. As we have seen already, this system of reward and punishment takes place both within the world and on the final day of judgment (see *Rec* 8.47.1-3).

But someone will say that rules of this sort are given by the philosophers also. Nothing of the kind; for indeed [commandments] concerning justice and sobriety are enjoined by them, but they do not know that God is the recompenser of good and evil deeds, and therefore their laws and rules only evade a public accuser, but cannot purify the conscience. For why should one who does not know that there is a witness and a judge of secret things be afraid to sin in secret? ... But also the philosophers say that God does not grow angry, unaware of what they say.

In other words, Peter is suggesting that the philosophers' demands for "justice and sobriety" may look remarkably like God's requirements on the surface.[97] However, the major difference between the ethical demands made by the protagonists and their philosophical opponents lies in their understanding of God's judgment. Because the philosophers deny that God punishes evil and rewards good deeds, their teachings focus only on what one does in public. As a result, such instruction cannot result in the purification of one's conscience.[98] In addition, the philosophers' insistence that God is not angry only teaches people *nullum habere vindictae alicuius vel iudicii metum, et per hoc tota peccantibus frena laxarent* ("to have no fear of any punishment or judgment, and through this they weaken all restraint for sinners"; *Rec* 10.50.1).[99] Moreover, the philosophers' claims about fate and chance have precisely the same effect (*Rec* 10.50.2-3):

> *aut quid illi humanum genus iuverunt, qui dixerunt non esse deum, sed casu omnia et fortuito agi? nonne ut haec audientes homines et arbitrantes nullum esse iudicem, nullum provisorem rerum, ad omne facinus, quod vel furor vel avaritia vel libido dictasset, neminem verendo praecipites agerentur?*

Or what have they done to help the human race, who have said that there is no God, but that all things happen by chance and accident? Is it not that human beings, hearing these

---

[97] Note the alignment of Peter and the other protagonists with God in this case.

[98] Cf. *Hom* 5, which contains an extended discussion between Clement and the philosopher Appion and repeatedly makes the point that philosophers' behavior is immoral because it is modeled on that of the Greek gods. Peter's statements in the *Recognitions* seem to be a misrepresentation of the demands of the philosophical life (in any of the schools), which were not particularly focused on outward appearances. On this point see Hadot, *The Inner Citadel*, passim. Peter's characterization seems to be more in line with Jesus' instructions about prayer in Matthew 6.5-6: "And whenever you pray, do not be like the hypocrites; for they love to stand in the synagogues and at the street corners, so that they may be seen by others. Truly I tell you, they have received their reward. But whenever you pray, go into your room and shut the door and pray to your Father who is in secret; and your Father who sees in secret will reward you." (NRSV)

[99] Cf. *Hom* 18.19.1 and *Hom* 20.4.2-3, where Peter argues that primordial people sinned by thinking they would not be subject to judgment, and that people continue to sin because of ignorance of the impending divine judgment that awaits them. Celsus argues in *Cels.* 4.99 that God is not "angry because of men any more than he is because of monkeys or mice; nor does he threaten them"; Origen responds that "he is not angry because of monkeys and mice; but he inflicts judgment and punishment upon men, seeing that they have gone against the impulses of nature."

things, and supposing that there is no judge, no provider of things, are driven headlong, without fear of anyone, to every rash deed which either passion, or greed, or desire may dictate?

Here Peter argues that the philosophers' rejection of providence – not to mention God's very existence – necessarily entails a denial of God's role as judge of humanity. The result is inescapable: because they fear no reprisals, people will have no reason to control their negative impulses. Without God's providential design and ability to reward or punish people according to their deeds, Peter argues, humanity has no reason to strive for the ideals that the philosophers are supposed to espouse. Such ideals make sense only within the framework of providence and judgment.

Based on this brief exploration of God's judgment and its role in fostering the type of just conduct prescribed by the philosophers, it is possible to offer a tentative conclusion about how the idea of judgment functions in the philosophical materials of the *Recognitions*. In the first place, the protagonists' argument about God's judgment is used to underscore the difference between philosophical expertise, and philosophy as a lived experience that has implications for one's conduct. Moreover, judgment is the crucial factor differentiating the protagonists' instructions on behavior from similar suggestions made by their philosophical rivals. Other philosophers may tell people to be chaste or just, but unless there is an omniscient providential God who rewards and punishes individuals based on their actions, there is little or no point in observing their teaching. In other words, philosophy falls short as a practical guide for living unless it is grounded in Peter's faith in a providential God who rewards and punishes. In Chapter 4, we shall see the most serious way in which rival philosophies fall short of the mark: their epistemology is built on shaky ground. Philosophical knowledge is not prophetic knowledge, no matter how much their truth-claims may coincide.

Conclusion

In conclusion, we can say that the *Recognitions* articulates its message in terms of philosophy in two rather different, but complementary, ways. In the first place, the protagonists' teaching is presented as providing the true answers to the philosophical quest. Not only are the heroes experts in philosophical discourse, but they also live the philosophical life and concern themselves with definite answers to philosophical questions about God and the world. By contrast, the philosophical opponents are sophists who are interested primarily in endless debate. In the second place, the *Recognitions* says that the protagonists' teaching *cannot* be obtained by philosophical inquiry, which depends on human conjecture. As we shall see in Chapter 4, the true knowledge found in Peter's message derives directly from the True Prophet, who is the only source of epistemological certainty available to human beings. These two coexisting strategies may seem contradictory at first, but returning once more to the notion of field may help to sort things out a bit. Both strategies are designed to undermine the current state of the field itself, because they divorce knowledge from expertise while suggesting that true knowledge does not – indeed *cannot* – be acquired from the institutional transmission recognized by the field. The project of undermining the institutions of the field, and challenging the participants' notions of capital within the field, is intended to allow the protagonists to disenfranchise their competitors and take over the field altogether. In the next chapter, we will see that such strategies are directed toward astrologers as well.

Chapter 3

Astrologers and the Problem with Astral Determinism

Introduction

In Chapter 2, we looked at the philosophical materials in the *Recognitions*, which argue that Peter and his followers, whose understanding of providence, creation, and judgment comes directly from the True Prophet, are the exclusive possessors of true knowledge. The text makes this argument by asserting that philosophers (1) are more interested in arguments than the truth; and (2) rely not on secure knowledge, but on human conjecture and opinion. Philosophers, however, are not the only group targeted in the *Recognitions*' campaign for epistemological predominance. The text also sets up confrontations between the protagonists and rival astrologers in the process of making its truth claims.

Why does the *Recognitions* polemicize against astrological knowledge? This question can be answered on two levels. If we think in terms of source materials, as many previous interpreters have done, we can conclude that the *Recognitions* inherits its interest in astrology from the *Grundschrift*. As I mentioned in Chapter 1, the *Grundschrift* appropriates over twenty chapters of the Bardesanite *Book of the Laws of the Countries* (or a text closely related to it). The presence of astrologically-oriented passages can thus be explained with reference to the *Recognitions*' major source, and could possibly be dismissed as material thoughtlessly repeated by the redactor of the *Recognitions*. However, we are not dealing with thoughtless repetition; the *Recognitions*' attitude toward astrology differs considerably from that of its predecessor.

The difference becomes clear when we consider the two texts' use of Bardaisan's ideas. An Edessan philosopher and theologian with ties to the royal court of Abgar VIII the Great, Bardaisan (ca. 154-222) had ties to Christianity and wrote a large number of hymns and prose works in Syriac.[1] Though none of his works survives, the *Book of the Laws of the Countries* is thought to represent fairly the main tenets of his thought. In addition to the *BLC*, the polemical works of Ephrem and the more

---

[1] For what little we know of Bardaisan's life, see Drijvers, *Bardaisan of Edessa*, 217-18.

flattering accounts in Eusebius' *Hist. Eccl.* 4.30 and *Praep. Evang.* 6.9.32 are important sources for Bardaisan's views.[2] According to Bardaisan, the human body is subject to fate; hence astrology can be used to explain why some people are born rich and others poor, some born healthy and others ill, and so on. Moreover, Bardaisan believes that horoscopes are important because the stars can tempt – but not compel – individuals to sin.[3]

Stanley Jones has argued convincingly that the *Grundschrift* embraces some of Bardaisan's astrological views. For example, the horoscope of Clement's mother Mattidia (*Rec* 9.32.5) explains the initial separation of her family, but the disastrous fate it portends is never realized.[4] The *Grundschrift* explains that the horoscope was not completely fulfilled because Mattidia's chastity pleased God, causing God to thwart the power of the stars. In other words, chaste behavior granted Mattidia "a special dispensation by God," which allowed her to overcome fate.[5] This is similar to Bardaisan's view that free will can frustrate the designs of astral determinism.[6] *Hom* 19.23.5 (cf. *Rec* 9.7.1-6) preserves the *Grundschrift*'s agreement with Bardaisan: it suggests that astral determinism is in control from a person's birth until the moment of baptism, at which point baptism allows one to escape the grip of fate. This idea resembles views expressed by other ancient Christians, and gives at least a limited role to the power of fate.[7]

---

[2] Steven K. Ross, *Roman Edessa: Politics and culture on the eastern fringes of the Roman Empire,* 114-242 CE (London and New York: Routledge, 2001) 119. As Ross notes, Eusebius' attitude is "still fairly complimentary, showing that in his time the boundaries of Christian orthodoxy were still somewhat flexible." Hippolytus' *Philosophoumena* also mentions Bardaisan. For a more complete discussion of the Greek sources for Bardaisan see Drijvers, *Bardaisan of Edessa,* 167-85; he also reviews Syriac, Arabic, and Armenian traditions on pp. 185-209.

[3] Jones, "Eros and Astrology," 62.

[4] Jones, "Eros and Astrology," 75. *Rec* 9.32.5 reads, *habuit enim Martem cum Venere super centrum, Lunam vero in occasu in domo Martis et finibus Saturni, quod schema adulteras facit et servos proprios amare, in peregre et in aquis defungi...* ("For she had Mars with Venus above the center, in fact the moon setting in the house of Mars and the boundaries of Saturn. This figure causes [women to be] adulteresses and to love their own slaves, and to die abroad and in waters...").

[5] Jones, "Eros and Astrology," 76.

[6] Jones, "Eros and Astrology," 76.

[7] Jones, "Eros and Astrology," 76-77. See, for example, Clement of Alexandria's *exc. Thdot.* 78.1: Μέχρι τοῦ βαπτίσματος οὖν ἡ Εἱμαρμένη, φασὶν, ἀληθής · μετὰ δὲ τοῦτο οὐκέτι ἀληθεύουσιν οἱ ἀστρολόγοι ("Until baptism, they say, Fate is real, but after it the astrologers are no longer right"). Robert Pierce Casey, *The Excerpta ex Theodoto of Clement of Alexandria* (Cambridge, MA: Harvard University Press, 1934) 88-89. On attempts by Gnostics to overcome the power of astral determinism see Horace Jeffery Hodges, "Gnostic Liberation from Astrological Determinism: Hipparchan 'Trepidation' and the Breaking of Fate," *Vigiliae Christianae* 51 (1997) 359-73.

Unlike the *Grundschrift*, the *Recognitions* tends to obscure the idea that human conditions can be ascribed to fate. For instance, *Rec* 9.7.1-6 practically eliminates the *Grundschrift* passage preserved by *Hom* 19.23.5, which seems to uphold the position held by Bardaisan.[8] Moreover, *Rec* 9.25.8 eliminates a statement from *BLC* col. 598 which clearly states that human beings are subject to the control of fate.[9] We can say, then, that while the *Recognitions* has taken over the astrological materials used by the *Grundschrift*, it has suppressed even the limited role assigned to fate by its predecessor; the *Recognitions'* interest in astrology cannot be dismissed as a careless repetition of its sources.

With this in mind, we must look for another explanation of the *Recognitions'* preoccupation with astrology. To understand our text's attitude toward astrology (and, ultimately, what "work" astrology does in the narrative), we should begin by looking at what other Christian authors have to say on the subject. While not all Christians were opposed to astrological ideas, many authors, including Tatian, Tertullian, Hippolytus, Gregory of Nyssa, Augustine, Methodius of Olympus and Arnobius of Sicca, engage in polemics against astrology and astral fate that are similar to what we find in the *Recognitions*.[10]

Though we must be careful not to assume that all Christians were uniformly opposed to astrological thinking, there was for many authors an inherent conflict between astrology and Christianity. Notions of astral fatalism were generally understood to exclude Christian ideas about divine providence and human free will. In addition, the philosophical doctrine of cosmic sympathy underlying astrology, which held that "everything in the cosmos is ... interconnected within one universal chain of action and reaction," was at variance with traditional Jewish and Christian notions of

---

[8] In the passage from *Hom* 19.23.5, Peter tells Simon: Εἰ ἦν αἰώνιος ταπείνωσις αὐτῶν, ἀτυχία ἂν ἦν μεγίστη · ἀλλὰ πρὸς τῷ κλήρῳ τὰ ταπεινώματα καὶ ὑψώματα ἀνθρώποις γίνεται ("If their humiliation were eternal, their misfortune would be very great. But the humiliations and exaltations of men take place according to lot..."). Jones, "Eros and Astrology," 63.

[9] Jones, "Eros and Astrology," 63. This will be discussed in more detail later in this chapter.

[10] Tatian, *orat.* 8-11; Tertullian, *De Idololatria* 9; Hippolytus, *haer.* 4.1-12; Methodius Olympius, *symp.* 13-16; Arnobius of Sicca, *Seven Books against the Heathen* 7.10. For a more comprehensive portrait of ancient Christian attitudes against (and in favor of) astrology, see Timothy Hegedus, "Attitudes to Astrology in Early Christianity: A Study Based on Selected Sources" (Ph.D. diss., University of Toronto, 2000), and Nicola Denzey, "Under a Pitiless Sky: Conversion, Cosmology, and the Rhetoric of 'Enslavement to Fate' in Second-Century Christian Sources (Ph.D. diss., Princeton University, 1998). Denzey, Hegedus, and Stanley Jones all note that it is incorrect to assume that Christians were uniformly opposed to astrology; see Denzey, "A New Star on the Horizon," 207-21, esp. 208-9.

a "divine creator who was external to the universe."[11] Finally, belief in the divinity of the stars, which was common in Greco-Roman astrology, clashed with Christian conceptions of monotheism and divine transcendence.[12] The author of the *Recognitions*, as we shall see, understands astrological views as incompatible with his religious perspective.

In order to understand what astrology accomplishes within the narrative of the *Recognitions*, we must return to Pierre Bourdieu's notion of *field* that figured so prominently in the last chapter. Recall that this term denotes "a field of objective relations among individuals or institutions *competing for the same stakes*."[13] We have already seen that the protagonists and their philosophical rivals can be placed in the field of Knowledge/Salvation, because both sets of competitors are vying for the same stakes. If we focus on the capital that is up for grabs – that is, true knowledge – we can begin to see how the inscribed astrologers of the *Recognitions* form a third competitive group in the field. Both philosophers and astrologers have one important thing in common: they both claim to have exclusive access to true knowledge (and hence sole possession of the capital contested within the field). Although their methods and areas of expertise are remarkably different, their concern for knowledge is strikingly similar. For both philosophers and astrologers in the *Recognitions*, "knowledge" involves a proper understanding of how the world works, correct interpretation of past and present events, as well as accurate predictions of future occurrences. As a result of their complementary epistemological claims, these two kinds of experts are able to mount a comprehensive and coherent attack on the ideas advanced by the *Recognitions*' protagonists.

Philosophers, astrologers, and Christians (not to mention members of other religious groups as well) vied for the allegiance of individuals in the same competitive spiritual marketplace. While it is not uncommon for modern interpreters to characterize astrology as a misguided kind of science, Luther H. Martin is probably more correct in stating that astrology was "the most important and widespread Hellenistic system of piety."[14] In other words, astrology can be understood as a *religious* movement of sorts,

---

[11] Hegedus, "Attitudes to Astrology," 1, 19.

[12] Hegedus, "Attitudes to Astrology," 19.

[13] Bourdieu, "Haute Couture," 133. Italics added.

[14] Luther H. Martin, "The Pagan Religious Background," in *Early Christianity: Origins and Evolution to A.D. 600*, ed. Ian Hazlett (London: SPCK, 1991) 59. Franz Cumont writes in detail about the religious characteristics of astrology in his *Astrology and Religion among the Greeks and Romans* (New York: G. P. Putnam, 1912). This paragraph and the next are indebted to Hegedus, "Attitudes to Astrology," 10-11.

with all the attendant qualities: Practitioners clearly viewed it as having divine origins (see e.g. Manilius' *Astronomica* 1.40ff). Moreover, as Hegedus argues, astrology had "authoritative, sacred writings" that were attributed to figures from the heroic past, and "astrologers were regarded as religious professionals in their own right."[15] Firmicus Maternus' *Mathesis* 2.30.1, for instance, instructs astrologers as follows: "It is necessary for him who daily speaks about the gods or with the gods to shape and furnish his mind so that he always approaches the imitation of divinity." According to Firmicus Maternus, astrologers not only have day-to-day relationships with divine beings but must cultivate a set of moral and household virtues appropriate for members of a priesthood (*Mathesis* 2.30.2).[16]

Astrology, then, was a *religious* enterprise, and a popular one at that. It grew in popularity among the Roman aristocracy beginning in the first century BCE and eventually "acquired an axiomatic validity" among the masses.[17] Astrology was no less popular after the rise of Constantine and the emergence of a so-called "Christian" empire, as Firmicus Maternus' *Mathesis*, Augustine's *Confessiones*, and the *Codex Theodosianus* all attest.[18] In fact, we know that many ancient Christians consulted astrologers, based on the testimony of authors who recognized that astrology was a force competing for the allegiance of the Christian faithful.[19] These considerations should make it unsurprising that Christians such as the author of the *Recognitions* represent themselves in conflict and competition not only with philosophers but with astrologers as well.

Once we have placed philosophers and astrologers within the same competitive field, we can begin to see similarities in the function of these two groups. The text speaks at length about the training required of philosophers and astrologers, and stresses the protagonists' extensive

---

[15] Hegedus, "Attitudes to Astrology," 16; Franz Cumont, *Les religions orientales dans le paganisme romain: conférences faites au collège de France en 1905*, 4th ed. (reprint of 1929 ed.; Paris: Librairie Orientaliste Paul Geuthner, 1963) 82, 152, 158.

[16] Translation by Hegedus, "Attitudes to Astrology," 16-17.

[17] A. Bouché-Leclercq, *L'Astrologie grecque* (Bruxelles: Culture et Civilisation, 1963) 546-48. Quote from Nock, *Conversion*, 100. See also Frederick H. Cramer, *Astrology in Roman Law and Politics* (Philadelphia: American Philosophical Society, 1954) 81-146.

[18] The *Mathesis* is addressed to Fl. Lollianus Mavortius, who was ordinary consul in 338; Augustine refers to the youthful interest in astrology of the proconsul Helvius Vindicianus (*Confessiones* 4.3.5, 7.6.8); and multiple laws of the *Codex Theodosianus* are directed against divination and astrology (see e.g. *CT* 9.16.4 in the year 357, 9.16.6 in the year 358, and 9.16.12 in the year 409). Hegedus, "Attitudes to Astrology," 14.

[19] Franz Boll, Carl Bezold and Wilhelm Gundel, *Sternglaube und Sterndeutung*, 6th ed. (Darmstadt: Wissenschaftliche Buchgesellschaft, 1974) 184-85.

instruction in both disciplines. In both cases, the text uses its heroes' expertise to mount a persuasive campaign against the competing specialists' claims to knowledge, arguing that (1) technical expertise in astrology and philosophy is not equivalent to knowledge and (2) prophetic knowledge is the only certain knowledge.

It is important to note that while astrologers belong in the same field with their philosophical compatriots, there are significant differences in their respective roles within the *Recognitions*. For example, the text uses different strategies to undermine the philosophers' and astrologers' skill. With the philosophers, we saw the text's assertions that their expertise has turned them into sophists rather than seekers after truth, and that their so-called "knowledge" is based on the fallible capacities of human beings. Like their philosophical counterparts, the astrologers have "knowledge" that is based on faulty assumptions about the world: they believe that the universe is deterministic, that there is no human free will or providence, and that the stars control the destiny of the world and its inhabitants. Unlike the philosophers, however, the astrologers' imperfect knowledge is based *not* on human conjecture, but on lies perpetuated by demonic forces. The *Recognitions* employs an entirely new strategy when it asserts that the source of the astrologers' knowledge and power is demonic activity rather than their own correct interpretation of the stars. This critique introduces a distinction between legitimate and illegitimate power that maps on to the existing dichotomy between true and false knowledge. These two vocabularies – knowledge and power – work together to differentiate the protagonists from their rivals, with the goal of granting the heroes exclusive possession of the epistemic capital and ultimately control of the field.

Astrological Expertise and Knowledge

In the ancient world, astrology was a realm usually restricted to highly-qualified specialists. Morris Jastrow writes of Babylonian astrology, "An astral theory of the universe is not an outcome of popular thought, but the result of a long process of speculative reasoning carried on in restricted learned circles. Even astrology, which the theory presupposes as a foundation, is not a product of primitive popular fancies but is rather an advanced scientific hypothesis."[20] Ramsay MacMullen makes a similar assessment of astrology in the Roman era:

---

[20] Morris Jastrow, *Die Religion Babyloniens und Assyriens* (Giessen: A. Töpelmann, 1905-1912) 236; cited in English translation by Franz Cumont, *Astrology and Religion among the Greeks and Romans* (New York and London: Knickerbocker, 1912) 6.

Astrology and allied arts could only be mastered through long study ... one can see the outlines of a true body of learning which could be lowered to the level of the racetrack crowds but which in its more technical forms came close to a science ... Rules, tables, calculations, and commentaries now known from a vast corpus of astrological writings lay far above the reach of casual charlatanism.[21]

I would like to suggest that the *Recognitions* characterizes both Clement and Faustinianus as such astrological experts. To this end it may be helpful to return to Bourdieu's idea of religious specialists, who are "socially recognized as the exclusive holders of the specific competence necessary for the production or reproduction of a *deliberately organized corpus* of secret (and therefore rare) knowledge."[22] While philosophers claimed to have secret and institutionally-transmitted information about the world, astrologers had even more cause to make this assertion: they too possessed specialized, esoteric, and widely-accepted knowledge about the universe and its workings.[23] Since Peter and his followers – the "newcomers" to the field – want to appropriate precisely this kind of knowledge possessed by the more established competitors, they must once again show that they have just as much specialized training as their opponents. After examining how the text constructs Faustinianus' credentials, I will argue that the text authenticates the heroes' astrological skill by alluding to formal training, referring explicitly to the agreement of Faustinianus, and by having the protagonists anticipate and summarize their opponent's arguments.[24]

The Opponent(s)

When Faustinianus first comes into contact with Peter, Clement, Niceta and Aquila, he offers *edocere quae recta sunt* ("to teach what is right"; *Rec* 8.1.4; cf. *Hom* 14.2.3). He reveals the content of this proposed instruction shortly thereafter: *fortuitus casus et genesis agunt omnia, sicut ego ex me ipso manifestissime conperi in disciplina mathesis prae ceteris eruditus* ("all things are done by fortuitous chance and fate, as I have discovered most clearly for myself, being educated beyond others in the discipline of astrology"; *Rec* 8.2.2).[25] This probably deserves a bit of explanation.

---

[21] Ramsay MacMullen, *Enemies of the Roman Order: Treason, Unrest, and Alienation in the Empire* (London and New York: Routledge, 1966) 137-38.

[22] Bourdieu, "Genesis and Structure of the Religious Field," 9. Italics in original.

[23] This will be discussed in more detail below.

[24] It is worth noting that the lineup of protagonists and opponents from the philosophical debates remains the same in the astrological discussion, although Clement's role becomes more prominent than that of his two brothers or Peter. Faustinianus continues to be the primary opponent, and the tone of their debate is friendly.

[25] Faustus makes a more direct claim about his education in *Hom* 14.3.2: οὔτε γὰρ θεός ἐστιν οὔτε πρόνοια, ἀλλὰ γενέσει τὰ πάντα ὑπόκειται, ὡς ἐγὼ ἐφ᾽ οἷς

Faustinianus is referring to one of the two main branches of predictive astrology according to Ptolemy's *Tetrabiblos* 2.1. While general astrology "relates to whole races, countries and cities" (καθ' ὅλα ἔθνη καὶ χώρας καὶ πόλεις), genethlialogy – the practice to which Faustinianus alludes – pertains to individuals.[26] Faustinianus' term *genesis*, which is a "technical term referring to an individual's (natal) horoscope," was the foundation of genethlialogy, which in turn was "arguably the most popular type of divination in the ancient world."[27] It is used by the Pseudo-Clementines and some other writings as a synonym for fate.[28] In this passage, then, Faustinianus is claiming to be a particularly accomplished student of genethlialogy.

Peter repeats a similar version of the old man's assertion in *Rec* 9.2.1: *te professus es gnarum esse positionis siderum et stellarum cursus* ("you profess to be expert in the position of the constellations and the courses of the stars"). Faustinianus' claim to expertise is corroborated a short while later in *Rec* 9.16.4 – 9.18, as he confesses that he is not yet convinced by Clement's arguments against astral fatalism: *conscius enim mihi sum quorundam, ex quibus bene novi, quia conpaginatione stellarum homines aut homicidae aut adulteri fiunt ceteraque perpetrant mala. Similiter autem et honestae ac pudicae feminae, ut bene agant, inde coguntur* ("...for I am cognizant of certain things from which I have come to know well, that by the joining of the stars people become either murderers or adulterers, and commit other evils; and similarly respectable and chaste women are compelled from that cause to act well"; *Rec* 9.16.4-5). He goes on to give the various stellar configurations that produce these conditions in *Rec* 9.17.1-4, which demonstrates his intimate familiarity with the technical details of astrology.[29]

These examples reveal that, in contrast to the philosophical materials, the astrological debates involve no references to named schools of thought in which the interlocutors have been trained. Nevertheless, Faustinianus clearly plays the role of astrological specialist in the *Recognitions*.

πέπονθα πεπληροφόρημαι, ἐκ πολλοῦ ἀκριβῶν τὸ μάθημα ("For there is neither God nor providence; but all things are subject to astral fate, as I have been fully assured because of the things I have myself endured, having for a long time inquired carefully of astrology").

26 Ptolemy, *Tetrabiblos*, trans. F. E. Robbins (LCL; Cambridge, MA: Harvard University Press, 1940). Unless otherwise noted, all English translations of Ptolemy's *Tetrabiblos* are by Robbins.

27 Hegedus, "Attitudes to Astrology," 20, 10.

28 On the equivalence of *genesis* and fate see A. J. Festugière, *L'Idéal religieux des Grecs et L'Évangile* (Paris: J. Gabalda, 1932) 111 n. 7.

29 Faustinianus' discourse in *Rec* 9.17.1-4 also appears in the writings of the sixth century monk Ps-Caesarius; on this see Rehm, *Rekognitionen*, 267-8.

Although Faustinianus is the only named astrologer in the narrative, Clement's responses at various points indicate that his father serves as a spokesperson for astrologers in general.[30] This representative function suggests that the old man should be interpreted as the established player in the field, or the competitor with the most epistemic capital. The protagonists, by contrast, are relative newcomers. Recall that the dynamics of the field require that the established players attempt to maintain their capital through "conservation strategies," while the newcomers try to topple the established players using "subversion strategies" to undermine the latter's epistemic authority. As we look more closely at the protagonists in the following section, we will find that this is precisely the case.

The Protagonists

Like their opponent, the protagonists have attained some measure of astrological instruction. Whereas in the philosophical discussions all the heroes could claim to have had philosophical training, in the debate on astrology Clement emerges as the primary astrological expert. One possible exception to this rule is found in *Rec* 8.22.4, where Niceta states that his arguments about divinely created order are based on *excelsorum disciplinis traduntur a Graecis* ["the knowledge of the heavens given by the Greeks"]. This may mean that Niceta's ideas come from the most respected circles of astrological knowledge, which in turn would suggest that he has had some kind of technical training in astrology. Another exception appears in *Rec* 8.58.1, where Clement appears to recognize his brothers' astrological skill when he tells Faustinianus that *cum his tibi erit sermo, qui expertes non sunt eius quam protuleris disciplinae* ("your discussion will be with those who are not without this knowledge that you will have advanced"). Clement, then, is not the only protagonist acquainted with astrology, but the many references to his credentials imply that he is the best qualified to debate Faustinianus. For example, in *Rec* 8.8.1 Clement tells the old man that he is familiar with the doctrine of *genesis*, or astral determinism (*est enim mihi notitia huius scientiae*). Later in *Rec* 9.18.2, Clement reiterates this point: "the science of astrology is known to me" (*scientia mihi mathesis nota est*). Aquila too acknowledges Clement's superior instruction in the subject when he defers to his brother, *qui*

---

30 Cf. *Hom* 14.11.2, where one of Faustus' close associates is the Egyptian Annubion, described as "the best of the astrologers" (ἀστρολόγων ἄριστος). See also *Hom* 20.11.3, where Faustus mentions that Clement and Annubion will have a future debate on the issue of astral fate; and *Hom* 20.21.1, where Peter declares that the protagonists will discuss *genesis* with Annubion when they arrive at Antioch. On the figure of Annubion see Bremmer, "Foolish Egyptians," 313-17.

plenius scientiam mathesis adtigit ("since he has more fully engaged in the science of astrology"; *Rec* 8.57.5).[31] Clement's appearance of authority is underscored when he judges the performance of his father in their debates about astrology: he tells Faustinianus that he has argued *doctissime et eruditissime* ("most skillfully and learnedly"; *Rec* 9.18.2), and that he is happy to talk *cum erudito viro* ("with a learned man"; *Rec* 9.18.2).

Of course, Clement believes that there are things his father ought to learn from him: *accipe ergo ad ea quae dixisti, ut evidenter agnoscas* ("Hear, therefore, while I reply to what you have said, that you may plainly acknowledge"; *Rec* 9.18.3). This statement introduces Clement's lengthy rehearsal of the contents of the *Book of the Laws of the Countries*. Toward the end of the *Recognitions* (10.7 and 10.9), Clement states that his qualifications allow him to use Faustinianus' own area of expertise to prove him wrong: he will debate his father *secundum ipsam...ut de his quae tibi in usu sunt accipiens rationem, citius adquiescas* ("according to that [science], so that, taking my method from those things which are in your experience, you may acquiesce more quickly"; *Rec* 10.9.1).[32] This claim is striking in comparison to Clement's recounting of his astrological expertise in *Homilies* 14.5.2-3: Εγω καὶ τὸ ἐμὸν φῦλον ἐκ προγόνων θεὸν σέβειν παρειληφὼς καὶ παράγγελμα ἔχων γενέσει μὴ προσανέχειν [λέγω δὴ τῷ τῆς ἀστρολογίας μαθήματι], διὰ τοῦτο οὐ προσέσχον. ὅθεν ἀστρολογίας μὲν οὐκ εἰμι ἔμπειρος ("I and my tribe, having received the worship of God from our ancestors, and having instruction not to devote ourselves to genesis (indeed I mean the science of astrology); because of this I did not devote myself to [it]. For this reason I am not experienced in astrology"). The *Recognitions*, in stark contrast to the *Homilies*, has a vested interest in demonstrating that the protagonists – especially Clement – believe themselves to be well-versed in astrological topics. Such demonstrations of "expertise," even if they amount to rehearsals of common knowledge, were widely employed in Christian anti-astrological polemics because they assured readers that the authors were knowledgeable about the practices they were attacking. For examples of

---

[31] The Latin *mathesis* can mean either mathematics or astrology (see Lewis and Short, *A Latin Dictionary*, s.v. *mathesis*). As Jean Rhys Bram notes, "This term, meaning learning in general, first came to be used for the mathematical sciences, then for astrology." (Firmicus Maternus, *Matheseos Libri VIII. Ancient Astrology: Theory and Practice*, trans. Jean Rhys Bram [Park Ridge, NJ: Noyes Press, 1975] 304 n. 10.) I have chosen to translate the term as "astrology," since this best conveys the *Recognitions'* understanding of the term to a modern audience.

[32] Cf. the strikingly similar claim of Basil's *Homiliae in hexaemeron* 6.5, where he writes: "I myself shall say nothing of my own, but I shall avail myself of what is theirs [i.e. the astrologers'] in order to refute them." Translation by Hegedus, "Attitudes to Astrology," 35.

this tactic see Augustine, *De Diversis Quaestionibus* 83, Qu. 45.2; Gregory of Nazianzus, *Poemata Arcana* 5.45-46; and especially Origen, *Philocalia* 23.17-18 (who unlike other Christian authors does seem to know a fair bit about astrology).

We can understand the *Recognitions'* concern for expertise in terms of *field*, since the competition within the field is a matter of specialized knowledge. Specifically, the text's highlighting of Clement's training is critically important for the placement of the protagonists within the field, since it suggests that the knowledge (or capital) possessed by the established players does not belong exclusively to them. The emphasis on Clement's astrological knowledge is designed to show that he too holds some of the capital that is at stake in the field. As a result, Clement is able to stand on equal footing with Faustinianus and the astrologers he represents. Of course, there is always the possibility that Clement should not be taken at his word. How do we know that Clement really *is* skilled in astrology, as he contends?

Clement's astrological proficiency is confirmed in the first place by the agreement of the other named expert inscribed in the text as his opponent: Faustinianus readily agrees that Clement *and* his brothers are right on target in their arguments about astrology. For example, in *Rec* 8.57.1 Faustinianus tells Aquila that his words are *validi* ("powerful"), although he disagrees with his son's ideas. He also declares that Aquila is *inbutum...in huiusmodi disciplinis* ("steeped in instruction of this sort"), even though Aquila chooses to demur by pointing out Clement's superior qualifications (*Rec* 8.57.4). Elsewhere, he assents to specific arguments put forth by Clement, telling him *Ita est, fili, nec aliter fieri potest* ("It is so, son; nor can it happen differently"; *Rec* 10.9.4); and *ita se...habet* ("it is so"; *Rec* 10.9.6). Hence not only do the protagonists allege that they have astrological knowledge, but their claims are also verified by a rival astrologer. This rhetorical strategy is clever, because it uses the expertise of Faustinianus not only to validate the protagonists' technical training, but also to support their side of the argument!

Clement's expert status is also confirmed by another method: he anticipates his opponent's arguments. For example, in *Rec* 8.47.1 Clement says to Faustinianus: *sed fortasse dices: Quid, quod in ista communi castigatione similia impii patiuntur et pii?* ("But perhaps you will say, 'Why [is it] that, in this common punishment, the impious and the pious suffer similar things?'"). In this case he has anticipated his father's objection before he even has a chance to give voice to it. Clement concedes that his father is correct (*verum est, etiam nos fatemur*; "It is true, indeed we ourselves acknowledge [it]"; *Rec* 8.47.2), but proceeds to demonstrate why this "common punishment" does not prove that the protagonists' ideas about reward and punishment are false. Elsewhere, in *Rec* 9.8.1, Clement makes a similar move: *sed fortasse dicas...quid de aegritudinibus dicemus et infirmitatibus, quae accidunt hominibus* ("But perhaps you will say...what shall we say of the sicknesses and infirmities which happen to human beings?") Just as before, Clement goes on to address the reservation he has just anticipated. This happens yet again in *Rec* 9.26.1, where Clement foresees an objection based on the expertise he and his father share: *Sed dicet aliquis eorum qui in disciplina mathesis adtentius eruditi sunt, genesim in septem partes dirimi, quae illi climata appellant* ("But someone of those who are carefully educated in the science of astrology will say that astral determinism is divided into seven parts, which they call climates"). Here again Clement voices and answers the objection before his father has been given a chance to speak.

On my reading, these instances where Clement anticipates his father's counter-arguments accomplish two things. In the first place, they effectively silence the opposition. Even though Faustinianus is a friendly rival, he barely has a chance to speak during the course of the debates. As a result, the term "debate" is itself a misnomer when applied to the astrological discourse. Like the philosophical discussions, the major characters' conversations about astrology are less like debates between two opponents whose ideas are equitably presented, and more akin to monologues delivered by one partner in the dialogue.

This brings us to the second and more important function of Clement's anticipatory strategy. Even though Clement ostensibly gives voice to Faustinianus' counterarguments, these anticipated objections do not work as equivalents to Faustinianus' own speech. Instead, they serve mainly to demonstrate *Clement's* expertise. They emphatically demonstrate that there is nothing Clement has failed to consider. He has thought about every possible problem in advance, and he has an answer ready for all potential objections. Because of this strategy, Faustinianus is a straw-man whose arguments are not supposed to provide Clement with any significant opposition.[33] The old man, who is ostensibly the established player in the field, finds himself silenced and outmaneuvered by a newcomer to the competition. The *Recognitions'* use of these strategies enables the

---

[33] In antiquity, there were many authors who argued in favor of astral fatalism; see for example the first book of Firmicus Maternus' *Mathesis*, which is a ready-made refutation of several common arguments against astral fatalism and astrology in general. The prevalence of arguments in favor of astral determinism suggests that the *Recognitions* probably knew of such materials. If this is the case, we can surmise that the *Recognitions* (and probably the *Grundschrift* before it) deliberately chose to make Faustinianus a weak opponent. He makes few arguments in favor of astrology, and those arguments that do find their way into the *Recognitions* are almost always placed in the mouth of Clement.

protagonists to challenge seriously their opponent's exclusive claim to the capital at stake in the field.

In addition to Faustinianus' statements of approval and Clement's anticipation of his rival's objections, there is a third way in which Clement's expert status is affirmed. In *Rec* 9, just after Clement tells Faustinianus to listen to what he has to say, Clement begins a prolonged recitation of twenty chapters from the Bardesanite *Book of the Laws of the Countries* (or a closely related text). Naturally, the author of the *Recognitions* presents this material not as an extended citation of a separate text, but as Clement's own words. Later in the chapter we will have occasion to look more closely at the contents of this astrological discourse appropriated by Clement. For now, however, it is sufficient to note that Clement's invocation of a well-known argument against astrology is designed to demonstrate that his own knowledge of the subject is beyond question. Clement is not comparing apples to oranges by attempting to refute astrology by means of some other discipline or set of texts; such a strategy might suggest that he opposes astrology simply because he does not understand it.[34] Instead, as he promises Faustinianus in *Rec* 10.9.1, he debates his opponent using only ideas taken from the latter's area of expertise. From a rhetorical point of view, this move is extremely important in establishing the protagonists' proficiency in multiple paths to knowledge. Such emphasis on their skills in philosophy and now astrology might seem to affirm the legitimacy of these two disciplines. However, just as we have seen in the case of philosophy, we will soon discover that the *Recognitions* uses this technique in order to make its protagonists better polemicists *against* astrology. Before we can understand this polemic, we must look at other elements of the *Recognitions* that seem to affirm the value of astrological knowledge.

Astrological Knowledge

We have just seen that the *Recognitions* makes a point of demonstrating that its interlocutors – especially Faustinianus and Clement – have specialized training in astrology. This emphasis on expertise implies that the text values astrology as a path to knowledge, at least in some respects. This conclusion is supported by sections of *Rec* 1 that unmistakably point to the reality of astrological knowledge. If the *Recognitions* ultimately intends to refute the idea that astrology produces real knowledge, what is

---

[34] Cf. *Hom* 14.5.2-3.

the purpose of these episodes? To find the answer, we need to look more closely at the passages in question.

Rec 1.28.1-2, which is part of an account of creation based largely on the book of Genesis, states that God placed the stars, sun and moon in *caelum istud visibile* ("that visible heaven") for two purposes: to provide light, and to be *indicio rerum praeteritarum, praesentium et futurarum. pro signis enim temporum facta sunt ac dierum, quae videntur quidem ab omnibus, intelleguntur autem ab eruditis et intellegentibus solis* ("an indication of past, present, and future things. For they have been made for signs of seasons and of days, which indeed are seen by all, but are understood only by the learned and intelligent"). The text gives no indication of what might constitute learnedness or intelligence, but it is clear that God created these celestial bodies so that certain individuals might be able to use them to understand past, present, and future events. The interpretive and predictive functions of these "stars" appear to support the most basic tenet of astrology, namely that there is a "link, causal or semiotic, between celestial and terrestrial events."[35] This affirmation of astrology is underscored a bit later in *Rec* 1.32.3, where Abraham is held up as an example: *ab initio tamen ceteris omnibus errantibus, ipse cum arte esset astrologus, ex ratione et ordine stellarum agnoscere potuit conditorem eiusque providentia intellexit cuncta moderari* ("Yet from the beginning, while all others were erring, he himself, [since] he was a skilled astrologer, was able to recognize the creator from the order and arrangement of the stars, and he understood that everything is guided by His providence"). Abraham, who has already been described as pleasing to God and a friend of God, is an astrologer. He appears to be precisely the kind of "learned and intelligent" person capable of understanding the stars as God intended them to be understood. It is probably safe to assume that Abraham, since he is characterized as an astrologer, was thought to use the stars as "signs of seasons and of days." This episode, together with the excerpt from the creation narrative, would seem to suggest that astrology is a favorable practice – after all, the stars were created by God as signs to be interpreted, and Abraham, an exemplary patriarch, is characterized as an astrologer and praised for his interpretation of the stars.

Many readers already will have noted that the Pseudo-Clementine *Recognitions* is not unique or even unusual in speaking of Abraham as an astrologer. Jubilees, Philo, and Josephus are all familiar with this line of interpretation, while the Sibylline Oracles and Genesis Rabba apparently know it well enough to suggest their opposition to it.[36] Abraham's

---

[35] Hornblower and Spawforth, *Oxford Classical Dictionary*, s.v. "astrology."

[36] Kugel, *Traditions of the Bible*, 244-74. Kugel lists Jub. 12.17-18, Philo *de Abr.* 69-71, and Josephus *AJ* 1.154-57 on pp 250-51, as well as *Sibylline Oracles* 3.218-28 and

widespread reputation as an astrologer probably derives from his Chaldaean background as narrated in Genesis; as is well known, "Chaldaean" was practically a synonym for "astrologer" in the ancient world.[37] Readers may also be aware that this particular section of *Rec* 1, which contains both the creation and Abraham stories, belongs to a separate source (typically demarcated as *Rec* 1.27-71, and sometimes identified as the *Anabathmoi Jakobou*)[38] that has been used by the *Grundschrift* and then passed on to the *Recognitions*. In some sense, then, one could argue that the positive evaluation of astrology we meet in the creation and Abraham stories has been inherited by the editor of the *Recognitions*. Since this editor is sometimes careless, this attitude toward astrology might not reflect his own stance at all; perhaps it should be written off as a source critical tension. To some extent, the *Recognitions'* astrological views *are* the product of its reliance on different sources, but I would like to suggest that we look at how these views work together rather than immediately dismissing them based on source critical considerations.

A closer look at these materials reveals that these two "rewritten Bible" episodes – even with their affirmation of astrology – have two important functions that are in keeping with the rest of the text. In the first place, both stories emphasize that the sun, moon, and stars are part of God's creation; this idea will become the foundation of one of the protagonists' arguments against astral determinism. In the second place, both stories reveal that when the sun, moon, and stars are interpreted properly, they point to the reality of God's providential care for the world. Astrologers interpret the stars based on their theory of astral determinism, or fate, which suggests that everything that happens has been determined in advance and cannot be changed. If they *really* understood what the stars indicated, however, they would arrive at the protagonists' conclusion that God's providence governs the world. Hence this positive assessment of the stars, as both instruments of God's creation and signs of God's providence, paves the way for the protagonists to use their opponent's astrological theories to prove the truth of their own ideas. If we articulate this rhetorical strategy in terms of Bourdieu's notion of field, we can begin to see how both the *Recognitions'* emphasis on its protagonists' astrological expertise and its affirmation of some astrological ideas make sense: they

---

Genesis Rabba 39.1 on pp 259-60. Since *Rec* 1.27-71 uses Jubilees as a source, this may explain in part its emphasis on Abraham as astrologer. See Scott, *Geography in Early Judaism and Christianity*, 99-114.

[37] *Astrologi, mathematici* and *Chaldaei* are more or less synonyms in Latin. MacMullen, *Enemies of the Roman Order*, 128.

[38] On this source, compare the assessments of van Voorst, *Ascents of James*, 29-46; and Jones, *Ancient Jewish Christian Source*, 111-55.

are simply part of a larger "subversion strategy" designed to devalue their opponent's capital, thereby increasing the value of the newcomers' epistemic authority.

Arguments for and against Astral Determinism

The opening lines of Ptolemy's *Tetrabiblos* describe astronomy – that is, astrology – as a means of prediction. It is "that whereby we apprehend the aspects of the movements of sun, moon, and stars in relation to each other and to the earth, as they occur from time to time" as well as "that in which by means of the natural character of these aspects themselves we investigate the changes which they bring about in that which they surround."[39] Astrology, on this definition, is largely about prediction, and its success depends on correctly understanding the significance of the sun, moon, stars, and planets' relative positions. At the heart of this system lies a fundamental presupposition about astral determinism: all events in the universe are destined to occur in a particular way, and when interpreted properly, the stars reveal precisely how such events will unfold. Therefore, astrologers' interpretive authority depends on the idea of an inflexibly deterministic universe whose future is signaled by the stars.[40] Ramsay MacMullen confirms this in speaking about the astrologers Tiberius Claudius Thrasyllus and Tiberius Claudius Balbillus: "a world in which men principally known for their astrological lore could rise to such influence and could found such a dynasty was a world quite dedicated to astral fatalism."[41] These two men, who were the friends and advisors to many members of the Roman imperial family, wielded an extraordinary amount of influence because they lived in a world where astral determinism was a fact taken for granted.

Because such a deterministic perspective was widely accepted in antiquity, astrologers' predictions of future events were considered by many to be undeniably and unavoidably true. MacMullen has shown that their epistemological power explains why astrologers' predictions were so troubling at various moments in the Roman Empire. For example, during the period from 33 BCE to 93 CE, all *mathematici, Chaldaei, astrologi, magi,* and *goetes* were expelled from the city of Rome approximately ten

---

[39] Ptolemy, *Tetr.* 3.

[40] Note, however, the qualification of this statement mentioned by Hegedus, who cites Ptolemy's *Tetr.* 1.3 in support of his point: "... such an all-embracing fatalism – though frequently assumed among Christian authors dealing with astrology – was not necessarily held by ancient astrologers themselves." Hegedus, "Attitudes to Astrology," 64.

[41] MacMullen, *Enemies of the Roman Order*, 141.

times.[42] The reason for the expulsions is suggested by Firmicus Maternus' advice to fellow astrologers in his *Mathesis* 2.30.4: "Be careful to say nothing about the condition of the state or the life of the emperor, if anyone should inquire; for that is forbidden; we must not, moved by criminal curiosity, speak of the condition of the country; and he who answers questions on the destiny of the emperor would be a wretch deserving of every punishment."[43] Because their knowledge of future events was thought to be certain, astrologers' predictions had the power and potential to be dangerous, even seditious.

The *Recognitions'* attack on astrology strikes at its epistemological foundation, by calling into question the very idea of a deterministic universe. For this reason, much of the discussion about astrology centers on the issue of astral determinism. While Faustinianus argues in favor of astral determinism, or *genesis*,[44] Clement is charged with defending the alternative view: a universe providentially governed by God and contingent on human free will.[45] In the following pages we will look at this debate in some detail, beginning with the case Faustinianus makes for astral determinism.

When he first arrives on the scene in *Rec* 8.2.2-3 (cf. *Hom* 14.3.3), Faustinianus states his intellectual position quite clearly: *neque deus est neque cultus hic aliquid est neque providentia in mundo, sed fortuitus casus et genesis agunt omnia.... nolite ergo errare; sive enim oretis, sive non oretis, quod genesis vestra continet, hoc erit vobis* ("...there is neither

---

[42] Part of this activity is detailed by Tacitus, *Ann.* 2.32; 12.52. MacMullen, *Enemies of the Roman Order*, 132-33. For a more detailed account of the relationship between astrologers and the Roman government during this era, see Cramer, *Astrology in Roman Law and Politics*, 233-81.

[43] Quoted by MacMullen, *Enemies of the Roman Order*, 132. Astrological studies in general were never banned in the Roman empire, but the production of individual horoscopes was outlawed in Rome. An edict of Augustus in the year 11 CE forbade any astrological inquiry concerning the emperor. Bram, *Ancient Astrology*, 5. Bram suggests that Firmicus Maternus' statement in *Mathesis* 2.30.4 means that "it is not only illegal but impossible to make a prediction in regard to the life of the Emperor since he belongs to a power higher than the stars." Bouché-Leclercq, *Astrologie grecque*, 567 maintains that legislation as late as the fourth century sections of the *Codex Theodosianus* was designed to quash attempts to determine the end of the emperor's life.

[44] The term *genesis* as it occurs within the *Recognitions* can mean astral determinism, but it can also denote a horoscope (or "nativity"). On this point see Cirillo and Schneider, *Reconnaissances du pseudo Clément*, 55: "L'auteur cherche à réfuter la croyance païenne en la fatalité astrologique; il combat l'idée que le destin serait imposé à l'homme par son horoscope, c'est-à-dire par la position de la constellation des astres au moment de sa naissance."

[45] The discussions about free will and astral determinism occur primarily in *Rec* 4, 5, 9 and 10. In addition, there are other relevant materials in *Rec* 1 and 8.

God, nor is there any worship here at all, nor [is there] providence in the world, but fortuitous chance and *genesis* drive all things... Therefore, make no mistake, for whether you pray or you do not pray, whatever your horoscope contains, this will happen for you"). As I have already indicated, however, Faustinianus is given little opportunity to advance a full argument in support of astral determinism. His participation in the "debate" is limited to occasional remarks about why he opposes the ideas of providence and human free will and supports the notion of fate. For instance, in *Rec* 8.4.6 he frames his belief in astral determinism in terms of his intellectual suspicions about providence: *ego dico non secundum providentiam dei gubernari mundum, quia multa in eo iniuste et inordinate geri videmus, sed genesim dico esse, quae omnia agit et continet* ("I say that the world is not governed according to the providence of God, because we see that many things in it are done unjustly and disorderly; but I say that it is *genesis* that does and regulates all things"). Faustinianus believes that, since providential governance presupposes that everything happens in accordance with the wishes of a just and rational God, the existence of injustice and disorder necessarily disprove the existence of providence. He reiterates this question in *Rec* 8.40.6-8 after a lengthy discourse by Niceta:

Igitur hesterno a te habitus sermo, qui adserebat quod arte et mensura et ratione cuncta constarent, non valde me suadet, mentem rationemque esse quae fecerit mundum; multa enim habeo, quae ostendam conpetenti mensura ac forma et specie constare, nec tamen per mentem condita et rationem. Tum praeterea video multa incondite, inconsequenter, iniuste geri in mundo et sine genesis cursu nihil fieri posse.

Therefore, the discourse produced by you yesterday, which claimed that all things consist in skill, and measure, and reason, does not greatly persuade me that it is mind and reason that have made the world; for I have many things that I will show to consist in appropriate measure, and form, and beauty, and yet were not founded by mind and reason. Then, besides, I see that many things are done in the world without order, consequence, or justice, and that nothing can be done without the course of fate.

Although Faustinianus does not elaborate on this point, here he has added another element to his argument against providence and in favor of *genesis*, or fate. Just as injustice and disorder call providence into question, according to Faustinianus there are many regular and orderly things that are not the result of "mind and reason" at all. Since the world contains disorder, and since order can exist without the help of reason, those who would argue in favor of providence cannot point to the orderliness of the universe and nature as conclusive proof of providential design. These are the two major intellectual objections Faustinianus makes against providence, but the reader quickly discovers that his personal experience is the real reason behind his belief in astral fatalism.

In *Rec* 8.57.1-2 Faustinianus tells Aquila that his academic arguments, though persuasive, will never be able to overturn the knowledge he has gained from his own familiarity with the workings of fate: *Ne aegre...accipias, fili, quod dicturus sum; sermones tui quamvis validi sint, non possunt tamen flectere me ut credam fieri aliquid posse extra genesim. scio enim omnia mihi necessitate genesis accidisse, et ideo suaderi mihi non potest* ("Do not accept reluctantly, my son, what I am going to say. Although your discourses are powerful, nevertheless they cannot persuade me to believe that anything can be done apart from *genesis*. For I know that all things have happened to me by the necessity of fate, and therefore it is not possible to persuade me"). Faustinianus is utterly convinced of the reality of astral determinism because he has watched it unfold in his own life. His experiences are – to his mind – irrefutable confirmation of the power of fate, and they cannot be supplanted by mere argumentation, no matter how powerful it may be. We can say, then, that Faustinianus' argument in favor of astral determinism is based not only on the technical skills he has acquired through formal training, but also on his first-hand, "eyewitness" experience of the workings of astral fatalism in his own life.[46]

The protagonists respond to Faustinianus' belief in astral determinism by addressing both his intellectual and experiential reasons for maintaining this view. Niceta and Clement make five major arguments against fate: (1) *genesis*, or astral determinism, means that prayer, worship, and virtuous practices are useless, and renders absurd the idea of God's righteousness; (2) when interpreted properly, the sun, moon, and stars – whose movements are purportedly signs of fate – actually point to and participate in God's righteous and providential care for the world; (3) fate only appears to be real because demonic activity perpetuates and supports it; (4) careful study of laws and customs from around the world reveals that they cannot be explained on the basis of astral fate; and (5) Faustinianus' personal experience of fate is an illusion produced by incorrect interpretation of events.[47] The remainder of this chapter examines each of these arguments in turn, paying special attention to the ways in which the *Recognitions* uses them to call all astrological knowledge into question.

---

[46] In the *Homilies*, Faustus' argument in favor of astral determinism is based much more on his personal experiences than on his claims to professional expertise. See e.g. *Hom* 14.3.3-4; 14.6.1 – 14.7.7, where his belief in *genesis* is explained with reference to his life circumstances.

[47] Hegedus lists and describes six arguments which Christian anti-astrological polemics adapted from Greek and Roman sources: 1) practical impossibility; 2) different destinies; 3) common destinies; 4) νόμιμα βαρβαρικά; 5) animals; 6) the moral argument. Hegedus, "Attitudes to Astrology," 23-110. The *Recognitions* makes use of most of these arguments and adds another – the argument that astrology is demonic in origin – that is common in Christian polemics against astrology.

Argument One: Prayer, Worship, and Human Virtue[48]

This argument, which is articulated almost exclusively by Niceta, draws on a long line of argumentation against fatalism that can probably be traced back to Carneades, the second century BCE head of the New Academy who developed a series of *topoi* against fate.[49] David Amand gives us a good sense of the content of this argumentative tradition when he writes, "Cette doctrine de l'εἱμαρμένη astrologique conduit nécessairement à la négation de notre liberté, à l'inaction et à l'indifférence radicale, à la suppression du mérite, à l'abrogation de la législation et des institutions judiciaires, enfin à la ruine de la morale."[50] Such attacks on astral fatalism were very widely adopted by ancient authors: "C'est l'argumentation 'éthique' antifataliste, qui a été adoptée et répétée par quelques moralistes de l'antiquité et surtout par les théologiens chrétiens."[51] The *Recognitions*, then, is in good company when it invokes elements of this argument in the course of its own "ethical" argument against astral determinism.[52]

Toward the beginning of his disputation with Faustinianus in *Rec* 8.12.2-3, Niceta observes that the old man's belief in *genesis* stands in contradiction to most practices of piety:[53]

cum immolant diis et exorant eos, sine dubio contra genesim se impetraturos aliquid sperant et per hoc genesim solvunt. cum vero rident eos qui ad virtutem provocant et ad continentiam cohortantur, et dicunt, quia nemo potest facere aliquid aut pati, nisi quod ei fato decretum est, omnem profecto cultum divinitatis abscidunt

---

[48] This corresponds to the "moral argument" discussed in Hegedus, "Attitudes to Astrology," 100-10, and examined in great detail by Amand, *Fatalisme et liberté, passim*.

[49] Boll, "Studien über Claudius Ptolemäus," is a history of the reception and transmission of arguments which may derive from Carneades. Christian writers, however, most likely derived their arguments from the doxographical literature that summarized the important opinions of philosophical schools. Hegedus, "Attitudes to Astrology," 21.

[50] Amand, *Fatalisme et liberté*, 49.

[51] Amand, *Fatalisme et liberté*, 49.

[52] For similar moral arguments made by Christian authors against astrology (and in particular astrological fatalism), see e.g. Cyril of Jerusalem, *catech.* 4.18 and Augustine, *Confessiones* 4.3.4, who state that astrology negates human free will and responsibility for evil; Ambrosiaster, Qu 115.59, who declares that belief in fate will lead to immorality; Origen, *philoc.* 23.1, who argues that astral fate challenges the idea that there will be divine judgment for human actions; and Augustine, *De Civitate Dei* 5.1, who states that belief in fate necessarily results in the cessation of worship and prayer given to God. For further examples see Hegedus, "Attitudes to Astrology," 100-10.

[53] Cf. *Hom* 14.4.4-5, where Clement makes a similar point in his brief discussion with the old man. In *Hom* 14.5 Clement makes two further arguments against astral determinism that are not present in the *Recognitions*: 1) prayer results in the cure of bodily deformities, whereas *genesis* has no power to heal (14.5.4-5); and 2) if human sin is caused by the stars, which were set in place by God, then sinfulness is ultimately caused by God (14.5.6).

when they sacrifice to the gods and appease them, without doubt they hope that they will obtain something in opposition to the horoscope, and by means of this they destroy the horoscope. But when they ridicule those who stir to virtue and encourage to self-control, and they say that no one can do or experience anything except what is decreed to him by fate, they cut off all worship of the divinity.

Here Niceta makes two separate but related arguments. First, he argues that people who participate in acts of (presumably pagan) piety such as sacrifice are contradicting the idea of fate; a similar point is made by Diodore of Tarsus, another fourth-century author.[54] Second, he makes the same point from an opposite angle: those who believe in fate are inclined to challenge the value of virtuous practices and self-control, which results in impiety. Augustine makes the same point in *De Civitate Dei* 5.1 when he tells Christians and others who want to worship the gods that they must reject belief in fate, because "what does this view bring about except that God would not be worshiped or prayed to at all?"[55] The upshot of Niceta's double-sided statement seems to be that those who champion astral fatalism cannot also be pious without implicating themselves in a performative contradiction. Since fate is unavoidable and unalterable, those who believe in its power have no rational reason to ask the gods to alter fate.

Rhetorically, this aligns the defenders of astral determinism with the impious, since these individuals would not pray or worship the gods if they could not logically hope to gain anything from such practices. But this implication can also be turned on its head: traditional practices of piety like prayer, worship and sacrifice cast doubt on the practitioners' claim to belief in *genesis* (fate), since they suggest that the outcome of events can be altered. To the extent that believers in astral determinism act piously, they compromise the validity of their intellectual position. The result of Niceta's argument is that those who support astral determinism are impious if they do not worship the gods, or inconsistent in their intellectual position if they do worship the gods.

However, astral determinism has even more serious implications, because it suggests that there is no point in pursuing virtue.[56] On the one

---

[54] Photius, *Bibliothèque*, trans. René Henry (Paris: Les Belles Lettres, 1959-1991) 37.

[55] *Haec enim opinio quid agit aliud, nisi ut nullus omnino colatur aut rogetur Deus?* Augustine, *De Civitate Dei*, 2 vols (CCL 47; Turnhout: Brepols, 1955) 128.15-21. Translation by Hegedus, "Attitudes to Astrology," 108. See also Origen, *philoc.* 23.2; Ambrosiaster, Qu 115.41; Augustine, *De Genesi ad Litteram* 2.17.

[56] This point is commonly made by Christian authors who attack astral fatalism. John Chrysostom, for example, says in his *Homily on 1 Timothy* 1.4: "Believe that there is a place of punishment, and a Kingdom, and you will not brave in a nativity that takes away our free agency, and subjects us to necessity and force. Neither sow, nor plant, nor according to the course of nativity! What need have we more of Prayer? And why should

hand, those who lead virtuous lives have not chosen to do so, but are merely acting in accordance with what fate has decreed to them. On the other hand, this also means that individuals who pursue their own vices or behave criminally are not to be held responsible for such actions.[57] Faustinianus confirms as much when he speaks about the adulterous behavior of his wife:[58] *neque enim inputandum ei est, quod eam genesis facere conpulit* ("of course, she should not be blamed for what her nativity compelled her to do"; *Rec* 9.33.3). Put another way, if people are not free to choose virtue or wrongdoing, they cannot be praised or blamed – and by implication cannot be rewarded or punished – for following the dictates of a fate assigned by the stars. This same argument is made many times by Augustine, who assails those who would assign responsibility for adultery to Venus instead of the adulterer himself.[59]

In his *Mathesis* 1.2.5, the astrologer Firmicus Maternus acknowledges that this "ethical" line of argumentation is potent: "But their most powerful argument against us is the one in which they say that our art removes all acts of virtue from human control if moderation, courage, wisdom, and justice are ascribed to the planets and not to our will." The widespread use of this *topos*, together with its acknowledged persuasiveness, indicates that it is designed to readily persuade the reader that the protagonists' position is correct. The same point can be made based on criteria internal to the *Recognitions*. In the first place, the argument builds on a point made earlier in the narrative during the philosophical discussions: intellectual systems such as philosophy and astrology may be academically interesting, but the real value of the institutionalized pursuit of knowledge is to be found in the impact it has on the individual's lived practices. If knowledge

---

you deserve to be a Christian, if there be this nativity? for you will not then be responsible." Translation from *A Select Library of the Nicene and Post-Nicene Fathers of the Christian Church*, ed. Philip Schaff and Henry Wace (Grand Rapids, MI: Eerdmans, 1978-1979) 13.411.

[57] Cf. Clement's statements to Appion in *Hom* 4.12.3-4 and 4.13.1-2. Tertullian says as much in *Apology* 1.11 when he argues that criminals admit that their behavior is caused by their sinful character, "but they lay the blame either on fate or on the stars." *Dinumerant in semetipsos mentis malae impetus, vel fato vel astris imputant.*

[58] Stanley Jones has argued convincingly that the *Grundschrift* (and by association the *Recognitions* as well) places great importance on chastity; hence adultery is a grave sin in this context. See Jones, "Eros and Astrology," 76. On the representation of women and family in the Pseudo-Clementines see Marie-Ange Calvet-Sébasti, "Femmes du roman pseudo-clémentin," in *Les personnages du roman grec: Actes du colloque de Tours, 18-20 novembre 1999*, ed. Bernard Pouderon, Christine Hunzinger, and Dimitri Kasprzyk (Lyon: Maison de l'Orient Méditerranéen-Jean Pouilloux, 2001) 285-97; and Kate Cooper, "Matthidia's Wish," 243-64.

[59] Augustine, *Enarratio in Ps.*40.6 (CCL 38) 453.24-27; *Enarratio in Ps.* 61.23 (CCL 39) 792.6-13; *Enarratio in Ps.* 140.9 (CCL 40) 2032.1-2, 6-9, 15-19.

of astral fatalism leads to the dissolution of morality, as many ancient authors claimed, such a doctrine is inherently problematic.

The *Recognitions'* case is founded on unstated agreements about the value of a virtuous life and intellectual integrity which give the argument about human responsibility and merit its persuasive power. It appears even more forceful because Faustinianus gives no response (or is not given a chance to respond) to these charges. If he were a serious opponent, he might have given a reply along these lines:

> For we make men fear and worship the gods; we point out the will and majesty of the gods, since we maintain that all our acts are ruled by their divine motion. Let us therefore worship the gods, whose origin has linked itself to us through the stars. Let the human race regard the power of the stars with the constant veneration of a suppliant. Let us call upon the gods in supplication and piously fulfill our vows to them so that we may be reassured of the divine nature of our own minds and may resist in some part the hostile decrees of the stars.[60]

Faustinianus' willingness to be silenced by Niceta's "ethical" argument against astral fatalism suggests that – at least within the competitive field of the *Recognitions* – there can be no adequate response to such an incredibly persuasive line of reasoning.

Argument Two: The Sun, Moon, and Stars

Thus far we have examined Niceta's use of a well-known *topos* which argues that astral fatalism has undesirable intellectual and ethical consequences. The second argument, which is articulated by Peter and all three of the brothers, suggests that the very celestial bodies that have been interpreted as signs of fate are, in fact, evidence of and participants in God's providential design. In other words, this argument appropriates the material basis for the astrologers' predictions, and uses it to question the validity of the fundamental astrological doctrine of *genesis*.

Long before Faustinianus has appeared on the scene, Peter addresses the idolatrous crowd at Tripolis about the sun, moon, and stars: *tu ergo adoras insensibilem, cum unusquisque habens sensum ne ea quidem credat adoranda, quae a deo facta sunt et habent sensum id est solem et lunam vel stellas omniaque quae in caelo sunt et super terram. ... gaudent enim etiam haec, cum ille adoratur et colitur* ("You therefore worship what is insensible, when everyone who has sense believes that not even those things that have been made by God and have sense – such as the sun, moon, and stars, and all things that are in heaven and upon earth – are to be worshipped. ... for even these things rejoice when he is adored and worshipped"; *Rec* 5.16.4-5). Peter's statement reveals that the sun, moon, and stars are all sentient parts of God's creation. Because they have sense

---

[60] Firmicus Maternus, *Mathesis* 1.6.1-2.

and because they are part of this creation, they are pleased when their creator is worshipped. This implies that the stars themselves are *displeased* when the creator is not venerated (as Peter states explicitly in *Hom* 11.10.2-3). Since we know that astral fatalism renders such piety pointless, this astrological doctrine can do nothing but offend the stars upon whose power it supposedly depends.

These heavenly bodies are not just opinionated bystanders, however. According to Peter, the sun actively participates in God's providential care for the world: *quod deus curam gerat humanarum rerum, ipsa mundi gubernatio testis est, cui sol cotidie deservit* ("That God does have concern for human affairs, his very government of the world testifies: the sun serves it daily"; *Rec* 5.29.2; cf. *Hom* 11.23.2). This same idea is underscored by Peter in *Rec* 6.7.6, where he again addresses a group of idolaters: *non propter te sol oritur et occidit et mutationes luna perpetitur?* ("Is it not for your sake that the sun rises and sets, and the moon undergoes changes?"). According to the protagonists, God's ongoing governance of the world proves that he has not set it on an unchangeable course and left it to its own devices, as the idea of astral fatalism would require. The sun and moon's indispensable role in human affairs, then, is not evidence in favor of astral determinism or the independent power of these heavenly bodies. On the contrary, Peter says that the work performed by the sun and moon attests to God's ongoing providential care for his creation.

Niceta adds yet another dimension to the text's use of the stars as evidence of providential design. In *Rec* 8.20.8 he makes a statement reminiscent of Abraham's discovery narrated earlier in *Rec* 1.32.3:

> *et ita quis invenietur insipiens, ut cum caeli opus inspiciat, splendorem solis cernat ac lunae, astrorum cursus et species et vias certis rationibus et temporibus videat definitas, non tam a sapiente haec artifice et rationabili quam ab ipsa sapientia et ratione clamet effecta?*

> And who can be discovered so foolish that, when he considers the work of heaven, and sees the brilliance of the sun and moon, and looks at the course and beauty of the stars and the paths assigned to them by fixed laws and periods, will not cry out that these things are made, not so much by a wise and rational craftsman, as by wisdom itself and reason?

According to Niceta, the regular periods and paths of the stars, together with the brilliance of the sun and moon, should be enough to convince anyone that these remarkable things could only have been produced by a "wise and rational craftsman." The regularity of the stars' movements – on which both the practice of astrology and the idea of astral determinism depend – is obvious evidence of God's existence and creative activity. Only a foolish person could interpret the evidence in such a way that supports fate or denies God's wise and rational creation. Niceta repeats this same idea shortly thereafter in *Rec* 8.22.2, 4:

quis astrorum cursus tanta ratione conposuit ortusque eorum et occasus instituit certisque et dimensis temporibus unicuique tenere caeli ambitum dedit? quis ad occasum aliis semper tendere, aliis etiam redire in ortum permisit? ... quis, inquam, tanti ordinis moderatricem non ipsam dei pronuntiet sapientiam?

Who fixed the course of the stars [with] so great reason, and arranged their rising and setting, and assigned to each one to keep the orbit of heaven in precise and measured times? Who granted to some to be always moving toward setting, and also to others to be returning to rising? ... Who, I say, would proclaim that the director of such order is not the wisdom of God itself?[61]

Although it may seem to be just a more detailed rehearsal of what Niceta has already said, this second version of the argument makes a direct appeal to specific elements of astrological knowledge.

To fully understand this alternative version of Niceta's argument, we need to look briefly at the branch of astrology known as *genethlialogy*. According to A. Bouché-Leclercq, "Le dogme fondamental et spécifique de la généthlialogie ... c'est l'idée que la vie de l'individu est déterminée tout entière, en qualité et en quantité, dans ses modes successifs et dans sa durée, par l'action des astres instantanément concentrée sur l'être vivant au moment précis où commence l'existence, moment marqué par l'Horoscope."[62] As this summary suggests, genethlialogy is based upon the rather specialized practice of producing horoscopes (or "nativities"), which calculate the positions of the celestial bodies at the moment of an individual's birth.[63] In order to create a horoscope, astrologers used astronomical tables to obtain two sets of data: (1) the positions of the seven planets[64] relative to each other and to the signs of the zodiac; and (2) "the position of the circle of the zodiac (and thus of the planets moving

---

[61] See also Peter's statements in *Hom* 3.33.2; 3.35.1-2; 10.9.5. Cf. Theophilus of Antioch, *Autol.* I.6: "Consider, O man, his works – the timely rotation of the seasons, and the changes of temperature; the regular march of the stars; the well-ordered course of days and nights, and months, and years ..."

[62] Bouché-Leclercq, *Astrologie grecque*, 372.

[63] Many ancient authors, Christian and otherwise, attacked the validity of genethlialogy based on the difficulty of producing a completely accurate nativity; see e.g. Cicero, *Div.* 2.44; Gregory the Great, *Sermo* 10; Hippolytus, *haer.* 4.3.5 – 4.5.3; Basil of Caesarea, *Hexaemeron* 6.5 (all cited by Hegedus, "Attitudes to Astrology," 25-26). As Hegedus notes, these polemics are misdirected because in Greco-Roman astrology "the fixing of the horoscope did not usually depend on actual celestial observation but was derived from astrological handbooks and tables." Hegedus, "Attitudes to Astrology," 26. See also Bouché-Leclercq, *Astrologie grecque*, 386-90.

[64] In antiquity, the seven "planets" included the sun and the moon, as well as Mercury, Venus, Mars, Saturn and Jupiter. Cumont, *Astrology and Religion among the Greeks and Romans*, 10.

round it) relative to a second circle of twelve 'places' ... whose cardinal points ... are the rising- and setting-points on the horizon and the zenith and nadir."[65] Once these positions and relationships have been determined, the astrologer uses such information to make pronouncements about the person's "destiny, character, and occupation."[66] From this brief summary we can see that both the *regularity* of the stars' movements and the *position* of the stars relative to the horizon are critically important for the production of horoscopes, which is the most important practice associated with the discipline of genethlialogy. Moreover, if we return to Niceta's statement cited above, it becomes clear that he is targeting the cornerstone of this branch of astrology. By suggesting that the stars' regular movements and their position relative to the horizon both testify to God's wise governance, Niceta is effectively using two basic assumptions of astrology to argue against astral determinism.

Just before his extensive citation from the *Book of the Laws of the Countries* (or a related text), Clement makes a brief remark that adds yet another dimension to the protagonists' discourse about the sun, moon and stars. In *Rec* 9.15.6-7 he states: *mare statutum terminum servat, ... stellae ordinem tenent et fluvii meatus ... et ne per singula sermonem longius producamus, intuere quomodo unumquodque timor dei continens, cuncta in <h>armonia propria et ordinis sui conpage custodiat* ("The sea keeps [its] established boundaries, ... the stars keep [their] order, and the rivers [keep their] channels ... And lest we should make the discourse more tedious by means of separate examples, consider how the fear of God, containing everything, keeps all things in lasting harmony, and in their fixed order"). Clement, like Peter and Niceta before him, points to the order of the stars as evidence of God's ongoing care for the world. However, Clement's point is slightly different from Niceta's suggestion that God gave the stars their orderliness and regularity: Clement argues that the stars keep *themselves* in order as a result of their fear of God. This remark is designed to show that the stars' "behavior," if you will, is controlled by their fear of God, just as the behavior of human beings is controlled *not* by fate but by fear of God and the coming judgment. The stars' order, then, points not to fate, but to providential governance and fear of God, as operative forces in the universe.

If we recall Faustinianus' criticisms of providence listed earlier in this chapter, we see that none of the protagonists' arguments thus far have addressed his questions about injustice and disorder. This task is left to

---

[65] Hornblower and Spawforth, *Oxford Classical Dictionary*, s.v. "astrology." For a more detailed account of this practice see Bouché-Leclercq, *Astrologie grecque*, 383-90.

[66] Hornblower and Spawforth, *Oxford Classical Dictionary*, s.v. "astrology."

Aquila, who uses the sun and moon as his examples in *Rec* 8.45.1-2, 4.[67]
Aquila says that the sun, moon, and stars were placed in heaven by God,
who had a purpose in mind for them. While it is easy for anyone to see that
the sun has an orderly course and is important for the functioning of the
world, those who are *imperitus* (unskilled, ignorant, or inexperienced)
believe the moon to be *inconpositus* (irregular) and *inordinatus*
(disordered). Is the ignorant person's impression of the moon's irregularity
correct? According to Aquila, the answer is no: *lunae cursus atque haec
quae imperitis videtur inordinata permutatio, incrementis frugum et
pecudum omniumque animantium commoda est* ("the course of the moon,
as well as that changing which seems to be disorderly to the ignorant, is
advantageous for the growth of crops, and cattle, and all living beings";
Rec 8.46.2). The moon's seeming disorder is designed to work in concert
with the growth of plants and animals, although the perfection of this
design is not immediately apparent to everyone. In other words, some
things seem disorderly only to those who lack the skill or knowledge to
view them correctly – that is, through the lens of providence. Individuals
like Faustinianus who would use the moon as an example of disorder and
irregularity, then, are characterized as ignorant and unskillful.

A few chapters later, the *Recognitions* adds an interesting twist to this
explanation of disorder. As it turns out, God *intends* for disorderly and
irregular events to cast doubt on the idea of providence! Aquila says as
much in *Rec* 8.52.2: *...et ei qui bonis gaudet bonorum ordinem, qui ad
fidem providentiae suae credentes adduceret, statuit, ei vero qui malis
gaudet, ea quae contra ordinem et inutiliter geruntur, ex quibus sine dubio
etiam providentiae fides in dubium veniat; et habita est per hoc a iusto deo
iusta divisio* ("To him who rejoices in good, he has appointed the ordering
of good things, whereby he might bring those who believe to the faith of
his providence; but to him who rejoices in evil, he has given over those

---

[67] Rec 8.45.1-2, 4 reads, *duo visibilia signa monstrantur in caelo, unum solis, aliud
lunae; haec sequuntur et aliae quinque stellae, diversos et proprios singulae explicantes
cursus. haec ergo deus posuit in caelo, quibus aeris temperies pro ratione temporum
dispensetur et ordo vicissitudinum permutationumque servetur. ... etenim palam est etiam
incredulis et imperitis, quod cursus solis utilis et necessarius mundo, per providentiam
datus, semper ordinatus habeatur; luna vero ad conparationem cursus solis in augmentis
et detrimentis suis apud imperitos inordinati cursus videtur et inconpositi.* ("Two visible
signs are shown in heaven – one of the sun, the other of the moon; and these are followed
by five other stars, each unfolding their own separate courses. These, therefore, God has
placed in the heaven, by which the temperature of the air may be regulated according to
the seasons, and the order of changes and revolutions may be kept. ... For it is well-
known even to the unbelieving and ignorant, that the course of the sun, which is useful
and necessary to the world, and which is assigned by providence, is always kept orderly;
but the moon, in comparison to the course of the sun, [has a] course [that] seems to the
ignorant to be disordered and irregular in its waxings and wanings.")

things which are done against order and uselessly, from which of course the faith of his providence comes into doubt; and by means of this a just division has been made by a just God").

Here Aquila is explaining the presence of both orderly and disorderly occurrences with reference to the Pseudo-Clementines' doctrine of the syzygies. Recall that, according to this idea, good and evil exist in oppositional pairs (of people, events, etc.) that are designed by God as a method for separating righteous people from those who are unrighteous. In this case, order and disorder are mapped onto good and evil, with the result that good and orderly events are intended to draw virtuous individuals to God, while evil and disorderly occurrences are supposed to draw wicked people away from belief in God and providence. Hence irregular events not only pose no difficulty for the idea of God's providential governance, but in fact such happenings are ultimately part of that governance in two ways: some irregularities (like that of the moon's course) are perfectly designed to work with the natural rhythms of the world, while others are intended to cast doubt on providence among those who "rejoice in evil." Aquila's counterargument, then, answers Faustinianus' initial question by showing how disorder and injustice – when properly interpreted – can be shown to fit perfectly into God's providential plan.

Argument Three: The Demon Connection

In the previous section we looked at the protagonists' use of the sun, moon and stars – central elements of the astrological system – in their arguments against astral determinism and in favor of providence. In this section we will look at another way in which the heroes question the validity of astrological practices: by suggesting that astrology, at its core, draws its power from demonic activity. To the extent that astrology is powerful, its power derives from an illegitimate and unholy source.[68] The *Recognitions'* campaign to associate astrology with demons begins very early on, in *Rec* 4.27.2-4, where Peter is retelling and elaborating on the Genesis narrative. Peter asserts that Zoroaster, who was one of the sons of Ham, was considered to be the first magician and was *astris multum ac frequenter intentus* ("very and frequently attentive to the stars"). When Zoroaster repeatedly attempted *scintillas quasdam ex stellis producere* ("to produce

---

[68] This argument can also be found among other ancient authors. It is, for example, very prominent in Tatian's *orat.*; see esp. 8-11. Elsewhere, Gregory of Nyssa's *fat.* is summarized by David Amand as follows: "C'est lui et les démons qui ont inventé l'astrologie et toutes les branches de la mantique. La vraie cause des prédictions astrologiques n'est donc pas l'εἱμαρμένη elle est à chercher dans la fraude et la perfidie des démons." Amand, *Fatalisme et Liberté*, 429. According to Hegedus, demonic activity was the most common explanation of the origins of astrology offered by early Christians. Hegedus, "Attitudes to Astrology," 111.

certain sparks from the stars"), he was set ablaze and consumed by the demon who had made such magical use of the stars possible.[69] Two observations can be made about this passage. In the first place, Peter creates an association between magic and attentiveness to the stars. This is significant because the *Recognitions*, like many other texts in antiquity, has a negative opinion of anything it calls "magic." It adopts the convention of using magic "to accuse particular groups of engaging in unpopular, undesirable activities."[70] Much like astrology, magic was considered to be dangerous precisely because it was so efficacious, and was punishable by death under Roman law.[71] Hence when the text establishes a connection between magic and study of the stars, it suggests that such attention to the stars is objectionable and should be avoided. In the second place, the *Recognitions* uses this text to assert that power which seems to derive from the stars is, in fact, demonic power. The stars themselves cannot make magical activity possible, but demons are willing – in fact, anxious (as we shall see below) – to make human beings believe in the stars' power.

Taken together, the connections made between astrology on the one hand, and magic and demons on the other hand, work to compromise the validity of astrology on two levels. On one level, they suggest that astrology relies on a bankrupt source of power, because the stars are incapable of any control over terrestrial events. Since astrology interprets the stars, and the stars have no such power, astrology does not grant its practitioners any interpretive purchase on the world. On another level, these arguments make it clear that astrology's power – to the extent that it exists – has malevolent and forbidden underpinnings: demonic and magical activity.

This connection between demonic activity and astrology is corroborated by *Rec* 5.20.2, where Peter says that *veteres Aegyptiorum, qui de caelesti cursu et astrorum natura rationem sibi visi sunt repperisse, obsidente sensus eorum daemone, omnibus nihilominus contumeliis nomen incommunicabile subiecerunt* ("the ancient Egyptians, who thought that they had discovered the calculation of the celestial course and the nature of the stars, because the demon was blocking up their senses, nevertheless

---

[69] According to *Rec* 4.29.3, Zoroaster was *indignatione daemonis cui nimis molestus fuerat conflagrasse* ("burned up by the indignation of the demon, to whom he had been too annoying"). Cf. *Hom* 9.4.1 – 9.5.2.

[70] Mihwa Choi, "Christianity, Magic, and Difference: Name-Calling and Resistance between the Lines in *Contra Celsum*," *Semeia* 79 (1997) 77. Choi makes the important point that identification of the precise activities denoted by the term "magic" is sometimes less important than the rhetorical force of accusations about magical arts.

[71] Choi, "Christianity, Magic, and Difference," 79.

subjected the incommunicable name to all reproaches"). The Egyptians' careful study of the stars *should* have led them to the same conclusion about God's providence that Abraham reached, but instead, demonic activity interfered, with the result that their study of the stars caused them to become idolaters (cf. *Hom* 10.16.1-2; 11.6.3). Hence although the stars – as an integral element of God's creation – are not themselves dangerous, demonic deeds underlie the stars' predictive power. Although the *Recognitions* does not associate astrology with magic in this case, it does forge connections between the stars, demonic power, and idolatry. Idolatry, like magic, is used as an umbrella term for impious and illegitimate practices; hence its association with the stars is designed to show that demons are eager to turn people's legitimate attentiveness to astronomical matters into an occasion for idolatry and sin.

The text's conviction about the demonic foundation of astrology[72] lies behind *Rec* 9.12.1-2, where Clement speaks about the fundamental problem with astrological knowledge:

igitur astrologi, ignorantes huiusmodi mysteria, putant stellarum cursibus ista contingere, unde et his qui accedunt ad eos, ut de futuris aliquid consulant, respondentes falluntur in plurimis; nec mirum, non enim sunt prophetae...

Therefore the astrologers, being ignorant of such mysteries, suppose that these things happen by the courses of the stars: whence also, in their answers to those who approach them to deliberate on something about future things, in answering they are usually deceived. Nor is it astonishing, for they are not prophets...

In this passage Clement is explaining why astrologers believe that human sinfulness should be attributed to astral determinism, rather than individual free will. The astrologers don't know or understand the "correct" explanation: God has granted free will to human beings, who can learn how to pursue the good and resist what is evil.[73] Because God wishes to reward those who are righteous, *quasdam contrarias oberrare mundum hunc et obluctari nobiscum permisit* ("he has allowed certain hostile [powers] to wander around this world, and to fight against us"; *Rec* 9.8.5). People sin of their own volition, because they choose to give in to these "contrary powers" whose existence is allowed by God. As a result of the astrologers' ignorance of these matters, they argue that people sin because they are compelled to do so by fate. But the astrologers are not just deceiving themselves – they in turn lead astray their clients, who look to

---

72 Cf. *Hom* 4.12.1-4, where *genesis* is listed among the examples of Greek *paideia*, which is described as having demonic origins.

73 Fate and human free will were, of course, important issues not just for Christians (or Jews), but also for the larger ancient world; see Albrecht Dihle, "Liberté et destin dans l'antiquité tardive," *Revue de théologie et de philosophie* 121 (1989) 129-47.

them for reliable predictions of future events.[74] There seem to be two
possible interpretations of this statement. On the one hand, it may be that
the astrologers are deceived because they misunderstand *why* things
happen; this could be the case even if they *are* able to forecast the future
accurately.[75] On the other hand, it may also mean that the astrologers'
predictions are sometimes incorrect because they cannot take human free
will into account.

I would like to suggest that – strange as it may seem – the *Recognitions*
supports *both* of these interpretations. Let's begin with the second
possibility (that is, that the accuracy of the astrologers' predictions is
sometimes compromised because they take no account of free will). This
option seems to be supported by the immediate context, where Clement
explains that astrologers are often deceived because they are not prophets.
To understand the contrast drawn by Clement, we need to understand that,
for the *Recognitions* as for other ancient texts, prophets are the mouthpiece
of God. Not only are they on the side of the one righteous God,[76] but they
also *always* speak the truth. Consider *Rec* 4.21.4-5, where Peter says: *sed
deus ... distinctionem falsi verique scire cupientibus in propatulo posuit.
est ergo ista distinctio: quod a vero deo dicitur sive per prophetas sive per
visiones diversas, semper verum est; quod autem a daemonibus
praedicitur, non semper* ("But God ... has made the distinction between
what is false and true open to those who desire to know. Therefore, this is
the distinction: what is spoken by the true God, whether by prophets or by
separate visions, is always true; but what is predicted by demons is not
always [true]"). We can deduce from this statement that the mark of a
prophet is true speech, or accurate prediction, while the mark of demonic
influence is occasional falsehood. At this point it makes sense for us to
return to the citation from *Rec* 9.12.1-2. If we read this as an assertion that
astrologers' predictive success is compromised by their disregard for free
will, we begin to see that the occasional inaccuracies of the astrologers
serve two purposes in the *Recognitions*' argument.

First, such inaccuracies demonstrate that astrologers are not prophets,
with the result that astrologers are constructed as the epistemological
inferiors of prophets (and those who rely exclusively on prophetic

---

[74] Moreover, although the text does not state this explicitly, one implication of this
seems to be that – rather than informing people of the need to guard against these "hostile
powers" – astrologers simply reinforce sinful behavior by suggesting that things could
not occur otherwise.

[75] This is the implication of Faustus' argument in *Hom* 14.11.4, though the old man is
speaking of the astrologers' acquaintance with astrological knowledge.

[76] This principle, which echoes Deut 13.1-3, is stated in *Rec* 2.45.7-8.

knowledge, as the protagonists do).[77] Second, the astrologers' mistakes reveal that demons are the source of their predictions, even if astrologers themselves believe that their knowledge is based on the movements of the stars. This last point is expressed clearly by Clement in *Rec* 9.12.3, just after he asserts that astrologers are not prophets:

> ... *ignorantes quod non stellarum cursus haec, sed daemonum gerit operatio, qui ad astrologiae errorem confirmandum deservientes, calculis mathesis decipiunt homines ad peccandum, ut cum, vel deo permittente vel legibus exigentibus, peccati dederint poenas, verum dixisse videatur astrologus.*

> ... since [the astrologers] do not know that it is not the course of the stars that governs these things, but the work of demons, who are devoted to confirming the error of astrology, and deceive people to sin by astrological calculations, so that when they assign the punishments to sinners, either by the permission of God or by legal requirements, the astrologer may seem to have spoken truth.

According to Clement, the astrologers are not only ignorant of the workings of providence and free will, but also are unaware of the very source of their predictive powers! Astrologers may think that their predictions are correct readings of fate that is signaled by the courses of the stars, but in fact this is not the case. We have already seen above that, because astrological predictions derive from demons, they are not always accurate. Their demonic derivation necessarily means that such forecasts are fallible. The present passage, however, suggests that this imperfection is in opposition to the demons' desires. According to this part of the text, demons *want* astrology to be as reliable as possible, because such consistency appears to confirm the truth of astrological knowledge. The appearance of truth, in turn, leads people to sin by following its practices.

We may gain better purchase on this idea if we return for a moment to Clement's statement that the astrologers "are usually deceived" (*Rec* 9.12.1). In addition to the interpretation we have already considered, I suggested the passage could mean that astrologers are deceived because they misunderstand *why* things happen, and that this might be so even if their forecasts are accurate. This second possibility seems to be precisely the situation described above. Astrologers may make correct predictions much of the time, but they are deluded because the real cause of their predictive success (demonic activity) is not what they imagine it to be (astral fatalism signaled by the stars' positions).

In the final analysis, the larger argument about astrology's demonic epistemological foundation cuts both ways. If astrology is inaccurate, the *Recognitions* takes this as proof of its demonic origin in order to contrast it negatively with the infallibility of prophetic knowledge. However, if astrology is reliable in its predictions, the text regards such accuracy as a

---

[77] This idea will be discussed in more detail in Chapter 4.

reflection of the will of demons, who want to induce more people to believe in (and sin in accordance with) astrology. In either case, this strategy accomplishes its goal of associating astrology with a demonic source of power. It calls the legitimacy of the entire astrological enterprise into question, thereby devaluing the epistemic capital its practitioners claim to possess.

Argument Four: Laws and Customs

Thus far we have looked at three of the five major arguments used by the protagonists against astral determinism. In this section, we will explore the protagonists' contention that *genesis* cannot explain the variety of laws and customs that exist around the world. Unlike the previous topics, where most of the protagonists contributed to the case being made, this line of reasoning is put forward entirely by Clement. Moreover, this argument stands in some relation to the Bardesanite *Book of the Laws of the Countries* (cf. Chapter 1 and earlier in this chapter). Whatever the precise literary relationship among these texts – and I do not propose to solve, or even address in detail, this problem in the following pages[78] – the material in *Rec* 9.19-29 almost certainly derives from an outside source. In the following paragraphs I will outline the major elements of Clement's argument, paying particular attention to what these individual points (and the text's use of outside source materials in general) accomplish for the *Recognitions*.

Let's begin by asking why our text might have incorporated an extended discourse taken from an outside source and placed it in the mouth of Clement.[79] One possible explanation is that the *Recognitions* intended Clement's speech to be recognized as material taken from another source. This line of reasoning makes sense because the argument contained in *Rec* 9.19-29 was widely known in antiquity. Assuming that the *Recognitions* is relying on a source that circulated in Bardesanite circles, we can look first to the importance of Bardaisan's writings in some ancient Christian circles.[80] For example, consider Eusebius' attack on astrology in *Praep. Evang.* 6.9.32-6.10.48. [81] He writes:

---

[78] For a detailed discussion of the question of the literary relationships, see Drijvers, *Bardaisan of Edessa*, 60-76.

[79] As I have already mentioned, because *Rec* 9.19-29 shares common material with *Hom* 14.3-7, 11, it is generally agreed that the *BLC* (or some related work) was used by the *Grundschrift*. The *Recognitions*, then, has inherited this discourse from its predecessor. However, the source material in *Rec* 9.19-29 is more extensive than that found in the *Homilies* parallel, which suggests that the *Recognitions* may have expanded (or, at the very least, preserved a more extensive version of) the text of the *Grundschrift*.

[80] The following section is dependent on Drijvers, *Bardaisan of Edessa*, 61-66. All English translations of ancient texts given in this section are taken from Drijvers. I am

But now it is also time to consider the arguments of the astrologers against the Chaldaeans, i.e. of those who present this pernicious imposture as a true study. And of this I shall give you proofs, borrowed from a man who is a Syrian by birth, and who attained to very great knowledge of the Chaldaean art.[82]

This passage prefaces Eusebius' own attack on fate, in which he uses two passages from a Greek text by Bardaisan that is almost identical to *BLC* 559.11-563.1, 583.5-611.8.[83] Eusebius, like the *Recognitions*, values Bardaisan's astrological expertise precisely because it can be used as an authoritative and incontrovertible tool for dismantling arguments in favor of fate. It goes without saying that numerous other ancient writers appropriated Eusebius' writings, and along with them Eusebius' use of Bardaisan: Hieronymus, for example, repeats some of Eusebius' testimony about Bardaisan in *De Viris illustribus* 33, adding that the dialogue on fate is *clarissimus et fortissimus*.[84] Theodoret of Cyrrhus also uses Eusebius' writing on Bardaisan in his *Haeretic. Fab. Comp.* 1.22, although he seems to have some first-hand knowledge of his own. He writes that "I, too, have handled writings of his, dealing with fate"[85] In addition to Eusebius' testimony about Bardaisan, we also have that of Epiphanius in *Panarion* 56.[86] All of these ancient patristic writers, regardless of their independence of one another, testify to what was at least a limited awareness of Bardesanite writings on fate. Moreover, knowledge of Bardaisan goes beyond these church fathers: Diodorus of Tarsus' *On Fate* 51 contains an attack on followers of Bardaisan and demonstrates the bishop's general knowledge of Bardaisan's teachings.[87] In addition, the fourth-century *Life of Aberkios* also exhibits familiarity with the *BLC* (or a similar text).[88]

---

assuming here that the references to Bardaisan preserved by patristic witnesses probably reflected – or at least produced – an awareness of Bardaisan's work among some ancient Christians.

[81] Drijvers, *Bardaisan of Edessa*, 61-62, 173. After mentioning Bardaisan's anti-heretical writings in *h.e.* 4.30, Eusebius states, "there is also his most excellent dialogue on Fate ..." Drijvers, *Bardaisan of Edessa*, 63.

[82] Drijvers, *Bardaisan of Edessa*, 62, 173.

[83] Drijvers, *Bardaisan of Edessa*, 62, 173.

[84] Hieronymous writes, "He wrote innumerable books against nearly all the heretics ... Among these is the very famous and influential book on Fate ..." Drijvers, *Bardaisan of Edessa*, 64.

[85] Drijvers, *Bardaisan of Edessa*, 64.

[86] Epiphanius is probably referring to the *BLC* when he writes, "In a conversation that he had with Awida [Bardaisan's conversation partner in the *BLC*], the astronomer, about fate, he adduced many arguments against it." Drijvers, *Bardaisan of Edessa*, 65.

[87] Drijvers, *Bardaisan of Edessa*, 62-63.

[88] Drijvers, *Bardaisan of Edessa*, 63. According to Drijvers, a dialogue within this text "correspond[s] in content and sequence with the questions which Awida puts to Bardaisan in the BLC."

Hence it is not unreasonable to suppose that the audience of the *Recognitions* may also have been familiar with Bardesanite writings on fate. This seems particularly likely if we imagine (with the majority of scholars) a Syrian origin for the *Grundschrift* and *Recognitions*, given the likelihood that the *BLC* was originally written in Syriac.

But there is another and more compelling reason to suppose that Clement's argument in *Rec* 9.19-29 would have been familiar to the *Recognitions'* audience: it is an example of the classic argument of the νόμιμα βαρβαρικά, which was used not just by Bardaisan, but by many ancient authors to challenge the validity of astrology. As Drijvers notes, "The point of the argument is a demonstration that the manners and customs of whole peoples are the same, so that the course of life and the qualities of an individual cannot be determined by the constellation of the stars at the hour of his birth."[89] The νόμιμα βαρβαρικά can be found in the writings of Panaetius, Cicero, Philo of Alexandria, Favorinus, Sextus, Diodorus of Tarsus, Pseudo-Caesarius, Origen, Ambrose, Gregory of Nyssa, Procopius of Gaza, and others;[90] Franz Boll and David Amand have affirmed that this argument can be traced back to Carneades.[91] Based on the prevalence of the νόμιμα βαρβαρικά argument and its long history in Greek philosophical and Christian apologetic circles, it is reasonable to suppose that this kind of argumentation was known to the readers of the *Recognitions*. Such familiarity may mean that the *Recognitions* knowingly uses an argument that will be recognized by its audience, a possibility that seems more likely given that the text makes no effort to disguise the boundaries of the source or integrate it more thoroughly into the immediate context.[92] Since this was a readily identifiable polemic against fate (and an argument in favor of human free will and responsibility), it could be used to underwrite Clement's claims about his astrological expertise.[93] Although

---

[89] Drijvers, *Bardaisan of Edessa*, 19.

[90] Boll, "Studien über Claudius Ptolemäus," 182; summarized by Drijvers, *Bardaisan of Edessa*, 18-19.

[91] Boll, "Studien über Claudius Ptolemäus," 181. Page 182 of Boll's article diagrams the genealogy of the νόμιμα βαρβαρικά as it has been reconstructed by the author. Amand also discusses the transmission of Carneades' arguments in some detail in his *Fatalisme et Liberté*, 55-60.

[92] This is not to say that the source material is out of place within the *Recognitions*, because in my view it is not. However, this does not change the fact that the parameters of the source are easily recognizable, even for a first-time reader of the *Recognitions*. One might object that if the *Recognitions* truly wanted the source to be known for what it is, the author could have mentioned the source by name. It seems, though, that an attribution this obvious would have detracted from the fiction that the discourse belongs to (even if it does not originate with) Clement.

[93] Such emphasis on Clement's familiarity with astrology is designed to address criticisms such as the one voiced by Firmicus Maternus in *Mathesis* 1.3.4: "First of all I

at first it might seem that Clement is merely "borrowing" his purported knowledge from somewhere else, rather than making his own arguments against fate, there is another way of looking at the issue. Clement's ability to recite from memory a famous and rather lengthy exposition against astral determinism shows that he has spent a great deal of time studying and thinking about the problem of astral fatalism.

This is all well and good, you might say, but what if the *Recognitions'* audience would not have recognized that Clement's speech was derived from an outside source? What if the *Recognitions* did not intend, or even want, its readers to understand that his discourse was not original? Even if we imagine such a scenario, it can still be argued that this material demonstrates Clement's knowledge about the world in general, and astrology in particular. First, the speech in question consists of a long list of empirical evidence, which is designed to show that astral determinism cannot possibly explain the diversity of laws and customs found in cultures around the world. If the reader assumes that this speech was created by Clement himself, then his appeal to the customs of these different global regions suggests that he has familiarized himself with these cultures through extensive study of writings about the regions. This detailed knowledge about the regions of the world contributes to the cosmopolitan image of the protagonists which the *Recognitions* tries to project: Clement's assertions are based on his broad awareness of what the world has to offer, and in no way reflect any ignorance on his part.

Second, and more specifically, this material demonstrates Clement's *astrological* knowledge. Recall Clement's statement to his father in *Rec* 9.18.2-3, which serves as an introduction to his speech: *ipsa me ratio invitat aliquid ad ea quae a te disserta sunt respondere, quoniam quidem scientia mihi mathesis nota est.... accipe ergo ad ea quae dixisti, ut evidenter agnoscas genesim ex stellis omnino non esse* ...("reason itself invites me to say something in reply to the things which have been discussed by you, since indeed the science of astrology is known to me ... Hear therefore, while I reply to what you have said, so that you may plainly acknowledge that fate is not at all from the stars"). This tells the reader that the speech introduced here is a product of Clement's acquaintance with astrology, and a spontaneous response to Faustinianus' assertions about astral determinism that comes out of Clement's astrological knowledge. Moreover, this introductory statement declares that Faustinianus – even though he is *in disciplina mathesis prae ceteris*

---

would like to ask this violent opponent of the astrologers whether he has any first-hand knowledge of the science." Elsewhere in *Mathesis* 1.3.8: "As for the one who refuses either to hear or to judge, he has no right to make any statement. He is not qualified to criticize what he is not willing to test."

eruditus ("educated beyond others in the discipline of astrology"; *Rec* 8.2.2) – has something to learn from the discourse Clement is about to deliver. Hence even if Clement's speech is understood by readers as a product of his own intellect, rather than a borrowing from another source, it demonstrates his extensive familiarity with astrology and global customs.[94]

To better understand how Clement's speech is used to demonstrate his astrological knowledge, we need to look closely at the structure of the argument contained within it. Clement's speech in *Rec* 9.19-29 is, on the whole, designed to make one point obvious: astral determinism simply cannot be real given the wealth of empirical evidence that argues against it. This evidence demonstrates that human laws and customs, together with the fear of God, are sufficient to prevent people from sinning, and thus are able to overcome whatever power fate might have. An important factor in the success of this overall argument is the configuration of the discourse itself: its length and endless details are designed to convince by overwhelming the hearer with evidence against astral determinism. The customs and laws invoked by Clement number in the double digits; when taken together they have a persuasive force that could not be matched by one or two counter-examples, no matter how well chosen they might be.

Upon closer inspection, it becomes clear that this deliberately relentless parade of examples can be divided into four parts: (1) people who follow similar laws and customs are not all born under the same astral configuration; (2) people in the same regions of the world have different customs and laws; (3) laws and customs change over time; and (4) laws and customs seem to override the compulsions of astral determinism. Let's take a closer look at Clement's argument, paying particular attention to how each of these points works within the larger narrative of the *Recognitions*.

The first part of Clement's argument in *Rec* 9.19-29 says that groups of people in different parts of the world all have their own laws and customs, *quas nemo facile transgreditur* ("which no one easily transgresses"; *Rec* 9.19.1). He uses the example of the Seres to make the point that *legum metus vehementior quam genesis constellatio* ("the fear of laws is more

---

[94] Nicola Denzey notes that the *BLC* served a similar function for Bardaisan: "On one level, this Hellenistic-style dialogue is a form of ethnographic literature, in which Philippus was able to show off his teacher's knowledge of other cultures' laws, religions, and traditions." Denzey, "Bardaisan of Edessa," in *A Companion to Second-Century Christian "Heretics,"* ed. Antti Marjanen and Petri Luomanen (Supplements to Vigiliae Christianae 76; Leiden: Brill, 2005) 159, 177. Denzey observes, however, that "one many wonder if Bardaisan and Philippus were really as learned in practical and theoretical astrology" as the *BLC* might suggest, given the pedestrian and derivative nature of the material; the same holds true for the *Recognitions*. Denzey, "Bardaisan of Edessa," 179.

powerful than the constellation of a horoscope"; *Rec* 9.19.5). The Seres have multiple laws against murder, adultery and the like, all of which are obeyed to the letter. Clement tells Faustinianus that astral configurations cannot prevail over the Seres' obedience to such laws, nor can it overcome their exercise of free will: *et tamen nullius libertas arbitrii conpulsa est secundum vos ab stella Martis ignita, ut ferro uteretur ad hominis necem, nec Venus cum Marte posita alienum matrimonium conpulit vitiari, cum utique apud eos per singulos dies Mars medium caeli circulum teneat* ("and yet no one's freedom of will is compelled, according to you, by the fiery planet of Mars, to use the sword for the murder of a human being; nor does Venus with Mars in position compel [anyone] to corrupt another's marriage, when assuredly with them Mars occupies the middle circle of heaven every day"; *Rec* 9.19.4). This sentence requires a bit of explanation. According to Babylonian astrology, Mars and Saturn were malefic stars.[95] This idea was passed on to the Hellenistic and Roman astrological traditions, as many texts attest.[96] In the passage just cited, Clement is referring to this common belief that the ascendance of Mars had a negative affect on human beings. Similarly, Clement's passing mention of Mars and Venus refers to another widespread astrological view: the conjunction of these two planets "indicates turbulent love."[97] For instance, Firmicus Maternus states in *Mathesis* 6.24.2: "Mars and Venus in the same sign will make seducers and adulterers."[98] In *Mathesis* 3.6.21-22 he is more expressive: "Mars strongly aspected to Venus in this house or in

---

[95] I. P. Culianu, "Astrology," in *The Encyclopedia of Religion*, vol. 1, 472; quoted in Jones, "Astrological Trajectory," 187 n. 12. Cf. Schoeps, "Astrologisches im pseudoklementinischen Roman," 94: "Tatsächlich gelten Mars und Saturn in der antiken Astrologie fast immer als Unheilsplaneten"; and Bouché-Leclercq, *Astrologie grecque*, 93-97, 98-99. In addition, some planets (Jupiter, Venus, and the earth's moon) were considered beneficent while others (Mercury and the sun) were somewhere in between beneficent and maleficent. Hegedus, "Attitudes to Astrology," 3; Bram, *Ancient Astrology*, 96.

[96] One well-known example is found in Claudius Ptolemaeus *Tetr.* 1.5: "[T]he ancients accepted two of the planets, Jupiter and Venus, together with the moon, as beneficent because of their tempered nature and because they abound in the hot and the moist, and Saturn and Mars as producing effects of the opposite nature, one because of its excessive cold and the other for its excessive dryness" (modified LCL). Another example is Firmicus Maternus, *Mathesis* 2.13.6: "[H]owever favorable the influence of the planet of Jupiter might be, if it be under the attack of Mars and Saturn, surrounded with hostile influences, it is not able to resist them alone. ... The dangerous and malevolent powers of the unfavorable planets must persist with increased hostility, so that the compound of the body can be dissolved." (Firmicus Maternus, *Matheseos Libri VIII. Ancient Astrology: Theory and Practice*, trans. Jean Rhys Bram, 43).

[97] Jones, "Eros and Astrology," 63.

[98] Bram, *Ancient Astrology*, 200.

conjunction with her makes well-known cases of scandal. A woman with Venus in this house will be oversexed, addicted to all kinds of pleasure – a prostitute who sets herself up in business or lets herself out to a pimp."[99] As Stanley Jones notes, the conjunction of these two planets was a well-known literary motif that can be traced back to Homer's *Odyssey* 8.266-366.[100] Clement's argument in *Rec* 9.19.1-5, then, uses two widespread astrological ideas in suggesting that the stellar configurations do not negate free will and cannot compel people to contravene their laws or customs. But Clement is not simply referring to ideas that are "in the air." Rather, his opening statement is intended as a direct rebuttal of Faustinianus' argument in *Rec* 9.17.1-4, which provoked Clement to make this speech in the first place.[101] There Faustinianus claimed that *cum Mars centrum tenens in domo sua ex tetragono respexerit Saturnum cum Mercurio ad centrum, Luna veniente super eum plena, in genesi diurna efficit homicidas* ("When Mars, occupying the center in his house, regards Saturn in quartile aspect, with Mercury towards the center, the full moon coming upon him, in the daily *genesis*, he produces murderers"; *Rec* 9.17.1). He also argued that *ipse rursus Mars ad Venerem schema tetragonum habens, ex parte ad centrum, non respiciente aliquo bonorum, adulteros efficit* ("On the other hand, Mars itself, having a quarterly position with respect to Venus, in part toward the center, while one of the good stars is not looking on, produces adulterers"; *Rec* 9.17.2). Clement, then, is attacking these well-known astrological principles introduced by Faustinianus by appealing to a "real-life example" in which people's fear of their laws, which they obey of their own free will, is more powerful than the effects of astral determinism. His appeal to the Seres shows that malefic stars cannot compel people to disobey laws that are good and just. In addition, Clement uses two examples, of non-Brahman Indians and "a certain country in the western parts of India" in *Rec* 9.20.3 to make a related point: *neque bonae stellae vetuerunt eos ab huiusmodi flagitiis et ab execrandis cibis* ("and good stars have not prevented these [people] from shameful acts of this sort and from

---

[99] Firmicus Maternus' statement here assumes some knowledge of astrology that deserves explanation. Hegedus articulates the principle clearly: "The influences of the planets were affected by their location *vis-à-vis* the zodiacal signs. For example, each planet 'rules' over a diurnal and a nocturnal 'house,' aside from the sun and moon which rule over the same house both day and night: the influence of the planet was increased and made more positive when it was located in its house." Hegedus, "Attitudes to Astrology," 5. A fuller explanation appears in Bouché-Leclercq, *Astrologie grecque*, 192-99.

[100] Jones, "Eros and Astrology," 63 n. 9.

[101] As we shall see shortly, Faustinianus' argument in *Rec* 9.17.1-4, which appears to be merely a recitation of astrological doctrines, has profoundly personal implications for the two partners in debate.

detestable food"). Hence in the same way that evil stars cannot compel people to disobey good laws, good stars cannot prevent people from following customs that are wicked.

As I mentioned earlier in this chapter, Clement's habit of anticipating Faustinianus' counter-arguments means that his opponent does not speak much, let alone provide a rebuttal, during their debate. This strategy serves the dual purpose of silencing Faustinianus and helping to demonstrate Clement's expert command of astrological argumentation. We can see this happening in *Rec* 9.21.1, where Clement says: *ne forte liceat his qui mathesim sequuntur uti illo perfugio quo dicunt, certas quas esse plagas caeli, quibus propria quaedam habere conceditur*... ("Lest perhaps those who attend to astrology be allowed to use that refuge by which they say that there are certain zones of heaven to which it is granted to have some things of their own ..."). It is interesting to note that Clement is not addressing Faustinianus directly; rather, he speaks in the third person about a set of imaginary astrological interlocutors.[102] To my way of thinking, this form of address tells us how Faustinianus functions in these debates: he represents the entire discipline of astrology rather than an individual astrologer. (For this reason, we should not look for a particular historical figure behind Faustinianus' character; doing so would obscure his representative role.) Hence when Clement rebuts his father's claims or anticipates his counter-arguments, he is speaking to all astrologers rather than a single individual: the phrase "those who attend to astrology" in *Rec* 9.21.1 means precisely what it says.

Moving on to the substance of the argument Clement has anticipated, in the passage above he attempts to shut down one avenue by which astrologers could contest his argument against astral determinism. When Clement suggested that people in particular regions of the world all follow their own customs and laws regardless of their horoscope, he left open the possibility that the regions of the world correspond to certain "zones of heaven," in which ruling stars are responsible for the laws and customs that seem contrary to fate. Here Clement is probably not speaking about the doctrine of *climata*, which holds that the world is divided into seven astrological zones, each of which corresponds to (and is under the influence of) one of the seven "stars."[103] Instead, he may be referring to the

---

[102] Although the rest of Clement's discourse matches up rather well with the content and sequence of Bardaisan's argument in the *BLC*, Bardaisan does not offer to anticipate counter-arguments as Clement does here. Moreover, although *Hom* 14.3-7, 11 does contain a brief conversation about fate, it contains nothing comparable to Clement's long list of examples derived from the *BLC*, nor does it mention the protagonists' anticipation of Faustinianus' counter-arguments. As a result, this feature of Clement's discourse can probably be assigned to the *Recognitions'* redactional activity.

[103] The notion of *climata* will be discussed in more detail below.

"five zones" into which the earth was commonly divided.[104] He responds to this imagined counter-argument by introducing the so-called Magusaei, or Persians, who have emigrated to different parts of the world while *incestae huius traditionis formam indeclinabilem servant ac posteris custodiendam transmittunt etiam cum plagam caeli mutaverint...*("they maintain an unchangeable form of this incestuous tradition, and transmit[ting] it to coming generations to be observed, even when they have moved away from [their] zone of heaven ..."; *Rec* 9.21.2).[105] The fact that the Persians have retained their customs even after moving to different regions of the world is evidence, according to Clement, that regional customs cannot be explained on the basis of "zones of heaven."

In *Rec* 9.22.1-3 Clement takes on yet another of Faustinianus' claims. At the end of *Rec* 9.17.4, the old man argued that *viros autem esse ut feminas nec quicquam virile gerere cacodaemonusa Venus cum Marte si sit in Ariete; efficit e contrario mulieres, si sit in Capricorno aut Aquario* ("Venus in the twelfth house with Mars, if it is in Aries, makes men to be as women, and not to carry on at all like men; on the other hand, if it is in Capricorn or Aquarius it produces women"). Clement responds by speaking about the Geli, whose customs seem to reverse the typical gender roles: their women are farmers and construction workers; they are promiscuous with the consent of their husbands; and they do not use ointments or wear shoes. The men, however, do use ointments and adorn themselves, *et haec non pro dissolutione virium, sunt enim bellicosissimi et venatores acerrimi* ("and this is not by virtue of weakness of manhood, for they are most warlike, and most keen hunters"; *Rec* 9.22.2). According to Clement, the existence of the Geli disproves Faustinianus' assertion: *nec tamen universae Gelorum mulieres in Capricorno aut Aquario cacodaemonusam Venerem nascentes habuere neque viri earum in Ariete cum Marte Venerem positam, per quod schema effeminatos et dissolutos nasci adserit viros Chaldaica disciplina* ("Yet the whole women of the Gelones did not have Venus in the twelfth house in Capricorn or Aquarius when they were born; nor did their men have Venus placed with Mars in Aries, by which configuration the Chaldean science asserts that men are born effeminate and licentious"; *Rec* 9.22.3). In other words, astral determinism cannot explain why such customs are kept by all the people in

---

[104] These consisted of two polar zones, two temperate zones, and one equatorial zone. Bram, *Ancient Astrology*, 303 n. 5. Pliny writes about these zones in his *HN* 2.68.173; cf. Strabo 2.23.

[105] The Persians' "incestuous tradition" has already been mentioned by Clement in *Rec* 9.20.4: *Est rursus mos apud Persas, matres accipere in coniugium et sorores et filias, et sub illo omni axe incesta Persae ineunt matrimonia* ("Again, there is a custom among the Persians to take mothers, and sisters, and daughters in marriage. In all that region the Persians enter into incestuous marriages").

a region, because not everyone has the same horoscope. Just as it is absurd to think that an entire country of people could be born on the same day, and at exactly the same time, so it is illogical to assert that the same astral configuration controls their behavior. Clement reinforces this point in *Rec* 9.23.1-5 with examples from Susae, "remoter parts of the East," and the Gauls. These additional illustrations perform yet another task: they demonstrate that people in different regions of the world have different customs, or different combinations of customs. For instance, while the Susian women may copulate freely like the women of the Gelones, the two groups' uses of bodily ornamentation are polar opposites.

Rec 9.24.1-5 continues Clement's explanation of the different laws and customs that are in effect throughout the various regions of the world. In this case he mentions the Amazons, all of whom customarily conceive their children around the time of the vernal equinox. Since many of these babies are born *unius temporis* ("in one season"; *Rec* 9.24.3), one would expect that they necessarily have the same horoscope. The Amazons, however, follow a custom that suggests these children could not possibly have the same fate: *et si marem pepererint abiciunt, feminas nutriunt. cumque ... absurdum est, ut in maribus quidem putetur Mars cum Saturno in tempore aequis esse portionibus, in feminarum vero genesi numquam* ("and if they give birth to a male, they cast [him] away, and raise only females. However ... it is absurd, of course, to suppose that among males Mars is at the time in equal portions with Saturn, but never in the horoscope of females"; *Rec* 9.24.2-3). How is it possible, Clement asks, for all the girls to have one fate and all the boys to have another?

Toward the end of the chapter (*Rec* 9.24.5) Clement addresses the belief that horoscopes can be used to predict people's occupations. This, like most of what has preceded it, agrees almost word-for-word with the parallel argument recorded in the *BLC*. The *BLC* makes it clear that after Bardaisan draws his conclusion about the Amazons, his comments about horoscopes and people's occupations pertain to the book of the Chaldaeans: "It is written in the Book of the Chaldaeans, that when Mercury stands with Venus in the house of Mercury, this gives rise to sculptors, painters and money-changers, but that when they stand in the house of Venus they produce perfumers, dancers, singers and poets."[106] The *Recognitions*, however, does not include this reference to the book of the Chaldaeans, with the result that Clement's comments about occupations appear to be a (rather puzzling) continuation of his discussion of the Amazons. Despite this minor confusion, his point is clear enough: if astral configurations are responsible for particular professions, then the

---

[106] *BLC* col. 595, lines 7ff. Translation by Drijvers, *Book of the Laws of the Countries*, 51.

absence of money-changers and sculptors in certain parts of the world means that *defecit apud eos Mercurii Venerisque constellatio* ("the constellation of Mercury and Venus has grown faint among them"; *Rec* 9.24.5). The implication, of course, is that if the stars do not have control over particular regions, they cannot really be all that powerful. Clement is suggesting that, since astrology depends on the idea that the stars have control over almost every area of the human experience, the stars' seeming lack of influence compromises the epistemic authority of astrology.[107] After citing still more examples of regional customs that cannot be explained on the basis of astral fatalism, Clement draws a conclusion in *Rec* 9.25.6-8:

> *ex quibus omnibus apparet, quia metus legum in unaquaque regione dominatur et arbitrii libertas quae est hominibus insita per spiritum, obtemperat legibus, nec cogere potest genesis aut Seres homicidium committere, aut Bragmanos carnibus vesci ... sed, ut diximus, unaquaeque gens suis legibus utitur pro libertatis arbitrio et decreta genesis legum severitate depellit.*

> From all this it appears that the fear of the laws has dominion in every region, and the freedom of will which is implanted in human beings by the Spirit obeys the laws, and fate cannot compel the Seres to commit murder, nor the Brahmans to eat flesh ... but, as we have said, each nation observes its own laws according to free will, and drives away the decrees of fate by the strictness of laws.

Here again Clement's speech agrees with the contours of the *BLC*, which (at least up to this point) draws a similar conclusion from the foregoing evidence.[108] He concludes that people's fear of their own laws and customs, which they follow according to their own individual free will, is more powerful than astral fatalism.[109] If people can choose to obey local

---

[107] In reality, astrologers varied considerably in their views of the stars' spheres of influence. For instance, Firmicus Maternus *Mathesis* 1.8.2-3 writes about a group of people who believe that fate controls birth and death, but that the rest of human life is governed by free will: "What we do while we are alive belongs to us; only our death belongs to Chance or Fate." Translation by Bram, *Ancient Astrology*, 27.

[108] In *BLC* col. 598 line 9ff, Bardaisan states: "In all places, every day and each hour, people are born with different nativities, but the laws of men are stronger than Fate, and they lead their lives according to their own customs. Fate does not force the Seres to commit murder if they do not want to ... But, as I have already said, in each country and each nation people use the liberty belonging to their nature as they please." Translation by Drijvers, *Book of the Laws of the Countries*, 53. *Rec* 9.25.8, however, does not include the next sentence in Bardaisan's discourse: "Yet they are subject to Fate and to nature, because of the body they are endowed with..." In omitting this statement, the *Recognitions* makes it clear that it does not accept the Bardesanite position that the human body is subject to fate.

[109] Clement's conclusion does seem to grant some measure of influence to the workings of fate, even though the text's omission of the latter part of Bardaisan's conclusion (see the previous note) would suggest that the *Recognitions* denies any power

laws and customs, thereby superseding fate's control over their lives, fate cannot be that powerful in the first place. Moreover, that people *choose* to obey laws necessarily means that human free will exists, and plays a role in human affaris.

However, what if these laws and customs are not instituted by human beings at all, or followed according to people's free will? What if regional customs are merely an expression of the stars' will? In *Rec* 9.26.1-2, Clement goes on to anticipate this potential objection:

Sed dicet aliquis eorum qui in disciplina mathesis adtentius eruditi sunt, genesim in septem partes dirimi, quae illi climata appellant, dominari vero unicuique climati unam ex septem stellis, et istas quas exposuimus diversas leges non ab hominibus positas, sed ab istis principibus secundum uniuscuiusque voluntatem; et hoc quod stellae visum est, legem ab hominibus observatam.

But someone of those who are very carefully educated in the science of astrology will say that genesis is divided into seven parts, which they call climates; in fact, one of the seven stars has dominion over each climate; and that those diverse laws which we have set forth are not made by human beings, but by those principal [stars] according to the will of each one, and that what pleases the star is observed by human beings as a law.

Earlier in this chapter, I argued that Clement's habit of anticipating his opponents' objections functions both to silence Faustinianus and to make Clement himself appear to be an expert in astrology. In this particular case, a glance at the parallel passage in *BLC* (col. 600 lines 5ff) reveals that the *Recognitions'* redactional activity supports such an interpretation.[110] In the *BLC*, the objection about *climata* is made by Awida and answered by Bardaisan.[111] As we have seen in *Rec* 9.26.1-2, however, our text turns what could have been Faustinianus' objection into a knowing remark by Clement.

Now that we have determined *why* this scene unfolds as it does, we need to consider the meaning of the objection Clement has introduced. As I

---

whatsoever to fate. This difficulty is resolved, however, if we recall that the text attributes the apparent workings of astral determinism to demonic activity.

[110] In this instance I am assuming that the *Recognitions* is directly dependent on the *BLC*. However, it stands to reason that even if our text is dependent on another similar dialogue on fate, the question-and-answer format would likely be a conversation between two people rather than a monologue, as it is in the *Recognitions*.

[111] After telling Bardaisan that his previous argument was both convincing and true, Awida asks, "Yet are you also aware that the Chaldaeans maintain that the earth is divided into seven parts named climates, and that one of the seven [stars] rules over each of these parts, and that in each of these regions the will of his government rules and is called law?" Translation from Drijvers, *Book of the Laws of the Countries*, 55 (slightly modified). Even if we assume a common ancestor for the *BLC* and *Rec* 9.19-29 (instead of proposing that the *Recognitions* has used the *BLC* directly), it still seems more likely that objections originally would have been raised by the second partner of the dialogue rather than anticipated and answered by a single individual.

mentioned above, the doctrine of "climates"[112] (Latin *climata*, from Greek κλίματα) stipulates that the world is divided into astrological zones. The number of zones ranged from five to twelve, although seven zones were usually identified.[113] Each of these zones corresponds to (and is under the influence of) one of the planets or signs of the Zodiac.[114] According to Drijvers, astrologers articulated this notion of *climata* as a defense against those authors who invoked the νόμιμα βαρβαρικά (see above). Recall that the νόμιμα βαρβαρικά argument stipulated that different groups' shared customs and practices invalidated astrology, because these shared customs compromised the predictive capacity of the horoscope for individuals. Astrologers, in turn, countered with the *climata*, which effectively transformed the νόμιμα βαρβαρικά from a critique of astrology into a defense of it. Thus shared laws and customs no longer posed a threat to astrological predictions about individuals – on the contrary, these customs could be explained as a result of a star's control over a particular region of the world. Returning to the *Recognitions*, we can now see that Clement is attacking the *climata*, which he has anticipated as an objection to his own use of the νόμιμα βαρβαρικά argument. He has a ready answer for those who wish to advance this kind of argument about astrological geography (*Rec* 9.26.3-4):

Ad haec ergo respondebimus, quod primo quidem non est in septem partes orbis terrae divisus, tum deinde, et si ita esset, in una parte et in una regione invenimus multas differentias legum, et ideo neque septem sunt secundum numerum stellarum neque duodecim secundum numerum signorum neque triginta et sex secundum numerum decanorum, sed sunt innumerae.

To this we shall answer, in the first place, that in fact the world is not divided into seven parts; and secondly, even if it were so, we find many differences of laws in one region and one area; and therefore there are neither seven [laws] according to the number of the

---

[112] The doctrine of *climata* is sometimes referred to as astrological geography, astrological ethnography, or climatology (which is, of course, not to be confused with modern climatology). According to Bram, the *climata* are mentioned first by Hipparchus' *Commentary on Aratus*, as well as Strabo 2.5.34 and Pliny the Elder's *HN* 6.33. Bram, *Ancient Astrology*, 308 n. 32. Drijvers, however, accepts Boll's argument that the doctrine of the seven *climata* can be traced back to Eratosthenes. Drijvers, *Bardaisan of Edessa*, 19 n. 2, citing Boll, "Studien über Claudius Ptolemäus," 188. Denzey apparently traces this idea to Basilides, as represented by Hippolytus *haer.* 5.15.6, though it is not clear whether she believes that this idea originates with Basilides. Denzey, "Bardaisan of Edessa," 177.

[113] For instance, Firmicus Maternus *Mathesis* 2.11.3-9 identifies the following regions: Alexandria, Babylonia, Rhodes, the Hellespont, Athens, Ancona, and Rome. Bram, *Ancient Astrology*, 40-42, 303 n. 5.

[114] Drijvers, *Bardaisan of Edessa*, 19.

stars, nor twelve according to the number of the signs,[115] nor thirty-six according to the number of the decans[116]; but they are innumerable.[117]

Clement's response to the argument about *climata* points out that in these so-called "climates," it is possible to identify more than one set of customs and laws. If the world were *really* divided into seven – even twelve or thirty-six – astrological zones, one would expect to find only seven (or twelve, or thirty-six) different sets of laws and customs followed by humanity. But in fact this is not the way things are at all. As Clement's prior exposition has already demonstrated, there are limitless variations in the laws and customs practiced in the different regions of the world. In order to strengthen his argument, Clement goes on in *Rec* 9.27.1-7 to recite some already-mentioned examples in support of his case. He notes that in one region of India there are both vegetarians and cannibals, and that the so-called "Magusaei" practice their incestuous customs not only in Persia, but also in other regions to which they have immigrated. In *Rec* 9.28.1 – 9.29.2, Clement continues this line of argumentation by referring to the Jews, who retain their customs no matter where they live and who cannot be compelled by fate to abandon circumcision or Sabbath observance, and to the new followers of the True Prophet, who have been persuaded by his teachings to reject their old ways of life when they returned home from Judea. These instances demonstrate that astrological zones have no control over such practices, *nec potuit ad crimina genesis conpellere, quos religionis doctrina prohibebat* ("nor has astral fate been able to compel those whom the teaching of religion restrained toward crimes"; *Rec* 9.29.2).

In *Rec* 9.27.4-7 Clement mentions the final chink in the armor of the doctrine of *climata*: the laws and customs of a particular region can change, due either to the decisions of *sapientes viri* ("wise men"), to voluntary abandonment as a result of corruption or difficulties of implementation, or to the changes put in place by conquering regimes. He uses the particular example of the Romans to make his point, noting that many nations who previously had their own laws and customs have been

---

[115] The "signs" mentioned here are the twelve divisions of the Zodiac, each of which consists of 30 degrees (because twelve equal parts of a 360° circle have 30° each). Bram, *Ancient Astrology*, 335.

[116] "Decans" are a further division of the signs just mentioned. Each sign has three decans, which consist of 10 degrees each for a total of 30 degrees. Bram, *Ancient Astrology*, 333. As Bouché-Leclercq, *Astrologie grecque*, 219-21 notes, ancient Egyptians believed the decans to be divine χρονοκράτορες, or time-guardians. Hegedus, "Attitudes to Astrology," 6.

[117] Once again, Clement's argument corresponds closely to what Bardaisan says to Awida in *BLC* col. 600 lines 10ff.

subjected to Roman law.[118] He concludes: *superest ergo ut et stellae gentium, quae a Romanis victae sunt, climata sua partesque perdiderint* ("It follows, therefore, that the stars of the nations which have been conquered by the Romans have lost their climates and their regions"; *Rec* 9.27.7). In other words, if regional customs stem from the influence of a particular star on a "climate," changes in such practices must mean that the governing star has lost its control over a region. Once again, Clement implies that this consummately logical conclusion renders absurd the idea of the stars' control over human customs and destinies. After all, a star that can lose its sphere of influence must not have been that powerful to begin with.

Although *Rec* 9.29.2 marks the last part of Clement's discourse shared by the *Recognitions* and the *BLC*, Clement continues his speech in *Rec* 9.30.1. There he returns to a theme already explored earlier in this chapter: the idea of astral determinism does not make sense in a world created and governed by a just and righteous God. He tells Faustinianus: *cum deus iustus sit et ipse fecerit hominum naturam, quomodo poterat fieri, ut ipse poneret genesim contrariam nobis quae nos cogeret ad peccatum, et rursus ulcisceretur ipse peccantes?... absurdissimum autem est dicere, quia ex natura nobis accidit pati mala, si non prius peccata praecesserint* ("Since God is just, and since he himself made the nature of human beings, how could it happen that he should establish for us a contrary astral fate which compels us to sin, and again that he himself should punish those who sin? ... But it is most absurd to say that it befalls us by nature to suffer evils, if sins had not gone before"; *Rec* 9.30.2, 5). In one sense, this is no different than the arguments we saw earlier in the chapter. Clement assumes (along with the *Recognitions* and its readers) that God is a righteous god who rewards people for good behavior and punishes them for their sins. Since divine reward and punishment necessarily depend on the exercise of human free will, it is unreasonable to believe that God would have devised a system of astral fatalism that compels people to sin. Why, asks Clement, would God punish people for sins for which they cannot be held responsible?

---

[118] In *BLC* col. 603 Bardaisan makes a similar, but more specific, example of the Romans: "Recently the Romans have conquered Arabia and done away with all the laws there used to be, particularly circumcision, which was a custom they used" (Drijvers, *Book of the Laws of the Countries*, 57). Drijvers notes that "this passage has often been used to date the *BLC*. One may think of the Arabian war of Septimius Severus in 195-6 or of that of Macrinus in 217-18." Drijvers, *Bardaisan of Edessa*, 92 n. 3. Hence either the *Recognitions* has made the example in the *BLC* less specific to suit its own purposes, or the *BLC* has used a more general example from its common source with the *Recognitions* to make a specific chronological reference.

Clement concludes his long discourse in *Rec* 9.31.1 with a call to action and a final addition to his argument:

et ideo si salutis curam gerimus, ante omnia scientiae debemus operam dare, certi quod, si mens nostra in ignorantia perseveret, non solum genesis mala, sed et alia extrinsecus quaecumque daemonibus visa fuerint perferemus, nisi metus legum et futuri iudicii obsistat omnibus desideriis et impetum peccandi refrenet.

And therefore, if we have concern for salvation, above all we ought to devote attention to knowledge, being certain that if our mind persists in ignorance, we shall endure not only the evils of fate, but also whatever other [evils] from outside the demons may please, unless fear of laws and of the future judgment resists all our desires, and restrains the impetus for sinning.

Here Clement speaks about one of the fundamental premises of the *Recognitions*: salvation is, first and foremost, the result of a quest for knowledge. The causal link between knowledge and salvation explains in part why the *Recognitions* has been so preoccupied with philosophers and astrologers, when it is ostensibly a collection of the salvific words of the True Prophet. Salvation is primarily a matter of knowledge, and as a result it makes sense for the protagonists to have been in dialogue with two major groups of epistemic rivals. In the quote from *Rec* 9.31.1 above, Clement mentions that ignorance has dire consequences because it leaves people open to evils imposed on them by demons, including fate. Once again, Clement may seem to be conceding that astral determinism is both real and powerful, but his claim must be read in light of the text's larger argument about demonic activity. Recall that for the protagonists, fate is a demonic device used to induce (but not compel) human beings to sin. They also regard it as a convenient strategy for excusing human sinfulness, since it suggests that people are not responsible for actions that are fated and hence unavoidable.

With these principles in mind, Clement's statement in *Rec* 9.31.1 begins to make more sense. Ignorance results in people's having to endure demonically-sponsored evils, but there is a solution to this problem: people's fear of laws and especially their fear of the coming divine judgment enable them to resist the sinful desires suggested to them by demons. Resistance of these impulses, in turn, enables individuals to safeguard themselves from sinning. *Rec* 9.31.4 states this idea more clearly: *sed his singulis obsistere et repugnare habet in natura sua mens, cum ei obfulserit veritatis agnitio, per quam scientia<m> et timor futuri iudicii datur, qui sit idoneus animae gubernator et qui eam possit a concupiscentiarum praecipitiis revocare* ("But the mind has it in its nature to oppose and fight against each one of these [errors], when the knowledge of truth shines upon it, by which knowledge is imparted fear of the future judgment, which is a suitable governor of the mind, and which can even call it back from the precipices of desires"). According to Clement, "knowledge of truth" enables the mind to fight against "errors," because knowledge produces fear of the coming judgment. This fear of judgment allows the individual to control his *anima*, or soul. This probably means that knowledgeable people can resist sinful desires, because they are aware that sins are subject to punishment in the final judgment. Hence for those who keep in mind their fear of judgment, it is possible to control the *anima* and resist sinful desires. In other words, though astral determinism (because of its demonic roots) may have power over the ignorant, those with true knowledge understand that actions ascribed to fate will be punished by God's judgment. Because they know of and fear such judgment, these persons are able to resist sinful desires instigated by demons.

As it is presented by the *Recognitions*, Clement's case against astral determinism appears to be airtight. Not only has he anticipated and addressed every conceivable argument that might be advanced against him, but he also has secured the agreement of his opponent on many points. How is it possible, then, that Faustinianus is not convinced? How can he continue to maintain that astral determinism is real? The answer lies in his conviction that his own personal experience of astral fate cannot be outweighed by the arguments of Clement. In the next section we will look more closely at Faustinianus' personal encounter with fate and the claim to epistemic authority inherent in his experience.

Argument Five: Personal Experience

If we look back over Faustinianus' conversations with the protagonists, it suddenly becomes clear that the connection between astral determinism and his own life has been telegraphed to the reader all along. Recall that when he first appears in the story, he declares to Peter and the others that "all things are done by fortuitous chance and fate, as I have discovered most clearly for myself..." (*Rec* 8.2.2). While it is true that this statement points to Faustinianus' astrological training,[119] it may be that the old man is alluding to the circumstances of his own life as well. This would seem to be confirmed by his answer to Clement's questions about his identity and background in *Rec* 8.2.5: *Quid, ait, hoc pertinet ad ea quae dixi vobis?* ("Why does this relate to the things which I have told you?"). The irony in this statement is palpable. As the reader already knows, Faustinianus' life and previous experience have *everything* to do with his profession of belief in astral determinism. Recall, too, Faustinianus' explicit statement of this in *Rec* 8.57.2, where he tells Clement that his powerful words are not

---

[119] The last part of the sentence states that Faustinianus is "educated beyond others in the discipline of astrology."

convincing, "[f]or I know that all things have happened to me by the necessity of fate, and therefore it is not possible to persuade me..."

The connection between Faustinianus' life experiences and his fatalistic beliefs becomes clearer in *Rec* 9.32. At this point Clement has just finished his lengthy refutation of astrology taken from the *Book of the Laws of the Countries* (or a related text), whose overwhelming length and detail are obviously designed to put an end to all the old man's convictions about astral determinism. Faustinianus' reply to his son again suggests that he can never be convinced by the protagonists' arguments:

Plenissime, ait, ostendisti, fili; sed ego, sicut dixi ex initio, omni huic inconparabili adsertioni tuae a propria conscientia prohibeor accommodare consensum. Novi enim et meam genesim et coniugis meae, et scio ea quae unicuique nostrum dictabat genesis accidisse, et ab his quae rebus et operibus conperta sunt mihi, nunc verbis transferri non possum.

You have argued most fully, my son, but I, as I said at first, am prevented by my own conscience from according agreement to all this incomparable declaration of yours. For I know both my own genesis and that of my wife, and I know that these things which have happened to every single one of us were dictated by genesis; and now I cannot be put off by words from those things which I have ascertained by facts and deeds. (*Rec* 9.32.2-3)

Faustinianus goes on to relate the horoscope of his wife, and to explain that this horoscope always leads women to adultery and death *in peregre et in aquis* ("abroad and in waters"; *Rec* 9.32.5). He tells Clement that everything has happened just as his wife's horoscope had predicted: his wife fell in love and ran away with one of her servants; after traveling abroad, they died in a shipwreck (*Rec* 9.32.6). As a result of his perfect certainty about this chain of events,[120] Faustinianus believes that *inpossibile est extra genesim fieri aliquid* ("it is impossible for anything to take place apart from fate"; *Rec* 9.34.4). As he has just stated in *Rec* 9.32.3, words cannot change Faustinianus' mind about things he has seen and experienced for himself.

Even though Faustinianus is convinced that his own experiences prove the truth of astral determinism, and insists that he cannot be persuaded otherwise, Peter shows him that there is another way of looking at the events that have happened. After he hears Faustinianus' life story and realizes what is really going on, Peter says in *Rec* 9.34.3: *Si tibi, inquit, hodie coniugem tuam castissimam consignavero cum tribus filiis tuis, credis quia potest pudica mens motus inrationabiles superare, et quod*

---

[120] When Clement questions Faustinianus about how he knows what happened to his wife after she went abroad, Faustinianus replies *Certissime...scio* that his wife's horoscope had been fulfilled, because of the testimony of his brother. Of course, Faustinianus' most certain knowledge rests on shaky ground, because his brother is lying to him about the cause of his wife's departure.

omnia quae a nobis dicta sunt, vera sint et genesis nihil sit? ("If today I make known to you your most chaste wife and your three sons, will you believe that a virtuous mind can overcome irrational impulses, and that all things that have been spoken by us are true, and that *genesis* is nothing?"; cf. *Hom* 15.4.1-6). Faustinianus replies that both the promised restoration and the consequent modification of his views are impossible. Peter then responds by saying, *omnem causam multo diligentius scio quam tu* ("I know the whole matter much more accurately than you do"; *Rec* 9.34.6). He proceeds to tell Faustinianus that his three companions (Clement, Niceta and Aquila), whom Faustinianus has been debating, are in fact his long-lost sons (*Rec* 9.35.1 – 9.36.9). Shortly thereafter, Faustinianus' wife Mattidia arrives on the scene, and the entire family is reunited (*Rec* 9.37.1-4).

How does this "recognition" work within the broad scope of the *Recognitions*' astrological discussions? Stanley Jones has argued that, on the level of the *Grundschrift*, the reunion of the family occurs because Mattidia's chastity persuades God to overcome the workings of fate (*Rec* 7.38.4-5, 7; par. *Hom* 13.13.2 – 13.14.3). Although fate has power over unbelievers, its spell can be broken when a person is baptized into the Christian faith (*Rec* 9.7.4, par. *Hom* 19.23.5).[121] Though I find Jones' argument about astrology in the *Grundschrift* convincing, I believe that more can be said about the purpose of the recognitions that take place in *Rec* 9.34-37.

First, the occurrence of this reunion demonstrates that the events predicted in Mattidia's horoscope did not come to pass. Although it had seemed incontrovertibly true to Faustinianus because he believed that his wife died as an adulteress in a shipwreck, this turned out not to be the case at all. Mattidia not only returned alive, but with her chastity still intact, effectively demonstrating that "Mars with Venus above the center, and the moon setting in the house of Mars and the boundaries of Saturn" did not produce the outcome predicted by astrologers. In one sense, then, the family's reunion is yet another example of the failed predictive power of horoscopes cast by astrologers. Second, we can say even more about the function of this recognition within the larger narrative. We have already seen that the protagonists' "intellectual" arguments against astral fatalism have overpowered Faustinianus' academic defense of the power of fate.

---

[121] Jones, "Eros and Astrology," 76-77. Tatian's *orat.* 8.1 makes a very similar argument: the stars control the destiny of non-Christians, but Jesus grants a new horoscope to those who have been baptized. The Valentinian Theodotus argues something slightly different: according to him, astral control of human destiny ended with the coming of Christ, so that providence had replaced fate altogether (Clement of Alexandria, *exc. Thdot.* 74). Denzey, "A New Star on the Horizon," 210-12.

The old man's case collapsed under the weight of the arguments against it. At first, it seems as though his own encounter with *genesis* is not subject to falsification in the same way. Faustinianus asserts that his own experience of fate, which consists of "facts" and "deeds," is beyond interpretation altogether, which makes it impossible for him to be persuaded by arguments to the contrary. However, when the reunion of Faustinianus' family occurs, it becomes apparent that the old man's "experiential evidence" is yet another case of incorrect interpretation. Faustinianus had believed that the separation of his family could only be interpreted through the prism of his wife's unfortunate horoscope. Yet, Peter has a unique understanding of God's providential design that allows him to see the true meaning of the events in question. While to Faustinianus' mind it appears that his family has been subject to the whims of fate, Peter "correctly" realizes that the series of seemingly unfortunate occurrences was part of God's larger plan to bring each family member to a knowledge of the truth. What looked like fate to the untrained eye has turned out to be providence after all.

Conclusion

To summarize, we can say that the *Recognitions* employs the astrological materials to make several important points. In the first place, the *Recognitions* enhances the perceived epistemological value of astrology in the service of its own agenda. For example, the protagonists and their opponent Faustinianus are depicted as expert astrologers who control a vast body of esoteric knowledge about the stars and the workings of fate. Moreover, the text states that the stars can be used to understand past, present, and future events, and asserts that Abraham was an astrologer. Although these passages might seem to compromise the *Recognitions'* overall polemic against astrology, they can be fruitfully read as part of a *subversion strategy*, in which the text appropriates building blocks of astrological knowledge in order to undermine them at a later point. The same can be said of the protagonists' use of their astrological expertise to argue against the power of astral determinism. Not only do they use a classic philosophical argument to demonstrate that fatalism has disastrous ethical consequences, but they also appeal to the celestial bodies as witnesses of God's providential design rather than participants in the workings of fate. They suggest that astrology is powerful because it has demonic underpinnings, while simultaneously using another well-known series of examples to argue that astral fatalism is demonstrably false. Finally, the text allows Peter to give an authoritative, and providentially-centered, interpretation of the separation and reunion of Faustinianus' family. This explanation forces the old man to admit that his own experience of fate was, in fact, part of God's providential design to lead his family to knowledge of the truth. If we articulate this polemic against astrology using the vocabulary of field, we can see that the *Recognitions'* strategy is designed to do two things that are identical to the goals of its polemic against philosophy. First, it appropriates for the protagonists whatever cultural capital can be gained from astrological expertise. This places the heroes on equal footing with their rivals, and implies that the newcomers to the field possess just as much capital as the established players. Second, this strategy is designed to undermine the existing state of the field itself. By suggesting that astrological expertise does not really count as knowledge of heavenly and earthly realities, the *Recognitions* makes it possible for the field itself to be taken over by the protagonists, who have unique access to a superior and more legitimate form of capital: prophetic knowledge.

Chapter 4

The Followers of the True Prophet

Introduction

Chapters 2 and 3 were concerned with philosophers and astrologers, two of the major groups who oppose the heroes of the *Recognitions*. The analyses focused on the debates among these rivals, which center on questions of knowledge. In particular, we studied how the protagonists undermine their opponents' claims to epistemological authority, either by invoking the problem of uncertainty or suggesting that demonic activity is involved. We also briefly examined the protagonists' claim that philosophical and astrological forms of expertise are inherently inadequate because they are not based on prophetic knowledge. Up to this point, however, we have not considered the rhetorical basis for the protagonists' own claims to such authority in any detail.

In Chapter 2 I mentioned that F. C. Baur and others have displayed an interest in authoritative claims made in the *Recognitions*. Baur focused above all on *Homily* 17, where Peter tells Simon Magus that true apostleship is based on personal acquaintance with Jesus rather than revelatory experience.[1] Baur understood this passage as strong evidence that the Pseudo-Clementines testify to a split of the early church into Pauline and Petrine factions.[2] Baur's views about these two apostolic and doctrinal trajectories may have declined in popularity over the years,[3] but

---

[1] In *Hom* 17.13.1, Simon Magus summarizes Peter's claim: ἱκανῶς νενοηκέναι σε τὰ τοῦ διδασκάλου σου λέγων, διὰ τὸ παρόντα ἐναργείᾳ ὁρᾶν καὶ ἀκούειν αὐτοῦ, καὶ ἑτέρῳ τινὶ μὴ δυνατὸν εἶναι ὁράματι ἢ ὀπτασίᾳ ἔχειν τὸ ὅμοιον. ("You say that you have sufficiently understood the things of your teacher because you were present to see and hear him clearly, and that it is not possible for any other to have anything similar by a vision or appearance.")

[2] Baur, "Die Christuspartei," 61-206. Georg Strecker provides a convenient summary of the views of the Tübingen School in his *Judenchristentum*, 1-34. There are several recent studies of anti-Pauline tendencies in the Pseudo-Clementines; on this see the initial footnote of Chapter 2.

[3] Stanley Jones speaks of two main lines of reaction to the Baur thesis: "(1) the tendency to maintain Baur's position by dating the Jewish Christian element early in the literary history of the PsCl and by emphasizing the importance of Jewish Christianity for the history of the church and (2) the tendency to refute Baur's evaluation of the PsCl

they serve as a useful starting-point for the argument of this chapter. I am convinced that Baur was right in placing special emphasis on Simon's and Peter's dispute over true apostleship.[4] Instead of considering this as evidence of an historical schism in early Christianity, however, I propose that we shift our attention to the broader implications of the question about how one comes to know and authoritatively transmit divine truth. I have already suggested that the protagonists' claims to authority not only pit them against Paul, but also oppose the *Recognitions'* version of Jesus' message to other philosophical and astrological rivals who declare that they too have special knowledge of divine truth. At this point we need to look more closely at Peter's emphasis on his personal acquaintance with Jesus, which forms the cornerstone of this larger oppositional dynamic.

The following pages spell out in some detail the content and ramifications of Peter's claim to personal acquaintance with Jesus. In the course of this analysis I intend to make three related points. First, Jesus' prophetic message is the "true knowledge" that philosophers and astrologers claimed to have, but which only followers of the True Prophet can actually possess. Second, the importance of Peter's relationship with Jesus lies in the continuity it establishes between Jesus' original message and the preaching of Peter. For the *Recognitions*, Peter's apostolic status means that whenever he speaks, his listeners hear Jesus' message as though Jesus himself were speaking. Third, the emphasis on Peter's direct connection to Jesus implies that the message contained in the *Recognitions* is – for all intents and purposes – identical to Jesus' message. Since the *Recognitions* is an exact and complete transcript of Peter's preaching, it can claim to be a reliable account of Jesus' words.

We can make begin to make sense of these three points if we think about Peter as a *delegate* for Jesus. Pierre Bourdieu has written at length about this vocabulary of *delegation*. According to Bourdieu, a "delegate ... is a person who has a mandate, a commission or a power of proxy, to represent – an extraordinarily polysemic word – in other words, to show and throw into relief the interests of a person or a group."[5] Put simply, the text says that Jesus' message is truth, and that Jesus has granted Peter the power to represent him and his message. It is important to understand the forcefulness of this claim, which may seem rather banal unless it is examined closely. Peter is not simply a disciple who is following in his

---

either by denying the Jewish Christian element in the PsCl or by relativizing its importance through the assignment of a late date to the Jewish Christian influence or through denial of the seriousness of this influence." Jones, "Pseudo-Clementines," 86.

[4] On this see Strecker, *Judenchristentum*, 191-94; and Côté, *Le thème de l'opposition*, 44-47.

[5] Bourdieu, *Language and Symbolic Power*, 203.

master's footsteps; he is not a "trainee or substitute who plays the part of the teacher...without having the qualifications."[6] Although Peter does speak of himself as the disciple of the True Prophet, the text makes it clear that he is not simply an apprentice. Rather, Peter is a legitimate spokesperson for Jesus himself, an individual vested with the power of the True Prophet.[7] This effectively makes Peter the character in the narrative who is the source of real knowledge about God, humanity, and the world.

In order for Peter to represent Jesus in this way, the text must show that Peter has received this authority from Jesus and is not merely usurping the privilege. As Bourdieu says, "the authorized spokesperson is only able to use words to act on other agents and, through their action, on things themselves, because his speech concentrates within it the accumulated symbolic capital of the group which has delegated him and of which he is the *authorized representative*."[8] When applied to the *Recognitions*, this means that Peter's message is effective only insofar as he can be shown to speak for Jesus. If Peter were preaching his own message, he would be unmasked as an impostor or an unqualified substitute, and his words would have no power. Moreover, Peter's status as Jesus' legitimate representative can be understood as the foundation for the *Recognitions'* claim to be an authoritative text. If the *Recognitions* preserves Peter's preaching as it was meant to be heard, and Peter's preaching is an exact transcript of what Jesus has said, then the *Recognitions* can claim to be a complete and accurate account of the prophetic knowledge passed down by Jesus. It is not difficult to see that there is a great deal at stake in the text's assertions about Jesus' preaching as well as Peter's relationship to Jesus.

In the first section of Chapter 4, we will explore the *Recognitions'* assertions that prophetic knowledge is the only certain knowledge, and that Jesus the True Prophet is the exclusive conduit of such knowledge. In sections two, three, and four, we will examine three arguments designed to show that Peter has flawlessly fulfilled his obligations as Jesus' delegate: (1) Peter was personally acquainted with Jesus and intimately familiar with his teachings; (2) Peter strengthens his natural gift for memorization by rehearsing Jesus' teachings on a regular basis, ensuring that he has not forgotten anything Jesus taught; and (3) Peter is careful to preserve the proper order of Jesus' teachings. A fifth and final section will discuss the

---

[6] Bourdieu, *Language and Symbolic Power*, 125.

[7] It is worth noting that Peter in the *Recognitions* never speaks of himself as a prophet, and that in *Hom* 18.7.6 Peter explicitly denies that he himself is a prophet.

[8] Bourdieu, *Language and Symbolic Power*, 109, 111 (italics in original). In this case, however, Peter is the delegate not of a *group* but of a *person*. While a United States Senator might be authorized by his constituents to represent the interests of the group, Peter is said to be authorized by Jesus to represent him and his message.

authentication of the prophetic knowledge passed on by Peter, focusing particularly on the text's insistence on James' approval of all teaching.

The True Prophet is the Only Source of Certain Knowledge[9]

We saw in Chapters 2 and 3 that the *Recognitions* values not expertise but *knowledge* – specifically, knowledge about divine and human matters – that has practical consequences for individuals' conduct in the world. The philosophers may seem wise because of their sophistical skill, but their reliance on opinion necessarily means that they have no true knowledge. Likewise, the astrologers may be proficient in esoteric technical matters, but their expertise relies on deceptions perpetuated by demons. We have also learned that the protagonists' extensive philosophical and astrological training is neither the source of their knowledge nor the real reason for their success in debating their opponents. What, then, is the source of their epistemological authority? According to the *Recognitions*, the True Prophet is the only conduit for real knowledge. Because Peter and his followers have access to the True Prophet, they possess prophetic (and therefore certain) knowledge which their opponents do not. In drawing a distinction between the heroes and their two groups of rivals, the *Recognitions* creates an opposition between philosophical and astrological knowledge on the one hand, and that provided by the True Prophet on the other hand.

I would like to suggest that this distinction between the protagonists and their opponents, based on the source of their knowledge, is an ingenious strategy designed to show that all who disagree with the *Recognitions'* contents are essentially rejecting the single source of epistemological certainty. To better understand this strategy, we must examine three characteristics of the knowledge provided by the True Prophet: it is

---

[9] Recall that within Pseudo-Clementine literature, "True Prophet" is the primary Christological title of Jesus (though the Syriac of *Rec* 1.34.4 refers to Moses as "the prophet of truth" as well). The title appears to derive from Deut 13.1, which Peter cites in *Hom* 16.13.2-4 and *Rec* 2.45.7. Not only is Jesus a prophet who possesses the kind of true knowledge sought in the *Recognitions*, he is also the most important and most knowledgeable of all the prophets. See Han J. W. Drijvers, "Adam and the True Prophet," 314-23; Charles A. Gieschen, "The Seven Pillars of the World," 67-81; idem, *Angelomorphic Christology*, 201-13; L. Cerfaux, "Le vrai prophète des Clémentines," *Recherches de Science Religieuse* 18 (1928) 143-63; and Strecker, *Judenchristentum*, 145-53. The *Recognitions'* acknowledgement of Moses as one of the prophets may stem from Stephen's speech in Acts 7.37. Loveday Alexander, "The Acts of the Apostles as an Apologetic Text," in *Apologetics in the Roman Empire*, 32.

undoubtedly true; it cannot be obtained from any other source; and it is superior to other purported forms of knowledge.

Prophetic Knowledge is Unquestionably True

The *Recognitions* makes a special point of showing that prophetic knowledge has been proven true, and therefore is to be believed without question. Consider, for example, what Peter says about Jesus to the crowds at Tripolis in *Rec* 5.10.3: *hic adnuntiavit regnum dei, cui nos de omnibus quae dicebat, tamquam vero prophetae credidimus, firmitatem fidei nostrae non solum ex verbis eius, sed et ex operibus adsumentes, quia et dicta legis, quae ante multas generationes de praesentia eius exposuerant, in ipso consignabantur* ("He proclaimed the kingdom of God, and we believed him as a True Prophet in all that he spoke, obtaining the strength of our belief not only from his words, but also from his works; and also because the sayings of the law, which many generations before had revealed his appearance, were placed beyond doubt by him").

Jesus' followers believed in the truth of his prophetic words for three reasons: (1) his words were themselves true, or were proven true as predictions of future events; (2) the power of his works confirmed that he must be acting in the name of God; and (3) he fulfilled "the sayings of the law" through his own speech and actions. Because Jesus' words have been ratified in these three ways, the *Recognitions* argues that everything Jesus says is to be believed without question. The unquestionable truth of the True Prophet's words is asserted again by Peter in *Rec* 8.60.1-4, 6. Because this passage is probably the clearest statement of this idea, it is worth quoting at some length:

si quis igitur vult omnia discere ... verum prophetam requirat. quem cum invenerit, non quaestionibus et disputationibus neque argumentis cum eo aget, sed si quid responderit, si quid pronuntiaverit, hoc certum esse non potest dubitari. et ideo quaeratur verus propheta ante omnia, et eius verba teneantur; in quibus illud tantummodo discutiendum unicuique est, ut satisfaciat sibi si vere prophetica eius verba sunt ... et cum his omnibus recto iudicio discussis verba constiterit esse prophetica, ita demum credi eis de omnibus quibus dixerint et responderint, debet.

Therefore, if anyone wishes to learn all things ... let him look for the True Prophet; when he has found him, let him discuss with him not by questions and debates, nor by arguments; but if he has said anything in reply, or uttered anything, it cannot be doubted that this is certain. And therefore, above all, let the True Prophet be sought, and let his words be held fast. In relation to these, only this should be discussed by every one, that he may satisfy himself if they are truly his prophetic words ... And when all these things have been discussed with proper judgment, and it is established that the words are prophetic, accordingly it is certainly necessary that they be believed about all things which they have said and answered.

Here Peter is saying that the True Prophet's statements are necessarily certain. His words are the key to knowledge of all things, and they are not to be doubted in any way. The proper response to the True Prophet's words is unquestioning belief. To Peter's way of thinking, the real issue is *not* the truth of Jesus' statements at all, since these words are presumed true from the start (cf. *Hom* 3.14.1-2; 19.7.1). Instead, Peter is concerned that some counterfeit, non-prophetic statements may be falsely attributed to the True Prophet – the task is not to prove the truth of Jesus' words, but rather to prove that sayings have been properly attributed to the True Prophet. The working assumption of the *Recognitions*, which has been placed on Peter's lips, is that all of the True Prophet's words are certain and true.

This same sentiment is immediately restated by Peter in *Rec* 8.61.3: *verecundis et simplicibus mentibus, cum viderint fieri quae praedicta sunt, satis abundeque sufficit, ut de certissima praescientia certissimam scientiam capiant et de cetero requiescant evidenti agnitione veritatis adsumpta* ("to modest and simple minds, when they see the things which have been foretold occur, it is sufficient and abundantly satisfying, that they obtain most certain knowledge from most certain prescience; and for the rest relax, having received evident knowledge of the truth"). Foreknowledge, which is the "sixth sense" belonging exclusively to prophets,[10] is a faculty that makes "prophetic" a modifier that is synonymous with "certain" and "evident." As was the case in the examples already cited, the certainty of prophetic knowledge seems to be an assumption, rather than a contentious issue, for the protagonists.

The True Prophet's Knowledge is Unique

In addition to insisting on the certainty of prophetic knowledge, the *Recognitions* asserts that the True Prophet is the only possible source for real knowledge. For example, in *Rec* 1.16.1-2 Peter declares: *verus propheta ... solus inluminare animas hominum potest, ita ut oculis suis viam salutis evidenter inspiciant. aliter enim inpossibile est, de rebus divinis aeternisque cognoscere, nisi quis ab isto vero propheta didicerit* ("the True Prophet ... alone can enlighten the souls of human beings, so that with their eyes they may plainly perceive the way of salvation. For otherwise it is impossible to understand divine and eternal things, unless

---

[10] Cf. *Hom* 3.11.1-3; 3.12.1-3; 3.13.1; 3.15.1. Peter tells Simon in *Rec* 2.51.5: *est enim et alius sextus sensus, id est praenoscendi; isti enim quinque sensus scientiae capaces sunt, sextus autem praescientiae est, quem habuerunt prophetae* ("there is also a sixth sense, that is, foreknowledge; for those five senses are capable of knowledge, but the sixth is [capable] of foreknowledge, which the prophets possessed").

one learns from that True Prophet").[11] Knowing Jesus is not simply the fastest or most direct route to knowledge – it is the only possible path.

Moreover, the knowledge given by the True Prophet is not just a matter of intellection. Such knowledge of "divine and eternal things" leads to salvation and the enlightenment of the soul. Those who desire to have knowledge, salvation and enlightenment must acquire such goods through the True Prophet (cf. *Hom* 3.54.1). This idea is reiterated in *Rec* 1.44.5, as Peter praises Clement for understanding the importance of Jesus' identity as the Christ: *Recte respondisti, inquit, o Clemens. sicut enim sine oculis cernere nemo potest nec sine auribus capere auditum vel absque naribus odoratum neque sine lingua gustum sumere aut absque manibus aliquid contrectare, ita inpossibile est, absque vero propheta quae deo placeant noscere* ("You have answered correctly, O Clement; for just as no one can see without eyes, nor hear without ears, nor smell without nostrils, nor taste without a tongue, nor handle anything without hands, so it is impossible, without the True Prophet, to know what is pleasing to God"). This passage suggests that each of the five senses provides a mode of unique access to the world.[12] For example, touch provides distinctive data that is not identical to the information provided by smell, and vice versa. Put differently, I could not smell that golden retriever puppies are soft, but touch would demonstrate that immediately. This means that some information is sense-specific: it can be gotten in only one way.

Just as each of the five senses provides particular and inimitable information, Jesus the True Prophet is said to provide knowledge of what is pleasing to God that cannot be obtained from any other source. Those who have not received such knowledge directly from Jesus cannot access it by means of another route, nor can they know what pleases God. The True Prophet's exclusive teaching about true knowledge and salvation is mentioned once more during Peter's speech to the crowds at Tripolis in *Rec* 5.4.4 – 5.5.3. First, he mentions the imposture of others who claim to have knowledge: *ita sunt ergo et hi qui ignorantes quod verum est, speciem tamen alicuius scientiae tenent et mala quasi bona gerunt atque ad perniciem quasi ad salutem festinant* ("Thus, therefore, are those also who do not know what is true, yet hold an outward appearance of some knowledge, and do evil things as if they were good things, and rush toward

---

[11] Cf. *Hom* 1.19.1-4; 2.4.3; 2.5.2-3; 2.8.2; 2.12.1-2; 3.11.1. See also the end of *Rec* 1.16.8: *... ita indubitatum est, a nullo alio nisi ab ipso solo sciri posse, quod verum est* ("... thus it is certain that what is true can be known from no other but him alone").

[12] Cf. Origen's account of divine sense perception in *Cels.* 1.48. Karl Rahner, "Le début d'une doctrine des cinque sens spirituels chez Origène," *Revue d'ascétique et de mystique* 14 (1932) 113-45; and Henri Crouzel, *Origène et la "connaissance mystique"* (Paris: Desclée de Brouwer, 1961).

destruction as if toward salvation"; *Rec* 5.4.4). Those who appear to know "divine and eternal things" do not really know what is true, and the consequence of such ignorance is disastrous.

By contrast, the True Prophet's knowledge leads not to destruction but salvation: *quaeri ergo magnopere debet veritatis agnitio, quam nemo alius potest adsignare nisi verus propheta. haec enim porta est vitae volentibus ingredi et iter operum bonorum pergentibus ad civitatem salutis* ("Therefore the knowledge of truth ought to be earnestly sought after, which no other except the True Prophet can confer. For this is the gate of life to those who wish to enter, and the road of good works for those proceeding to the city of salvation"; *Rec* 5.5.3). Such knowledge, which (the text emphasizes again) is the True Prophet's alone to confer, leads to good works and ultimately to salvation.

Finally in *Rec* 9.1.4-5, Peter introduces Clement's disputation with Faustinianus by summarizing his own discourse from the day before:

de voluntate dixi et consilio dei, quam habuit priusquam mundus esset, et quo consilio fecerit mundum, tempora statuerit, legem dederit, iustis ad bonorum remunerationem futurum saeculum promiserit, iniustis poenas ex iudicii sententia statuerit; hoc ego dixi consilium et hanc voluntatem dei ab hominibus inveniri non posse, quia nemo hominum potest sensum dei coniecturis et aestimatione colligere, nisi propheta ab eo missus enuntiet.

I spoke about the will and plan of God, which he had before the world existed, and by which plan he made the world, appointed times, gave the law, promised a future age to the righteous for the rewarding of good [deeds], and established punishments to the unrighteous according to a judicial sentence. I myself said that this plan and this will of God cannot be found out by human beings, because no human being can gather the mind of God from conjectures and estimation, unless a prophet sent by him reveals it.

In this statement Peter is speaking not about the True Prophet specifically, but about prophetic knowledge in general. Ordinary human beings cannot know God's purpose or will, because their knowledge is conjectural. A prophet, however, *can* know the will of God, because prophetic knowledge is not based on opinion. Prophetic knowledge, then, is the only certain knowledge that can be had by human beings.

Over the last few pages we have examined the text's assertions about the proven truth and the exclusivity of prophetic knowledge. I would like to conclude this section by noting that these two claims serve an important purpose: they work to make prophetic knowledge *a rare and therefore valuable commodity*. To understand this more clearly, we need to recall Bourdieu's definition of *religious specialists*: they are "socially recognized as the exclusive holders of the specific competence necessary for the production or reproduction of a *deliberately organized corpus* of secret (and therefore rare) knowledge."[13] The *Recognitions'* agenda, which involves establishing the dominance of its own protagonists (or, if you like, religious specialists) over their epistemic competitors, depends partly on this idea that Peter and his followers have access to rare and valuable knowledge. It is *this* knowledge, rather than other forms of expertise, that ultimately counts as capital within the competitive field of the *Recognitions*.

Prophetic Knowledge is Superior to Other Forms of Knowledge

The exclusivity and certainty of the True Prophet's knowledge not only makes it a valuable commodity, but also ensures that it is inherently better than other kinds of knowledge. This conviction is evident in the *Recognitions'* attacks on other forms of expertise in general, but it is most apparent when the protagonists' prophetic knowledge is juxtaposed with the philosophical and astrological arts in particular.[14] First, let's briefly consider the text's evaluation of non-prophetic knowledge in *Rec* 9.1.6, immediately after Peter says that prophets, as opposed to conjectures, are the only way for human beings to know God's will (see above): *non ergo de quibuscumque disciplinis aut studiis dixi, quia inveniri sine propheta aut sciri non possint, quippe qui sciam et artificia et disciplinas sciri et exerceri ab hominibus, quas non a vero propheta, sed a magistris hominibus didicerint* ("Therefore I did not say that any sciences or studies whatsoever cannot be learned or understood without a prophet; since I know that both professions and sciences are understood and practiced by human beings, which they have learned not from the True Prophet, but from human instructors").

In other words, it is possible for people to master various sciences or paths of study, but these disciplines are of human origin and involve instruction by human beings. This kind of knowledge, however, is to be distinguished from prophetic knowledge, because such skills are not

---

[13] Bourdieu, "Genesis and Structure of the Religious Field," 9. Italics in original.

[14] Luigi Cirillo has noted the contrast between philosophical and prophetic knowledge in the *Recognitions*: "La section initiale (*Rec* I, 1-11) révèle clairement une idée maîtresse du roman de Clément: l'impossibilité de trouver la vérité dans la philosophie des différentes écoles de l'époque, d'où la nette opposition qui est tracée entre la 'philosophie' et la 'prophétie', opposition qui se traduit dans la doctrine du vrai Prophète.... L'opposition philosophie-prophétie, ainsi que la nécessité du vrai Prophète, sont affirmées de manière beaucoup plus vigoureuse et constante dans les *Reconnaissances* ... C'est l'une des caractéristiques de cette rédaction" Cirillo and Schneider, Reconnaissances *du pseudo Clément*, 33. I agree with Cirillo on this point, but would add that astrology, much like philosophy, is also opposed to prophetic knowledge in the view of the *Recognitions*.

revealed by a prophet or learned from a prophet.[15] Peter does not mention any of these "human" disciplines by name, which suggests that he is referring to *all* non-prophetic knowledge. Another example of this evaluation of non-prophetic knowledge is found in *Rec* 5.4.4, which has already been cited above. In this case, Peter is speaking not of a dichotomy between *human* and *prophetic*, but instead is making a differentiation between *knowledge* and *ignorance* (or *a semblance of knowledge*).[16] According to this passage, all knowledge that does not originate with the True Prophet only appears to be real knowledge, when in fact it is mere ignorance; it may appear true, but in fact is false (cf. *Hom* 2.7.1-4).

The protagonists' devaluation of other forms of knowledge becomes even more pointed when they take on philosophy and astrology, the two disciplines that have been the subject of much of this book. Let's look first at the attack on philosophical knowledge. We know from Chapter 2 that, according to the *Recognitions*, philosophers are more interested in arguments than truth, and their so-called knowledge is mere opinion. However, this characterization only hints at the fundamental flaw of philosophical knowledge: philosophers are not prophets, nor do they rely on prophetic knowledge. The best example of this epistemological principle is found in a statement made by Peter in *Rec* 10.51.2-3, where he attacks the philosophers: *praesentia quidem et visibilia nosse hominis est rationabilis, praeterita vero et futura et invisibilia scire solius propheticae praescientiae est. non ergo haec coniecturis et opinionibus colligenda sunt, in quibus valde falluntur homines, sed fide propheticae veritatis, sicut se habet haec nostra doctrina* ("It is indeed the mark of a rational person to know present and visible things, but it is the nature of prophetic foreknowledge alone to know past, future, and invisible things. Therefore, these things should not be gathered from conjectures and opinions, in which people are greatly deceived, but from faith in prophetic truth, as this

---

[15] Athenagoras' *leg.* 7 contains a similar contrast between prophetic and philosophical knowledge: "...the poets and philosphers have proceeded by conjecture. ... They were able, indeed, to get some notions of reality, but not to find it, since they did not deign to learn about God from God, but each one from himself. For this reason they taught conflicting doctrines about God, matter, forms, and the world. We, on the contrary, as witnesses of what we think and believe, have prophets who have spoken by the divine Spirit about God and the things of God." The same argument occurs in chapter 9 ("Were we satisfied with such reasoning, one would think our doctrine was human. But prophetic voices confirm our arguments") and in chapter 24 ("...we say nothing without authority and speak only of what the prophets have told"). Translation from Richardson, *Early Christian Fathers*. Theophilus of Antioch, *Autol.* II.8, 12 contains an argument remarkably similar to Athenagoras'.

[16] Cf. *Hom* 11.19.2, where Peter speaks of the True Prophet destroying ignorance by knowledge (ἀναιρεῖ τὴν ἄγνοιαν τῇ γνώσει).

teaching of ours is"; cf. *Hom* 2.7.1-2; 2.8.3). According to this passage, the philosophers are presumptuous in speaking about God (as well as the origin and end of the world). Because they are reasonable men, they can know things that are present and visible. However, their so-called knowledge is merely deceptive supposition to the extent they claim to know things they haven't seen and heard for themselves.

Peter and his followers, however, are able to preach a message based on fact rather than opinion, because of their faith in prophetic truth. In contrast to the philosophers, Peter and his followers have access to *propheticae praescientiae* ("prophetic foreknowledge"), which makes it possible for them to know past, future, and invisible things with certainty.[17] As we saw above in *Rec* 5.5.3, the *Recognitions* asserts that the protagonists' message is based on the teaching of the True Prophet and hence contains *veritatis agnitio* ("knowledge of truth"). According to the *Recognitions*, then, prophetic knowledge is superior to philosophical knowledge. The distinction made here deprives philosophers of *any* special claim to epistemic authority, because it credits them with the ability to understand *only* occurrences that are present and visible, which is available to any "reasonable" person. Only those with prophetic knowledge can truly know past and future events, or understand things that cannot be seen.

Peter makes a similar point in *Rec* 1.16.2-4, when he says to Clement:

fides rerum causarumque sententiae pro ingeniis magis defendentium ponderantur.... ista de causa religionis ac pietatis fides veri prophetae praesentiam postulavit, ut ipse nobis diceret de singulis, prout se ipsa veritas habet, et doceret quomodo oporteat de singulis credi.

The belief of things, and the opinions of matters, are weighed more in proportion to the talents of [their] supporters ... For this reason, the confirmation of religion and piety demanded the presence of the True Prophet, so that he himself might tell us about each one, just as the truth itself is, and that he might teach us what must be believed about each one.

Here Peter is invoking Clement's judgment about the philosophical schools he frequented, which can be found in *Rec* 1.3.1-5. He agrees with Clement that true knowledge cannot be obtained from philosophers, who are more interested in winning arguments than they are in the truth. The difficulty of finding the truth in philosophical circles "demanded the presence" of the True Prophet, who has the power to tell human beings what should be believed as true. The True Prophet's knowledge is reliable and certain in a way that philosophical expertise is not.[18]

---

[17] Cf. *Hom* 2.6.1-4; 2.10.1-3. Note that *Hom* 2.6.4 mentions the exception of πολιτεία, which can be known by a reasonable person.

[18] Clement, too, shares Peter's judgment about the superiority of prophetic knowledge. In *Rec* 1.18.5, he tells Peter, *adversum prophetiam etenim neque argumenta*

Of course, it should come as no surprise that philosophers are not the only epistemic competitors whose knowledge is unfavorably compared to that of the True Prophet. The *Recognitions* also makes a point of arguing that astrologers' technical skills are inferior to prophetic knowledge. The most obvious example of this is found in *Rec* 9.12.1-2, which has been cited already in Chapter 3. Clement says: "Therefore the astrologers, being ignorant of such mysteries, suppose that these things happen by the courses of the stars: whence also, in their answers to those who approach them to deliberate on something about future things, in answering they are usually deceived. Nor is it astonishing, for they are not prophets." Unlike prophets, astrologers do not have the "sixth sense" of foreknowledge. Whereas prophets can use their prescience to accurately predict future events, astrologers must rely on their interpretations of the stars and their understanding of astral determinism to make predictions. Prophetic predictions are always correct, but astrologers are frequently mistaken when they rely on such faulty methods to produce information about future events.

The astrologers' mistakes confirm that demons are the source of their understanding, according to Peter in *Rec* 4.21.5: "what is spoken by the true God, whether by prophets or by separate visions, is always true; but what is predicted by demons is not always [true]." By associating astrologers with demons, the *Recognitions* sets up a dichotomy with the true God, prophets, and visions on one side, and astrologers and demons on the other side. Prophetic knowledge, then, is always reliable and correct, and has God as its source. It is diametrically opposed to the kind of information provided by astrology, which is often erroneous and has demonic underpinnings.

This section has explored the *Recognitions'* assertions about the exclusivity, reliability, and superiority of prophetic knowledge in contrast to all other ways of understanding the world. All three of these arguments are designed to increase the value of prophetic knowledge, which is the kind of knowledge the protagonists claim to possess. While Peter and his followers can match their rivals' philosophical and astrological expertise, thereby compromising the competitors' exclusive claim to epistemic capital, the philosophers and astrologers cannot counter by claiming to possess this prophetic knowledge. The *Recognitions*, as we shall see, makes such a counter-claim nearly impossible because of its relentless emphasis on personal acquaintance with the True Prophet as a condition for the possession of prophetic knowledge.

---

neque ars ulla stare sufficiet neque sofismatum syllogismorumque versutiae ("For neither arguments nor any art is sufficient to stand against prophecy, nor the subtleties of sophisms and syllogisms"). Cf. *Hom* 1.21.5-6.

Personal Companionship

According to the argument I'm calling Personal Companionship, Peter's role as Jesus' disciple ensures that he has heard Jesus' message – which is the "prophetic knowledge" already mentioned – as Jesus intended it to be heard. Moreover, it means that Peter has had the opportunity to understand Jesus' message completely. As a result, Peter is a reliable witness to Jesus' words and actions, and can claim to know the prophetic truth Jesus preached.[19] The implication of this, of course, is that those who have not heard Jesus' teaching for themselves cannot say that they truly represent Jesus, nor can they claim to know the meaning of what he taught. This would seem to suggest that individuals like Paul, who professed to know Jesus by means of revelation rather than personal acquaintance, are not true mouthpieces for Jesus' prophetic message. Likewise, written accounts that claim to preserve Jesus' words are not always to be believed. Nothing is to be trusted except the account of those who saw and heard with their own eyes and ears.

Peter Was the Disciple of the True Prophet

The *Recognitions* goes to great lengths to emphasize the face-to-face, master-disciple relationship between Jesus and Peter. This can be understood in the light of training techniques employed by ancient philosophical schools.[20] As Pierre Hadot writes, "True education is always oral because only the spoken word makes dialogue possible, that is, it makes it possible for the disciple to discover the truth himself amid the interplay of questions and answers and also for the master to adapt his teaching to the needs of the disciple."[21] To be properly considered the follower of a philosophical teacher, one had to be physically present at the master's side. The *Recognitions*' insistence on personal acquaintance can thus be understood in terms of philosophical instruction, since it implies

---

[19] This concurs with the judgment of Luigi Cirillo, who (in the context of discussing the opposition between philosophy and prophecy in the *Recognitions*) writes: "Mais le problème capital, surtout dans les *Reconnaissances*, pour ce qui est de la recherche de la vérité, est celui de l'interprétation de la tradition transmise par le vrai Prophète. L'interprète par excellence est Pierre." Cirillo and Schneider, Reconnaissances *du pseudo Clément*, 34.

[20] Although much of the *Recognitions*' material on Peter's discipleship is taken from the New Testament Gospels, its strong interest in depicting the protagonists as philosophers justifies this analogy with philosophical schools.

[21] Hadot, *Philosophy as a Way of Life*, 62.

that Peter could have learned Jesus' teaching completely and thoroughly as a result of their interaction as master and disciple.[22]

Many interpreters, however, have read this material in a rather different light. The Pseudo-Clementines' understanding of apostolic authority has long been the subject of scholarly discussion, most often in connection with analyses of "Ebionite" theology and ecclesiology.[23] Consider for example Hans von Campenhausen's disapproving estimation of the Ebionite apostolate:

> In other words, the teaching of Jesus is the ultimate revelation of truth and righteousness, and all that now remains is to follow it. Jesus is explicitly hailed as the 'new Moses', and for this reason the Jewish Christian church, just like rabbinic Judaism, can declare that henceforward no prophet is justified in saying anything new. In her life she no longer has any need of direct spiritual assistance; in her 'synagogues' the concern is simply with precise exegesis and casuistic application of the numerous legal prescriptions.... Here the apostles are the authorised founders of the Church's tradition and legislation, and absolutely nothing more. Any sort of direct 'authority' bestowed upon them, and especially on their own ideas and insights, is explicitly rejected; all that matters is what they 'learned' during their intimacy with Jesus.[24]

Von Campenhausen's remarks identify the Pseudo-Clementine view of apostolic authority as "Jewish Christian." Though von Campenhausen does not mention anti-Paulinism in his rather brief remarks on the Ebionites, the analyses of F. C. Baur and the Tübingen school regard the Pseudo-Clementines' "Jewish Christian" understanding of apostolic authority as diametrically opposed to that held by Paul.

One rationale for reading our text's insistence on Peter's relationship to Jesus in the light of "Jewish Christian" and anti-Pauline ideas can be found

---

[22] This reading suggests that the *Recognitions* may be understood in the light of a specific category of ancient lives of philosophers. Charles H. Talbert argues that one species of philosophical biography "attempted by their succession lists or narratives to say where the true followers of the founder were to be located in the present. The living voice is to be found with individual D because he received the tradition from C who got it from B who in turn had it passed to him by A who got it from the founder." Charles H. Talbert, "Biographies of Philosophers and Rulers as Instruments of Religious Propaganda in Mediterranean Antiquity," in *Aufstieg und Niedergang der römischen Welt: Geschichte und Kultur Roms im Spiegel der neueren Forschung*, vol. 2.16, ed. Hildegard Temporini and Wolfgang Haase (Berlin and New York: Walter de Gruyter, 1980) 1645.

[23] On the methodological and historical difficulties presented by the term "Ebionite," see Leander E. Keck, "The Poor among the Saints in Jewish Christianity and Qumran," *Zeitschrift für die Neutestamentliche Wissenschaft* 57 (1966) 54-78, esp. 55-66; and J. M. Magnin, "Notes sur l'Ébionisme," *ProcheOrient chrétien* 24 (1974) 225-50.

[24] Hans von Campenhausen, *Ecclesiastical Authority and Spiritual Power in the Church of the First Three Centuries*, trans. J. A. Baker (Stanford: Stanford University Press, 1969) 180. On p. 181 he goes on to conclude that "this could never provide the basis for a vital development of spiritual authority." Cf. Schoeps, *Theologie und Geschichte*, 289ff.

in one of the *Recognitions'* sources – the New Testament book of Acts.[25] In Acts 1.21-22, where Matthias is chosen as Judas' replacement to complete the number of the Twelve, it is clear that an apostle is someone who physically accompanied Jesus during his entire ministry and also witnessed his resurrection.[26] Bruce Chilton and Jacob Neusner seem to be following Acts' line of thought when they write, "Jesus was the principal agent of the kingdom of God. Personal, continuous contact with him was therefore … a matter of discipleship, that following of Jesus which could enable one to enter into the kingdom oneself."[27]

As is well known, Acts' view of discipleship stands in marked contrast to that of Paul.[28] The opponents in Paul's letters never ceased to point out that Paul did not obtain his message from the earthly Jesus as the other apostles had. Paul tells his addressees in Galatians 1.11-12: "For I want you to know, brothers, that the gospel that was proclaimed by me is not of human origin; for I did not receive it from a human source, nor was I taught it, but I received it through a revelation of Jesus Christ." To Paul's way of thinking, his knowledge of the message he preached was based on a visionary experience, and he seemed to regard this as a kind of direct access to Jesus. Indeed, he seemed to regard this revelation as a more direct path to the truth than mere instruction by another human being. Our text holds a view of discipleship very similar to the one found in Acts (and thus different from that held by Paul). In the *Recognitions'* view, one who lacks personal acquaintance with Jesus necessarily has knowledge that is less secure. Knowing comes only from seeing and hearing Jesus for oneself.

Robert J. Hauck has questioned the reading of the *Homilies* offered by Baur and the Tübingen school. He argues that Simon's and Peter's dispute

---

[25] Stanley Jones has made a convincing case for the Pseudo-Clementines' dependence on Acts in his "Ancient Jewish Christian Rejoinder," 223-45. See also the analysis of Scott, *Geography in Early Judaism and Christianity*, 114-23.

[26] "So one of the men who have accompanied us during all the time that the Lord Jesus went in and out among us, beginning from the baptism of John until the day when he was taken up from us – one of these must become a witness with us to his resurrection." (Acts 1.21-22, NRSV.) Because Paul did not know the earthly Jesus, he is almost never called an apostle in Acts. The sole exception to this rule, of course, is Acts 14.14 (and possibly 14.4). C. K. Barrett, "Pauline Controversies in the Post-Pauline Period," *New Testament Studies* 20 (1973-1974) 240 argues that this was not intended as a denigration of Paul's status.

[27] Bruce Chilton and Jacob Neusner, *Types of Authority in Formative Christianity and Judaism* (London and New York: Routledge, 1999) 41.

[28] Jean-Noël Aletti, "L'autorité apostolique de Paul: théorie et pratique," in A. Vanhoye, *L'Apôtre Paul: Personnalité, Style et Conception du Ministere* (Leuven: Leuven University Press, 1986) 229-46, discusses the early Christian debates on apostolic authority.

about discipleship in *Hom* 17 is best understood *not* (or not exclusively) as a dramatization of the conflict between Jewish (Petrine) and Gentile (Pauline) Christianity, but as a debate "carried out in philosophical language common in the late antique thought world and in pagan-Christian dialogue" that is "occupied with the relative trustworthiness of sense knowledge, various sorts of visions, and the divine knowledge present in the soul of the sage."[29] Hauck's argument is an important corrective to interpretations of the *Homilies* that would read it only as a "Jewish Christian" document, because he demonstrates that the text is participating in a much broader philosophical conversation about the value of sensory knowledge. To this extent, his analysis also can be usefully extended to the *Recognitions*: as we have seen, it too is embedded in philosophical and epistemological discussions that extend well beyond the sectarian concerns of a "Jewish Christian" group.

I am not convinced, however, that Hauck's assessment of the relative unimportance of Peter's relationship to Jesus in the *Homilies* also applies to the *Recognitions*. He contends that the Clementine Peter "does not argue for a reliance on simple sense knowledge in place of visions," nor does he "rely on the knowledge he had by seeing Jesus." Instead, Peter "argues that divine truth dwells in his soul continuously, without the need for vision."[30] As the following paragraphs attempt to demonstrate, though the *Recognitions* is clearly interested in more than the dramatization of a debate between Peter and Paul, it is nevertheless the case that Peter's personal acquaintance with Jesus is the foundation of the apostle's epistemic authority.

Throughout the narrative, Peter insists on the importance of the personal instruction implicit in the master-disciple, or teacher-student, relationship. According to Peter, *nemo potest discere aliquid qui non docetur* ("no one who is not taught can learn anything"; *Rec* 5.36.1). Truly reliable knowledge, then, must be handed down directly, through the process of instruction. In these instances Peter is referring to his relationship with Jesus, as well as his own instruction of Clement and the others.

The importance of one-on-one instruction is underscored when Peter scolds Simon Magus for his mistaken beliefs in *Rec* 2.55.1: *Solent ista, o Simon, absurda adversum deum meditari hi qui legem non magistris tradentibus legunt, sed semetipsos doctores habent et putant se intellegere posse legem, quam sibi non exposuit ille qui a magistro didicerit* ("O

---

[29] Robert J. Hauck, "'They Saw What they Said they Saw': Sense Knowledge in Early Christian Polemic," *HTR* 81.3 (1988) 248.

[30] Hauck, "Sense Knowledge," 246-47. It is important to note that Hauck writes exclusively about Origen and the *Homilies*. Though he does speak of the "Clementine Peter," he does not claim that his analysis applies to the *Recognitions*.

Simon, the ones who usually consider such absurdities against God are those who read the law without being taught by masters, but consider themselves teachers, and think that they can understand the law, though he who has learned from the master has not explained it to them").[31] In this case Simon, who is altogether familiar with the Mosaic law both he and Peter believe to be authoritative, has made the terrible mistake of supposing that there is another more powerful God besides the God who created the world and wrote the law.

In the *Recognitions'* view, Simon's attempt to understand the law without the aid of a master's instructions has led him to commit the most grievous sin of all: denying the reality of the one almighty and righteous creator God. Peter, in contrast to Simon, *has* received proper instruction from the master.[32] He tells Simon in 3.18.3, *non indigeo abs te doceri, habeo enim magistrum a quo omnia didici* ("I do not need to be taught by you, for I have a master from whom I have learned all things"). Peter has no need to learn anything from Simon, because as Jesus' disciple he has had an opportunity to learn "all things" directly from the unique source of prophetic truth.

In addition to Peter's emphasis on having been taught directly by the True Prophet, his personal acquaintance with Jesus is established in another way. On a number of occasions Peter provides "eyewitness accounts" about Jesus known to us from the Gospel traditions.[33] In each

---

[31] Cf. Theophilus of Antioch, *Autol.* I.8: "And what art or knowledge can anyone learn, unless he first applies and entrusts himself to the teacher?" Translation from Roberts and Donaldson, *Ante-Nicene Fathers* (slightly modified).

[32] *Hom* 1.15.2 and 4.5.2 speak of Peter as the "most esteemed" (δοκιμώτατος) of Jesus' disciples. Cf. *Hom* 3.29.5; 12.7.1; 17.19.4.

[33] There is greatest agreement that the Pseudo-Clementines used Matthew and Luke. For a discussion of these matters as they pertain to the *Homilies*, see the history of research given in Leslie L. Kline, *The Sayings of Jesus*, 1-11; A. Hilgenfeld, *Kritische Untersuchungen über die Evangelien Justin's, der clementinischen Homilien und Marcion's: Ein Beitrag zur Geschichte der ältesten Evangelien-Literatur* (Halle: C. A. Schwetschke und Sohn, 1850) 307f; and Hendrik Marius van Nes, *Het Nieuwe Testament in de Clementinen* (Amsterdam: de Roever Kröber-Bakels, 1887) 1-11 (n.v.). On the use of the Gospel of John by *Rec* 1.33-71, see J. Louis Martyn, "Clementine Recognitions 1,33-71, Jewish Christianity, and the Fourth Gospel," in *God's Christ and His People: Studies in Honour of Nils Alstrup Dahl*, ed. Jacob Jervell and Wayne A. Meeks (Oslo: Universitetsforlaget, 1977) 265-95. Most recently, Frédéric Amsler has revisited the issue of the Pseudo-Clementines' Gospel citations, especially as they have been treated by Waitz and Strecker. See his "Les citations évangéliques dans le roman pseudo-clémentin. Une tradition indépendante du Nouveau Testament?" in *Le canon du Nouveau Testament: Regards nouveaux sur l'histoire de sa formation*, ed. Gabriella Aragione, Eric Junod, and Enrico Norelli (Geneva: Labor et Fides, 2005) 141-67. Amsler argues for the methodological importance of distinguishing between direct and indirect citations.

case he uses a kind of loose introductory formula to indicate his presence alongside Jesus:

propter hoc denique verus propheta cum esset praesens nobiscum et quosdam ex divitibus neglegentes erga dei cultum videret, huius rei ita aperuit veritatem: »Nemo potest,« inquit, »duobus dominis servire, non potestis deo servire et mammonae«; mammona patria eorum voce divitias vocans.

Precisely because of this *the True Prophet, when he was present with us,* and saw certain people who were neglecting the worship of God because of [their] wealth, thus disclosed the truth of this matter: 'No one,' he said, 'can serve two masters; you cannot serve God and mammon,' calling riches 'mammon' in the language of his country (*Rec* 5.9.3-4).

Elsewhere he makes a similar statement:

Hic ergo est verus propheta, qui in Iudaea nobis apparuit ut audistis; qui stans publice sola iussione faciebat caecos videre, surdos audire, fugabat daemones, aegris sanitatem reddebat et mortuis vitam. cumque nihil ei esset inpossibile, etiam cogitationes hominum pervidebat, quod nulli est possibile nisi soli deo.

He therefore is the True Prophet, who appeared to us in Judea, as you have heard, who, standing before the people, by a single command made the blind see, the deaf hear, cast out demons, restored health to the sick, and life to the dead; and since nothing was impossible for him, he even perceived the thoughts of human beings, which is possible for none but God only (*Rec* 5.10.1-2).

Although the words used to introduce these episodes are not precisely the same, both opening statements have the same effect because they make Peter an eyewitness of events known from the Gospels.[34]

In yet another instance, Simon continues in his role as foil for Peter. His ongoing refusal to believe Peter (in this case, about God's judgment) is attributed to his lack of instruction by Jesus: *et Simon: Cur ergo mihi non persuadetur? Petrus ait: Quia verum prophetam non audisti dicentem: »Quaerite primo iustitiam eius, et haec omnia adponentur vobis«* ("And Simon: 'Why, then, am I not convinced [that there will be a judgment]?' Peter said: Because you have not heard the True Prophet saying, 'Seek first his righteousness, and all these things will be added to you'"; *Rec* 3.41.4). Peter repeats Jesus' words here as one intimately familiar with them; this familiarity, as well as his confidence in their truthfulness, stems from his

---

The issue of the Pseudo-Clementines' dependence on earlier gospel traditions is a vexed one, in part due to the complexity of the "Jewish Christian Gospel" question. There is a helpful overview of the evidence for Jewish-Christian Gospels in Hennecke-Schneemelcher, *New Testament Apocrypha*, I.134-78; and a more detailed exposition in A. F. J. Klijn and G. J. Reinink, *Patristic Evidence for Jewish-Christian Sects* (Leiden: E.J. Brill, 1973).

[34] Amsler observes that in the *Recognitions*, Peter functions almost exclusively as the spokesperson for Jesus' sayings, which produces the following effect: "Pierre reste le témoin privilégié de l'enseignement de Jésus, puisqu'il est le rapporteur exclusif des paroles du Maître." Amsler, "Citations évangéliques," 157.

having heard them directly from Jesus. This strategy is thus designed to convince the reader that the Peter in this text is the same Peter of the New Testament Gospel accounts who stood beside Jesus and heard his words.

As noted above, many interpreters of the Pseudo-Clementines have understood this emphasis on Peter's personal acquaintance with Jesus (and the epistemological restrictions it entails) as hostility toward Paul. This is especially true because Simon is often considered to be a thinly veiled stand-in for Paul. While I do not wish to argue against the presence of anti-Pauline sentiment in some early layers of the Pseudo-Clementines,[35] I would like to suggest that we can understand the text's insistence on Peter's face-to-face interaction with the True Prophet as a broader polemic against other types of knowledge. Peter's personal acquaintance with Jesus – chronicled in the *Recognitions* by Peter's quotation of Gospel traditions as well as his emphasis on his role as Jesus' disciple – is the foundation for all of the truth claims made by the protagonists of the *Recognitions*.

As I hope to have demonstrated in the last two chapters, these truth claims are set forth not only in opposition to Paul, but indeed *all* epistemic competitors who claim to have knowledge about things divine and human. Simon may to some extent be intended to signify Paul, but this representative function surely does not exhaust his role in the *Recognitions*. I prefer to argue that Simon functions as more than just a single adversary in his debates with Peter. Although he is a straw man who makes an easy target, he also seems designed to raise every possible objection to the protagonists' message. Simon is not just Paul, but also a magician, an idol-worshipper, and a philosopher.[36] He's a paper doll who can be dressed in different career clothing to suit Peter's needs. Rather than attempting to pin down the precise historical figures whom Simon is supposed to represent, I find it more useful (and more true to the *Recognitions'* rhetorical aims) to think of him as a moving target who corresponds to many possible epistemic competitors.

Peter Was Sent by the True Prophet

In the previous section we examined the *Recognitions'* interest in establishing that Peter was the True Prophet's disciple and constant companion. This is not, however, the only assertion our text makes about Peter's connection to Jesus. In addition to insisting on Peter's personal ties

---

[35] Cf. A. Salles, "La diatribe anti-Paulinienne dans le 'Le roman pseudo-Clémentin' et l'origine des 'Kérygmes de Pierre,'" *Revue Biblique* 64 (1957) 516-51; Cullmann, *Problème littéraire*, 154-55; Strecker, *Judenchristentum*, 187-96.

[36] Simon is perhaps better known as a "Gnostic" or "Marcionite," terms not present in the *Recognitions* but commonly employed by modern scholars to describe Simon's beliefs.

to Jesus, the *Recognitions* also maintains that he and the other apostles
were sent out to preach the message of the True Prophet. It is significant
for our purposes that representation and delegation are implied in the
apostolic role. Chilton and Neusner make this point clearly: "in the
institution of the apostle or delegate, the *shaliaḥ*, Jesus broke new ground.
What had been a matter of occasional representation by a delegate ...
becomes in the practice of Jesus a programmatic method of extending what
he says and does in regard to the kingdom to a new constituency beyond
the range of his personal contact."[37] In other words, the apostles, who were
in the best position to have heard Jesus' words in the first place, were
called by their master to represent him and to transmit his message to
others, most of whom will never have the opportunity to see and hear Jesus
for themselves. The apostles' representative function is clear in Peter's
version of Jesus' commission to the apostles, given to Simon Magus in *Rec*
2.33.3-5. It is surely no coincidence that this account recalls Matthew
28.19-20 in its opening words:

*dominus noster mittens nos apostolos ad praedicandum praecepit nobis, ut doceamus
omnes gentes de his quae mandata sunt nobis. neque ergo dicere ea, ut ab ipso nobis
dicta sunt, possumus. non enim dicere, sed docere ea in mandatis habemus et ex ipsis
ostendere, quomodo unumquodque eorum veritate subnixum sit. neque rursus proprium
nobis aliquid dicere permissum est. sumus enim missi, et necessario qui missus est, illud
quod missus est nuntiat et voluntatem mittentis exponit.*

Our Lord, when he sent us apostles to preach, instructed us that we should teach all
nations about these things which have been entrusted to us. Therefore we cannot speak
those things as they were spoken to us by him. For we have a commission not to speak,
but to teach those things, and from them to show how each and every one of them is
resting upon truth. Nor, again, are we permitted to speak anything of our own. For we are
sent; and of necessity he who is sent reports that for which he has been sent, and sets
forth the will of the sender.

This passage is essential for understanding several of the rhetorical devices
that attach to the idea of Peter's apostleship. For the moment, however, I
want to continue focusing upon the idea that the apostles were *sent* by the
True Prophet. Peter tells Simon Magus that the apostles were sent to
preach, and to teach "all nations" the message entrusted to them. Note the
differentiation he makes between *dicere* and *docere*. Although the
overlapping semantic domains of these two words make it difficult to be
certain about the distinction being drawn here, we can make a reasonable
inference based on the broader context of the *Recognitions*' statements
about apostolic responsibilities.

According to Lewis and Short, *dicere* can be used in a rhetorical or
juridical sense to mean "pronounce, deliver, rehearse, speak," which

---

[37] Chilton and Neusner, *Types of Authority*, 41.

implies that this kind of language is a rehearsal or delivery of a fixed speech, such as those learned in rhetorical schools.[38] This definition makes sense in light of Peter's statement that the apostles cannot repeat Jesus' words exactly as they were given. The point of this seems to be that the apostles are not simply reciting Jesus' statements without first having understood them properly. The apostles' understanding and mastery of Jesus' words is implied in *docere*, which Lewis and Short translates as "teach, instruct, inform."[39] The apostles, then, have been entrusted with the task of teaching and explaining Jesus' message to others. They have not simply memorized his words, but in fact have received from Jesus an authoritative *understanding* and *interpretation* of his words.

In addition, Peter's statement tells us that a true apostle makes clear, unadorned statements about the True Prophet's words. He establishes the truth of the message, but cannot alter any part of that message to suit his own desires. The force of this language about *being sent*, then, is to emphasize that Peter's message is not his own – he has been entrusted with the words of the True Prophet, and it is from this commission that all of his preaching derives. At the same time that the language of *sending* is used to authorize the preaching of Peter specifically, it is also used to argue that believing in Peter's message is not merely a matter of fidelity to an individual – it is adherence to divine truth as manifested in Jesus himself.[40]

In *Rec* 2.33.6-8, Peter continues his discourse about what it means to be an apostle by saying the following:

nam si aliud dicam, quam praecepit mihi ille qui me misit, falsus ero apostolus, qui non illud dico quod missus sum dicere, sed quod mihi videtur. quod qui facit, utique se meliorem vult ostendere quam est ille a quo missus est, et est sine dubio praevaricator. si vero ea quae iussus est prosequatur eorumque adsertiones manifestissimas proferat, apostoli opus exequi videbitur.

For if I say anything other than what he who has sent me has taught me, I will be a false apostle, because I do not say that which I have been sent to say, but what seems good to me. He who does these things certainly wishes to show himself to be better than that one by whom he has been sent, and without doubt is an apostate. If, however, he proceeds with the things that he has been commanded, and brings forward most clear assertions of them, he will be regarded as accomplishing the work of an apostle.

Here Peter argues that to be considered a true apostle, one must be both taught by, and sent out by, Jesus. His first criterion recalls the *Recognitions'* emphasis on personal acquaintance with the True Prophet as a condition of discipleship, while the second qualification underscores that

---

[38] Lewis and Short, *A Latin Dictionary*, s.v. *dico*.

[39] Lewis and Short, *A Latin Dictionary*, s.v. *doceo*.

[40] I will return to this idea below, in the section entitled "Peter Preaches What Jesus Taught."

his authority comes not just from companionship with Jesus, but also a direct commission from Jesus.

Rec 4.35.2-3 adds another criterion that is designed to exclude others from the ranks of those who possess prophetic knowledge. Peter admonishes: *sed neque propheta neque apostolus in hoc tempore speretur a vobis aliquis alius praeter nos. unus enim est verus propheta, cuius nos duodecim apostoli verba praedicamus. ipse est annus domini acceptus, nos apostolos habens duodecim menses* ("But neither a prophet nor an apostle [nor] anyone other than us should be expected by you at this time. For there is one True Prophet, whose words we twelve apostles preach; for he is the accepted year of the Lord, having us apostles as his twelve months"). According to the narrative of the *Recognitions*, at the time Peter preaches the number of the True Prophet's messengers is complete and does not need to be increased. It is unclear if such an increase is considered to be impossible, unnecessary, or unwelcome, but in any case the number twelve denotes completeness. This implies that anyone who attempts to insinuate himself into this circle of authorized messengers would be breaking ranks, so to speak: such harmony with the cosmos is divinely intended and not to be trifled with.[41]

Indeed, it is interesting that the number of twelve "apostles" is maintained constantly, almost like a thermostat. In *Rec* 1.60.5 the reader encounters the common idea that Judas was replaced by *Barnabas qui et Mathias* ("Barnabas, who [is] also Matthias") in order to make the twelve complete once more. There is a more unusual occurrence of the motif of twelve apostles in *Rec* 3.68.1, where the persons listed are not the followers of Jesus, but a group of twelve gathered around Peter: Zacchaeus and Sophonias, Joseph and Michaeus, Eleazar and Phineas, Lazarus and Eliseus, Clement and Nicodemus, Niceta and Aquila. When Peter decides to keep four of these individuals beside him, he replaces them with four others *expleri ... duodecim numerum* ("to complete ... the number of twelve"; *Rec* 3.68.6). That Peter has twelve followers, just as Jesus had twelve apostles, is obviously a narrative fiction designed to create a parallel between Jesus and Peter. Jesus entrusted his immediate followers with prophetic knowledge, and these twelve are commissioned to transmit Jesus' teachings without modification. Similarly, Peter – as one of the apostles sent out to teach what Jesus said – hands down the traditions of prophetic knowledge to his own twelve followers.

Peter and his band of twelve men, then, are officially commissioned to preach "the word of Christ." *Rec* 4.36.1 tells the reader that these

---

[41] There is of course a great deal of literature on the concept of the apostle, and the Twelve more specifically. A helpful list of important older works is listed in Hennecke-Schneemelcher, *New Testament Apocrypha* II.5.

messengers *and no others* must be received: *causae autem quibus maculetur istud indumentum hae sunt: si quis recedat a patre et conditore omnium deo, alium recipiens doctorem praeter Christum, qui est solus fidelis ac verus propheta quique nos duodecim apostolos misit ad praedicandum verbum ...* ("But these are the ways in which this garment[42] may be stained: If anyone withdraws from God the father and creator of all, receiving another teacher besides Christ, who alone is the faithful and True Prophet, and who has sent us twelve apostles to preach the word ...."). According to this passage, an individual forfeits her entrance into the kingdom by "receiving another teacher besides Christ," which can only be understood to mean *receiving another apostle who has not been sent and authorized by Christ.* In other words, anyone who receives an apostle whose message differs from Peter's does so at the risk of eternal damnation (cf. *Hom* 17.19.4). It is striking that the penalty for this reception of false teachers is presented in such stark terms. It is also remarkable that receiving another (false) apostle is equated – at least in terms of penalty or outcome – with murder and eating at the table of demons, the latter of which is a heinous crime according to the *Recognitions.*[43]

The point, ultimately, of the reiterated vocabulary of *sending* and *being sent* is to underscore the exclusive connection that exists between the True Prophet and the limited number of messengers authorized to transmit his message. It denotes a close relationship between Jesus and his followers, and suggests that the True Prophet has entrusted these apostles with his prophetic knowledge. Moreover, the language of *sending* is used to close the ranks of those who have knowledge of the truth and are authorized to impart it to others. No one who is not counted among these approved messengers can claim to have access to prophetic truth.

---

[42] That is, the *indumenta nuptialia* ("wedding garments") of baptism (*Rec* 4.35.5), which recall the parable of the marriage feast in Matt 4.10 and Luke 4.8.

[43] Rejection of sacrifices is a common theme mentioned by ancient authors with regard to Jewish Christianity: Epiphanius (*Pan.* 19.3.6, 30.16.5, 30.16.7), Jerome (*Epist.* 112.13; *in Hier.* 3, 14-16), Augustine (*Epist.* 116.16.1), Rufinus (*Expos. Symb.* 37). Naomi Janowitz observes that this opposition to animal sacrifice, which was not limited to Jewish Christianity or indeed any religious tradition, "was in full swing by the first century B.C.E." She goes on to cite the judgment of Henry Chadwick that "the Late Antique trope that daimons feed on sacrifices was 'universal'"; authors such as Porphyry (*Abst.* 2.42), Origen (*Cels.* 8.62), and Philo (*On the Decalogue* 74), for example, share this view. Naomi Janowitz, *Icons of Power: Ritual Practices in Late Antiquity* (Magic in History series; University Park, PA: Pennsylvania State University Press, 2002) 98-99, citing Chadwick, *Origen: Contra Celsum*, 146 n. 1.

Clement Was a Faithful and Constant Disciple of Peter

In the previous section, I noted briefly that the *Recognitions* makes a connection between Jesus' initial twelve apostles and Peter's twelve faithful followers and companions. The narrative nowhere mentions that Jesus himself commissioned the second group of apostles, but they – like the initial twelve – are said to be "sent by Christ." As a result, the *Recognitions* must have in mind some other method by which Jesus' initial charge to his apostles was extended to Peter's followers. When one looks for clues in the *Recognitions* about why Peter's followers are empowered to preach in the same way as Peter, one begins to notice a parallel in the text's characterization of Peter and Clement. Just as the *Recognitions* places a fair amount of emphasis on Peter's personal acquaintance with the True Prophet, it works hard to demonstrate that Clement was an inseparable companion to Peter.[44]

Even before Clement has met Peter, Barnabas is so impressed with Clement that he tells Peter all about him. Barnabas says to Clement in *Rec* 1.12.6-7, *Hic est, inquit, Petrus, quem tibi maximum esse in dei sapientia dicebam cuique de te rursus sine cessatione locatus sum. ingredere igitur tamquam bene ei cognitus* ("This is Peter, who I told you is the greatest in the wisdom of God, and to whom again I have spoken constantly of you. Therefore enter as one well known to him"). Peter "knows" and approves of Clement even before they meet, making it seem as though their personal acquaintance lasted longer than the time they were together.[45]

Peter quickly invites Clement to be present at all his discourses, which causes the reader to imagine Clement alongside Peter, traveling with him from the beginning of their acquaintance onward. Peter is convinced that Clement's faith is certain – even though Clement has not yet been baptized – and will not be shaken if Peter should falter in the upcoming debates: *disputans, etiam si forte inferior visus fuero, non verebor, ne forte tu de his, quae tibi a me sunt tradita, in dubium venias, quia etiamsi ego visus fuero superari, non tamen idcirco ea, quae nobis verus propheta tradidit, infirma videbuntur* ("when I dispute, even if by chance I shall seem to have

---

[44] There has been a fair amount of scholarly discussion about the Pseudo-Clementines' motives for choosing Clement as Peter's successor, but the most obvious and compelling rationale must have been Clement's role as the first bishop of Rome ordained by Peter. On this see Jones, "Clement of Rome and the *Pseudo-Clementines*," 154-55.

[45] Stanley Jones has observed that Clement's conversion to Christianity in Rome during Jesus' lifetime (*Rec* 1.7.3 par. *Hom* 1.7.2) serves an important purpose in this regard: it makes "the star witness to [the Pseudo-Clementines'] variety of Christianity, Clement, the constant companion of Peter from the earliest days of his mission onwards." Jones, "Clement of Rome and the *Pseudo-Clementines*," 151.

been inferior, I shall not be afraid that you are falling into doubt about these things which were passed on to you by me, because even if I shall seem to be overcome, yet for that reason, those things which the True Prophet has transmitted to us shall not seem weak"; *Rec* 1.17.6).

In the following chapter (*Rec* 1.18.2) Clement reinforces Peter's assessment of his unshakable faith: *verumtamen de me in tantum debes esse securus, quod de his quae didici abs te, in dubium venire non possim, ut si tu ipse velis aliquando fidem meam a vero propheta transferre, omnino non possis; ita pleno spiritu hausi, quae tradidisti* ("Nevertheless, you should be secure about me to such a degree, that I cannot fall into doubt about the things that I have learned from you; so that if you yourself should ever wish to turn my faith away from the True Prophet, you absolutely could not, because I have drunk in the things which you have taught with a full spirit"). Clement takes in every word of Peter's like a sponge,[46] and he is present for everything Peter says. His constant presence beside Peter ensures that he has not missed anything Peter says and does.

Clement, then, is Peter's regular companion. In addition, Clement and the other members of the group are eager to listen to Peter night and day. They are not mere hangers-on, but instead possess an insatiable hunger to hear Peter's message. *Rec* 3.31.1 says that Peter, who rises before dawn, awakens to find Clement and the others already waiting for him to teach them. In fact, they would prefer to lose sleep rather than miss even a moment of Peter's words – since he habitually wakes up in the middle of the night, they do too (*Rec* 2.2.5; 3.32.2)![47] Peter's followers may seem like sycophants to readers of the *Recognitions*, but their toadying serves an important purpose: they never miss a word he says.

All of Peter's close companions share Clement's eagerness to learn, but only Clement is allowed to remain with Peter at all times. This ensures that Clement is present to hear Peter's every word, in addition to demonstrating that Peter – while showing no favoritism – believes Clement ought to have a special place next to him, *mecum semper esse, quia ex gentibus veniens audiendi verbi grande desiderium gerit* ("always with me, because coming from the Gentiles, he has a great desire to hear the word"; *Rec* 3.68.5; cf. *Hom* 12.4.1).

Peter's insistence on keeping Clement beside him suggests that he has chosen Clement for a reason. But what is it? The answer to this question

---

[46] For more on Clement's capacity for memorization, see the section "Faithful Memory" below.

[47] Cf. *Hom* 20.1.1; 20.12.1. These episodes may be compared to an incident recounted in Plato's *Protagoras*. *Prt.* 310b describes Hippocrates barging in on the sleeping Socrates at dawn, because he is so excited at the prospect of joining Protagoras' group of students.

appears in *Rec* 1.17.2, where Clement, who is the narrator of the *Recognitions*, tells James the addressee that *unde et iubente ipso, ea quae ad me locutus est, in ordinem redigens, librum de vero propheta conscripsi eumque de Caesarea ad te, ipso iubente, transmisi* ("by [Peter's] command, bringing back into order the things he has said to me, I composed a book about the True Prophet, and sent it from Caesarea to you by his command"). According to Clement, Peter has assigned Clement to write an account of his preaching about the True Prophet, so that it can be sent to James. Because he was always with Peter, Clement was able to become familiar with Peter and his message in a very short period of time. In fact, he understood Peter's preaching so completely and accurately that he was asked to carry out the important task of preserving such prophetic knowledge for future generations. Since the *Recognitions* itself purports to be an account of Peter's preaching composed by Clement, the accuracy and completeness of Clement's record is of paramount importance for the text's claim to authenticity.

A close look at the text's emphasis on the master-disciple relationships between Jesus, Peter and Clement tells us something important about the truth-claims of the *Recognitions*: our text makes personal acquaintance the cornerstone of what it means to be an authorized messenger of the True Prophet's word, and an indispensable criterion for the possession of prophetic knowledge. Peter, as Jesus' disciple, came *rebus divinis aeternisque cognoscere* ("to know divine and eternal things"; *Rec* 1.16.2) and was sent out by Jesus to transmit this knowledge to others. Just as he required a master for this instruction, Clement also needed to learn the truth – as written in the *Recognitions* – from his own teacher. Clement, like Peter, was beside his master throughout his travels and discourses, and as a result the reader is assured that Clement missed nothing of what Peter had to say. The strategy of Personal Companionship, in light of this information, can be said to establish a set of historical connections between the three major characters of the narrative (the True Prophet, Peter, and Clement). These connections are neither incidental nor insignificant: they convey a sense that both the messenger and his message of prophetic knowledge have been approved by the True Prophet himself.

Faithful Memory

If Peter's historical acquaintance with Jesus made him an eyewitness and firsthand observer of Jesus' words, and his travels with Clement ensured that Clement received a thorough transmission of Jesus' message, this would certainly go a long way toward excluding others from the small circle of authorized messengers. A critic might, however, still be able to accuse these apostles of forgetting what they'd heard from Jesus as the years passed. An ancient reader could also argue that they made deliberate alterations to the original message, with the result that the apostles did not accurately pass on what they'd heard directly from Jesus. As a result of such potential concerns, the *Recognitions* employs a second argument I've labeled Faithful Memory.

This line of reasoning is designed to show that, once Peter received Jesus' message directly, he retained it fully and transmitted it carefully (right down to the reader of the *Recognitions*). According to this argument, Peter and Clement have remarkable capacities for memorization. Not only are they naturally talented in this regard, but they also go to great lengths to meditate on the words of Jesus and recite them as often as possible. This is evidence of their piety as well as their trustworthiness as messengers of prophetic knowledge. Moreover, nothing is added to or subtracted from Jesus' words. The reader of the Pseudo-Clementine *Recognitions* receives Jesus' words directly, with as few alterations as possible.

Clement Has a Good Memory

In *Rec* 1.26.1-2, Peter tells Clement that he has confidence in the latter's ability to remember his message of prophetic truth. Clement's good memory is critically important, because there is a great deal at stake in remembering the "words of salvation" contained in Peter's version of the True Prophet's message:

Magnifice, inquit, delector, o Clemens, quod tam tuto cordi verba committam; memorem namque esse eorum quae dicuntur, indicium est in promptu habere operum fidem: cui vero malus daemon salutis verba furatur et de memoria rapit, etiam si velit salvari non poterit; perdidit enim viam, qua pervenitur ad vitam.

I am magnificently delighted, O Clement, that I entrust [my] words to such a secure heart; for in fact to be mindful of the things that are spoken is evidence of having ready the faith of works. But he from whom the evil demon steals the words of salvation and snatches [them] from memory, cannot be saved, even if he wishes; for he has lost the way by which life is reached.

Forgetfulness, as this passage suggests, is not an indication of mere absentmindedness. Instead, it reflects something far more insidious – a loss of "the way by which life is reached," due to a kind of demonic theft. Salvation is impossible to attain without a grasp of the prophetic knowledge given by Jesus to Peter. For this reason, it would be catastrophic for Clement to forget any of the things Peter had passed on to him. At the same time it emphasizes the dreadful consequences of poor memory, however, the passage above also shows that Clement is in no danger of forgetting anything spoken by Peter. Clement's remarkable capacity for memorization is underscored further in *Rec* 1.25.10, where Clement tells Peter that he is able to recite Peter's entire account of world history: *et si placet, possum memoriter universa retexere* ("and if you please, I can repeat the whole from memory"). Clement even goes so far as to say that Peter's account of eternity is impossible to forget: *Nihil, inquam, o Petre, aliquando retinebo, si hoc omittere aut oblivisci potuero* ("O Peter, I will not ever remember anything, if I can let go of or forget this"; *Rec* 1.22.6; cf. *Hom* 1.21.1-2).

It is not simply that Clement has retained Peter's words through rote memorization. In fact, Clement has so internalized what Peter preaches that he is able to give Peter a full accounting in his own words: *et omnium paene quae exposuisti, sensum integrum servo, etiamsi verba non omnia, quia tamquam vernacula animae meae et ingenita effecta sunt, quae dixisti* ("and of almost all things that you have explained, I retain the complete meaning, although not all the words; because the things that you have said have been made native to my soul, so to speak, and inborn"; *Rec* 1.23.3). This sounds a bit like *Rec* 2.33.3-5, where Peter intimated that the apostles were not sent out to recite Jesus' words as though they were a fixed canon of ready-made speeches; instead, his close followers were charged with transmitting and explaining Jesus' message in their own words. Like the apostles before him, Clement has thoroughly understood and memorized the meaning of the prophetic knowledge entrusted to him. He has an excellent memory partly because of an innate ability to remember, and partly because of his profound grasp of the subject matter. His memory is not of a superficial kind, but reflects his deep understanding and appreciation of what he has been asked to recall.

Peter and Clement Recite and Meditate on the True Prophet's Words

Up to this point, the discussion has centered on Clement's inborn capacity for memorization of prophetic truth. Memory, however, is more than just a natural ability in the context of the *Recognitions*. A good memory may be an innate talent, but above all it is a skill that must be cultivated through practice and repetition. According to *Rec* 2.1.6, Peter practices his memorization skills, often when his desire for Jesus' words wakes him up at night: *in consuetudine habui verba domini mei, quae ab ipso audieram, revocare ad memoriam, et pro ipsorum desiderio suscitari animis meis et cogitationibus imperavi, ut evigilans ad ea et singula quaeque recolens ac retexens possim memoriter retinere* ("I have been in the habit of recalling to memory the words of my Lord, which I had heard from him; and because of [my] longing for them, I command my mind and my thoughts to be awakened, so that, awaking to them, and recalling and repeating them one by one, I may be able to preserve them accurately"). This passage tells us several important pieces of information. First, Peter presents himself as one who longs incessantly for the teachings of his master. He has even trained himself to forgo sleep in order to recite and meditate on Jesus' words. Like his own followers, he finds this preferable to missing a moment of reflection on such teachings. Second, Peter is recalling and meditating on words that he has heard firsthand from his master. As we have already seen, the *Recognitions* insists on this point because it is essential in establishing the validity of the prophetic traditions passed down by Peter. Third, Peter is methodical when he meditates on Jesus' words. This tells us that his habit is not a casual, haphazard occurrence, but a thoughtfully developed practice undertaken for two specific purposes: edification and memorization.

Peter not only takes it upon himself to practice this kind of recitation and meditation, but also uses this technique with others as a pedagogical device. He often repeats teachings he has already given his followers, in order to help them remember: *volo tibi rursus ea quae dicta sunt breviter iterare, ut magis tibi ad memoriam revocentur* ("I wish to repeat briefly to you again the things which have been spoken, so that they may be more completely applied to your memory"; *Rec* 1.22.4). He also asks his disciples to recite such teachings for him, and rejoices when their recollection is good: *dic quae retines ex his, quae ... a nobis dicta sunt* ("Tell [me] what you retain from these things which were spoken by us"; *Rec* 1.23.2). Elsewhere he recites the True Prophet's teachings in tandem with his followers: *propter quod eo magis repetamus quae dicta sunt, et confirmemus ea in corde tuo ... breviter ergo tibi haec eadem firmioris causa memoriae retexemus* ("On account of this, let us all the more repeat what has been said, and let us confirm these things in your heart... therefore we shall repeat these same things briefly to you, for the sake of more faithful memory"; *Rec* 1.26.3, 5).

I would like to suggest that we think of the protagonists' habit of memorization and recitation in the light of another custom that is familiar to students of ancient philosophy: the practice of creating ὑπομνήματα, or "memoranda."[48] Pierre Hadot characterizes ὑπομνήματα as "notes written on a daily basis for the author's own personal use,"[49] as opposed to "artfully (or even deceitfully) well-composed and well-edited pieces of writing."[50] This tells us that ὑπομνήματα were not intended for public consumption. But what exactly does it mean to say they were written for

---

[48] I am grateful to Annewies van den Hoek for pointing me toward this idea in her comments on an earlier version of this chapter.

[49] Hadot, *Philosophy as a Way of Life*, 179.

[50] Annewies van den Hoek, "Techniques of Quotation in Clement of Alexandria: A View of Ancient Literary Working Methods," *Vigiliae Christianae* 50 (1996) 225.

"personal use"? (After all, in modern parlance "notes" can mean everything from grocery lists to email messages.) Hadot gives another, more instructive definition that is better suited to our present purposes as he critiques Michel Foucault's examination of "the literary genre of *hypomnemata*, which one could translate as 'spiritual notebooks,' in which one writes down other people's thoughts, which may serve for the edification of the person writing them down."[51] The notes we're talking about, then, are reminders of edifying statements that have been made by other people.

Hadot believes that Foucault has misunderstood the purpose of ὑπομνήματα when he asserts that their function is to "capture what-has-already-been-said," or "to allow one to turn back towards the past."[52] On the contrary, argues Hadot, the writing of ὑπομνήματα depends on an understanding that things said in the past, often by the founders of a philosophical school, were in fact "that which reason itself has to say *to the present*."[53] Put differently, these notes are important not just as records of what was said by one's teachers in the past, but in fact as a method of actualizing the workings of reason – which are manifested in their words – in the present moment.

We should be careful in applying this notion of ὑπομνήματα to the *Recognitions*, since such "notes" intersect with the protagonists' memorization strategies in different ways. Peter, according to our text, does not seem to have made any such written notes about the True Prophet's teaching at all. Peter retains everything he has learned from Jesus in his memory, rather than in writing. However, Clement – as the putative author of the *Recognitions* – has been commanded by Peter not only to commit Jesus' words to memory as he himself as done, but also to keep a written record of everything that the apostle says and does (*Rec* 3.74.4). Although it may not be difficult to see how Clement's written account could parallel the creation and use of ὑπομνήματα, Peter's memorization techniques apparently involve no writing at all.

How, then, might these ὑπομνήματα map on to Peter's practice of reciting and meditating on Jesus' words? And – more to the point – does the use of this notion tell us anything that we could not have discovered by reading the text all by itself? I am convinced that this second question can be answered in the affirmative. We have already learned that, according to the *Recognitions*, Peter repeats and reflects on Jesus' words to enhance his own memory. This is an important point, since it reflects the text's interest

---

[51] Hadot, *Philosophy as a Way of Life*, 209.

[52] Hadot, *Philosophy as a Way of Life*, 209, quoting Michel Foucault, "L'écriture de soi," *Corps écrit* 5 (1983) 8.

[53] Hadot, *Philosophy as a Way of Life*, 210. Italics in original.

in affirming the authenticity and completeness of the prophetic traditions handed down by Peter. By categorizing Peter's memorization practices as ὑπομνήματα, we can add yet other layers to the meaning assigned by the *Recognitions* itself. Recall that ὑπομνήματα, in Hadot's interpretation, are intended to actualize the words of the original speaker in the present moment. If we read Peter's recitation of the True Prophet's words in this light, we can see something new: Peter, by enumerating Jesus' statements to himself and in the presence of others, is essentially making the words of the True Prophet *real* and *active* in those instances. In other words, the protagonists' intense focus upon Jesus' words can be understood not just as a focus on the past, but as a strategy to help them understand the present world through the eyes of the True Prophet. Their efforts at memorization and recitation work to create and sustain the presence of the True Prophet as an interpretive prism and a guide for daily living.[54]

In addition, if we accept Annewies van den Hoek's observation that ὑπομνήματα stand in direct contrast to "artfully (or even deceitfully) well-composed and well-edited pieces of writing,"[55] we discover something else by analyzing Peter's rehearsal of Jesus' words through this lens. Recall that Peter, as a true apostle, has been commissioned to preach the words of Jesus. Since his own preaching is based on a memorized list of Jesus' statements that resembles the form of ὑπομνήματα, his use of such memoranda as the foundation for his preaching reinforces the *Recognitions'* claim that Peter speaks straightforwardly and without dialectic artifice.

Our examination of Peter's and Clement's memorization strategies and the comments on Clement's naturally excellent memory serve to underscore a number of important points. First, because of their natural capacities Peter and especially Clement are incapable of forgetting even large quantities of information. Second, Peter and Clement clearly understand what it is they know by heart; their memorization is no substitute for understanding, but rather an aid to it. Third, Peter and Clement take special care to exercise their memories, meditating on and reciting Jesus' words whenever possible. This recitation not only improves their grasp of the message with which they are entrusted, but also works to shape their interpretation of the world through the eyes of the True Prophet himself. Thus far such strategies have been designed to show that these true apostles *lost* none of what Jesus taught, but there is one final method

---

[54] This understanding of the protagonists' efforts at memorization and recitation of the True Prophet's words suggests that von Campenhausen's disparaging estimation of the Pseudo-Clementine apostolate (cited above) is mistaken.

[55] van den Hoek, "Techniques of Quotation in Clement of Alexandria," 225.

used by the *Recognitions* to argue that Peter and Clement have *neither changed nor added anything* to Jesus' preaching.

Peter Preaches What Jesus Taught

At a number of points in the narrative, Peter states that his commission requires him to faithfully transmit the words of his master, speaking nothing except the message he has been commanded to preach. The most detailed example of this is in *Rec* 2.33.3-5, which has already been cited at length above. This passage is essentially a speech about what it means to be a true apostle, and contains two ideas that are crucial to the text's larger rhetorical aims. First, it claims that true apostles are not allowed to speak anything of their own; they can neither add to nor change any part of the original message. All true apostles are really just "playback machines" for Jesus: they recorded his teachings when they were with him, and all their subsequent preaching is an exact replica of these teachings, albeit in the words of the apostles themselves. They say nothing except what they have been taught by their master, because a "false apostle" is someone who adds anything – anything at all – to the message with which he has been entrusted. True apostles do not put forth their own teachings as though they were in accordance with God's will, but rather are bearers of a message whose content has been determined beforehand by their master.[56]

Peter's discourse in *Rec* 2.33.3-5 also contains a second idea which is important for the *Recognitions'* agenda: true apostles are commissioned to carry out the will of the one who sent them, rather than their own will. This language suggests that a true apostle, even if he found the message to be in conflict with his own desires, would nevertheless deliver his charge as he was instructed. As a result of these two notions, it is practically impossible to impugn the message of a true apostle, because such a message is of divine origin and contains none of the trappings of human derivation.

Similar claims appear at other places in the *Recognitions*. In *Rec* 2.34.6, for example, Peter states that *nos enim apostoli illius qui nos misit, verba exponere missi sumus et adfirmare sententias, proprium vero dicere aliquid non habemus in mandatis, sed verborum illius, ut dixi, aperire veritatem* ("we apostles are sent to explain the words and confirm the views of him who has sent us; but we do not have a commission to say anything of our own, but to demonstrate the truth of his words, as I have said").[57] Elsewhere, in *Rec* 3.41.6, Peter claims to be unable to disobey the

---

[56] This strategy requires that the content of the apostles' preaching – but *not its form* – be identical to that put forward by Jesus. This is because the *Recognitions* makes a point of stating that the apostles explain Jesus' teachings in their own words, as we have already seen.

[57] Cf. *Hom* 1.10.5-6, where Barnabas speaks of a similar apostolic commission.

instructions of the True Prophet. In *Rec* 2.28.1, Peter states that *Magister, inquit, noster, qui erat verus propheta et sui in omnibus memor, neque sibi contraria locutus est neque nobis ab his quae ipse gerebat diversa mandavit* ("Our master, who was the True Prophet, and mindful of himself in every respect, neither spoke things contrary to himself nor commanded us [to do] things different from what he himself did"). In other words, Jesus' commission to the apostles was directly in line with his own life and teachings. Because the apostles never do anything outside of what they have been instructed to do, one must conclude that they are the closest possible approximation to the presence of Jesus that can be had. This is particularly interesting in light of Manichaean traditions which argue that "the eye-witnesses falsified Jesus' words and doctrine and that only some *electi* in later generations, among whom is Mani in the first place, had the right understanding of Jesus' preaching."[58]

In *Rec* 8.37.3, Peter ensures that his own followers receive the same commission that he obtained from Jesus himself: *nec aliquid proprium et quod vobis non est traditum proloquamini, etiamsi vobis verisimile videatur, sed ea, ut dixi, quae ipse a vero propheta suscepta vobis tradidi, prosequimini* ("You should not say anything which is your own, and which has not been handed down to you, even if it may seem to you to be true; but proceed with those things, as I have said, which having been received from the True Prophet, I myself have passed on to you"). Peter's charge to his hearers means that just as Peter says and does only those things entrusted to him by the True Prophet, so too his own followers can be trusted as reliable delegates of Jesus. He reiterates this point toward the end of the narrative, in *Rec* 10.14.4: *hoc tamen unum profitemur ea nos scire, quae a vero propheta didicimus; ea autem a vero propheta nobis esse tradita, quae sufficere humanae scientiae iudicavit* ("Yet we profess only this: that we know those things which we have learned from the True Prophet; and that those things have been handed down to us by the True Prophet, which he judged to be sufficient for human knowledge"). Since Peter is here referring to his companions Clement, Niceta, and Aquila, it is clear that he regards his immediate followers as obeying the same commission from Jesus himself. Peter *and* his companions are reliable spokesmen for Jesus and the prophetic knowledge he has imparted to them.

---

[58] H. J. W. Drijvers, "Facts and Problems in Early Syriac-Speaking Christianity," *Second Century* 2 (1982) 164. On this aspect of Manichaean literature see A. Böhlig, "Christliche Wurzeln im Manichäismus," in idem, *Mysterion und Wahrheit: Gesammelte Beiträge zur spätantiken Religionsgeschichte* (Leiden: Brill, 1968) 202-21. Chapter 5 of the present work deals with possible historical referents of the *Recognitions'* polemical agenda.

I believe that Peter's claim to speak for Jesus, using only the statements made by Jesus, is an example of what Bourdieu has termed the *oracle effect*. In speaking about priestly claims to represent God, he argues that "it is in abolishing himself completely in favour of God or the People that the priest turns himself into God or the People."[59] Put another way, Peter's claim to be nothing more than Jesus' spokesperson – his contention that his words come *only* from Jesus – effectively makes him equivalent to Jesus himself. Although this strategy makes it seem as if Peter is casting off any claims to personal importance, in reality this claim makes him a quintessentially significant individual, because agreement with Peter's message becomes the sole point of differentiation between *true* and *false apostleship*. Since Peter is a true apostle, any other true apostle of Jesus would necessarily preach the same message as that offered by Peter. If Peter's preaching comes directly from Jesus with no alteration or mediation, then anyone whose words differ from those taught by Peter – such as Simon's "unauthorized version" of spiritual matters – must necessarily be a false apostle. As Bourdieu says of religious experts like ministers, "If I am an incarnation of the collective, of the group, and if this group is the group to which you belong, which defines you, which gives you an identity, which means you are *really* a teacher, *really* a Protestant, *really* a Catholic, etc., you *really* have no choice but to obey."[60] If we translate this into the language of the *Recognitions*, it means that if Peter and the apostles are Jesus' legitimate representatives, those who disagree with them (and persist in preaching ideas contrary to theirs) are not *really* apostles or followers of Jesus.

Moreover, since Jesus' message is the prophetic knowledge that provides certainty about "divine and human things," and since Peter has unique purchase on the content of that message, no one whose information differs from Peter's can claim to have certain knowledge. This point is the linchpin of the *Recognitions'* entire epistemological agenda. Secure knowledge is *impossible* for those without access to Jesus and the prophetic truth he imparts, and hence *impossible* for those who disagree with the protagonists' understanding of God, the world, and human events. This is ultimately the reason why I believe that our text has targeted philosophers and astrologers alongside rival apostolic claimants: they all purport to have certain knowledge about divine and human things, and their epistemic assertions immediately place them in conversation with the text's claims about Peter and the knowledge he has passed down to others.

---

[59] Bourdieu, *Language and Symbolic Power*, 211.
[60] Bourdieu, *Language and Symbolic Power*, 212.

Everything in its Right Place

The third and final strategy used by the *Recognitions* to underscore Peter's command of prophetic truth centers on the idea of *order*. Our text has a pronounced interest in the organization of divine knowledge, particularly as it is transmitted by teachers to their disciples. This orderliness is necessary for a correct understanding of divine truth, and only the teacher who passes his teachings directly to his students can provide such order. Proper understanding, in turn – together with the actions that result from it – is the key to salvation. The following section discusses the *Recognitions'* concern for the proper arrangement of divine knowledge, as well as the correct order of Peter's teaching of that knowledge.

Divine Knowledge Has a Proper Order

In *Rec* 3.34.2-3 Peter speaks of the acquisition of divine knowledge as a quest. According to this passage, which in its larger context suggests that a guide or teacher is always necessary, an individual's steps on the "way of knowledge" must begin in the proper place:

et ideo in primis ordo servandus est, si tamen hoc proposito quaeramus, ut possimus quod quaerimus invenire. etenim qui rectum initium viae acceperit, etiam secundum locum consequenter advertet et ex secundo tertium facilius inveniet; et quanto ultra processerit, tanto magis ei via agnitionis apertior fiet, usquequo ad ipsam quo tendit et desiderat urbem perveniat veritatis.

And therefore order should be observed above all, at least if we seek for this purpose, that we should be able to find what we seek. For he who has taken the correct entrance of the road consequently will turn to the second place, and from the second will more easily find the third; and the further he will have proceeded, the more the way of knowledge will become open to him, all the way until he arrives at that city of truth which he travels to and longs for.

Here Peter is saying that it is not enough to search for knowledge. (After all, this is precisely the kind of quest undertaken by philosophers and astrologers, and neither group has been able to find the kind of certain knowledge they were seeking.) The starting point of one's quest is critically important for a successful outcome; if one begins the search for knowledge in the wrong place, one is likely to be led down the wrong path altogether.

To understand what Peter is talking about, let's imagine being on a scavenger hunt at Harvard University where one receives a set of instructions, each part of which only works in relation to the other. If the intended starting point is Andover-Harvard Library, let's say, and the next instructions read "walk fifty paces to the south and enter the building on your right," anyone who started at Widener Library would be hopelessly out of the game even before it began! The same idea seems to be at work in the *Recognitions'* conception of the quest for the "city of truth."[61] If Peter had tried to find this city of truth without beginning his search in the right place, he would have ended up somewhere else entirely. Although it is not stated explicitly in this context, it seems likely that "enter[ing] rightly upon the road" speaks to the importance of seeking the True Prophet at the beginning of one's quest for knowledge. In any case, it is apparent that the quest for true knowledge necessarily entails observing proper order.

The meaning of this idea becomes a bit clearer in *Rec* 3.36.1, where Peter says, *Si quidem per ordinem et consequenter audiat, potest scire quod verum est* ("if indeed one hears in an orderly and suitable manner, he can know what is true"). In other words, divine knowledge not only requires a proper starting-point, but also demands a specific method of acquisition. In order for the message of truth to be recognized by its hearers, it must be presented in the correct arrangement. A short while later in *Rec* 3.36.4, Peter makes a similar statement: *Qui audierint per ordinem sermonem veritatis, contradicere omnino non possunt, sed sciunt verum esse quod dicitur, si tamen libenter etiam vitae instituta suscipiant* ("Those who hear an orderly statement of the truth certainly cannot contradict it, but know that what is spoken is true, if in the same way they also willingly undertake the regulations of life"). This underscores Peter's contention that the truth, if it is to be understood as such, must be unfolded in the proper order. When it is communicated in an orderly way, it is impossible to contradict. When taken together, these statements reveal that there is a proper order intrinsic to prophetic truth. Hence the strict arrangement observed by Peter in the *Recognitions* is not peculiar to his teaching, but instead is necessitated by the message of the True Prophet. Should this order be neglected or confused, someone on the path toward knowledge would be delayed at best and, at worst, *extra vitae ianuas remanebit* ("he shall remain outside the gates of life"; *Rec* 3.34.4).[62]

Peter and his Followers Teach in Proper Order

Because the stakes are so high and the need for proper order so great, Peter in the *Recognitions* takes great care to teach his followers the message of the True Prophet in the right sequence. As he says in *Rec* 3.51.5, *necesse est enim ut sermo doctrinae ab initio per ordinem currens et singulis quibusque quaestionibus obvians cuncta aperiat et cuncta dissolvat et perveniat* ("For it is necessary that the discussion of teaching, moving

---

[61] I understand the "city of truth" to mean the possession of true (prophetic) knowledge which, when combined with the practice of good deeds, leads to salvation.

[62] Cf. *Hom* 3.14.2, where disorderly prediction is mentioned as a characteristic of false prophecy.

along in order from the beginning, and meeting each individual question, should explain all things, and answer and arrive at all things"). Peter goes on to say that this kind of discourse should allow its hearers to exhaust every question that arises for them, and at various points he is portrayed as patiently answering the questions of those around him.[63] In those cases, however, he is careful that such questions do not interfere with the sequence he intends. For example, he occasionally tells someone to hold his question because it will be answered shortly, or provides a brief response to a question while stating that a full answer will be given at a more appropriate time.

One example of Peter's concern for order is to be found in his repetition. Recall that Peter rehearses parts of Jesus' teaching with his followers, so that they might better remember what has been discussed. In addition to this, Peter consistently repeats and reworks his message to present it in proper order to Clement and his other followers. Because of Simon's "contentiousness" and "unskillfulness," Peter is generally unable to control the sequence of their disputes. As a result, he is concerned that his followers (who were present for the debates) have not heard a clear and complete presentation of the doctrines in question. His solution to the problem is this: *volo vobis ea tantum quae hesterno sparsim dicta sunt, repetens diligentius et cum suo ordine explicare* ("I wish to repeat to you more carefully, and to explain in their order, the things that were spoken here and there just yesterday"; *Rec* 3.32.4; cf. *Hom* 2.41.4). In this case, Peter wishes his hearers not only to remember but also to fully understand the message he preaches. And for him this full understanding can only be achieved when the message is presented in its correct arrangement. He says this explicitly in *Rec* 3.34.1:

totius doctrinae disciplina habet certum ordinem, et sunt quaedam quae prima tradenda sunt, alia vero quae secundo in loco, et alia tertio, et sic singula quaeque per ordinem, quae utique si per consequentiam tradantur manifesta fiunt, extra ordinem vero si proferantur etiam contra rationem dicta videbuntur.

The teaching of all science has a specific order, and there are certain things which should be taught first, but there are others which are in the second place, and others in the third, and in this way all are in order; and at least if they are taught in sequence, they become clear, but if they are mentioned out of order, they certainly will seem to be spoken against reason.

---

[63] This recalls the characterization of philosophical education by Pierre Hadot, which was mentioned earlier in this chapter: "True education is always oral because only the spoken word makes dialogue possible, that is, it makes it possible for the disciple to discover the truth himself amid the interplay of questions and answers and also for the master to adapt his teaching to the needs of the disciple." Hadot, *Philosophy as a Way of Life*, 62.

Peter wants his teaching to sound reasonable, and he wants to be clearly
understood by his hearers; both of these goals require that he explain the
tenets of his message in strict order.

The organization of Peter's preaching and teaching is underscored by
the narrative's repeated suggestion that Simon is disorderly (*Rec* 3.16.7; cf.
Hom 3.41.2; 16.1.3; 16.3.2). This juxtaposition of Peter's care for order
with Simon's disorderliness is significant because it establishes Peter as a
more authoritative teacher than Simon. The connection between order and
authority is confirmed by *Rec* 3.18.2, where Peter asserts his authority over
Simon using this vocabulary of order: *habeo quod te prius doceam, ut per
consequentiam et ordinem doctrinae veniens, ex te ipso intellegas quid sit
malum* ("I must first teach you something, so that when you attain [it] by
consequence and the order of teaching, you may understand for yourself
what evil is"). Simon, whose intellectual jousting with Peter is disruptive
of the established order, needs to learn not only correct teaching, but also
proper order, from Peter.[64] Elsewhere, Peter states that Simon is a traveler
in a foreign country who needs the help of the native – in this case Peter
himself, of course – for guidance in seeking the *via veritatis* ("way of
truth"; *Rec* 3.34.4).[65] Peter's grasp of the proper order in which his
message should be taught functions much like a roadmap, which is
designed to lead people to knowledge of prophetic truth. Only someone
with access to this internal map can be a guide on this "way of truth."

Because Peter does know the order in which prophetic knowledge
should be revealed, he is able to pass this on to his followers. Consider
Clement's estimation of the sequence of Peter's teaching in *Rec* 1.23.5-6:
*iam nunc quae dicta sunt in memoriam revocabo; in quo me plurimum
iuvat ordo disputationis tuae. etenim quia consequenter directa sunt et
librate ordinata, quae dicis, idcirco et facile ad memoriam ordinis sui
lineis revocantur* ("I shall now recollect the things which were spoken, a
matter in which the order of your argument helps me very much; for

---

[64] Of course, Simon is not the type to let such an affront to his authority go
unchallenged. In *Rec* 3.39.3 he tells Peter that although he has relentlessly bragged about
his command of proper order, his own teaching is out of order.

[65] These ideas might fruitfully be explained with reference to recent scholarship that
uses notions of geography and mental mapping to analyze late antique texts; see e.g.
Loveday Alexander, "Mapping Early Christianity: Acts and the Shape of Early Church
History," *Interpretation* 57 (2003) 163-75; Judith Perkins, "Social Geography in the
Apocryphal Acts of the Apostles," in *Space in the Ancient Novel*, ed. Michael Paschalis
and Stavros Frangoulidis (Ancient Narrative Supplementum 1; Groningen: Barkhuis,
2002) 118-31; and Simon Goldhill, ed., *Being Greek under Rome: Cultural Identity, the
Second Sophistic and the Development of Empire* (Cambridge: Cambridge University
Press, 2001). The text's claims about Peter's native knowledge of the *via veritatis* use his
experiences rhetorically to authorize his arguments against Simon.

because the things that you say have been arranged logically, and deliberately ordered, for that reason they are easily recollected by the lines of their order"). Here Clement affirms that Peter teaches the contents of prophetic knowledge in an orderly fashion, so that each part of the discussion follows logically after what has gone before.

Clement's statement is important not only as a verification of Peter's claims about orderly narration, but also for two other reasons as well: Peter's systematic account ensures that his hearers are better able to understand and memorize what he has said, and it also means that his followers are able to replicate this same sequence when they transmit the prophetic message they have received from Peter to others. Clement in particular possesses a natural talent for reproducing the kind of orderly account given by Peter. After he gives a particularly lengthy recitation of Peter's version of world history, in *Rec* 1.25.2 Clement tells Peter that *Narrandi ordinem et lucidius quae res expetit proferendi eruditio nobis contulit liberalis* ("liberal instruction has given us the order of narrating and mentioning clearly the things which the circumstance requires").[66] Clement, who has been charged with producing a written version of the message preached by Peter, is particularly adept at reproducing his master's sequential description and explanation of things. However, in *Rec* 4.4.4 Peter encourages not just Clement but *all* his immediate companions to master the art of giving an orderly account: *propter quod deprecor vos conservos et adiutores meos, ut discatis adtentius praedicandi ordinem ... ut possitis salvare animas hominum* ("Because on this I beg you, my fellow-servants and assistants, that you might learn carefully the order of preaching ... so that you may be able to save the souls of human beings"). Hence it is that Peter, who has an exquisite command of the proper order of divine truth, has passed this knowledge on to his own circle of followers.

Peter's orderly teaching of the truth, then, accomplishes several things for the *Recognitions*. First, it shows he understands that divine knowledge can only be grasped if approached in the correct order. Second, it asserts that he is a good teacher and preacher, because he takes great pains to unfold these divine truths to his listeners in the appropriate arrangement. Peter's orderly teaching, and the repetition of the message made necessary by his demand for orderly instruction, ensures that his listeners will not only remember but also fully comprehend his teaching of the divine wisdom. Third, Peter's grasp of the proper order of divine knowledge indicates that he fully understands the message entrusted to him. This further implies that his grasp of prophetic truth must derive from his

---

[66] Although Clement uses the first person plural here, it is unclear who (if anyone) else is implicated in his statement.

instruction by the True Prophet himself. Finally, Peter passes on his command of sequential narration to his followers. This is particularly important in the case of Clement, who is charged with providing a written account of Peter's preaching of prophetic knowledge and submitting it to James for his approval.

James as Authenticator of Prophetic Knowledge

Up to this point in Chapter 4, we have examined various strategies used by the *Recognitions* to argue that Peter has a complete and reliable understanding of the prophetic knowledge transmitted to him by Jesus. As we have seen, the *Recognitions* understands this prophetic truth as the only possible form of certain knowledge that human beings can possess. This means that Peter's preaching is not only more trustworthy than the accounts of rival apostolic claimants, but also more authoritative than the so-called "knowledge" about divine and human things possessed by epistemic competitors such as philosophers and astrologers. By interpreting the various source layers together, as integral elements of a broad rhetorical agenda about true knowledge, we have been able to see that the *Recognitions* makes far-reaching claims about the epistemic authority of the prophetic truth preached by Peter. However, we have not had an opportunity to examine the role of James the brother of Jesus, who is the implied addressee of the *Recognitions* and the one empowered by Jesus to accept or reject those who claim to teach Jesus' message.

James[67] is an important figure in our text for two reasons. In the first place, James is the head of the Jerusalem church, and as such he alone has the authority to accept or reject those who claim to preach the message of the True Prophet. This is especially interesting because, although the vast majority of the *Recognitions'* pages are given over to Peter's actions and speeches, it remains the case that the Pseudo-Clementines "clearly subordinate Peter to James."[68] In the second place, he is the person who

---

[67] On the figure of James see Wilhelm Pratscher, *Der Herrenbruder Jakobus und die Jakobustradition* (Göttingen: Vandenhoeck & Ruprecht, 1987); Scott Kent Brown, "James: A Religio-Historical Study of the Relations between Jewish, Gnostic, and Catholic Christianity in the Early Period through an Investigation of the Traditions about James the Lord's Brother" (Ph.D. diss., Brown University, 1972); K. L. Carroll, "The Place of James in the Early Church," *BJRL* 44 (1961) 49-67; and F. Stanley Jones, "Hegesippus as a Source for the History of Jewish Christianity," in *Le judéo-christianisme dans tous ses états*, 201-12.

[68] Oscar Cullmann, *Peter: Disciple, Apostle, Martyr. A Historical and Theological Study*, 2nd rev. ed., trans. Floyd V. Filson (Philadelphia: Westminster, 1962) 229. This is also the view of Jones ("Clement of Rome and the *Pseudo-Clementines*," 156); Schmidt,

commissions Peter to dispute with Simon Magus, and who asks for a written account of everything Peter says and does on his mission.[69] This makes him the intended recipient of Clement's written accounts of Peter's words and deeds, and hence the implied reader of the *Recognitions* as well. Let's take a closer look at both of these functions assigned to James.

According to *Rec* 1.43.3,[70] James was appointed bishop of the Jerusalem church by Jesus himself:[71] *et ecclesia dei*[72] *in Hierusalem constituta copiosissime multiplicata crescebat per Iacobum, qui a domino ordinatus est in ea episcopus, rectissimis dispensationibus gubernata* ("and the church of God established in Jerusalem was very abundantly multiplied and grew, being guided with most righteous ordinances by James, who was ordained bishop in it by the Lord"). James, as bishop and head of the Jerusalem church, appears to be in a position of some authority over Jesus' original twelve apostles. In their dispute with the Jewish leaders, Gamaliel and the high priest both address James as a representative of and spokesperson for the apostles (*Rec* 1.66.5, 1.68.2). Moreover, the apostles report to James as if he is a supervisor, telling him what they have said and done while preaching Jesus' message (*Rec* 1.44.1; 1.66.1). James' role as overseer and authorizer of those who teach Jesus' words is made explicit in *Rec* 4.35.1-2 (cf. *Hom* 11.35.4):

propter quod observate cautius, ut nulli doctorum credatis, nisi qui Iacobi fratris domini ex Hierusalem detulerit testimonium, vel eius quicumque post ipsum fuerit. nisi enim quis illuc ascenderit et ibi fuerit probatus quod sit doctor idoneus et fidelis ad praedicandum Christi verbum, nisi, inquam, inde detulerit testimonium, recipiendus omnino non est.

Studien zu den Pseudo-Clementinen, 108ff and 322ff; Schoeps, *Theologie und Geschichte*, 122ff; and Strecker, *Judenchristentum*, 58-62. This appears to be a relatively stable consensus. However, cf. the opinion of Jean Daniélou: "Il n'y a pas de subordination de Pierre à Jacques. Mais il y a nécessité d'être en communion avec l'Eglise de Jérusalem, comme Eglise mère. Et les Apôtres eux-mêmes s'acquittent de ce devoir. Il y a là un primat ecclésial de Jacques." He goes on to note the methodological importance of distinguishing between different source layers in the texts. Jean Daniélou, "Pierre dans le judéo-christianisme hétérodoxe," in *San Pietro: Atti della XIX Settimana biblica* (Brescia: Paideia, 1967) 449.

[69] For a discussion of the relationship between Peter and James in the Pseudo-Clementines, see Henri Clavier, "La primauté de Pierre d'après les pseudo-clémentines," *Revue d'histoire et de philosophie religieuses* 36 (1956) 298-307, esp. 303-306.

[70] All of the material from *Rec* 1.27-71 mentioned here belongs to an early Jewish-Christian source layer, used first by the *Grundschrift* and then adopted by the *Recognitions*. For a detailed analysis of this source see Jones, *Ancient Jewish-Christian Source*, 111-55; and van Voorst, *Ascents of James*, 30-45.

[71] There has been some debate about the uniqueness of this passage, which suggests that Jesus himself instituted the office of bishop. On this see Jones, *Ancient Jewish-Christian Source*, 130 n. 62.

[72] Other mss read *domini* instead of *dei* here. See Rehm, *Rekognitionen*, 33.

Because of this, be very careful that you believe no teacher, except he who brings down from Jerusalem the testimonial of James the Lord's brother, or of whoever may be after him. For unless he has gone up to that [place], and has been approved there because he is a suitable and faithful teacher for preaching the word of Christ – unless, I say, he brings down a testimony from there, he should absolutely not be accepted.

This passage tells us that James serves as a gatekeeper of sorts – a watchdog entrusted with the duty of distinguishing faithful teachers from those who are deemed unfit. James has the power to approve and reject those who claim to speak in Jesus' name, and his decision is portrayed by the *Recognitions* as final and absolute. As a result, James' endorsement of Peter's message is critically important as an authorizing mechanism, a "seal of approval," from the highest (human) authority of all.

Because the approval of James is essential to the legitimacy of those who speak in Jesus' name, it should come as no surprise that the *Recognitions* records James' support of Peter at every turn. In fact, James is the one who appoints Peter to debate with Simon Magus. In *Rec* 1.72.5-6, 7 James tells Peter, *Multi sunt ergo ... o Petre, quorum salutis causa proficisci te oportet et arguere magum ac sermonem veritatis docere ... dato sane operam, ut per singulos annos praecipua quaeque ex dictis gestisque tuis scripta mittas ad me, et maxime per septimanas annorum* ("Therefore there are many..., O Peter, for the sake of whose salvation it is right for you to go and to refute the magician, and to teach the discourse of truth ... Every year you certainly should send me a special written account of your sayings and doings, and especially every seven years"). Because Peter's activities in the *Recognitions* are a direct result of his commission from James, the reader assumes that James has confidence in Peter's command of this "discourse of truth." This passage suggests that James acts in a supervisory capacity with Peter, just as he had with the other apostles, because he asks Peter to report back to him in writing. In fact, James' request that Peter provide this written account is repeated often enough in the *Recognitions* to be called a motif; I will mention each of these occurrences briefly.

We have already had occasion to consider the passage in *Rec* 1.17.2-3 where Clement, who has been charged with recording Peter's words, tells James that

unde et iubente ipso, ea quae ad me locutus est, in ordinem redigens, librum de vero propheta conscripsi eumque de Caesarea ad te, ipso iubente, transmisi. dicebat enim mandatum se accepisse abs te, ut per singulos annos, si qua a se essent dicta gestaque, ad te descripta transmitteret

by [Peter's] command, bringing back into order the things he has said to me, I composed a book about the True Prophet, and sent it from Caesarea to you by his command. For he said that he had received a command from you, that every year he should send you a written account of the things that had been said and done by him.[73]

Because Peter's preaching consists entirely of the words of Jesus, Clement's written account of this preaching is essentially a book about the True Prophet himself.

This same motif appears again in *Rec* 3.74.4, immediately before the controversial "table of contents" in *Rec* 3.75.1-12:[74] *simul et imperat mihi, quia intellexit me studiosius quae audirem memoriae commendare, libris singula quaeque quae memoratu digna videbantur conprehendere et mittere ad te, mi domine Iacobe, sicut et feci parens eius praeceptis* ("And at the same time, because he understood that I studiously committed to memory what I heard, he commanded me to recount in books whatever things seemed worthy of mention, and to send [it] to you, my lord James, as also I have done, being obedient to his command"). Just as in the previous passage, Peter fulfills James' request through Clement: because Clement has memorized everything Peter says and does, he is the one entrusted with the task of writing the account and sending it to James. The idea appears once more in the next chapter (*Rec* 3.75.11): *de his ergo singulis quae apud Caesaream disserta sunt a Petro, iubente, ut dixi, ipso decem conscripta ad te transmisi volumina* ("Therefore, concerning these individual things which were discussed by Peter at Caesarea, by [his] command, as I have said, I have sent them to you written in ten volumes").

These four passages, which are strikingly similar to one another, form what Stanley Jones has called a "framing motif" that highlights the importance of James in the source material found in *Rec* 1.27-71.[75] While it is undoubtedly true that James is far more prominent in this section of the *Recognitions* than he is elsewhere in the narrative,[76] I would like to suggest that this technique of invoking James as an authoritative figure is significant in terms of the larger rhetorical agenda of our text as well. As one who reads and approves Clement's account of Peter's preaching, James plays a crucial role in the verification and sanctioning of Peter's authority. Moreover, the figure of James is invoked for another reason as well. Because the *Recognitions* presents itself as Clement's compilation of

---

[73] *Hom* 1.20.2-7 contains a similar set of instructions given to Peter by James.

[74] This so-called table of contents, in which Clement enumerates the contents of the account he has already sent to James, has been the subject of a great deal of scholarly debate. One major point of contention is whether the "table of contents" recapitulates the contents of *Rec* 1 (and reflects an earlier source), or is merely a literary fiction. For a discussion of this question, see Jones, "Pseudo-Clementines," 15ff.

[75] Jones, *Ancient Jewish-Christian Source*, 150 n. 130.

[76] Of the twenty times James is mentioned by name in the *Recognitions*, at least half occur in the context of this source.

Peter's preaching,[77] the rhetorical effect of this appeal to James takes on new significance: James' vigilant eye supervises and approves the *Recognitions* as a proper account of the True Prophet's message. In other words, by repeatedly suggesting that James has sanctioned the record of Peter's preaching contained within the *Recognitions*, our text effectively makes a claim about its own importance: it is an account of the True Prophet's teaching that has been approved and endorsed by James, the highest human authority.

Conclusion

In this chapter, we finally reached the heart of the *Recognitions'* epistemological program, which contrasts the prophetic and certain knowledge possessed by Peter with the uncertain and dubious "knowledge" claimed by rivals such as philosophers and astrologers. We have looked closely at the various strategies by which the text establishes and authenticates Peter's relationship to Jesus, all of which are designed to demonstrate that the prophetic knowledge contained within its pages has been accurately and completely handed down. The line of transmission runs from the True Prophet to Peter to Clement, and then directly to the readers and hearers of the text. Any understanding of human and divine things that conflicts with this presentation is, according to the *Recognitions*, necessarily incorrect.

Thus far we have spent a great deal of time looking at the text itself, in an effort to uncover how the *Recognitions* uses earlier source materials in the service of an identifiable epistemic agenda. We have not, however, begun the process of looking *behind* the text to understand its socio-historical context, and as a result some important questions remain unanswered: What circumstances led to the production of the *Recognitions*? Can we identify the "texts," broadly construed, with which the *Recognitions* is in conversation? Does our text's polemical and apologetic agenda tell us anything about the world in which it was produced and reproduced? The next and final chapter of this book seeks to answer these questions.

---

[77] The *Recognitions* undoubtedly purports to be Clement's account of Peter's preaching, so the rhetorical effect of the "framing motif" arguably remains the same even if Clement is referring to other, separate accounts he has previously sent to James.

Chapter 5

The *Recognitions* and its
Fourth-Century Syrian Context

Thus far I have looked in great detail at the narrative of the *Recognitions*, but have not situated it within the larger social, historical, and theological framework of Christianity in the first four centuries CE. This chapter explores the *Recognitions'* late antique Syrian context in an attempt to understand why the text is preoccupied with questions of epistemology, authenticity, and Petrine authority. In particular, I am concerned with Antioch and Edessa, two prominent Syrian cities that may have produced the *Recognitions*. I argue that, in the third and fourth centuries, these cities were competitive religious environments which entailed conflict, competition, and conversation among Christians, Jews, and pagans of many stripes. This situation may help us to understand better the *Recognitions'* multifaceted polemical agenda as well as its interest in establishing a proper chain of custody for Jesus' prophetic teaching.[1]

On one level, the question of the socio-historical context of the *Recognitions* is enormously difficult. The redactional history of the Pseudo-Clementines involves two fourth-century Syrian spinoffs of a third-century Syrian novel, which itself relies on a number of earlier sources that clearly derive from yet other times and places,[2] suggesting not one environment but indeed multiple milieux for these materials. To deal with these many embedded contexts in all their complexity is beyond the scope of this book, and in any event I am interested primarily in the fourth-century context of the *Recognitions* in its "final" form.[3] This rather focused

---

[1] Portions of this chapter appeared in an earlier publication: Kelley, "Problems of Knowledge and Authority," 315-348.

[2] For recent attempts to shed new light on the literary history of the Pseudo-Clementines, see chapter 1 of Meinolf Vielberg's *Klemens in den pseudoklementinischen Rekognitionen*, and J. Wehnert, "Abriss der Entstehungsgeschichte des pseudoklementinischen Romans," *Apocrypha* 3 (1992): 211-35; a recent summary of the history of scholarship on this issue can also be found in Côté, *Le thème de l'opposition*, 7-18.

[3] The fourth-century *Sitz im Leben* of these texts has received scant attention in scholarship, probably because there has been little interest in the fourth-century texts themselves. For instance, the latest studies by Côté and Vielberg provide an excellent

inquiry will allow us to examine how the *Recognitions* uses earlier materials as a resource for thinking about Christian identity and group definition in fourth-century Syria.

Locating the Recognitions

Philip Sellew's work on Thomas traditions in early Christianity suggests that we must be cautious in moving unreflectively from texts to communities "behind" those texts.[4] For a text such as the *Recognitions*, it is not difficult to imagine distinctive communities behind some source layers,[5] but it is more challenging to envision what sort of interpretive community might have been served by the text as it now stands. For this reason I am generally hesitant to speak of a "community" of Christians that might lie behind the *Recognitions*, preferring instead to think only about how the text fits into its environment. With what communities, texts and ideas was the *Recognitions* in conversation? How does the text situate itself relative to these concerns? I do not claim to have definitive answers to these questions, but what follows should begin to shed some light on the text's socio-historical context and its significance for understanding the *Recognitions'* epistemological agenda.

As I mentioned in Chapter 1, both Antioch and Edessa (or somewhere in between) seem plausible candidates for the location of the *Recognitions*. Already in 1854 Gerhard Uhlhorn argued forcefully for the Syrian

---

framework for analyzing the common narrative of the *Homilies* and *Recognitions* in the context of the larger intellectual currents of the third century, while focusing only to a limited degree on the life of these texts in the fourth century. I've placed the word "final" in scare quotes because, as my friend and colleague David Levenson likes to point out, texts (and their attendant manuscript traditions) are not static entities.

[4] Philip Sellew, "Thomas Christianity: Scholars in Quest of a Community," in *The Apocryphal Acts of Thomas*, ed. Jan Bremmer, Studies on Early Christian Apocrypha 6 (Leuven: Peeters, 2001), 11-35, esp. 18-27. On pp. 24-25 he writes, "One of the key questions of method ... is whether or how we can use a literary narrative as a transparent 'window' through which to gaze on some other world, or, less optimistically perhaps, as a reflective 'mirror' by which we at least get glimpses, admittedly distorted, of that other world. The assumption of much discussion of the 'communities' lying behind early Christian texts seems often to be that the narratives can indeed function as one of these types of glass." See also S. Barton, "Can We Identify the Gospel Audiences?" in *The Gospels for All Christians: Rethinking the Gospel Audiences*, ed. R. Bauckham (Grand Rapids, MI: W. B. Eerdmans, 1998), 173-94.

[5] The clearest example of this is *Rec* 1.27-71; see van Voorst, *Ascents of James*, 174-80.

provenance of the *Grundschrift* and the *Homilies*,[6] and these arguments were appropriated by subsequent scholars to support a Syrian origin for the *Recognitions* as well.[7] We cannot know for certain *where* in Syria these texts were produced, but Antioch probably should be preferred because of its association with traditions about Petrine authority.[8] Paul's testy account in Galatians 2 mentions that Peter (assuming Cephas = Peter in 2.11) came to Antioch, and Acts 11.19 states that some of those scattered during the persecution following Stephen's death ended up in Antioch (but cf. Acts 8.1, which excludes the apostles from this diaspora). This is hardly enough information to establish a Petrine foundation of the church in Antioch, but the tradition – which is, after all, what's important in the present context – nevertheless appears fairly early in Origen's *Homily on Luke* 6.1 (*PG* XIII, cols. 1814-15) and somewhat later in sources such as Eusebius' *Hist. Eccl.* 3.36.2, 22.[9] In addition to this material we also have other texts such as the Gospel of Matthew, which gives a special place to Peter among the apostles (see esp. Mt 16.17-19) and can probably can be located in Western Syria, if not Antioch specifically. Though Edessan traditions typically do not claim Peter as "their" apostle,[10] and though we should be cautious not to conflate the circumstances that obtained in these two cities,

---

[6] Gerhard Uhlhorn, *Die Homilien und Recognitionen des Clemens Romanus nach ihrem Ursprung und Inhalt dargestellt* (Göttingen: Dieterische Buchhandlung, 1854), 381-429.

[7] See e.g. Strecker, *Judenchristentum*, 255ff. Joseph Langen argued that the *Recognitions* should be located in Antioch; his judgment has been adopted by Waitz and others. Joseph Langen, *Klemensromane*, 145-46; Waitz, *Pseudoklementinen*, 372.

[8] Cf. Jan N. Bremmer, "Foolish Egyptians," 316. The Western Syrian interest in Petrine authority (e.g. in the Gospel of Matthew, the Gospel of Peter, and the so-called Kerygmata Petrou) is examined by Helmut Koester in his influential essay "ΓΝΩΜΑΙ ΔΙΑΦΟΡΟΙ: The Origin and Nature of Diversification in the History of Early Christianity," *HTR* 58 (1965) 284-90. A more wide-ranging discussion of Peter's role in the early church is undertaken by Oscar Cullmann in the classic study *Peter*, 34-70, 228-42.

[9] For a more complete list see Cullmann, *Peter*, 54 n. 60; and Glanville Downey, *A History of Antioch in Syria from Seleucus to the Arab Conquest* (Princeton, NJ: Princeton University Press, 1961) 583-86.

[10] This is not absolute; see e.g. Sebastian Brock's point about the *Doctrina Addai*: "First is the concern to establish a link with the see of Rome, which is achieved by the statement that Addai's second successor, Palut, was consecrated bishop by Serapion of Antioch (190/191-211/212), who was in turn consecrated (a patent anachronism!) by Zephyrinus of Rome (198-217), whose priesthood went back to Simon Peter." He observes that the same line of succession appears in the Acts of Barsamya; see W. Cureton, *Ancient Syriac Documents* (London: Williams and Norgate, 1864) 71, lines 17-30. Sebastian Brock, "Eusebius and Syriac Christianity," in *Eusebius, Christianity, and Judaism*, ed. Harold W. Attridge and Gohei Hata (Detroit: Wayne State University Press, 1992) 227-28.

it is still true that Antioch and Edessa faced similar theological, philosophical and sociological challenges in late antiquity.[11] As a result, we may find that information about Edessa helps to shed light on the context of the *Recognitions*.[12]

Religious Diversity in Fourth-Century Syria

Despite criticisms of his theses about the development of orthodox and heterodox varieties of Christian belief, Walter Bauer's observations about Syrian Christianity remain trenchant: in late antique Edessa, we find a variety of competing Christian communities, some of which were already well-established by the second century.[13] Stephen K. Ross captures this diversity when he describes Edessa as "a laboratory in which the thinking of philosophers including Marcion, Bardaiṣan and Mani was further developed and then propagated."[14] The hallmark of Edessan Christianity was a series of extended theological contests waged by different heterodox groups, as Ephrem (ca. 306-373) realized when he arrived there after Rome surrendered his native Nisibis to the Persians in 363 CE.[15] Much to Ephrem's dismay, he discovered that Christians of his stripe "were lost among a throng of followers of other teachers of a more or less 'heretical'

---

[11] H. J. W. Drijvers speaks repeatedly of a "continuous exchange of ideas" between Antioch and Edessa. See e.g. his "East of Antioch: Forces and Structures in the Development of Early Syriac Theology," in idem, *East of Antioch: Studies in Early Syriac Christianity* (London: Variorum, 1984) I.3-4, 13-14, 17.

[12] On this point see Drijvers, "East of Antioch," 5. Cf. Bauer, *Orthodoxy and Heresy*, 19-20. Note, however, Koester's word of caution about speaking of Edessa and Western Syria as if they were homogeneous. Koester, "ΓΝΩΜΑΙ ΔΙΑΦΟΡΟΙ ," 299.

[13] Bauer, *Orthodoxy and Heresy*, 1-43, esp. 28ff. For criticisms of the Bauer thesis see e.g. Strecker, "On the Problem of Jewish Christianity," 241-85; and Thomas A. Robinson, *The Bauer Thesis Examined: The Geography of Heresy in the Early Christian Church* (Lewiston, NY: E. Mellen Press, 1988).

[14] Ross, *Roman Edessa*, 127. The *Chronicon Edessenum* mentions Marcion, Bardaisan, and Mani in its list of important religious developments in Edessa. Drijvers, "East of Antioch," 4.

[15] H. J. W. Drijvers, *Cults and Beliefs at Edessa* (Leiden: E. J. Brill, 1980) 194; Ross, *Roman Edessa*, 118. For biographical information about Ephrem see E. Beck, "Ephrem le syrien (saint)," *Dictionnaire de Spiritualité: ascétique et mystique, doctrine et histoire*, vol. IV, ed. M. Viller et al. (Paris: G. Beauchesne, 1959) cols. 788-90; Sidney H. Griffith, "Ephraem, the Deacon of Edessa, and the Church of the Empire," in *Diakonia: Studies in Honor of Robert T. Meyer*, ed. Thomas Halton and Joseph P. Williman (Washington, D.C.: Catholic University of America Press, 1986) 22-52, esp. 24-29; and Christine C. Shepardson, "In the Service of Orthodoxy: Anti-Jewish Language and Intra-Christian Conflict in the Writings of Ephrem the Syrian" (Ph.D. diss., Duke University, 2003) 5-16.

bent," with each group taking the name of its founder.[16] Ephrem was particularly vexed by the followers of Bardaisan, Marcion, and Mani,[17] but so-called "Arians"[18] and "Jewish-Christians"[19] were also important factors in the religious landscape. Christians were not the only groups vying for preëminence and converts. Philosophical schools, adherents of native Syrian religions,[20] and Jews[21] must also be viewed as competitors in the religious marketplace of fourth-century Syria. As H. J. W. Drijvers says of Edessa,

Es war eine Stadt mit einer autochthonen semitischen Bevölkerung, die hauptsächlich arabischer Herkunft war; wo Juden und Griechen wohnten; wo die Parther einen grossen Einfluss ausübten; wo das Judentum, der Paganismus und das Christentum nebeneinander

---

[16] Ross goes on to note (correctly) that Ephrem's need to assert his own group's primacy "makes clear for us that 'orthodox' Christians, if not in the minority, were still only a shaky majority at that time in Edessa." Ross, *Roman Edessa*, 123-24.

[17] Ephrem writes a number of hymns directed against Marcion, Mani, and Bardaisan. In particular, Ephrem seems to know of a community of fourth-century Bardaisanites; see E. Beck, "Bardaisan und seine Schule bei Ephram," *Le Muséon* 91 (1978) 271-333. On Ephrem's polemics against Jews and Christians see Shepardson, "In the Service of Orthodoxy," 39-210.

[18] On Arianism in Antioch, see Rowan Williams, *Arius: Heresy and Tradition*, rev. ed. (Grand Rapids, MI: Eerdmans, 2001), 158-66. R. P. C. Hanson, *The Search for the Christian Doctrine of God: The Arian Controversy, 318-381* (Edinburgh: T&T Clark, 1988), xvii-xviii; Joseph T. Lienhard, "The 'Arian' Controversy: Some Categories Reconsidered," *TS* 48 (1987) 415-37; and Rebecca Lyman, "A Topography of Heresy: Mapping the Rhetorical Creation of Arianism," in *Arianism after Arius*, ed. Michael R. Barnes and Daniel H. Williams (Edinburgh: T&T Clark, 1993) 45-62 address the terminological problems associated with "Arianism," which tends to ascribe all subordinationist Christologies indiscriminately to Arius. As Rowan Williams puts it, "Arius' role in 'Arianism' was not that of the founder of a sect. It was not his individual teaching that dominated the mid-century eastern Church. 'Arianism', throughout most of the fourth century, was in fact a loose and uneasy coalition of those hostile to Nicaea in general and the *homoousios* in particular." Williams, *Arius*, 165-66. Ephrem's views on Arius and his followers are addressed in Griffith, "Ephraem, the Deacon of Edessa," 37-47.

[19] On the existence of Jewish Christians in the fourth century, as well as the definitional problems associated with the term Jewish Christianity, see Reed, "Jewish Christianity," *passim*.

[20] Drijvers gives a more complete picture of the indigenous religions of Edessa in his *Cults and Beliefs at Edessa, passim*; cf. Kevin Butcher, *Roman Syria and the Near East* (London: British Museum, 2003), 335-98 for a more comprehensive (if somewhat problematic) account of "the pious world" of Syria generally.

[21] Robert L. Wilken, *John Chrysostom and the Jews: Rhetoric and Reality in the Late 4th Century* (Berkeley: University of California Press, 1983); Wayne A. Meeks and Robert L. Wilken, *Jews and Christians in Antioch in the First Four Centuries of the Common Era* (Missoula, MT: Scholars, 1978).

lebten; wo man sich der Astrologie und der Philosophie widmete, so dass die Stadt das Athen des Orients genannt wurde.[22]

Clearly, Edessa was a melting-pot. The same diverse and contentious environment existed in Antioch and throughout Syria. My argument is that, at this point in late antiquity, these locales constituted a competitive marketplace – or, as Bourdieu might put it, a *field* – that is reproduced in particular and strategic ways within the *Recognitions*. Let's now take a closer look at a few of these Christian and non-Christian groups, with an eye toward how the *Recognitions* might situate itself in regard to the overall situation in Antioch and Edessa.[23]

Bardesanites

Ephrem's preoccupation with Marcionites, Bardesanites, and Manichees suggests just how popular these groups were in his generation. This is especially striking because, like Marcion, Bardaisan lived nearly two centuries before Ephrem encountered his followers. Although his views were products of the second century, "nearly 150 years after Bardaisan's death, the Edessan philosopher and his 'school' were in the thick of the cosmological, theological, and soteriological disputes of the day."[24] Why were the Bardesanites and their views[25] so problematic for Christians such as Ephrem? A quick look at some aspects of Bardesanite thought reveals some major points of contention.

Bardaisan was familiar with Greek philosophy, though his thought betrays a range of influences from Persian religion to astrology to so-called "gnostic" ideas.[26] Bardesanite cosmology, for example, takes from Greek

---

[22] H. J. W. Drijvers, "Edessa und das jüdische Christentum," *Vigiliae Christianae* 24 (1970) 4.

[23] What follows is a very limited sketch of the religious landscape of fourth-century Syria, which is designed to highlight certain elements that may be important for understanding the *Recognitions*.

[24] Ross, *Roman Edessa*, 124.

[25] It is important to note, however, that Bardesanite beliefs and teachings were not uniform, even during the time of Bardaisan. Ephrem, for example, tells us that there were differences between the teachings of Bardaisan and his son Harmonius. Drijvers, *Bardaisan of Edessa*, 227.

[26] H. J. W. Drijvers, "Syrian Christianity and Judaism," in *The Jews Among Pagans and Christians*, ed. Judith Lieu, John North and Tessa Rajak (London & New York: Routledge, 1992) 126, notes that Bardaisan's ideas on fate and free will were influenced by the Peripatetic philosopher Alexander of Aphrodisias. Denzey argues that much of the *BLC*'s cosmological, anthropological and astrological concerns are rooted in traditions of exegesis of Plato's *Timaeus*, as well as ideas prevalent in Stoic circles. Denzey, "Bardaisan of Edessa," 168-80.

philosophy its notion of four essences that combine to form matter,[27] but it also employs Persian ideas about a fifth principle (darkness) that is the source of evil. This fifth principle was the foundation for Mani's dualistic system.[28] Ephrem's hostility to the Bardesanites stems in part from this connection to Manichaeism, which the Syrian heresiologist regarded as a grave threat to orthodox belief. But even without the Manichaean connection, ideas such as Bardaisan's fifth principle seemed to challenge the unity of God, a fundamental tenet of Ephrem's Christianity.

According to later authors, Bardaisan's Christology denied the suffering of Jesus together with his bodily resurrection.[29] Such docetic ideas, which were problematic for Christians such as Ephrem,[30] were an outgrowth of Bardaisan's tripartite anthropology, which held that human beings were composed of spirit, soul, and body. The human body, in the Bardesanite view, was composed of a mixture of the elements and darkness, which meant that "it perishes at death and does not rise again."[31] Moreover, Bardesanite anthropology affirmed human free will and moral responsibility while ascribing a limited role to the influence of astral fate. While human beings are free in the sense that they have been given the gift of free will, they are also "unfree in that [they are] subject to nature and [their] horoscope[s]."[32] The human spirit "is of divine origin and joins the soul when the latter descends through the seven spheres of the planets to the human body at the moment of birth."[33] While the spirit is

---

[27] This idea is repeated in the Pseudo-Clementine *Grundschrift*; see e.g. *Hom* 3.33.1; 19.12.3; 20.3.8; 20.8.2-3.

[28] Ross, *Roman Edessa*, 126. Based on an examination of the extant evidence about Bardaisan's thought, Drijvers, *Bardaisan of Edessa*, 220 says that "Tradition vacillates as to whether darkness is itself an element, or whether it only consists in the confusion of the four pure elements, in keeping with the ambivalent nature of evil." On Mani's adaptation of Bardaisan's cosmology see Drijvers, *Bardaisan of Edessa*, 225-26.

[29] It is not altogether clear that such docetic ideas can be traced back to Bardaisan himself. As Denzey notes, "we have no reliable Christology whatsoever that derives directly from Bardaisan or a Bardesanite." Denzey, "Bardaisan of Edessa," 171. On the conflicting accounts of Bardaisan's relationship to Christianity and Valentinianism generally, see Denzey, "Bardaisan of Edessa," 164-65; Sebastian Brock, "Didymus the Blind on Bardaisan," *Journal of Theological Studies* 22 (1971) 530-31; Drijvers, *Bardaisan of Edessa*, 167-71, 183-85.

[30] This Christology seems to be the target of Ephrem's polemicizing in *Against Bardaisan* 10-15 *et passim*. The material in this paragraph depends on Ross, *Roman Edessa*, 126.

[31] Drijvers, *Bardaisan of Edessa*, 220. Bardaisan appears to have believed that the spirit and soul were released from their bodily prison at death, "to ascend upward to unite with the source of their origin, in the 'Bridal Chamber of Light.'" Denzey, "Bardaisan of Edessa," 174, referring to Ephrem, *Prose Refutations* 32-40.

[32] Drijvers, *Bardaisan of Edessa*, 220.

[33] Drijvers, *Bardaisan of Edessa*, 219.

"ontologically free,"[34] the human body is subject to the laws of nature, and "the soul is endowed by the seven planets with various qualities, depending on the constellation at the hour of birth, which determine the outward fortunes of human life, wealth or poverty, power or subjection, a long or short life, health or sickness."[35] This was undoubtedly problematic for many like Ephrem, who felt that Bardesanite views were not only a concession to the demonic enterprise of astrology, but also inconsistent with Christian notions of an omnipotent God who metes out divine reward and punishment.[36] Bardaisan, at least, did not seem convinced of the incongruity of his astrological and philosophical/theological convictions. As H. H. Schaeder writes:

> es ist nicht angängig ... eine allgemeine Ablehnung der Astrologie und der aus ihr hergeleiteten philosophischen Bestimmung des Sternenzwanges gegenüber einer früheren Periode der Astrologie-Freundlichkeit bei Bardesanes herzuleiten. ... Die unbedingte Astrologiefeindschaft der Kirche weist er ausdrücklich ab. ... ist Bardesanes zwar ein Kritiker der Astrologie, aber nicht ihr Gegner geworden.[37]

It is thus clear that Bardaisan and his followers were able to find a satisfying answer (at least for themselves) to the typical Syrian questions about free will and determinism, fate and providence. As Ephrem's writings attest, the Bardesanites still existed in his day, and in Drijvers' judgment they "constituted a formidable power." By this time, some Bardesanites were giving even more prominence to astrology than they had previously done.[38]

The early fifth-century *Doctrina Addai*, together with the various pagan and Christian accounts of Bardaisan and the Bardesanites (most notably Ephrem's polemical writings), provides evidence of the continuing appeal

---

[34] Denzey, "Bardaisan of Edessa," 173.

[35] Drijvers, *Bardaisan of Edessa*, 219.

[36] For a nuanced treatment of Bardaisan's views on free will and fate, see Tim Hegedus, "Necessity and Free Will in the Thought of Bardaisan of Edessa," *Laval théologique et philosophique* 59.2 (2003) 333-44.

[37] H. H. Schaeder, "Bardesanes von Edessa in der Überlieferung der griechischen und der syrischen Kirche," in *Studien zur orientalischen Religionsgeschichte*, ed. Carsten Colpe (Darmstadt: Wissenschaftliche Buchgesellschaft, 1968) 124, as cited by Hegedus, "Necessity and Free Will," 335.

[38] Drijvers says that "Ephrem tells us of developments approaching the views of the Audians. ... Bardaisan's single potency is divided into three, which together with the four pure elements complete the heptad. These seven are then brought into relation with the Seven planets, including Sun and Moon, who are looked upon as creators of man." According to the *Vita* of Rabbula, the Bardesanites still existed in the time of bishop Rabbula of Edessa (d. 435), who forcibly converted them and destroyed their meeting-place. Drijvers, *Bardaisan of Edessa*, 227; Paul Bedjan, ed., *Acta martyrum et sanctorum*, vol. 4 (Paris: Harrasssowitz, 1890-1897) 431-32. The "still influential and threatening" legacy of Bardaisan is also noted by Denzey, "Bardaisan of Edessa," 160.

of astrology in fourth-century Syria.[39] For example, in the *Doctrina Addai* the eponymous hero exhorts his followers to "be ye indeed also far removed from...magic arts, which are without mercy, and from soothsaying, and divination, and fortune-tellers; and from fate and nativities, in which the erring Chaldaeans boast; and from planets and signs of the Zodiac, on which the foolish trust."[40] This injunction against astrological practices attests to the existence of such sympathies among the inhabitants of Edessa.

Given the prominence of the Bardesanites and the prevalence of astrological leanings among fourth-century Syrian Christians, it is hardly surprising that the *Recognitions* makes astrology a polemical target in its epistemological campaign. What is surprising, however, is that the *Recognitions* – which disagrees with Bardaisan's views on fate and which has an identifiable (if somewhat inconsistent) interest in presenting its views as orthodox – would employ a very large section of the Bardesanite *Book of the Laws of the Countries* in its ninth book.

Marcionites

One answer to this question lies with the Pseudo-Clementine *Grundschrift*, which unlike the *Recognitions* does not disagree with Bardaisan's position on fate: it probably used the *Book of the Laws of the Countries* as a weapon in its anti-Marcionite polemic.[41] Bardaisan was apparently well-known as an opponent of Marcionites. According to Eusebius' *Hist. Eccl.* 4.30, Bardaisan composed dialogues against Marcion.[42] Though these have not survived, fragments of these dialogues survive in the *Vita* of Aberkios, a famous opponent of Marcionites in Syria.[43]

Of course, others polemicized against the Marcionites as well. An anti-Marcionite polemic appears in Adamantius' *De Recta Fide in Deum*, written somewhere in Syria around 300 C.E., and in the third-century *Odes of Solomon* (see e.g. 3.6, which opposes the Marcionite notion of the jealous creator god).[44] The *Odes* repeatedly insist on the guiding hand of

---

[39] See e.g. Hippolytus *Philosophoumena* 6.35; the testimony of Eusebius which has been discussed in previous chapters; the *Vita* of Aberkios; Adamantius, *De Recta Fide in Deum*; Hieronymus, *Adv. Jov.* 2.14; Epiphanius, *Panarion* 56; Sozomen, *Hist. eccl.* 3.16. On these and others see Drijvers, *Bardaisan of Edessa*, 167-209.

[40] Translation from Cureton, *Ancient Syriac Documents*, 15 (lines 7-13).

[41] H. J. W. Drijvers, "Marcionism in Syria: Principles, Problems, Polemics," *Second Century* 6 (1987-1988) 155.

[42] Hippolytus, *Ref.* 7.31.1 and Theodoret *Her.* 1.22 indicate that the Marcionites likewise did their share of polemicizing against Bardaisan.

[43] See H. Grégoire, "Bardesane et S. Abercius," *Byzantion* 25-27 (1955-1957) 363-368.

[44] Drijvers, "Marcionism in Syria," 156.

divine providence, and they consistently assert that "God the creator is also God the Saviour."[45] The list would not be complete without Ephrem, who is one of our most important sources for Marcion's ideas. Ephrem (to give just two examples among many) addresses Marcion's notion of the Stranger in his *Third Discourse to Hypatius* and argues against Marcion's cosmology in *Hymns contra Haereses* 48.[46] This rather vibrant and longstanding series of polemical exchanges testifies to the powerful influence of Marcionite views in Syria.

In fact, it may be that "die Marcioniten sind die ältesten Christen in Edessa," as Drijvers and Bauer have argued.[47] In any case, Marcionism was widespread in Edessa probably by the end of the second century and certainly by the early third century.[48] Theodoret (*H. E.* 5.31) informs us of the existence of entire Marcionite villages in the fifth century.[49] The corroboration of Ephrem's testimony by Theodoret and Adamantius makes it safe to assume that Marcionism was alive and well in fourth-century Syria during the time that the *Recognitions* was written.

The basic outline of Marcion's views, which are largely based on the writings of Paul, is well-known: the Jewish Creator God proclaimed by the law and the prophets was a harsh and jealous god, too weak to create a better human being or to eradicate evil, and too inferior and ignorant to be aware of the existence of the highest God (the "Stranger"). Marcion rejected the Christian Old Testament because it concerned the demiurge, but he maintained that some elements of its teachings were written for the sake of Christians. Christ, in Marcion's view, had been sent by the good God to redeem all of humanity – not just the Jews – from the lawgiver (and the law and the prophets). As von Harnack puts it, "by means of his death Christ purchased mankind from the creator of the world."[50]

Marcion's views are very similar to Middle Platonic views that derive in part from Plato's *Timaeus* 31b, "where the difference between the invisible God and the visible world is essential. Marcion's Stranger, an unknown and even unknowable God of perfect goodness, shows all the typical features of the highest unknown God of Middle Platonism, who does not

---

[45] Drijvers, "East of Antioch," 6.

[46] Drijvers, "Marcionism in Syria," 156-61 talks at some length about Ephrem's presentation of Marcion's views.

[47] Drijvers, "Edessa und das jüdische Christentum," 5; Bauer, *Orthodoxy and Heresy*, 21-22.

[48] Ross, *Roman Edessa*, 121, 128.

[49] Adolf von Harnack, *Marcion: The Gospel of the Alien God*, trans. John E. Steely and Lyle D. Bierma (2d ed.; Durham, NC: Labyrinth Press, 1990) 102.

[50] von Harnack, *Marcion*, 87. For a fuller and more nuanced exposition of Marcion's views see von Harnack, *Marcion*, 65-92.

have any contact with our visible reality."[51] It is probably not a coincidence, then, that Platonic views are prevalent in the *Recognitions*, nor is it accidental that *Rec* 8.20.2 mentions the *Timaeus* by name and that Simon Magus gives voice to Marcion's views in some of his conversations with Peter.[52] Given the status and influence of Syrian Marcionite communities throughout late antiquity, and given the diametrical opposition between the Marcionite perspective on God, humanity, and the world and that espoused by the Pseudo-Clementines, we must conclude that at least part of the *Recognitions'* polemic would have been directed at Marcion and his followers. But this leaves an important question unanswered: why does none of Pseudo-Clementine literature mention Marcion or Marcionites by name? We will return to this in a moment.

Manichees

Thus far we have looked at Bardesanites and Marcionites, two of the three groups targeted by Ephrem as the chief heresies in Edessa. We now turn to the Manichees, who were likely regarded by Ephrem as the most serious local threat to orthodoxy. Manichaeism, the movement founded by Mani (216-76), was an eclectic synthesis of gnostic, Zoroastrian, Elchasaite, and Christian elements (among others).[53] The Manichaean religious system took as its starting point a radical dualism of two primordial principles, light and darkness, not unlike that found in other gnosticizing systems.[54] The Manichees had elaborate mythologies explaining how "the enlightened souls of men which are of divine origin came to be clothed in the body of matter which is evil."[55] The Manichaean elect, with the financial support of the sect's "hearers," traveled as itinerant missionaries throughout the eastern Roman empire.[56] They engaged in ascetic practices such as vegetarianism, avoidance of wine, sexual abstinence, avoidance of certain

---

[51] Drijvers, "Marcionism in Syria," 161-62.

[52] See e.g. A. Salles, "Simon le Magicien ou Marcion?" and Drijvers, "Adam and the True Prophet."

[53] For a fuller treatment of Mani's thought see Samuel N. C. Lieu, *Manichaeism in the Later Roman Empire and Medieval China: A Historical Survey* (Manchester, UK: Manchester University Press, 1985) 5-54.

[54] Lieu, *Manichaeism*, 8; Pheme Perkins, "Mani, Manichaeism," in *Encyclopedia of Early Christianity*, ed. Everett Ferguson (New York and London: Garland Publishing, Inc., 1990) 562-63.

[55] Lieu, *Manichaeism*, 8.

[56] Augustine of Hippo is probably the most famous Manichaean "hearer." Perkins notes that the itinerant missionaries of Manichaeism were a "Christianization" of the movement's organizational structure, which came about as a result of the persecution of Mani and his followers under the Zoroastrian Bahram I (274-77). Perkins, "Mani, Manichaeism," 562-63.

types of work, and extended periods of fasting.[57] The goal of these practices was to effect the redemption of the particles of light, which are trapped in the material world, by freeing them for their return to the heavenly world. The figure of Jesus takes on multiple roles in Manichaeism, including Mani's guardian angel, the revealer who informed Adam of his soul's divine origins and bodily captivity, the historical and wholly divine forerunner of Mani, and the one whose apparent suffering, death and resurrection were "an *exemplum* of the suffering and eventual deliverance of the human soul."[58]

Manichaeism was targeted by Christian heresiologists. The anonymous Christian writer dubbed Ambrosiaster, referring to Diocletian's edict against the Manichaeans in 302, warns his flock about a "heresy (*haeresis*) from Persia."[59] In one sense, we may attribute the targeting of Manichaeism in the anti-heresiological Christian writings of Ambrosiaster, Augustine, and Ephrem, as well as the *Doctrina Addai* and the *Odes of Solomon*, to the presence of Manichees throughout the Roman Empire, probably owing to the missionary character of the movement. As Drijvers observes, "Manichaeism spread quickly and everywhere in the Syrian area Manichaean communities came into existence, among other places, at Edessa."[60] But two aspects of Manichaean thought, which are relevant for our understanding of the *Recognitions*, may have made the threat seem especially urgent.

The first is a connection to the biggest theological debate among Christians in the early fourth century. Samuel N. C. Lieu writes, "The Manichaean view of Jesus as an emanation of the Father of Greatness stood surprisingly close to the principle of consubstantiality (ὁμοούσιος) as laid down by the First Ecumenical Council of Nicaea in 325 against Arius."[61] This is clearly the view of the heresiologist Epiphanius, who quotes part of the Nicene Creed in *Panarion* 66.42.2: "We [i.e. the orthodox] use the same language as they [i.e. the Manichaeans] do, that the Good Off-spring of the Good Father, Light of Light, God of God, True God of True God came to us in order to save us."[62] Later in *Panarion* 69, Epiphanius preserves a letter of Arius to Alexander, in which Arius argues

---

[57] These ascetic practices were referred to as the "Seal of the Mouth," the "Seal of the Hands," and the "Seal of the Breast." Lieu, *Manichaeism*, 19-20; Perkins, "Mani, Manichaeism," 563.

[58] Lieu, *Manichaeism*, 127.

[59] Ambrosiaster, *in ep. ad Tim. ii.*3.6-7.2. On Diocletian's rescript as well as the statement of Ambrosiaster see Lieu, *Manichaeism*, 91-95.

[60] Drijvers, "Syrian Christianity and Judaism," 134.

[61] Lieu, *Manichaeism*, 96.

[62] Translation by Lieu, *Manichaeism*, 96.

that the Nicene view of the consubstantiality of Father and Son borders on Manichaeism.[63] On the one hand, the Manichees' Christology was obviously regarded as heretical because it mapped onto already-existing markers of heresy, such as docetism (a hallmark of Marcionism and other forms of gnosticizing Christianity) and an incarnational theology that would have given Irenaeus a heart attack. On the other hand, (in the estimation of both sides!) Manichaean Christology more closely resembled the Nicene view than the subordinationism of Arius, blurring further the distinctions between heresy and orthodoxy in a time when the so-called "Arian" controversy had already rendered such boundaries dangerously uncertain. This situation may have motivated the heresiologists to focus even more intensely on Manichaeism. Whatever the cause, it is clear that Manichaeism "gave the impetus to a counter-movement on the part of other Christians which would develop into a fourth-century orthodoxy having close links with Antioch."[64]

The second aspect of Manichaeism that deserves our attention here is its connection to astrological beliefs and practices. Mani's thought contains astrological elements, owing partly to the influence of Elchasai and Bardaisan. The Cologne Mani Codex makes it clear that Mani was raised as a member of the Elchasaite sect, whose *Book of Elchasai* espouses katarchic astrology and encourages believers to organize their Christian practices around the alignment of the stars and planets.[65] Mani's own *Book of Mysteries* contains references to Bardaisan, which confirms Ephrem's statements about the existence of a connection between Bardaisan's and Mani's teachings.[66] As a result of Mani's use of astrology, the Manichaean

---

[63] Lieu, *Manichaeism*, 96.

[64] Drijvers, "Syrian Christianity and Judaism," 134-35. Drijvers has argued persuasively that the *Doctrina Addai* targets Manichaeism and its well-known missionary Adda(i), who traveled around Syria and Mesopotamia in the latter half of the third century. He has made similarly persuasive arguments about the *Odes of Solomon*. See e.g. "Odes of Solomon and Psalms of Mani. Christians and Manichaeans in Third-Century Syria," in *East of Antioch*, X.117-30.

[65] *CMC* 94.10-12; see Lieu, *Manichaeism*, 28-37. Katarchic astrology "deals with determining whether a particular moment ... is appropriate for commencing an action." Jones, "Astrological Trajectory," 186. This paragraph depends on Jones' treatment of Mani in "Astrological Trajectory," 194-99.

[66] Jones, "Astrological Trajectory," 194. See also Iain Gardner and Samuel N. C. Lieu, *Manichaean Texts from the Roman Empire* (Cambridge, UK: Cambridge University Press, 2004) 4, 28, 75, 155, 261. On the relationship between Bardaisan and Mani see e.g. H. J. W. Drijvers, "Mani und Bardaisan: Ein Beitrag zur Vorgeschichte des Manichäismus," *East of Antioch*, XIII, 459-69; B. Aland, "Mani und Bardesanes – Zur Engstehung des manichäischen Systems," in *Synkretismus im syrisch-persischen Kulturgebiet: Bericht über ein Symposion in Rheinhausen bei Göttingen in der Zeit vom*

cosmogony "abounds in astrological details."[67] *Kephalaia* 69 contains a summary of this teaching on the cosmos, in which Mani asserts that the zodiac is the cause of all evil. The result of this is that, for the Manichees, all the stars and planets, with the exception of the sun and moon, are malefic.

Strikingly, in *Kephalaia* 48 Mani's disciples state that the vicissitudes of human life occur as a result of one's horoscope. This same sentiment can be found in *BLC* col. 570 and (in a modified form) in *Rec* 9.7.1-6. Mani responds, however, that the sun and the moon rule over and are capable of restraining the power of the stars and the zodiac. Elsewhere (back in *Kephalaia* 69) Mani mentions an ἐπίτροπος, or steward, who is above the zodiac and stars and has some control over their effects on human life. Though Mani's astrological views differ from those of Bardaisan, it is clear that astrology plays an integral role in his cosmology. This is confirmed by Ephrem's *Second Discourse to Hypatius*, which addresses in some detail Manichaean teachings on the sun and moon.

Even if Mani's application of astrological ideas is "amateurish," by the time of Augustine's early fifth century squabbles with the Manichees, members of the sect in the West had acquired a reputation as astrologers.[68] That the Manichees had a strong presence in fourth-century Antioch and Edessa is established by the polemical writings of John Chrysostom and Ephrem, among others.[69] Might it be the case that the *Recognitions*, which was probably written in the mid-fourth century, is targeting the followers of both Bardaisan and Mani (and possibly others as well) with its anti-astrological rhetoric? I am inclined to say yes, and to add other groups or individuals with astrological leanings, including Syrian worshipers of Bêl and Nebo, to the list of potential targets of this polemic (see below).

"Arians"

A study of Christian groups in fourth century Syria would not be complete without a brief account of the Arian party, which much recent research has shown was neither Arian nor a party. Indeed, the whole notion of an Arian party may be attributed to the polemical penstrokes of Nicene proponents, as Rowan Williams observes: "The anti-Nicene coalition did not see themselves as constituting a single 'Arian' body: it is the aim of works like

---

4. bis 8. Oktober 1971, ed. A. Dietrich (Göttingen: Vandenhoeck & Ruprecht, 1975) 123-43.

[67] Lieu, *Manichaeism*, 141.

[68] Lieu, *Manichaeism*, 141-42.

[69] See e.g. John Chrysostom, *Hom. in Mt* (*PG* 58.975-1058); *S. Ephraim's Prose Refutations of Mani, Marcion and Bardaisan*, ed. and trans. C. W. Mitchell (London: Williams and Norgate, 1912-1921). On Manichaeism in Syria generally see Samuel N. C. Lieu, *Manichaeism in Mesopotamia and the Roman East* (Leiden: Brill, 1994) 38-53.

Athanasius' *de synodis* to persuade them that this is effectively what they are, all tarred with the same brush."[70] Whatever we choose to call them, the opponents of Nicaea were – together with Nicene supporters – engaged in a theological debate that would divide Christians throughout the Roman empire during the fourth century and beyond.

Though the debate proper began with Arius and Alexander in Alexandria, a good deal of the controversy can be associated with anti-Nicene figures in Antioch, such as Lucian of Antioch (d. 312), whose subordinationist views were employed in various ways by Arius and Eusebius of Nicomedia; Aetius (ca. 300-370), who was a native of Antioch and a founder of the Anomoean party; Eunomius (ca. 325 – ca. 395), who at times resided in Antioch; and Euzoius, who was bishop of Antioch from 361 until 376. Throughout the fourth century, Antioch was at the heart of this struggle for control of the church.[71] It is telling that in 380 and 381, Theodosius I's anti-Arian edict *Cunctos Populos* pointedly omits the bishop of Antioch from a list of bishops authorized to "serve as arbitrators of the norm by which orthodoxy would be judged."[72] Antioch was a city divided.

There is evidence that the controversy divided Edessa as well. For example, the emperor Julian wrote a letter to the inhabitants of Edessa "admonishing them to desist from their factional quarrels," which included the disagreements between Constantius' Arian party and the followers of Valentinus.[73] Ephrem had been troubled by Manichees, Marcionites and Bardesanites in Nisibis, but his arrival in Edessa after 363 put him in conversation, and conflict, with "Arians" and their theological views.[74] Edmund Beck has shown that Ephrem's *Hymns on Faith*, though they do not name Arians directly, have Arian teachings as their target.[75]

It is of course not possible to do justice to the complexities of the *homoousios* debate in this context. For our purposes, there are two ways in

---

[70] Williams, *Arius*, 166.

[71] Wilken attributes Antioch's central role in the Arian controversy to "its central location, its hegemony over the churches of northern Syria, and its symbolic importance as a Christian city." He notes that this was not just an argument among intellectuals, but a series of disputes that "turned on the competing loyalties of the populace and [was] symbolized by possession of buildings and by rituals." Wilken, *John Chrysostom and the Jews*, 11, 13.

[72] Wilken, *John Chrysostom and the Jews*, 14.

[73] Ross, *Roman Edessa*, 124, referring to Julian, *Ep.* 40. See *L'Empereur Julien: oeuvres complètes*, ed. J. Bidez and G. Rochefort (Paris: C. Lacombrade, 1924-63).

[74] Griffith, "Ephraem, the Deacon of Edessa," 40.

[75] Griffith, "Ephraem, the Deacon of Edessa," 38. Edmund Beck, *Die Theologie des hl. Ephraem in seinen Hymnen über den Glauben*, Studia Anselmiana philosophica theologica 21 (Città del Vaticano: Libreria Vaticana, 1949), esp. 62-80.

which the dispute is important for understanding the *Recognitions*. In the first place, the Arian controversy framed the contestation of orthodoxy and heresy for much of eastern Christendom in the fourth century. Heresiological discourse took on a new importance in the newly Christian empire,[76] becoming a central mode of establishing and negotiating religious identities, even when non-Christians were the object of discussion.[77] As Daniel Boyarin puts it:

> The fourth century seems particularly rich in the proliferation of technologies for the production of self and other: Christian orthodoxy versus its other, so-called heresy (including prominently the 'Judaizing' heresies); rabbinic Jewish orthodoxy versus its major (br)other, Christianity and Christian Judaism (its 'twin'); and even the ongoing issue of the fuzzy separation between Christianity and so-called paganism.[78]

Though Boyarin is talking about the role of martyrdom in the production and contestation of Jewish and Christian identities, he could just as easily have been writing an introduction to the *Recognitions*. Our text participates in this larger discourse about orthodoxy and heresy, as is evident from its interest in the apostles as guarantors of tradition, as well as its use of Simon Magus – who from the time of Irenaeus was regarded as the father of all heresies – as a foil for Peter. There is yet another way the *homoousios* debates are relevant for our understanding of the *Recognitions*: the controversy was very much concerned with the role of the non-scriptural vocabulary of philosophy (and especially Platonism) in the articulation of Christian thought and doctrines.

Philosophers

Philosophical currents ran strong in both Antioch and Edessa. Edessa, which had a famous school of philosophy and rhetoric, was nicknamed "the Athens of the East."[79] Many of the inhabitants of Edessa likely had some knowledge of Greek philosophy, and Stoicism in particular.[80] Likewise, Antioch – the home of the famous rhetor Libanius and his

---

[76] Note, however, Robert Wilken's observation that for Christians in the fourth century, "The march of emperors between Constantine and Theodosius I ... gave no one cause to think Constantine stood at the beginning of a new age." Wilken, *John Chrysostom and the Jews*, 129. Cf. Ephrem's perspective on the matter as characterized by Sidney H. Griffith, "Ephraem the Syrian's Hymns 'Against Julian': Meditations on History and Imperial Power," *VC* 41 (1987) 245.

[77] This, in part, is the argument of Shepardson, "In the Service of Orthodoxy," esp. 163-210.

[78] Daniel Boyarin, *Dying for God: Martyrdom and the Making of Christianity and Judaism* (Stanford, CA: Stanford University Press, 1999) 18.

[79] Drijvers, "Syrian Christianity and Judaism," 126.

[80] Drijvers, *Bardaisan of Edessa*, 216.

student John Chrysostom[81] – has been described by Robert Wilken as "the embodiment of Greek culture and civility."[82] Wilken finds that, in the fourth century,

> Hellenism was still very much alive in cities such as Antioch, not only in the writings of intellectuals, but in the schools and other social institutions, the mores of the citizens, the art that adorned people's homes and the architecture that graced the streets, and the values that shaped people's ideas and attitudes.[83]

Late antique Antioch still retained all the trappings of a Hellenistic city, including temples and shrines to pagan deities, festivals and games in honor of the Greek gods, and a Greek educational system.[84]

These academic currents were important in the development of Syrian Christianity. The philosophical leanings of Bardaisan toward Stoic thought, the influence of Platonism on Marcion and his followers' view of the world, the eclectic (if rather pedestrian) philosophical ideas espoused in the Pseudo-Clementines, and the *homoousios* debate all suggest that Greek philosophy formed part of the *lingua franca* of late antique Syria. Ephrem's eighty-seven *Hymns on Faith*, composed after he arrived in Edessa in 363, reveal how the grammar of philosophy played an important role in the discourses of orthodoxy and heresy that emerged anew in the fourth century Christological debates. As Sidney Griffith argues,

> A major purpose of the *Hymns on Faith* ... was to cultivate among the faithful a profound distaste for dialectics in religion, or indeed for any sort of philosophical inquiry governed by academic logic rather than by a fundamental faith in the scriptures. ... To admit the language of the academy was to admit another measure of truth, and to attempt to state Christian convictions in nonscriptural, academic terms was to espouse non-Christian doctrines. For Ephraem, the Arians were the prime example of those who had given in to this temptation. [85]

Hence the question of one's attitude toward Greek philosophy and its relation to Christian teaching – always an important question for the church fathers[86] – took on a new urgency in the fourth century as pro-Nicene and anti-Nicene Christians engaged in theological debate. Little wonder, then, that the *Recognitions* takes a strong position on the epistemological value of philosophical thought. Even if much of its philosophical material was inherited from earlier sources, including the

---

[81] For a thorough analysis of Greek *paideia* in Antioch, see A. J. Festugière, *Antioche païenne et chrétienne: Libanius, Chrysostome et les moines de Syrie* (Paris: Éditions E. de Boccard, 1959) esp. 91-140 and 211-40.

[82] Wilken, *John Chrysostom and the Jews*, 5.

[83] Wilken, *John Chrysostom and the Jews*, xvii.

[84] Wilken, *John Chrysostom and the Jews*, 18.

[85] Griffith, "Ephraem, the Deacon of Edessa," 43, 46.

[86] See e.g. Chadwick, *Early Christian Thought, passim.*

Grundschrift, it is clear that these matters were relevant, even urgent, for Christians living in late antique Syria.

Pagans[87]

Now let's turn briefly to yet another element in the competitive religious marketplace of Syria: a variety of native Syrian religious beliefs and practices.[88] As with the followers of Bardaisan, the adherents of these indigenous cults may help us to understand how the *Recognitions'* interest in astrology and the stars was especially relevant in its environment. Astrology was important not only in the thought of Bardaisan, but also in a number of Syrian cults, particularly the one associated with Nebo and Bêl. As Drijvers observes of Edessa,

> The religious scene was dominated by the cult of Nebo and Bêl, the first the Babylonian god of wisdom and human fate, the latter the kosmokrator, lord of planets and stars, who guided the world and gave it fertility. ... In his cult astrological practice kept an organic place, because astrology made known the plans and guidance of the divine creator of order.[89]

The prominence of Nebo and Bêl is clear in the *Doctrina Addai*, where Addai gives a speech against idolatry and performs signs that cause the chief priests of the city to "thr[o]w down the altars on which they sacrificed before Nebu and Bel, their gods, except the great altar in the midst of the city."[90] This may be an allusion to fourth-century Edessan pagan temples, which were still standing and "still maintained their central position."[91] The persistence of these beliefs is confirmed by Ephrem, who argues against pagan practices such as astrology and the use of amulets.[92] Ephrem's concern for these customs suggests that Christians in Edessa were drawn to them. Pagan practices, especially those associated in some

---

[87] Though I have isolated paganism and philosophy as separate movements for the sake of clarity, I agree with Wilken's statement that "To the citizens of Antioch, Hellenism did not appear as a 'separate' religion, the faith of a particular community; it was woven into the fabric of life." Wilken, *John Chrysostom and the Jews*, 21.

[88] As Drijvers notes, our evidence for these beliefs and practices is less than ideal: "Our sources thus are meager, often silent or contradictory, and at best make known only the surface of a whole religious world-view, but do not give any clear insight into the structural pattern on which the cult of the pagan gods and human behavior in general is based." Drijvers, "The Persistence of Pagan Cults and Practices in Christian Syria," in idem, *East of Antioch*, XVI, 35.

[89] Drijvers, "The Persistence of Pagan Cults," 37.

[90] Translation from Cureton, *Ancient Syriac Documents*, 14 (lines 11-15).

[91] Drijvers, "The Persistence of Pagan Cults," 39.

[92] Drijvers, *Cults and Beliefs at Edessa*, 195. See e.g. Ephrem, *Hymns against Heresies* 5.14, 19; 8; 9.8.

way with the stars and astrology, had a long history in Syria and were perceived by many Christians as a threat to orthodox practice and belief.

Jews and "Judaizing Christians"

In addition to the bewildering array of Christian and pagan religious groups in fourth-century Syria, archaeological and literary evidence reveals that there were also communities of Jews living in both Antioch and Edessa.[93] None of these religious groups lived in isolation:

> There was therefore a permanent interaction between the various population groups which lived densely packed within the walls of the usually small towns, where privacy was rare. ... In a small town like Edessa, Gentiles, Jews and Christians walked along the same streets, did their shopping at the common market-place, suffered from the same diseases, epidemics and wars, and therefore shared a lot of ideas and concepts about which they talked with each other.[94]

Jews were present when the city of Antioch was founded in 300 BCE, and may have lived in the region prior to this date.[95] As the above quote suggests, Jews were well-integrated into Antioch's social, political, and religious life, and throughout their history in ancient Antioch there were Jews in all social and economic classes.[96] Though we know a fair bit about the history of the Jewish community in Antioch, our evidence regarding late antique Syrian Judaism is far from complete.[97] Much of the literary evidence derives from Christian sources that are hardly complimentary to Jews, such as the writings of John Chrysostom, Ephrem, and the *Doctrina Addai*. Though these materials may tell us a limited amount of information about late antique Jewish praxis, they reveal a Judaism very much in conversation and competition with the Christian groups already discussed.

In the early part of the fourth century (esp. 324-337), Constantine's legislation pertaining to Jews suggests a certain degree of competition for

---

[93] See H. Pognon, *Inscriptions sémitiques de la Syrie, de la Mésopotamie et de la région de Mossoul* (Paris: Imprimerie Nationale, 1907) 78ff; Drijvers, "Jews and Christians at Edessa," 90. The literary evidence will be partially discussed below.

[94] Drijvers, "Syrian Christianity and Judaism," 127-28.

[95] Bernadette J. Brooten, "The Jews of Ancient Antioch," in *Antioch: The Lost Ancient City*, by Christine Kondoleon (Princeton, NJ: Princeton University Press, 2000) 29.

[96] Brooten, "Jews of Ancient Antioch," 29.

[97] Drijvers, "Syrian Christianity and Judaism, 141: "As in Antioch, we do not know much about the situation in Edessa in the fourth century." Wilken's assessment differs somewhat. While he agrees that we know very little about second- and third-century Judaism after the Bar Kokhba revolt, he states that "the later fourth century ... is the best documented of any period." Wilken, *John Chrysostom and the Jews*, 43. Helpful and concise summaries of the history of Jews in Antioch can be found in Brooten, "Jews of Ancient Antioch," 29-37; and Wilken, *John Chrysostom and the Jews*, 34-65.

adherents among Jews and Christians. While very much in keeping with Roman legal tradition, some of Constantine's laws during this period "are more explicitly designed to dissuade people from affiliating with Judaism."[98] Perhaps under the influence of Christian bishops, Constantine sought to limit Christians' contact with Jews (and, by implication, their attraction to and affiliation with Judaism). Other such legislation indicates that some Jews may have been abandoning Judaism for Christianity. *CT* 16.8.5, for instance, states that "It shall not be permitted that Jews harass or attack in any kind of injury him who became Christian from Jew."[99] Constantine's successor Constantius enacted similar legislation (*CT* 16.8.1; 16.8.6; 16.9.2).[100] This suggests that in the first half of the fourth century, Jewish and Christian communities throughout the empire perceived themselves to be competing for converts.[101]

We find a similar situation in both Antioch and Edessa during the latter half of the century. John Chrysostom's famous sermons *Against the Judaizers* (or, perhaps less accurately, *Against the Jews*), delivered to his congregation in Antioch, reveal that close ties existed between the Jewish synagogue and some of the members of John's flock. In the fall of 386, John declared that a certain disease was rampant among Christians: "What is this sickness? The festivals of the wretched and miserable Jews that follow one after another in succession – Trumpets, Booths, the Fasts – are about to take place. And many who belong to us and say they believe our teaching attend their festivals and even share in their celebrations and join

---

[98] See e.g. *CT* 16.9.1, which forbids the circumcision of a Christian (or otherwise non-Jewish) servant by a Jew: "Emperor Constantine Augustus to Felix, Praefectus Praetorio: If any one of the Jews shall buy and circumcise a Christian slave or of any other sect, he shall on no account retain the circumcised in slavery, but he who suffered this shall acquire the privileges of liberty." Wilken, *John Chrysostom and the Jews*, 51. Translation of Codex Theodosianus from Amnon Linder, ed. and trans., *The Jews in Roman Imperial Legislation* (Detroit, MI: Wayne State University Press, 1987) 141.

[99] Translation from Linder, *Jews in Roman Imperial Legislation*, 142. This legislation may reflect a social reality in which some Jews converted to Christianity, but it may also be participating in a rhetorical statement about the inevitable attraction of Christianity to non-Christians and the disruptive nature of the Jews.

[100] Linder, *Jews in Roman Imperial Legislation*, 126, 144-51. The situation changed after Constantius: "the law codes record almost no legislation on the Jews until the end of the century," and Theodosius I's leglislation from 379 onwards "exhibits genuine respect for the Jews and their traditions." Wilken, *John Chrysostom and the Jews*, 52.

[101] I am not arguing that late antique Jews were aggressively proselytizing, as some have done. My point here is more about Christian *perceptions* of competition with Jews, whether or not Jews were actively seeking out converts. On the question of proselytizing see Shepardson, "In the Service of Orthodoxy," 63; and Miriam Taylor, *Anti-Judaism and Early Christian Identity: A Critique of the Scholarly Consensus* (New York: Brill, 1995).

in their fasts" (*Jud.* 1.1).[102] John's eight sermons against Judaizing Christians[103] reveal that Christians competed not only among their own factions, but also with Jews, for adherents.

The infamous and equally incendiary anti-Jewish rhetoric of Ephrem Syrus suggests a similar situation in late fourth-century Nisibis and Edessa.[104] Consider, for example, one segment of the last of Ephrem's nineteen *Hymns on Unleavened Bread*:

16. Do not take, my brothers, that unleavened bread from the People whose hands are covered with blood,

17. Lest it cling to that unleavened bread from the filth that fills their hands.

18. Although flesh is pure, no one eats from that which was sacrificed [to idols], because it is unclean.

19. How impure therefore is that unleavened bread that the hands that killed the Son kneaded![105]

In this hymn, Ephrem draws a comparison between the continuing presence of Christ's blood in the Eucharist, and the perpetual contamination of the Jews' unleavened bread, which was kneaded by the hands of those who killed Christ. This passage is interesting for our purposes because it reveals that Ephrem believed that some Christians were engaging in practices that he regarded as "too close to Judaism." It appears that some of his audience may have celebrated Easter on 14 Nisan, the date of Passover, and Ephrem writes to construct "a clear boundary that appears not yet to exist along the lines that he wishes between local 'Judaism' and 'Christianity.'"[106] The writings of Ephrem, like those of John Chrysostom, are meant for internal Christian consumption and were

---

[102] Translation from Meeks and Wilken, *Jews and Christians in Antioch*, 86.

[103] The definitional problems associated with Jewish Christianity and Judaizing Christians are notorious. See e.g. the discussion in Reed, "Jewish Christianity," 190-91 (esp. notes 4 and 5); A. F. J. Klijn, "The Study of Jewish Christianity," *New Testament Studies* 20 (1974) 419-31; Joan E. Taylor, "The Phenomenon of Early Jewish-Christianity: Reality or Scholarly Invention?" *Vigiliae Christianae* 44 (1990) 313-34; and Simon C. Mimouni, "Pour une définition nouvelle du judéo-christianisme ancien," *New Testament Studies* 38 (1992) 161-86. On the presence of "Jewish Christians" in Antioch's earlier history, see Clayton N. Jefford, "Reflections on the Role of Jewish Christianity in Second-Century Antioch," in *Le judéo-christianisme dans tous ses états*, 147-67.

[104] Shepardson is surely right, however, in suggesting that some of Ephrem's anti-Jewish rhetoric functions as part of an "intra-Christian debate" and does not necessarily tell us about interactions between Christians and Jews in Nisibis and Edessa. Shepardson, "In the Service of Orthodoxy," 39-112.

[105] Translation by Shepardson, "In the Service of Orthodoxy," 59-60.

[106] Shepardson, "In the Service of Orthodoxy," 64. On the so-called Quartodeciman practices of ancient Christians, see Shepardson, 61-64.

not directed at a Jewish audience.[107] But they reveal that Judaism was appealing to Christians, many of whom had regular contact with their Jewish neighbors and saw little if any conflict between religious practices which, for church leaders such as Chrysostom and Ephrem, belonged to two separate religions whose boundaries were not fuzzy but crystal clear.

Annette Reed has proposed that the Pseudo-Clementine *Homilies* and *Recognitions*, which are often regarded as Jewish-Christian texts that deviate from normative Judaism and normative Christianity, should be regarded as participants in this larger discourse about the relationship between Christianity and Judaism.[108] Reed's point is important, and very much in line with my own view of the Pseudo-Clementines, but in light of what we've covered in this chapter I'd like to expand even further on her observation. While it is true that the *Recognitions* is participating in a discourse about the relationship between Christianity and Judaism, we need to broaden the discursive framework a bit. Our text is negotiating Christian identity by using not just Judaism, but a variety of religious groups, to think with.

Julian

Up to this point I have provided a general sketch of religious life in fourth-century Antioch and Edessa, in an attempt to explore the contentious and competitive environment in which late antique Christians found themselves. For the sake of clarity I've artificially separated different Christians groups from Jews and pagans, though it is not difficult to see that these religious communities were participating in a single discourse about religious belief, practice, and authority. Indeed, nowhere is the intersection between Christianity, Judaism, and paganism clearer in late antique religious discourse than during and immediately after the reign of the emperor Julian (361-363 CE).

Julian, sometimes dubbed "the Apostate," was a nephew of Constantine, the first Christian emperor of Rome.[109] Born ca. 331 into a Christian household, Julian studied rhetoric and philosophy and "converted" to paganism in the form of Neoplatonism and theurgy around the year 351. He was appointed Caesar in 355 and was acclaimed Augustus by his troops in 360; by late 361, when Constantius died, Julian was the sole emperor. During his brief reign, Julian attempted to reverse the nascent imperial

---

[107] Drijvers, "Syrian Christianity and Judaism," 141.

[108] Reed, "Jewish Christianity," 202-3. See also Baumgarten, "Literary Evidence," 39-50.

[109] I have consulted the summary of Julian's life in Rowland Smith, *Julian's Gods: Religion and philosophy in the thought and action of Julian the Apostate* (London and New York: Routledge, 1995) 1-9; the details in this paragraph can be found there.

trend that had supported Christianity and repressed traditional religious practices. To cite a few of the more well-known examples, he proclaimed religious tolerance, in an effort to restore pagan cultic sacrifices (forbidden by Constantius in 341) and to exacerbate the tensions among Christians involved in the *homoousios* debates. He forbade Christians to teach philosophy and classical literature in the schools. Most famously, he began a failed attempt to rebuild the Jewish Temple in Jerusalem.[110] It seems that he wanted Jews to be able to honor their God with sacrifices and, in so doing, to undermine the triumphalist claims of Christians who argued that the destruction of the Temple in 70 CE was proof of God's judgment on the Jews and a mark of the transfer of divine favor to Christians. His plan outraged Christians at the time, who saw it as "an extremely threatening act which undermined the very foundations of Christianity."[111] Indeed, Christians such as Ephrem, who wrote during and immediately after Julian's brief reign, spent a great deal of time and effort responding to the issues raised by Julian.[112] Might the *Recognitions* also have been regarded as a response to such issues, either by its author or subsequent audiences? In my view this is altogether possible.

The events of Julian's reign intersect and overlap with several of the main ideas put forward by the *Recognitions*. First, Julian's personal commitments and public actions raised a host of questions about the relationship between philosophy and paganism on the one hand, and Christian truth-claims on the other hand. Julian, who had a Greek education in rhetoric and philosophy that was typical for the literate elite, held philosophy in high regard.[113] He was also an initiate into the mysteries of Cybele and (possibly) Mithras, and a devotee of Iamblichan Neoplatonism.[114] And, of course, Julian was a vocal critic of Christianity.

---

[110] On the evidence for this attempt see David B. Levenson "Julian's Attempt to Rebuild the Temple: An Inventory of Ancient and Medieval Sources," in *Of Scribes and Scrolls: Studies on the Hebrew Bible, Intertestamental Judaism, and Christian Origins presented to John Strugnell on the occasion of his sixtieth birthday*, ed. Harold W. Attridge, John J. Collins, and Thomas H. Tobin (New York and London: Lanham, 1990) 261-79; and more recently, idem, "The Ancient and Medieval Sources for the Emperor Julian's Attempt to Rebuild the Jerusalem Temple," *JSJ* 35 (2004) 409-60.

[111] Jan Willem Drijvers, "The Syriac Julian Romance. Aspects of the Jewish-Christian Controversy in Late Antiquity," in *All Those Nations ...: Cultural Encounters within and with the Near East. Studies presented to Han Drijvers at the occasion of his sixty-fifth birthday by colleagues and students*, ed. H. L. J. Vanstiphout et al. (Groningen: Styx Publications, 1999) 36-37.

[112] On the importance of the Temple in fourth-century Christian thought see Shepardson, "In the Service of Orthodoxy," 101-10.

[113] For a detailed and nuanced account of Julian's philosophical education and views see Smith, *Julian's Gods*, 23-90.

[114] Smith, *Julian's Gods*, 91-178.

His *Against the Galileans*, written from Antioch in 362-363, was designed "to show all men that the Galilaean fabrication is a human fiction contrived by evil."[115] Among other things, the preserved parts of this polemical treatise deal with many of the same issues raised in the *Recognitions*. For example, one of its sections addresses human ideas about the divine.[116] There Julian criticizes biblical ideas about the nature of God and his reasons for creating the world, including a critique of the creator that is not unlike that found in Marcion's thought (*CGa* 89a; 94a).[117] Another section of *Against the Galileans* involves comparisons of Jewish and Greek conceptions of the divine. Here Julian writes about Jewish and Greek accounts of the creation of the world (*CGa* 96ce; 49a-66a), including an exposition of Genesis and Plato's *Timaeus*; the question of the relationship of Christians' one god to the multiplicity of peoples in the world; and a description of the variety of nations and cultures in the world, each of which has its own laws and its own presiding god (*CGa* 116a; 131b; 138b; 143b).[118] As we have seen in the previous chapters of this book, many of these issues recur frequently throughout the *Recognitions* as well.

We must be extremely cautious, I think, not to reach unwarranted conclusions about these similarities. I am not proposing that the *Recognitions* was written as a response either to Julian's religio-political program or to his treatise *Against the Galileans*. This is not least because the topical similarities – and they are only that – are commonplaces of apologetic and polemical exchanges among Jews, Greeks, and Christians in late antiquity. I am, however, suggesting that the Julian episode provides us with a crucial instance when the *Recognitions'* rhetorical agenda would have seemed not just relevant, but acutely important, for its Christian audience living in fourth-century Antioch or Edessa. This may become clearer if we consider two more aspects of Julian's religious beliefs and political actions.

One of these aspects has to do with Julian's views on blood sacrifice and the Jerusalem Temple. As Jan Willem Drijvers states,

The emperor, as a Neoplatonist of the school of Iamblichus, believed that sacrifices were essential to religion, which explains his sympathy for the ritual aspect of Judaism. According to Mosaic law Jews were only allowed to sacrifice in the Temple in Jerusalem.

---

[115] *CGa* 39a, as cited in Smith, *Julian's Gods*, 190.

[116] On the argument of Julian's *Against the Galileans* see Smith, *Julian's Gods*, 189-207.

[117] Smith, *Julian's Gods*, 192-94.

[118] Smith, *Julian's Gods*, 193-96.

However, since the destruction of the Temple in 70 CE no Jewish sacrifices could be performed.[119]

Julian's attempt to rebuild the Jerusalem Temple stemmed not only from his desire to undermine the triumphalist claims of Christians over Jews and pagans, but also from his theurgic commitment to ritual sacrifice. While Julian is clearly in favor of animal sacrifice, the *Recognitions* opposes it. Its argument against animal sacrifices (see *Rec* 1.36-39, for example) belongs primarily to the identifiable source layer *Rec* 1.27-71, and is considered to be a hallmark of Jewish-Christian belief. It may very well be the case that this aspect of the *Recognitions* testifies to the ongoing existence of a Jewish-Christian community in the fourth century, as Reed has argued.[120] It is also possible, in light of what we know about Julian's activities, to situate the *Recognitions'* arguments against animal sacrifice in the broader framework of the Roman empire. In other words, perhaps the audience of the *Recognitions* understood its statements on ritual sacrifice to refer not only to Judaism, but also to paganism in the form of the Neoplatonist theurgy of Julian and his proposed reinstatement of sacrifices in Jerusalem.

One final aspect of Julian's religious beliefs needs to be considered here. Julian, a worshipper of Helios and possibly an initiate into the Mithraic mysteries, was an astrologer of sorts. Julian's astrological leanings are addressed in Ephrem's *Hymns against Julian*:

This one, too, who followed in his footsteps,

who loved Chaldeans – [God] surrendered him to the Chaldeans.

He worshipped the sun and fell before the servants of the sun.[121]

In this stanza Ephrem states that since Julian loved Chaldeans (a synonym for astrologers), he was handed over by God to the Persians. The Persians, who worshipped the Sun just as Julian did, caused the emperor's death.[122] Other passages in Ephrem's fourth hymn against Julian discuss astrological topics such as the Julian's use of the Zodiac.[123] The *Recognitions'*

---

[119] Jan Willem Drijvers, "Syriac Julian Romance," 36.

[120] Reed, "Jewish Christianity," 224-31.

[121] Ephrem, *Hymns against Julian* 4.8. Translation by Kathleen E. McVey, *Ephrem the Syrian: Hymns* (New York: Paulist Press, 1989) 252.

[122] H. J. W. Drijvers, "The Syriac Romance of Julian: Its Function, Place of Origin and Original Language," in *VI Symposium Syriacum (1992)*, ed. R. Lavenant (Orientalia Christiana Analecta 247; Rome: Pontificio Istituto Orientale, 1994) 205.

[123] Griffith, "Ephraem the Syrian's 'Hymns against Julian'," 260 states that the final stanza of these hymns echoes "Ephraem's hope to see in the emperor Julian's fate the final defeat of every force opposed to the triumph of a Christian empire.":

opposition to astrology, which we have explored at some length in Chapter 3 of this book, would have proven newly relevant in light of Julian's interest in astrological practices. The audience of the *Recognitions*, who may have encountered our text during Julian's heyday, would have thought of its polemics against astrology, philosophy and sacrifice not as vestiges of an earlier era of Christian history, but as entirely applicable to the fourth century.

The *Recognitions* in the Light of Fourth-Century Syria: Four Observations

This sketch of religious life in fourth-century Syria reveals that the *Recognitions* was constructed in the midst of an intensely competitive and diverse religious marketplace. In addition to the points I've already made, I'd like to conclude this chapter by highlighting four ways in which this agonistic environment is important for our understanding of the *Recognitions*.

Observation One

It is significant that Christian authors contemporary with the *Recognitions*, such as Ephrem and Aphrahat,[124] direct so much of their polemical energy at second- and third-century figures whose thought has continued to be influential well into the fourth century. This suggests that the *Recognitions*' polemical agenda, which is likewise oriented around concerns raised by the same second- and third-century persons,[125] is not

---

Who will ever again believe in
fate and the horoscope?
Who will ever again affirm
diviners and soothsayers?
Who will ever again go astray,
after auguries and Zodiacal signs?

All of them have been wrong in everything.

So that the Just One will not have to instruct
each one who goes astray,
He broke the one who went astray,
so that in him those who have gone astray might learn their lesson.

[124] Much like Ephrem his contemporary, Aphrahat condemns Marcion, Valentinus and Mani in his *On Fasting* 9 (written ca. 336-37).

[125] Côté, *Le thème de l'opposition*, 95-134, is an important treatment of the Pseudo-Clementine portrait of Peter and Simon in light of second- and third-century ideas about magic and philosophy.

merely a vestige of its debt to the *Grundschrift*. The text's interest in providence, fate, and the nature of God (to take just a few examples) reflects the author's own situation in fourth-century Syria, which was characterized by the continued existence and power of religious movements begun in earlier times and a "general pattern ... where philosophical and religious debates on body and soul, God and the world, freedom of will and determinism, and related matters were common practice in large groups of the population."[126] In other words, the *Recognitions* shows us that topics attributed to the "age of the apologists" continued to be relevant in new ways for fourth-century Christians: its interest in fate and providence makes sense in light of the continued influence of Bardaisan's ideas, its concern with the nature of God may reflect an ongoing concern with Marcionite (and, in the case of *Rec* 3.2-11, possibly Arian or Eunomian) beliefs, and its preoccupation with the intersection of philosophical ideas and Christian belief, which it shares with Christian apologists from the second century onward, may signal how important such issues were for late antique Christians involved in debates about the precise nature of the Godhead. In addition, during the reign of Julian the *Recognitions'* entire polemical and apologetic agenda may have served as a Christian response to the beliefs and activities of the emperor himself. This brings me to the next point.

Observation Two

It is noteworthy that the *Recognitions* emerges at a time when new forms of competition were being introduced into the Syrian religious marketplace. As we have seen, Syrian cities like Antioch were deeply implicated in the Christological controversies of the fourth century and experienced no small degree of conflict and schism as a result.[127] Heresiological discourses, a feature of Christian writing since the time of Irenaeus, became more prominent than ever. A number of Christian groups, especially in Antioch, were rivals in these contests of orthodoxy. Such emerging religious conflict and competition may have created an environment in which the *Recognitions'* multifaceted polemical agenda, with its emphases on apostolic tradition and absolute prophetic truth, became relevant in new ways. This is strongly suggested by the example of the early fifth-century *Doctrina Addai*, if Sebastian Brock's explanation of the creation and promotion of the Addai/Thaddaeus legend is correct. He argues that

---

[126] Drijvers, "Marcionism in Syria," 172.

[127] See e.g. Downey, *History of Antioch*, 317-449; Kelley McCarthy Spoerl, "The Schism at Antioch since Cavallera," in *Arianism after Arius*, 101-26; Rowan Williams, *Arius: Heresy and Tradition*, 158-67.

One quite likely suggestion is that early Christianity in Edessa covered a wide spectrum of groups, some of whom (such as the followers of Marcion and of Bardaisan) later came to be regarded as heretical; according to this view, members of the group which emerged in the late third and early fourth century as 'orthodox' sought to promote their authority by circulating a narrative concerning Addai's mission to Edessa in order to provide themselves, not only with a respectable apostolic origin, but also with a direct link to Jesus himself.[128]

This is, of course, precisely what the *Recognitions* seems to be doing as well! Like the *Doctrina Addai*, our text has an interest in promoting beliefs and practices it deems orthodox, and it advances its agenda and underwrites its own authority by recounting the missionary activity of Peter. The *Recognitions* is not attempting to establish an apostolic origin for a church in a particular locale, as the *Doctrina Addai* is, but it is most certainly intent on creating an apostolic foundation for its teaching. Moreover, this apostolic foundation does not stop with Peter but can be traced back to Jesus himself. These rather striking similarities make it all the more curious that, while virtually every treatment of Syria in the third and fourth centuries discusses in some detail the *Doctrina Addai*, Chrysostom, and Ephrem (together with the 'heterodox' figures Bardaisan, Marcion, Mani, and Arius), few studies bother to talk about the Pseudo-Clementines. Like other texts produced in this environment, these writings are an important witness to the continuing development of discourses of orthdoxy and heterodoxy, and their attendant concerns of apostolic authority and authentic traditions, in fourth-century Syria. This brings me to my third point.

Observation Three

Given the large number of rival religious groups in late antique Syria, it is significant that the *Recognitions* uses Simon Magus and Faustinianus as spokespersons for a number of competing views that are more or less lumped together. As I mentioned at the outset of the book, there are no Marcionites, Arians or Bardesanites identified as such in the narrative of the *Recognitions*. I see this "grouping" technique as a rhetorical strategy of sorts. In an environment characterized by a multitude of competing truth-claims, the *Recognitions* functions as a multi-pronged attack not just against *one* group such as the Marcionites or Pauline Christians, but

---

[128] Brock, "Eusebius and Syriac Christianity," 227. Drijvers makes essentially the same point when he states that the *Doctrina Addai* "does not inform us about historical events during the first, second and third century A.D., but champions a kind of orthodoxy that must be considered the preliminary final phase of a long development of Christian and pagan controversies and doctrinal discussions and fights in the Christian community of Edessa." Drijvers, *Cults and Beliefs at Edessa*, 195. See also Ross, *Roman Edessa*, 118.

against several different varieties of belief.[129] In this way the text redescribes the field of competition, so that it ceases to be a bewildering array of rival religious claimants and becomes something more manageable: a choice between prophetic and false knowledge, and ultimately a choice between salvation or damnation.[130]

Observation Four

The *Recognitions'* religiously competitive Syrian environment may explain (at least in part) its use of sources that seem to be poorly integrated into the narrative as a whole.[131] It is not unreasonable to think that the text's haphazard integration of sources produces a reading that is not haphazard at all: the *Recognitions* is, in a sense, designed to have recognizable sources and readily identifiable themes and *topoi*. The dialogue between Faustinianus and the protagonists in *Rec* 9, for example, agrees almost word-for-word with much of the conversation between Bardaisan and Awida in the *Book of the Laws of the Countries*.[132] The romantic and novelistic subplot that tells the story of Clement and his family is, by all accounts, remarkably similar to other examples of the Hellenistic novel.[133] Simon Magus makes statements that are obvious summaries of the views of Marcion.[134] Peter's rejection of animal sacrifice is often considered to be an expression of a "Jewish-Christian" sensibility,[135] but it might also be understood with reference to common late antique ideas expressed not only by Elchasai and the Ebionites, but also by Porphyry and Origen.[136]

---

[129] This polemical variety is evident also in the writings of Ephrem; see Drijvers, *Cults and Beliefs at Edessa*, 195; and now Shepardson, "In the Service of Orthodoxy," 163-210 *et passim*.

[130] This claim is to be differentiated from the idea, common in older scholarship, that the Pseudo-Clementines follow Irenaeus in regarding Simon Magus as the father of all heresies. See e.g. Koester, "ΓΝΩΜΑΙ ΔΙΑΦΟΡΟΙ ," 289.

[131] Not every apparent redactional difficulty in the Pseudo-Clementines can be explained on these grounds. For instance, I agree with previous scholars who have identified any number of literary seams and temporal difficulties created by the author's rather careless editorial practices. I am claiming only that some larger narrative purpose may have been served by the text's awkward juxtaposition of such sources.

[132] Rehm, *Rekognitionen*, 271-317 shows clearly the extensive parallels between the two texts.

[133] See the discussion above.

[134] Drijvers, "Adam and the True Prophet," 314-23.

[135] See e.g. *Rec* 1.36.1 – 1.39.3; 1.64.1-2. On the rejection of animal sacrifice as a hallmark of Elchasaite and Ebionite beliefs, see Epiphanius *Panarion* 19.3.6 and 30.16.5, respectively.

[136] On the general late antique association between sacrifice and demons, see Jonathan Z. Smith, "Towards Interpreting Demonic Powers in Hellenistic and Roman

We may fault the redactor(s) of the text for a lack of originality and editorial finesse, but these all-too-apparent connections serve an important purpose: they allow readers to re-situate familiar but competing religious texts and truth claims. In other words, the *Recognitions* targets an audience that knows of the ideas of Marcion, Bardaisan, Arius and perhaps other religious and philosophical competitors as well. Its readers may have had more than just a general awareness of such ideas – they might have read or heard the competing texts for themselves. By re-positioning these ideas and texts within the framework of a story where the competitors are always wrong, Peter and his companions are always right, and the only valuable commodity is Peter's prophetic knowledge of God's providential design, the *Recognitions* demands that readers abandon their previous understanding of such ideas in favor of its own truth claims.

Apostolic Authority and the Rhetoric of Authenticity in Fourth-Century Syria

As we have seen, the *Recognitions* suggests that Peter has near-exclusive control of prophetic knowledge and an unparalleled understanding of providential design, which he is able to impart to his close followers. The Pseudo-Clementines, of course, are only one segment of a range of ancient Christian writings that claim such authority on Peter's behalf; one thinks immediately of texts such as the Gospel of Matthew, 2 Peter, the Acts of Peter, and the Apocalypse of Peter. Other texts, such as the Gospels of Mary, Thomas, and John, inadvertently witness to Peter's importance in their attempts to challenge it. [137]

Obviously there is a set of traditions ascribing a central role to the apostle Peter. But why does the *Recognitions*, in particular, place such emphasis on the authority of Peter? Is this feature of the text just a careless repetition of earlier Christian ideas, or can we uncover ways in which this idea may have been newly-relevant for the *Recognitions*? On the one hand, it is most certainly inherited – inherited directly from the *Grundschrift*, [138]

Antiquity," in *ANRW* II.16.1, ed. Hildegard Temporini and Wolfgang Haase (Berlin and New York: Walter de Gruyter, 1978) 428; Janowitz, *Icons of Power*, 98-100.

[137] For summaries of the roles of Peter in these and other texts, see Lapham, *Peter: The Myth, the Man and the Writings*; Pheme Perkins, *Peter: Apostle for the Whole Church* (Columbia, SC: University of South Carolina Press, 1994), 151-67; Terence V. Smith, *Petrine Controversies in Early Christianity: Attitudes towards Peter in Christian Writings of the First Two Centuries* (WUNT 2.15; Tübingen: J. C. B. Mohr [Paul Siebeck], 1985); and Daniélou, "Pierre dans le judéo-christianisme hétérodoxe," 443-58.

[138] The Pseudo-Clementine emphasis on Petrine authority can be traced back even further to the second-century *Kerygmata Petrou*, if it did in fact exist; I am inclined to

which already contains much of the narrative about Peter, and inherited indirectly from other Christian texts and communities (many of them probably located in Syria) that regarded Peter as "the spokesperson for the understanding of Christian truth held by the majority of Christians" and "the model for those who seek to defend that tradition."[139]

On the other hand, our text's interest in Peter might fruitfully be understood with reference to its fourth-century Syrian context. Petrine authority, already an important ecclesiastical issue in the third-century,[140] may have had a renewed importance by the time the *Recognitions* was created in the fourth century. This is suggested by the much-discussed sixth canon of the Council of Nicaea (325 CE), which "recognized the preeminent rights and privileges of the churches of Antioch and Alexandria, which, by virtue of the apostolic foundation that they could claim, were to be allowed to exercise greater rights than other churches."[141]

If the *Recognitions* can be dated to some point in the mid-fourth century CE, it follows that our text was written at a time when apostolic connections continued to be used as a tool for legitimizing and ratifying the authoritative claims of specific Christian communities.[142] As Lapham notes, "those churches which could legitimately boast apostolic foundation were in a position to claim superior authority and greater theological credibility."[143] This would have been especially pertinent at a time when the imperially-sanctioned pursuit of "orthodoxy," begun in earnest at Nicaea, continued to dominate the Christian landscape. What better way to ratify one's beliefs at the expense of competing religious ideas than to

---

believe that it did not. On the *KP* source see Georg Strecker, "Appendix 1: On the Problem of Jewish Christianity," in Bauer, *Orthodoxy and Heresy*, pp. 241-85, esp. 257-71.

[139] Perkins, *Peter*, 159.

[140] Smith, *Petrine Controversies*, 20-24; Perkins, *Peter*, 173-76.

[141] Downey, *History of Antioch*, 351. It is beyond the scope of the article to offer an analysis of the sixth canon, which raises complex interpretative problems; see Henry Chadwick, "Faith and Order at the Council of Nicaea: A Note on the Background of the Sixth Canon," *Harvard Theological Review* 53 (1960) 171-95. The canon itself refers to "ancient customs" (ἀρχαῖα ἔθη) without stating explicitly that the cities' apostolic foundation is the reason for their preëminence, but it seems safe to say that this reasoning forms part of the implicit rationale behind the canon. Consider, for example, the various ancient sources that report on Peter's ties to Antioch offered in Downey, *History of Antioch*, 583-86.

[142] Strecker and Waitz date the *Recognitions* to 350 CE. Strecker, *Judenchristentum*, 270; Waitz, *Pseudoklementinen*, 372. On the complexity of the interpretation of *Rec* 3.2-11 and its significance for the question of dating the text, see the history of scholarship given in Jones, "Pseudo-Clementines," 76-79. The use of apostolic genealogies as a legitimizing strategy is not, of course, peculiar to the fourth century.

[143] Lapham, *Peter: The Myth, the Man and the Writings*, 93.

appeal to Jesus' foremost apostle and his successor Clement[144] as guarantors of authenticity and truth? This is especially the case if Perkins' assertions about second- and third-century Christian views of Peter, cited in the previous paragraph, also hold true for the fourth century. If Peter's authority continues to be associated with "the understanding of Christian truth held by the majority of Christians," then we can understand why a text such as the *Recognitions* – which is clearly interested in presenting its teachings as "orthodox," and was written at an historical moment when the pursuit of orthodoxy was at its height – would have appropriated the figure of Peter for its own purposes. This is supported by the appearance of Peter in apostolic genealogies found in two other Syrian texts that are nearly contemporary with the *Recognitions*: the *Doctrina Addai* and the Martyrdom of Barsamya.

Recall that according to Drijvers, the *Doctrina Addai* "does not inform us about historical events during the first, second and third century A.D., but champions a kind of orthodoxy that must be considered the preliminary final phase of a long development of Christian and pagan controversies and doctrinal discussions and fights in the Christian community of Edessa."[145] Although the narrative purports to tell its readers about earlier events in Christian history, it is a later text using an archaizing strategy to legitimate its story. The same is true, of course, for the *Recognitions*, which presents itself as an account of events that took place shortly after Jesus' death, but is really a product of the fourth century and its attendant controversies. It is probably no accident, then, that the *Recognitions* devotes much of its space creating a genealogy from Clement to Peter to Jesus, and the *Doctrina Addai* relates the following:

And because [Addai] died suddenly and quickly ... he was not able to lay his hand upon Palut, and Palut himself went to Antioch, and received the Hand of Priesthood from Serapion, Bishop of Antioch, which Hand Serapion himself also received from Zephyrinus, Bishop of the city of Rome, from the succession of the Hand of Priesthood of Simon Cephas, who had received it from our Lord, and was bishop there in Rome twenty and five years in the days of that Caesar who reigned there thirteen years.[146]

Just like the *Recognitions*, the *Doctrina Addai* sets up an apostolic pedigree for the leader of its community and the source of its teachings, as

---

[144] Tertullian, *De Praescrip. Haer.* 32, preserves the tradition that Clement was directly ordained by Peter as bishop of Rome. Cf. *Apostolic Constitutions* 7.46. On these issues see W. Ullmann, "Some Remarks on the Significance of the *Epistola Clementis* in the Pseudo-Clementines," in *Studia Patristica* 4: *Papers presented to the Third International Conference on Patristic Studies held at Christ Church, Oxford, 1959*, ed. F. L. Cross (TU 79; Berlin: Akademie-Verlag, 1961) 330-37.

[145] Drijvers, *Cults and Beliefs at Edessa*, 195.

[146] Translation from Cureton, *Ancient Syriac Documents*, 23 (lines 6-13).

a strategy for establishing its own orthodoxy. If Drijvers is correct, though the *Doctrina Addai* never mentions Manichaeism explicitly, it nevertheless "should be explained against the background of a historical situation in Edessa in which the Manichaean version and interpretation of Christian belief was the most powerful rival of a nascent 'orthodox' vision of the same tradition." He concludes that the constant allusions to Manichaean ideas and practices "might refer to a situation in which the 'orthodox' ... formed a minority that played a subordinate role in the local religious pattern."[147] Like the *Recognitions*, the *Doctrina Addai* finds itself strategically asserting the authenticity and orthodoxy of its claims, in an environment where its author and (presumably) audience may have considered themselves to be part of a minority religious group.

The Martyrdom of Barsamya, which purportedly relates events that occurred during the reign of the emperor Trajan (98-117 CE), is the story of the near-martyrdom of Barsamya, the bishop of Edessa.[148] The material in the text, most of which is commonly found in other martyr acts and apologetic literature, is less important than the line of descent that is traced at the very end of the narrative. It states that Barsamya received the "hand of priesthood" from Abshelama the bishop of Edessa, who in turn received it from Palut, who received it from Serapion the bishop of Antioch, who received it from Zephyrinus the bishop of Rome, who received it from a succession of individuals ending in Simon Peter, who received it from "our Lord."[149] Like the *Doctrina Addai* and the *Recognitions*, this text likewise constructs a genealogy that is designed to guarantee the authority of an individual and his teachings – and hence the preëminent place of the group attached to this leader – and which relies on a transmission of authority from Jesus to Peter and then on to others.[150]

These examples suggest that in the religiously competitive environment of fourth-century Syria, the general association of Peter with approved Christian teachings and the recent assertion of the ecclesiastical power of

---

[147] Drijvers, "Facts and Problems," 166.

[148] The text was probably written in the fourth or early fifth century. Susan Ashbrook Harvey ("Sacred Bonding: Mothers and Daughters in Early Syriac Hagiography," *JECS* 4.1 (1996) 27-56, 37 n. 37) lists the story of Barsamya as a fifth-century creation, though Ignatius Aphram I Barsoum (*The Scattered Pearls: A History of Syriac Literature and Sciences*, 2d rev. ed., trans. Matti Moosa [Piscataway, NJ: Gorgias Press, 2003] 159, 162) places them in the mid-fourth century. I am inclined to agree with Harvey on the basis of the similarities between this text and the Abgar/Addai cycle. I am grateful to David Levenson for his characteristic generosity in helping me to track down this information.

[149] Cureton, *Ancient Syriac Documents*, 71 (lines 17-30).

[150] Susan Ashbrook Harvey characterizes the Acts of Barsamya (along with other similar martyr acts) as "an apparent attempt by Edessa's aristocracy to upgrade their own past." Harvey, "Sacred Bonding," 37 n. 37.

Antioch – no doubt derived from its claim to have Peter as its first bishop – make the *Recognitions'* emphasis on Peter a timely and effective rhetorical strategy, and not just a vestige of its debt to earlier source materials.

Conclusion

As we have seen, fourth-century Syria was a hotbed of religious and philosophical rivalry, and a point of intersection for many cultural, social and political currents of the time. In other words, Syria at this point in Christian history constituted a competitive religious marketplace that is reproduced in particular and strategic ways within the *Recognitions* itself. This chapter has attempted to show that the text's multifaceted polemical program, which we examined in Chapters 2 and 3 of this book, reflects not just competition between so-called Jewish Christians and gentile Christians, or between Christians and Jews, but a complex rivalry between several types of Christian and non-Christian groups such as that found in fourth-century Antioch or Edessa.

I will conclude this study by mentioning a couple of the implications of this study for future research on the Pseudo-Clementines and late antique Syrian Christianity. First, my hope is that future scholars will pay closer attention to the *Recognitions* and its narrative. Given the size and the unwieldy nature of the text, it is only natural that many previous interpreters focused only on selected portions of the storyline. But the *Recognitions* has much to say to those who have the patience to listen to it, and I have no doubt only scratched the surface. Second, my hope is that the text will be viewed by future interpreters as something more than a Jewish-Christian text, existing on the fringes of a normative tradition that rejected some of its more eccentric doctrinal propositions, and valuable only insofar as it preserves earlier Christian materials. I have tried to re-situate the *Recognitions*, placing it not just in a conversation among small groups of marginal Jews and Christians, but in a centuries-long and empire-wide set of discourses about orthodoxy and heresy, authority and authenticity, and proper religious practice and belief that took place not only among Christians of all stripes but also among their Jewish and pagan neighbors. This re-positioning of the text means that the *Recognitions* should count as a resource for those who seek to understand fourth-century Syrian Christianity, and a central participant in its attendant discourses that seek to establish what it means to be a Christian, a Jew, a pagan.

Bibliography

1. Critical Editions and Translations

Apuleius. *The Golden Ass: Being the Metamorphoses of Lucius Apuleius.* Translated by W. Adlington and revised by S. Gaselee. Loeb Classical Library, ed. T. E. Page and others. Cambridge, MA: Harvard University Press, 1958.

– *The Isis-Book (Metamorphoses Book XI).* Edited and translated by J. Gwyn Griffiths. Etudes préliminaires aux religions orientales dans l'Empire romain 39. Leiden: Brill, 1975.

Augustine. *De Civitate Dei.* 2 volumes. Corpus Christianorum Series Latina 47. Turnhout: Brepols, 1955.

Bardaisan of Edessa. *The Book of the Laws of Countries: Dialogue on Fate of Bardaisan of Edessa.* Translated by H. J. W. Drijvers. Assen: Van Gorcum, 1964.

– *Liber legum regionum.* Edited by F. Nau. Patrologia Syriaca 1.2. Paris: Didot, 1907.

– *Le Livre des Lois des Pays.* Translated with introduction and notes by F. Nau. Paris: Librairie Orientaliste Paul Geuthner, 1899.

Bedjan, Paul, ed. *Acta martyrum et sanctorum.* 7 vols. Paris: Harrasssowitz, 1890-1897.

Clement of Alexandria. *Excerpta ex Theodoto.* Edited and translated by Robert Pierce Casey. Studies and Documents 1, ed. Kirsopp Lake and Silva Lake. London: Christophers, 1934.

– *The Exhortation to the Greeks, The Rich Man's Salvation,* and *To the Newly Baptized.* Translated by G. W. Butterworth. Loeb Classical Library, ed. T. E. Page and others. Cambridge, MA: Harvard University Press, 1960.

Cirillo, Luigi, and Schneider, André. *Les Reconnaissances du pseudo Clément: Roman chrétien des premiers siècles.* Turnhout: Brepols, 1999.

Cureton, William. *Ancient Syriac Documents.* Amsterdam: Oriental Press, 1967.

de Lagarde, Paulus Antonius, ed. *Clementis Romani Recognitiones Syriace.* Osnabrück: Otto Zeller, 1966.

Diels, H., and Kranz, W. *Die Fragmente der Vorsokratiker,* volume 2. 6th ed. Zürich: Weidmann, 1985.

Dodds, E. R. *Plato, Gorgias: A Revised Text with Introduction and Commentary.* Oxford: Clarendon, 1959.

Ephrem the Syrian. *Hymns.* Translated and introduced by Kathleen E. McVey. New York: Paulist Press, 1989.

– *S. Ephraim's Prose Refutations of Mani, Marcion, and Bardaisan.* Translated by C. W. Mitchell. Volume I: The Discourses Addressed to Hypatius. London: Williams and Norgate, 1912.

Firmicus Maternus, Julius. *Matheseos Libri VIII. Ancient Astrology: Theory and Practice.* Translated by Jean Rhys Bram. Park Ridge, NJ: Noyes Press, 1975.

Frankenberg, Wilhelm. *Die syrischen Clementinen mit griechischem Paralleltext: Eine Vorarbeit zu dem literargeschichtlichen Problem der Sammlung.* Texte und Untersuchungen zur Geschichte der altchristlichen Literatur 48.3. Leipzig: J. C. Hinrichs, 1937.

Gardner, Iain, and Lieu, Samuel N. C., eds. *Manichaean Texts from the Roman Empire.* Cambridge, UK: Cambridge University Press, 2004.

Hennecke, Edgar, and Schneemelcher, Wilhelm, eds. *New Testament Apocrypha. Volume Two: Writings Related to the Apostles; Apocalypses and Related Subjects.* Rev. ed. Translated by R. McL. Wilson. Tübingen: Mohr (Siebeck), 1989.

Julian. *L'Empereur Julien: oeuvres complètes.* Edited by J. Bidez and G. Rochefort. Paris: C. Lacombrade, 1924-63.

Origen. *Contra Celsum.* Translated with an introduction and notes by Henry Chadwick. Cambridge: At the University Press, 1965.

– *Origène: sur le libre arbitre: Philocalie 21-27.* Translated by Éric Junod. Sources Chrétiennes 226. Paris: Éditions du Cerf, 1976.

Ortiz de Urbina, Ignatius. *Patrologia Syriaca.* Rome: Pontifical Institute of Oriental Studies, 1958.

Norlin, George. *Isocrates.* Loeb Classical Library, ed. T. E. Page and others. Cambridge, MA: Harvard University Press, 1980.

Paschke, Franz. *Die beiden griechischen Klementinen-Neuausgabe der Texte.* Texte und Untersuchungen zur Geschichte der altchristlichen Literatur 90. Berlin: Akademie, 1966.

Photius. *Bibliothèque.* Translated by René Henry. Paris: Les Belles Lettres, 1959-1991.

Plato. *Plato: Lysis, Symposium, Gorgias.* Translated by W. R. M. Lamb. Loeb Classical Library, ed. T. E. Page and others. Cambridge, MA: Harvard University Press, 1961.

Ptolemy, Claudius. *Tetrabiblos.* Edited and translated by F. E. Robbins. Loeb Classical Library, ed. G. P. Goold and others. Cambridge, MA: Harvard University Press, 1980.

Rehm, Bernhard, and Strecker, Georg, eds. *Die Pseudoklementinen I: Homilien,* 3d ed., rev. Die griechischen christlichen Schriftsteller der ersten Jahrhunderte 42. Berlin: Akademie, 1992.

–, and Strecker, Georg, eds. *Die Pseudoklementinen II: Rekognitionen in Rufins Übersetzung,* 2d ed, rev. Die griechischen christlichen Schriftsteller der ersten Jahrhunderte 51. Berlin: Akademie, 1994.

Richardson, Cyril F. *Early Christian Fathers.* New York: Collier, 1970.

Roberts, A., and Donaldson, J., eds. *The Ante-Nicene Fathers.* 10 volumes. Grand Rapids, MI: Eerdmans, 1975.

Schaff, Philip, and Wace, Henry, eds. *A Select Library of the Nicene and Post-Nicene Fathers of the Christian Church.* 2d series. 14 volumes. Grand Rapids, MI: Eerdmans, 1978-1979.

Strecker, Georg, ed. *Die Pseudoklementinen III: Konkordanz zu den Pseudoklementinen.* 2 volumes. Die griechischen christlichen Schriftsteller der ersten Jahrhunderte. Berlin: Akademie, 1986-89.

2. General Bibliography

Adamik, T. "The Image of Simon Magus in the Christian Tradition." In *The Apocryphal Acts of Peter: Magic, Miracles, and Gnosticism,* ed. Jan N. Bremmer, 52-64. Leuven: Peeters, 1998.

Adler, William. "Apion's 'Encomium of Adultery': A Jewish Satire of Greek Paideia in the Pseudo-Clementine *Homilies.*" *Hebrew Union College Annual* 64 (1993) 15-49.

Aland, B. "Mani und Bardesanes – Zur Engstehung des manichäischen Systems." In *Synkretismus im syrisch-persischen Kulturgebiet: Bericht über ein Symposion in Rheinhausen bei Göttingen in der Zeit vom 4. bis 8. Oktober 1971*, ed. A. Dietrich, 123-43. Göttingen: Vandenhoeck & Ruprecht, 1975.

Aland, K. „The Problem of Anonymity and Pseudonymity in Christian Literature of the First Two Centuries." *Journal of Theological Studies* n.s. 12.1 (1961) 39-49.

Aletti, Jean-Noël. "L'Autorité apostolique de Paul: Théorie et Pratique." In *L'Apôtre Paul: Personnalité, Style et Conception du Ministère*, ed. A. Vanhoye, 229-46. Leuven: University Press, 1986.

Alexander, Loveday. "Mapping Early Christianity: Acts and the Shape of Early Church History." *Interpretation* 57 (2003) 163-75.

Amand, David. *Fatalisme et liberté dans l'antiquité grecque. Recherches sur la survivance de l'argumentation morale antifataliste de Carnéade chez les philosophes grecs et les théologiens chrétiens des quatre premiers siècles.* Amsterdam: Adolf M. Hakkert, 1973.

Amsler, Frédéric. "Les citations évangéliques dans le roman pseudo-clémentin. Une tradition indépendante du Nouveau Testament?" In *Le canon du Nouveau Testament: Regards nouveaux sur l'histoire de sa formation*, ed. Gabriella Aragione, Eric Junod, and Enrico Norelli, 141-67. Geneva: Labor et Fides, 2005.

– "Les *Reconnaissances* du Pseudo-Clément comme catéchèse romanesque." In *La Bible en récits: l'exégèse biblique à l'heure du lecteur*, ed. D. Marguerat, 442-55. Geneva: Labor et Fides, 2003.

Anderson, R. Dean, Jr. *Ancient Rhetorical Theory and Paul.* Contributions to Biblical Exegesis & Theology 18. Kampen, Netherlands: Pharos, 1996.

Attridge, Harold W. *The Interpretation of Biblical History in the Antiquitates Judaicae of Flavius Josephus.* Harvard Dissertations in Religion 7. Missoula, MT: Scholars, 1976.

Aune, David E. "Magic in Early Christianity." In *Principat*, ed. Wolfang Haase, 1507-57. *Aufstieg und Niedergang der römischen Welt: Geschichte und Kultur Roms im Spiegel der neueren Forschung*, vol. 2.23, ed. Hildegard Temporini and Wolfgang Haase. Berlin and New York: Walter de Gruyter, 1980.

Bammel, Ernst. "Rufins Einleitung zu den Klemens zugeschriebenen Wiedererkennungen." In *Storia ed esegesi in Rufino di Concordia*, 151-63. Udine: Arti grafiche friulane, 1992.

Bardy, Gustave. "Origene et la magie." *Recherches de Science Religieuse* 18 (1928) 126-42.

Barnes, Michael R., and Williams, Daniel H. *Arianism after Arius.* Edinburgh: T&T Clark, 1993.

Barrett, C. K. "Light on the Holy Spirit from Simon Magus (Acts 8, 4-25)." In *Les Actes des Apotres: traditions, rédaction, théologie*, ed. Jacob Kremer, 281-95. Bibliotheca Ephermeridum Theologicarum Lovaniensium 48. Louvain: Leuven Univ Press, 1979.

Barsoum, Ignatius Aphram I. *The Scattered Pearls: A History of Syriac Literature and Sciences.* 2d rev. ed. Translated by Matti Moosa. Piscataway, NJ: Gorgias Press, 2003.

Barton, S. "Can We Identify the Gospel Audiences?" In *The Gospels for All Christians: Rethinking the Gospel Audiences*, ed. R. Bauckham, 173-94. Grand Rapids, MI: Eerdmans, 1998.

Bauer, Walter. *Orthodoxy and Heresy in Earliest Christianity*, 2d ed. Translated by the Philadelphia Seminar on Christian Origins. Philadelphia: Fortress, 1971.

Baumgarten, Albert. "Literary Evidence for Jewish Christianity in the Galilee." In *The Galilee in Late Antiquity*, ed. L. Levine, 39-50. New York: Jewish Theological Seminary of America, 1992.

Baumstark, Anton. *Geschichte der syrischen Literatur mit Ausschluß der christlich-palästinensischen Texte.* Bonn: A. Marcus and E. Webers Verlag, 1922.

Baur, Ferdinand Christian. *Die christliche Gnosis oder die christliche Religions-Philosophie in ihrer geschichtlichen Entwicklung.* Tübingen: C. F. Osiander, 1835.

- "Die Christuspartei in der Korinthischen Gemeinde, der Gegensatz des petrinischen und paulinischen Christenthums in der ältesten Kirche, der Apostel Paulus in Rom." *Tübinger Zeitschrift für Theologie* 4 (1831) 61-206.

- *Paul, the Apostle of Jesus Christ: His Life and Works, His Epistles and Teachings: A Contribution to a Critical History of Primitive Christianity.* 2d ed. Translated by Eduard Zeller and A. Menzies. London: Williams and Norgate, 1873-1875.

Beck, E. "Bardaisan und seine Schule bei Ephram." *Le Muséon* 91 (1978) 271-333.

- *Die Theologie des hl. Ephraem in seinen Hymnen über den Glauben.* Studia Anselmiana philosophica theologica 21. Città del Vaticano: Libreria Vaticana, 1949.

Bergmann, J. "Les éléments juifs dans les Pseudo-Clémentines." *Revue des Études juives* 46 (1903) 89-98.

Berner, Ulrich. "The Image of the Philosopher in Late Antiquity and in Early Christianity." In *Concepts of Person in Religion and Thought*, ed. Hans G. Kippenberg, Yme B. Kuiper, and Andy F. Sanders, 125-36. Religion and Reason 37. Berlin: de Gruyter, 1990.

Bett, Richard. "The Sophists and Relativism." *Phronesis* 34.2 (1989) 139-69.

Beyschlag, Karlmann. *Clemens Romanus und der Frühkatholizismus. Untersuchungen zu I Clemens 1-7.* Beiträge zur historischen Theologie 35. Tübingen: Mohr (Siebeck), 1966.

- "Das Jakobusmartyrium und seine Verwandten in der frühchristlichen Literatur." *Zeitschrift für die Neutestamentliche Wissenschaft* 3/4 (1965) 149-78.

- *Simon Magus und die christliche Gnosis.* Wissenschaftliche Untersuchungen zum Neuen Testament 16. Tübingen: Mohr, 1974.

- "Zur Simon-Magus-Frage." *Zeitschrift für Theologie und Kirche* 68.4 (1971) 395-426.

Bigg, Charles. "The Clementine Homilies." In *Studia Biblica et Ecclesiastica: Essays Chiefly in Biblical and Patristic Criticism*, vol. 2, 157-93. Oxford: At the Clarendon Press, 1890.

Birdsall, J. Neville. "Problems of the Clementine Literature." In *Jews and Christians: The Parting of the Ways A.D. 70 to 135*, ed. J. D. G. Dunn, 347-61. Grand Rapids: Eerdmans, 1992.

Blum, G. G. *Tradition und Sukzession. Studien zum Normbegriff des Apostolischen von Paulus bis Irenäus.* Arbeiten zur Geschichte und Theologie des Luthertums 9. Berlin: Lutherisches Verlagshaus, 1963.

Böhlig, A. *Mysterion und Wahrheit: Gesammelte Beiträge zur spätantiken Religionsgeschichte.* Leiden: Brill, 1968.

Bohman, James. *New Philosophy of Social Science: Problems of Indeterminacy.* Cambridge, MA: MIT Press, 1991.

Boll, Franz. "Das Eingangsstück der Ps.-Klementinen." *Zeitschrift für die Neutestamentliche Wissenschaft* 17 (1916) 139-48.

- "Studien über Claudius Ptolemäus: ein Beitrag zur Geschichte der griechischen Philosophie und Astrologie." Jahrbücher für classische Philologie, Supplementary volume 21 (1894) 4-243.

– Carl Bezold, and Wilhelm Gundel. *Sternglaube und Sterndeutung: die Geschichte und das Wesen der Astrologie*. 6th ed. Darmstadt: Wissenschaftliche Buchgesellschaft, 1974.

Bornkamm, Günther. "The Stilling of the Storm in Matthew." In *Tradition and Interpretation in Matthew*, by Günther Bornkamm, Gerhard Barth, and Heinz Joachim Held, 52-57. Translated by Percy Scott. Philadelphia: Westminster, 1963.

Bouché-Leclercq, A. *L'Astrologie grecque*. Bruxelles: Culture et Civilisation, 1963.

Bourdieu, Pierre. "Genesis and Structure of the Religious Field." *Comparative Social Research* 13 (1991) 1-43.

– *Language and Symbolic Power*. Edited and introduced by John B. Thompson. Translated by Gino Raymond and Matthew Adamson. Cambridge, MA: Harvard University Press, 1991.

– *Sociology in Question*. Translated by Richard Nice. London: Sage Publications, 1993.

–, and Wacquant, Loïc J. D. *An Invitation to Reflexive Sociology*. Chicago: University of Chicago, 1992.

Bousset, Wilhelm. "Die Wiedererkennungs-Fabel in den pseudoklementinischen Schriften, den Menächmen des Plautus und Shakespeares Komödie der Irrungen." *Zeitschrift für die neutestamentliche Wissenschaft* 5 (1904) 18-27.

Bowersock, G. W., ed. *Approaches to the Second Sophistic: Papers Presented at the 105th Annual Meeting of the American Philological Association*. University Park, PA: American Philological Association, 1974.

– *Greek Sophists in the Roman Empire*. Oxford: Clarendon, 1969.

– *Roman Arabia*. Cambridge and London: Harvard University Press, 1983.

Boyarin, Daniel. *Dying for God: Martyrdom and the Making of Christianity and Judaism*. Stanford, CA: Stanford University Press, 1999.

Bremmer, Jan N. "Foolish Egyptians: Apion and Anoubion in the *Pseudo-Clementines*." In *The Wisdom of Egypt: Jewish, Early Christian, and Gnostic Essays in Honour of Gerard P. Luttikhuizen*, ed. Anthony Hilhorst and George H. van Kooten, 311-29. Leiden: Brill, 2005.

Brock, Sebastian. "Didymus the Blind on Bardaisan." *Journal of Theological Studies* 22 (1971) 530-31.

– *From Ephrem to Romanos: Interactions between Syriac and Greek in Late Antiquity*. Aldershot, UK: Ashgate, 1999.

– "Eusebius and Syriac Christianity." In *Eusebius, Christianity, and Judaism*, ed. Harold W. Attridge and Gohei Hata, 212-34. Leiden: Brill, 1992.

– *The Holy Spirit in the Syrian Baptismal Tradition*. 2d ed. Syrian Churches Series 9. Pune: Anita, 1998.

Brooks, E. C. "The Translation Techniques of Rufinus of Aquileia." In *Studia Patristica 17: Papers presented at the Eighth International Conference on Patristic Studies, Oxford, Sept. 3-8, 1979*, ed. Elizabeth A. Livingstone, I.357-364. 3 volumes. Elmsford, NY: Pergamon Press, 1982.

Brown, Scott Kent. "James: A Religio-Historical Study of the Relations between Jewish, Gnostic, and Catholic Christianity in the Early Period through an Investigation of the Traditions about James the Lord's Brother." Ph.D. diss., Brown University, 1972.

Bultmann, Rudolf. Review of *Theologie und Geschichte des Judenchristentums*, by Hans Joachim Schoeps. *Gnomon* 26 (1954) 177-89.

Butcher, Kevin. *Roman Syria and the Near East*. London: British Museum, 2003.

Cadiou, René. "Origène et les "Reconnaissances clémentines." *Recherches de Science Religieuse* 20 (1930) 506-28.

Calvet-Sébasti, Marie-Ange. "Femmes du roman pseudo-clémentin." In *Les personnages du roman grec. Actes du colloque de Tours, 18-20 novembre 1999*, ed. Bernard Pouderon, Christine Hunzinger, and Dimitri Kasprzyk, 285-97. Lyon: Maison de l'Orient Méditerranéen-Jean Pouilloux, 2001.

Calzolari, Valentina. "La tradition arménienne des Pseudo-Clémentines. État de la question." *Apocrypha* 4 (1993) 263-93.

Cambe, Michel, ed. *Kerygma Petri*. Corpus Christianorum Series Apocryphorum 15. Louvain: Brepols, 2003.

– "La *Prédication de Pierre* (ou: Le *Kérygme de Pierre*)." *Apocrypha* 4 (1993) 177-95.

Carroll, K. L. "The Place of James in the Early Church." *Bulletin of the John Rylands Library* 44 (1961) 49-67.

Cerfaux, Lucien. "Le vrai prophète des Clémentines." *Recherches de Science Religieuse* 18 (1928) 143-63.

Chadwick, Henry. *Early Christian Thought and the Classical Tradition: Studies in Justin, Clement, and Origen*. Oxford and New York: Oxford University Press, 1984.

– "Faith and Order at the Council of Nicaea: A Note on the Background of the Sixth Canon." *Harvard Theological Review* 53 (1960) 171-95.

Chapman, John. "On the Date of the Clementines," *Zeitschrift für die Neutestamentliche Wissenschaft* 9 (1908) 21-34, 147-59.

– "Origen and the Date of Pseudo-Clement." *Journal of Theological Studies* 3 (1902) 436-41.

Chilton, Bruce, and Neusner, Jacob. *Types of Authority in Formative Christianity and Judaism*. Routledge: London and New York, 1999.

Choi, Mihwa. "Christianity, Magic, and Difference: Name-Calling and Resistance between the Lines in *Contra Celsum*." *Semeia* 79 (1997) 75-92.

Cirillo, Luigi. "L'antipaolinismo nelle Pseudoclementine. Un riesame della questione." In *Verus Israel: Nuove prospettive sul giudeocristianesimo. Atti del Colloquio di Torino (4-5 novembre 1999)*, ed. Giovanni Filoramo and Claudio Gianotto, 280-303. Brescia: Paideia Editrice, 2001.

– "La littérature pseudo-clémentine: un aperçu." Unpublished paper presented at the annual meeting of the Association for the Study of Apocryphal Christian Literature, 24 June 1988.

Clarke, G. W. "The Literary Setting of the Octavius of Minucius Felix." *Journal of Religious History* 3 (1965) 195-211.

Clavier, Henri. "La primauté de Pierre d'après les pseudo-clémentines." *Revue d'histoire et de philosophie religieuses* 36 (1956) 298-307.

Contreras, Carlos A. "Christian Views of Paganism." In *Principat*, ed. Wolfang Haase, 974-1022. *Aufstieg und Niedergang der römischen Welt: Geschichte und Kultur Roms im Spiegel der neueren Forschung*, vol. 2.23, ed. Hildegard Temporini and Wolfgang Haase. Berlin and New York: Walter de Gruyter, 1980.

Conzelmann, Hans. *The Theology of St. Luke*. Translated by Geoffrey Buswell. New York: Harper & Brothers, 1960.

Cooper, Kate. "Matthidia's Wish: Division, Reunion, and the Early Christian Family in the Pseudo-Clementine *Recognitions*." In *Narrativity in Biblical and Related Texts/La narativité dans la Bible et les textes apparentés*, ed. G. J. Brooke and J.-D. Kaestli, 243-64. Leuven: Leuven University Press, 2000.

Côté, Dominique. "Une critique de la mythologie grecque d'après L'*Homélie pseudo-clémentine* IV." *Apocrypha* 11 (2000) 37-57.

– "La fonction littéraire de Simon le Magicien dans les Pseudo-Clémentines." *Laval théologique et philosophique* 57 (2001) 513-23.

– *Le thème de l'opposition entre Pierre et Simon dans les Pseudo-Clémentines.* Études Augustiniennes, Série Antiquités 167. Paris: Institut d'Études Augustiniennes, 2001.

Courcelle, Pierre. "La figure du philosophe d'après les écrivains latins de l'Antiquité." *Journal des Savants* (1980) 85-101.

Cox, P. *Biography in Late Antiquity: A Quest for the Holy Man.* The Transformation of the Classical Heritage 5. Berkeley: University of California Press, 1983.

Cramer, Frederick H. *Astrology in Roman Law and Politics.* Philadelphia: American Philosophical Society, 1954.

Crouzel, Henri. *Origène et la "connaissance mystique."* Paris: Desclée de Brouwer, 1961.

Cullmann, Oscar. *Peter: Disciple, Apostle, Martyr. A Historical and Theological Study.* 2d rev. ed. Translated by Floyd V. Wilson. Philadelphia: Westminster, 1962.

– "Die neuentdeckten Qumrantexte und das Judenchristentum der Pseudoklementinen." In *Neutestamentliche Studien für Rudolf Bultmann zu seinem siebzigsten Geburtstag am 20. August 1954,* ed. Walther Eltester, 35-51. Berlin: Alfred Töpelmann, 1954.

– *Le problème littéraire et historique du roman pseudo-clémentin: Étude sur le Rapport entre le Gnosticisme et le Judéo-Christianisme.* Études d'histoire et de philosophie religieuses publiées par la faculté de théologie protestante de l'Université de Strasbourg 23. Paris: Librairie Félix Alcan, 1930.

Cumont, Franz. *Astrology and Religion among the Greeks and Romans.* American Lectures on the History of Religions 8. New York and London: Knickerbocker Press, 1912.

– *Les religions orientales dans le paganisme romain: conférences faites au collège de France en 1905.* 4th ed. Paris: Librairie Orientaliste Paul Geuthner, 1963.

Daniélou, Jean. "Pierre dans le judéo-christianisme hétérodoxe." In *San Pietro. Atti della XIX Settimana biblica,* 443-58. Brescia: Paideia, 1967.

– *The Theology of Jewish Christianity.* Translated and edited by John A. Baker. A History of Early Christian Doctrine before the Council of Nicea 1. Philadelphia: Westminster, 1964.

de Romilly, Jacqueline. *Magic and Rhetoric in Ancient Greece.* Cambridge, MA: Harvard University Press, 1975.

Denzey, Nicola. "Under a Pitiless Sky: Conversion, Cosmology, and the Rhetoric of 'Enslavement to Fate' in Second-Century Christian Sources." Ph.D. diss., Princeton University, 1998.

Dibelius, Martin. *From Tradition to Gospel.* Translated by Bertram Lee Woolf. New York: Charles Scribner's Sons, 1935.

Dihle, Albrecht. "Liberté et destin dans l'antiquité tardive." *Revue de théologie et de philosophie* 121/2 (1989) 129-47.

Downey, Glanville. *A History of Antioch in Syria from Seleucus to the Arab Conquest.* Princeton, NJ: Princeton University Press, 1961.

Drijvers, Jan Willem. "The Syriac Julian Romance. Aspects of the Jewish-Christian Controversy in Late Antiquity." In *All Those Nations...: Cultural Encounters within and with the Near East. Studies presented to Han Drijvers at the occasion of his sixty-fifth birthday by colleagues and students,* collected and edited by H. L. J. Vanstiphout with the assistance of W. J. van Bekkum, G. J. van Gelder and G. J. Reinink, 31-42. Groningen: Styx Publications, 1999.

–, and Watt, John W., eds. *Portraits of Spiritual Authority: Religious Power in Early Christianity, Byzantium and the Christian Orient.* Leiden: Brill, 1999.

Drijvers, H. J. W. "Adam and the True Prophet in the Pseudo-Clementines." In *Loyalitätskonflikte in der Religionsgeschichte: Festschrift für Carsten Colpe,* ed.

Christoph Elsas and Hans G. Kippenberg, 314-23. Würzburg: Königshausen & Neumann, 1990.

- *Bardaisan of Edessa*. Assen: Van Gorcum & Co., 1966.
- *Cults and Beliefs at Edessa*. Leiden: E. J. Brill, 1980.
- "Early Syriac Christianity: Some Recent Publications." *Vigiliae Christianae* 50 (1996) 159-77.
- *East of Antioch: Studies in Early Syriac Christianity*. London: Variorum, 1984.
- "Edessa und das jüdische Christentum." *Vigiliae Christianae* 24 (1970) 3-33.
- "Jews and Christians at Edessa." *Journal of Jewish Studies* 36 (1985) 88-102.
- "Marcionism in Syria: Principles, Problems, Polemics." *Second Century* 6 (1987-1988) 153-72.
- "The Saint as Symbol. Conceptions of the Person in Late Antiquity and Early Christianity." In *Concepts of Person in Religion and Thought*, ed. Hans G. Kippenberg, Yme B. Kuiper and Andy F. Sanders, 137-57. Religion and Reason 37. Berlin: de Gruyter, 1990.
- "The Syriac Romance of Julian: Its Function, Place of Origin and Original Language." *VI Symposium Syriacum (1992)*, ed. R. Lavenant, 201-14. Orientalia Christiana Analecta 247. Rome: Pontificio Istituto Orientale, 1994.
- "Syrian Christianity and Judaism." In *The Jews Among Pagans and Christians*, ed. Judith Lieu, John North and Tessa Rajak, 124-46. London and New York: Routledge, 1992.
Edwards, M. J. "The *Clementina*: A Christian Response to the Pagan Novel." *Classical Quarterly* 42 (1992) 459-74.
- "*Locus Horridus* and *Locus Amoenus*." In *Homo Viator: Classical Essays for John Bramble*, ed. Michael Whitby, Philip Hardie, and Mary Whitby, 267-76. Bristol, U.K.: Bristol Classical Press, 1987.
- "Simon Magus, the Bad Samaritan." In *Portraits: Biographical Representation in the Greek and Latin Literature of the Roman Empire*, ed. M. J. Edwards and S. Swain, 69-91. Oxford: Clarendon, 1997.
-, M. Goodman, and S. Price, eds. *Apologetics in the Roman Empire: Pagans, Jews, and Christians*. New York: Oxford, 1999.
Faivre, Alexandre. "Les Fonctions ecclésiales dans les écrits pseudo-Clémentins." *Revue des Sciences Religieuses* 50 (1976) 97-111.
Ferreiro, Alberto. "Simon Magus: The Patristic-Medieval Traditions and Historiography." *Apocrypha* 7 (1996) 147-65.
Festugiere, A. J. *Antioche païenne et chrétienne. Libanius, Chrysostome et les moines de Syrie*. Paris: Éditions E. de Boccard, 1959.
- *L'Idéal religieux des Grecs et L'Évangile*. Paris: J. Gabalda, 1932.
Feyerabend, Paul. *Against Method*. New York and London: Verso, 1993.
- *Realism, Rationalism, and Scientific Method: Philosophical Papers*, volume 1. Cambridge: Cambridge University Press, 1981.
Fitzmyer, Joseph A. "The Qumran Scrolls, The Ebionites and Their Literature." *Theological Studies* 16 (1955) 335-72.
Foucault, Michel. *The Archaeology of Knowledge*. Translated by A. M. Sheridan Smith. New York: Pantheon Books, 1972.
- "L'écriture de soi." *Corps écrit* 5 (1983) 3-23.
Fowden, Garth. "The Pagan Holy Man in Late Antique Society." *Journal of Hellenic Studies* 102 (1982) 33-59.

Gagarin, Michael. "Probability and persuasion: Plato and early Greek rhetoric." In *Persuasion: Greek Rhetoric in Action*, ed. Ian Worthington, 46-68. London and New York: Routledge, 1994.

Geertz, Clifford. *The Interpretation of Cultures.* New York: Basic Books, 1973.

Gerth, H. H., and Mills, C. Wright, eds. *From Max Weber: Essays in Sociology.* New York: Oxford, 1946.

Gieschen, Charles A. "The Seven Pillars of the World: Ideal Figure Lists in the Christology of the Pseudo-Clementines." *Journal for the Study of the Pseudepigrapha* 12 (1994) 47-82.

– *Angelomorphic Christology: Antecedents and Early Evidence.* Leiden: Brill, 1998.

Gleason, Maud W. *Making Men: Sophists and Self-Presentation in Ancient Rome.* Princeton, NJ: Princeton University Press, 1995.

Goldhill, Simon, ed. *Being Greek under Rome: Cultural Identity, the Second Sophistic and the Development of Empire.* Cambridge: Cambridge University Press, 2001.

Grant, Robert M. *Irenaeus of Lyons.* London and New York: Routledge, 1997.

Grébaut, Sylvain. "Littérature éthiopienne pseudo-clémentine." *Revue de l'Orient Chrétien*, 2d series, 10 (1915-1917) 33-37.

Grégoire, H. "Bardesane et S. Abercius." *Byzantion* 25-27 (1955-1957) 363-68.

Griffith, Sidney H. "Ephraem, the Deacon of Edessa, and the Church of the Empire." In *Diakonia: Studies in Honor of Robert T. Meyer*, ed. Thomas Halton and Joseph P. Williman, 22-52. Washington, D.C.: Catholic University of America Press, 1986.

– "Ephraem the Syrian's Hymns 'Against Julian': Meditations on History and Imperial Power." *Vigiliae Christianae* 41 (1987) 238-66.

Hadot, Pierre. *The Inner Citadel: The* Meditations *of Marcus Aurelius.* Translated by Michael Chase. Cambridge, MA and London: Harvard University Press, 1998.

– *Philosophy as a Way of Life: Spiritual Exercises from Socrates to Foucault.* Edited and with an Introduction by Arnold I. Davidson. Translated by Michael Chase. Oxford: Blackwell, 1995.

Hägg, T. *Narrative Technique in Ancient Greek Romances. Studies of Chariton, Xenophon Ephesius and Achilles Tatius.* Stockholm: P. Aström, 1971.

– *The Novel in Antiquity.* Oxford: Blackwell, 1983.

Halliwell, Stephen. "Philosophy and rhetoric." In *Persuasion: Greek Rhetoric in Action*, ed. Ian Worthington, 222-43. London and New York: Routledge, 1994.

Hammond, C. P. "The Last Ten Years of Rufinus' Life and the Date of His Move South from Aquileia." *Journal of Theological Studies* n.s. 28 (1977) 372-429.

Hanson, R. P. C. "The Christian Attitude to Pagan Religions up to the Time of Constantine the Great." In *Principat*, ed. Wolfang Haase, 910-973. *Aufstieg und Niedergang der römischen Welt: Geschichte und Kultur Roms im Spiegel der neueren Forschung*, vol. 2.23, ed. Hildegard Temporini and Wolfgang Haase. Berlin and New York: Walter de Gruyter, 1980.

– *The Search for the Christian Doctrine of God: The Arian Controversy, 318-381.* Edinburgh: T&T Clark, 1988.

Harris, Rendel. "Notes on the Clementine Romances." *Journal of Biblical Literature* 40 (1921) 125-45.

Harvey, Susan Ashbrook. "Sacred Bonding: Mothers and Daughters in Early Syriac Hagiography." *Journal of Early Christian Studies* 4.1 (1996) 27-56.

Hauck, Robert J. "'They Saw What they Said they Saw': Sense Knowledge in Early Christian Polemic." *Harvard Theological Review* 81.3 (1988) 239-49.

Hazlett, Ian, ed. *Early Christianity: Origins and Evolution to A.D. 600.* London: SPCK, 1991.

Headlam, A. C. "The Clementine Literature." *Journal of Theological Studies* 3 (1902) 41-58.

Hegedus, Tim. "Necessity and Free Will in the Thought of Bardaisan of Edessa." *Laval théologique et philosophique* 59 (2003) 333-44.

– "Attitudes to Astrology in Early Christianity: A Study Based on Selected Sources." Ph.D. diss., University of Toronto, 2000.

Heintz, Florent. *Simon "Le Magicien": Acts 8,5-25 et l'accusation de magie contre les prophètes thaumaturges dans l'antiquité.* Paris: J. Gabalda, 1997.

Heintze, Werner. *Der Klemensroman und seine griechischen Quellen.* Texte und Untersuchungen zur Geschichte der altchristlichen Literatur 40.2. Leipzig: J. C. Hinrichs, 1914.

Hilgenfeld, A. *Bardesanes, der letzte Gnostiker.* Leipzig: T. O. Weigel, 1864.

– *Die clementinischen Recognitionen und Homilien nach ihrem Ursprung und Inhalt dargestellt.* Jena: J. B. Schreiber – Leipzig: Chr. E. Kollmann, 1848.

– *Kritische Untersuchungen über die Evangelien Justin's, der clementinischen Homilien und Marcion's: Ein Beitrag zur Geschichte der ältesten Evangelien-Literatur.* Halle: C. A. Schwetschke und Sohn, 1850.

Hodges, Horace Jeffery. "Gnostic Liberation from Astrological Determinism: Hipparchan 'Trepidation' and the Breaking of Fate." *Vigiliae Christianae* 51 (1997) 359-73.

Hornblower, Simon, and Spawforth, Anthony, eds. *The Oxford Classical Dictionary.* 3d ed. Oxford and New York: Oxford University Press, 1996.

Hort, F. J. A. *Judaistic Christianity: A Course of Lectures.* Cambridge, London, and New York: MacMillan and Co., 1894.

Howard, George. "The Pseudo-Clementine Writings and Shem-Tob's Hebrew Matthew." *New Testament Studies* 40 (1994) 622-28.

Jaeger, Werner. *Early Christianity and Greek Paideia.* Cambridge, MA: Belknap Press, 1961.

James, M. R. "A Manual of Mythology in the Clementines." *Journal of Theological Studies* 33 (1932) 262-65.

Janowitz, Naomi. *Icons of Power: Ritual Practices in Late Antiquity.* University Park, PA: Pennsylvania State University Press, 2002.

Jastrow, Morris. *Die Religion Babyloniens und Assyriens.* Giessen: A. Töpelmann, 1905-1912.

Jones, C. P. *Plutarch and Rome.* Oxford: Clarendon, 1971.

– *The Roman World of Dio Chrysostom.* Cambridge, MA: Harvard University Press, 1978.

Jones, F. Stanley. "The Ancient Christian Teacher in the *Pseudo-Clementines.*" In *Early Christian voices: in texts, traditions, and symbols: essays in honor of François Bovon,* ed. David H. Warren, Ann Graham Brock, and David W. Pao, 355-64. Boston: Brill, 2003.

– "An Ancient Jewish Christian Rejoinder to Luke's Acts of the Apostles: Pseudo-Clementine Recognitions 1.27-71." *Semeia* 80 (1997) 223-45.

– *An Ancient Jewish Christian Source on the History of Christianity: Pseudo-Clementine Recognitions 1.27-71.* Atlanta: Scholars, 1995.

– "The Astrological Trajectory in Ancient Syriac-Speaking Christianity (Elchasai, Bardaisan, and Mani)." In *Atti del Terzo Congresso Internazionale di Studi "Manicheismo e Oriente Cristiano Antico,"* ed. Luigi Cirillo and Aloïs van Tongerloo, 183-200. Manichaean Studies III. Louvain and Naples: Brepols, 1997.

– "Clement of Rome and the *Pseudo-Clementines:* History and/or Fiction." In *Studi su Clemente Romano: Atti degli Incontri di Roma, 29 marzo e 22 novembre 2001,* ed.

Philippe Luisier, 139-61. Orientalia Christiana Analecta 268. Rome: Pontificio Istituto Orientale, 2003.

– "Clementines, Pseudo-." In *The Anchor Bible Dictionary*, vol. 5, ed. David Noel Freedman, 1061-62.

– "Early Syriac Pointing in and behind British Museum Additional Manuscript 12,150." In *Symposium Syriacum VII: Uppsala University, Department of Asian and African Languages, 1-14 August 1996*, ed. René Lavenant, 429-44. Orientalia Christiana Analecta 256. Rome: Pontificio Istituto Orientale, 1998.

– "Eros and Astrology in the *Periodoi Petrou*: The Sense of the Pseudo-Clementine Novel." *Apocrypha* 12 (2001) 53-78.

– "Evaluating the Latin and Syriac Translations of the Pseudo-Clementine *Recognitions*." *Apocrypha* 3 (1992) 237-57.

– "Jewish-Christian Chiliastic Restoration in Pseudo-Clementine *Recognitions* 1.27-71." In *Restoration: Old Testament, Jewish, and Christian Perspectives*, ed. James M. Scott, 529-47. Leiden: Brill, 2001.

– "A Jewish Christian Reads Luke's Acts of the Apostles: The Use of the Canonical Acts in the Ancient Jewish Christian Source behind Pseudo-Clementine *Recognitions* 1.27-71." *Society of Biblical Literature Seminar Papers* 34, ed. E. H. Lovering, Jr., 617-35. Atlanta: Scholars Press, 1995.

– "PsCl Concordances: Mistakes/Corrections." *Zeitschrift für antikes Christentum* 1 (1997) 126-28.

– "The Pseudo-Clementines: A History of Research Part I," and "The Pseudo-Clementines: A History of Research Part II." *Second Century* 2 (1982) 1-33, 63-96.

Keck, Leander E. "The Poor among the Saints in Jewish Christianity and Qumran." *Zeitschrift für die neutestamentliche Wissenschaft* 57 (1966) 54-78.

Kelley, Nicole. "Problems of Knowledge and Authority in the Pseudo-Clementine Romance of Recognitions." *Journal of Early Christian Studies* 13.3 (2005) 315-48.

Kennedy, George Alexander. *The Art of Persuasion in Greece*. Princeton, NJ: Princeton University Press, 1963.

– *The Art of Rhetoric in the Roman World, 300 B.C. – A.D. 300*. Princeton, NJ: Princeton University Press, 1972.

– *New Testament Interpretation through Rhetorical Criticism*. Chapel Hill, NC: University of North Carolina Press, 1984.

Kerényi, Karl. *Die griechisch-orientalische Romanliteratur in religionsgeschichtlicher Beleuchtung: Ein Versuch mit Nachbetrachtungen*. Darmstadt: Wissenschaftliche Buchgesellschaft, 1962.

Kerferd, G. B. *The Sophistic Movement*. Cambridge: Cambridge University Press, 1981.

Klijn, A. F. J. *The Acts of Thomas*. Leiden: Brill, 1962.

– "The Pseudo-Clementines and the Apostolic Decree." *Novum Testamentum* 10 (1968) 305-12.

– "The Study of Jewish Christianity." *New Testament Studies* 20 (1974) 419-31.

–, and Reinink, G. J. *Patristic Evidence for Jewish-Christian Sects*. Supplements to Novum Testamentum 36. Leiden: E. J. Brill, 1973.

Kline, Leslie L. *The Sayings of Jesus in the Pseudo-Clementine Homilies*. Society of Biblical Literature Dissertation Series 14. Missoula, MT: Scholars, 1975.

Koester, Helmut. "ΓΝΩΜΑΙ ΔΙΑΦΟΡΟΙ: The Origin and Nature of Diversification in the History of Early Christianity." *Harvard Theological Review* 58 (1965) 279-318.

Kohler, K. "Dositheus, the Samaritan Heresiarch, and his Relations to Jewish and Christian Doctrines and Sects." *American Journal of Theology* 15 (1911) 404-35.

Kolenkow, Anitra Bingham. "A Problem of Power: How Miracle Doers Counter Charges of Magic in the Hellenistic World." In *Society of Biblical Literature Seminar Papers* 10, ed. G. MacRae, 105-10. Missoula, MT: Scholars Press, 1976.

Kondoleon, Christine. *Antioch: The Lost Ancient City.* Princeton, NJ: Princeton University Press in association with the Worcester Art Museum, 2000.

Kortekaas, G. A. A. "The *Historia Apollonii Regis Tyri* and Ancient Astrology." *Zeitschrift für Papyrologie und Epigraphik* 85 (1991) 71-85.

Kotarbinski, Thadée. "L'éristique – cas particulier de la théorie de la lutte." In *La théorie de l'argumentation: perspectives et applications*, 19-29. Louvain: Nauwelaerts, 1963.

Kugel, James L. *Traditions of the Bible: A Guide to the Bible As It Was at the Start of the Common Era.* Cambridge, MA and London: Harvard University Press, 1998.

Langen, Joseph. *Die Klemensromane: Ihre Entstehung und ihre Tendenzen aufs neue untersucht.* Gotha: Friedrich Andreas Perthes, 1890.

Lanham, Richard A. *A Handlist of Rhetorical Terms: A Guide for Students of English Literature.* Berkeley: University of California Press, 1968.

Lapham, F. *Peter: The Myth, the Man and the Writings. A Study of Early Petrine Text and Tradition.* Journal for the Study of the New Testament Supplement Series 239. London: Sheffield Academic Press, 2003.

Le Boulluec, Alain. "Hors de la μοναρχία pas de salut. Les refus de Pierre dans les *Homélies pseudo-clémentines.*" In *Nier les dieux, nier dieu. Actes du colloque organisé par le Centre Paul-Albert Février (UMR 6125) à la Maison Méditerranéenne des Sciences de l'Homme, les 1er et 2 avril 1999*, ed. Gilles Dorival and Didier Pralon, 263-77. Aix-en-Provence: Publications de l'université de Provence, 2002.

– "Les citations de la Septante dans l'Homélie XVI pseudo-clémentine: une critique implicite de la typologie?" In *Kata tous o' selon les Septante: trente études sur la Bible grecque des Septante en hommage à Marguerite Harl*, ed. Gilles Dorival and Olivier Munnich, 441-61. Paris: Cerf, 1995.

Leclercq, J. "Pour l'histoire de l'expression 'philosophie chrétienne'." *Mélanges de Science Religeuise* 9 (1952) 221-26.

Légasse, Simon. "La polémique antipaulinienne dans le judéo-christianisme hétérodoxe." *Bulletin de Littérature Ecclésiastique* 90 (1989) 5-22, 85-100.

– *L'antipaulinisme sectaire au temps des pères de l'église.* Cahiers de la Revue Biblique 47. Paris: J. Gabalda, 2000.

Levenson, David B. "The Ancient and Medieval Sources for the Emperor Julian's Attempt to Rebuild the Jerusalem Temple." *Journal for the Study of Judaism* 35 (2004) 409-60.

– "Julian's Attempt to Rebuild the Temple: An Inventory of Ancient and Medieval Sources." In *Of Scribes and Scrolls: Studies on the Hebrew Bible, Intertestamental Judaism, and Christian Origins presented to John Strugnell on the occasion of his sixtieth birthday*, ed. Harold W. Attridge, John J. Collins, and Thomas H. Tobin, 261-79. New York and London: Lanham, 1990.

Lienhard, Joseph T. "The 'Arian' Controversy: Some Categories Reconsidered." *Theological Studies* 48 (1987) 415-37.

Lietzmann, Hans. *The Beginnings of the Christian Church.* Translated by Bertram Lee Woolf. Rev. ed. New York: Charles Scribner's Sons, 1949.

Lieu, Samuel N. C. *Manichaeism in Mesopotamia and the Roman East.* Religions in the Graeco-Roman World 118. Leiden: Brill, 1994.

– *Manichaeism in the Later Roman Empire and Medieval China: A Historical Survey.* Manchester, UK: Manchester University Press, 1985.

Linder, Amnon, ed. *The Jews in Roman Imperial Legislation.* Detroit, MI: Wayne State University Press, 1987.

Lüdemann, Gerd. "The Acts of the Apostles and the Beginnings of Simonian Gnosis." *New Testament Studies* 33 (1987) 420-26.

– *Paulus, der Heidenapostel,* vol 2, *Antipaulinismus im frühen Christentum.* Göttingen: Vandenhoeck & Ruprecht, 1983.

MacDonald, Dennis R., ed. *The Apocryphal Acts of Apostles. Semeia* 38 (1996).

MacIntyre, Alisdair. "Epistemological Crises, Dramatic Narrative, and the Philosophy of Science." *Monist* 60 (1977) 453-72.

MacMullen, Ramsay. *Enemies of the Roman Order: Treason, Unrest, and Alienation in the Empire.* London and New York: Routledge, 1966.

Magnin, J. M. "Notes sur l'Ébionisme." *Proche Orient chrétien* 24 (1974) 225-50.

Malingrey, Anne Marie. *"Philosophia." Étude d'un groupe de mots dans la littérature grecque, des Présocratiques au IVe siècle après J.-C.* Paris: C. Klincksieck, 1961.

Marjanen, Antti, and Luomanen, Petri, eds. *A Companion to Second-Century Christian 'Heretics.'* Supplements to Vigiliae Christianae 76. Leiden: Brill, 2005.

Mansour, Tanios Bou. "La défense éphrémienne de la liberté contre les doctrines marcionite, bardesanite et manichéenne," *Orientalia Christiana Periodica* 50 (1984) 331-46.

Marrou, H. I. *Histoire de l'éducation dans l'antiquité.* 7th ed. Paris: Éditions du Seuil, 1971.

Martyn, J. Louis. "Clementine Recognitions 1,33-71, Jewish Christianity, and the Fourth Gospel." In *God's Christ and His People: Studies in Honour of Nils Alstrup Dahl,* ed. J. Jervell and W. A. Meeks, 265-95. Oslo, Bergen, and Tromsö: Universitetsforlaget, 1977.

Marxsen, Willi. *Mark the Evangelist: Studies on the Redaction History of the Gospel.* Translated by James Boyce, Donald Juel, and William Poehlmann, with Roy A. Harrisville. Nashville and New York: Abingdon, 1969.

Meeks, Wayne A. "Simon Magus in Recent Research." *Religious Studies Review* 3 (1977) 137-42.

–, and Wilken, Robert L. *Jews and Christians in Antioch in the First Four Centuries of the Common Era.* Missoula, MT: Scholars, 1978.

Merx, A. *Bardesanes von Edessa, nebst einer Untersuchung über das Verhältniss der clementinischen Recognitionen zu dem Buche der Gesetze der Länder.* Halle: C. E. M. Pfeffer, 1863.

Millar, Fergus. *The Roman Near East 31 BC – AD 337.* Cambridge, MA and London: Harvard University Press, 1993.

Mimouni, Simon C. "Pour une définition nouvelle du judéo-christianisme ancien." *New Testament Studies* 38 (1992) 161-86.

–, and Jones, F. Stanley, eds. *Le judéo-christianisme dans tous ses états: Actes du colloque de Jérusalem, 6-10 juillet 1998.* Paris: Éditions du Cerf, 2001.

Mingana, A. "A New Document on Clement of Rome, His Relations and His Interview with Simon Peter," *Expositor* 8 (8th series; 1914) 227-42, 90-108.

– "Some Early Judaeo-Christian Documents in the John Rylands Library." *Bulletin of the John Rylands Library* 4 (1917-18) 59-118.

Molland, Einar. "La circoncision, le baptême et l'autorité du décret apostolique (*Ac* 15,28 sq.) dans les milieux judéo-chrétiens des Pseudo-Clémentines." *Studia Theologica* 9 (1955) 1-39.

Momigliano, Arnaldo, ed. *The Conflict between Paganism and Christianity in the Fourth Century.* Oxford: Clarendon, 1963.

Morgan, J. R., and Stoneman, Richard., eds. *Greek Fiction: The Greek Novel in Context*. London and New York: Routledge, 1994.

Moss, Cyril. *Catalogue of Syriac Printed Books and Related Literature in the Britism Museum*. London: Trustees of the British Museum, 1962.

Murray, James Stuart. "Interpreting Plato on Sophistic Claims and the Provenance of the 'Socratic Method'." *Phoenix* 48 (1992) 115-34.

Murray, Robert. "Defining Judaeo-Christianity." *Heythrop Journal* 15 (1974) 303-10.

Nehamas, Alexander. "Eristic, Antilogic, Sophistic, Dialectic: Plato's Demarcation of Philosophy from Sophistry." *History of Philosophy Quarterly* 7.1 (1990) 3-16.

Niewöhner, F. "Epikureer sind Atheisten: Zur Geschichte des Wortes apikuros in der jüdischen Philosophie." In *Atheismus im Mittelalter und in der Renaissance*, ed. F. Niewöhner and O. Pluta, 11-22. Wiesbaden: Harrassowitz, 1999.

Nock, A. D. *Conversion: The Old and the New in Religion from Alexander the Great to Augustine of Hippo*. Oxford: Clarendon Press, 1933.

Noegel, Scott, Joel Walker, and Brannon Wheeler, eds. *Prayer, Magic, and the Stars in the Ancient and Late Antique World*. University Park, PA: Pennsylvania State University Press, 2003.

Norelli, Enrico. "Situation des Apocryphes pétriniens." *Apocrypha* 2 (1991) 31-83.

Ory, Georges. "Réflexions sur les écrits clémentins: Qui était Clément?" *Cahiers du Cercle Ernest-Renan* 32 (1984) 33-38.

Perkins, Judith. "Social Geography in the *Apocryphal Acts of the Apostles*." In *Space in the Ancient Novel*, ed. Michael Paschalis and Stavros Frangoulidis, 118-31. Ancient Narrative Supplementum 1. Groningen: Barkhuis, 2002.

Perkins, Pheme. *Peter: Apostle for the Whole Church*. Columbia, SC: University of South Carolina Press, 1994.

Perry, Ben Edwin. *The Ancient Romances: A Literary-Historical Account of Their Origins*. Sather Classical Lectures 37. Berkeley and Los Angeles: University of California Press, 1967.

Pognon, H. *Inscriptions sémitiques de la Syrie, de la Mésopotamie et de la région de Mossoul*. Paris: Imprimerie Nationale, 1907.

Potter, David. *Prophets and Emperors: Human and Divine Authority from Augustus to Theodosius*. Cambridge, MA and London: Harvard University Press, 1994.

Pouderon, Bernard. "Clément de Rome, Flavius Clemens et le Clément Juif." In *Studi su Clemente Romano: Atti degli Incontri di Roma, 29 marzo e 22 novembre 2001*, ed. Philippe Luisier, 197-218. Orientalia Christiana Analecta 268; Rome: Pontificio Istituto Orientale, 2003.

– "Dédoublement et création romanesque dans le roman Pseudo-Clémentin." In *Les personnages du roman grec. actes du colloque de Tours, 18-20 novembre 1999*, ed. Bernard Pouderon, Christine Hunzinger and Dimitri Kasprzyk, 269-83. Lyon: Maison de l'Orient Méditerranéen-Jean Pouilloux, 2001.

– "Flavius Clemens et le proto-Clément juif du roman Pseudo-Clémentin." *Apocrypha* 7 (1996) 63-79.

– "Origène, le Pseudo-Clément et la Structure des *Periodoi Petrou*." *Apocrypha* 12 (2001) 29-51.

Pratscher, W. *Der Herrenbruder Jakobus und die Jakobustradition*. Göttingen: Vandenhoeck & Ruprecht, 1987.

Quispel, G. "L'Évangile selon Thomas et les Clémentines." *Vigiliae Christianae* 12 (1958) 181-96.

Rahner, Karl. "Le début d'une doctrine des cinq sens spirituels chez Origène." *Revue d'ascétique et de mystique* 14 (1932) 113-45.

Reardon, B. "The Greek Novel," *Phoenix* 23 (1969) 291-309.

Reed, Annette Yoshiko. "'Jewish Christianity' after the 'Parting of the Ways': Approaches to Historiography and Self-Definition in the Pseudo-Clementines." In *The Ways that Never Parted: Jews and Christians in Late Antiquity and the Early Middle Ages*, ed. Adam H. Becker and Annette Yoshiko Reed, 189-231. Tübingen: Mohr Siebeck, 2003.

Rehm, Bernhard. "Bardesanes in den Pseudoclementinen." *Philologus* 93 (1938) 218-47.

– "Clemens Romanus II (Ps Clementinen)." In *Reallexicon für Antike und Christentum: Sachwörterbuch zur Auseinandersetzung des Christentums mit der antiken Welt*, vol. 3, ed. Theodor Klauser, 197-206. Stuttgart: Hiersemann, 1957.

– "Zur Entstehung der pseudoclementinischen Schriften." *Zeitschrift für die neutestamentliche Wissenschaft* 37 (1938) 77-184.

Reinink, G. J., and Klugkist, A. C., eds. *After Bardaisan: Studies on Continuity and Change in Syriac Christianity in Honour of Professor Han J. W. Drijvers*. Leuven: Peeters, 1999.

Riad, Eva. *Studies in the Syriac Preface*. Studia Semitica Upsaliensia 11. Uppsala: Almqvist & Wiksell, 1988.

Richardson, Ernest Cushing. "The History of Clement." *Presbyterian and Reformed Review* 6 (1895) 108-13.

Riegel, Stanley K. "Jewish Christianity: Definitions and Terminology." *New Testament Studies* 24 (1977-1978) 410-15.

Risch, Franz Xaver. "Was tut ein Epitomator? Zur Methode des Epitomierens am Beispiel der pseudoclementinischen *epitome prior*." *Das Altertum* 48 (2003) 241-55.

Rius-Camps, J. "Las Pseudoclementinas. Bases filológicas para una nueva interpretación." *Revista Catalana de Teologia* I (1976) 79-158.

Robins, William. "Romance and Renunciation at the Turn of the Fifth Century." *Journal of Early Christian Studies* 8 (2000) 531-557.

Robinson, Thomas A. *The Bauer Thesis Examined: The Geography of Heresy in the Early Christian Church*. Lewiston, NY: E. Mellen Press, 1988.

Rohde, Erwin. *Der griechische Roman und seine Vorläufer*. 5th ed. Hildesheim and New York: Georg Olms, 1974.

Ross, Steven K. *Roman Edessa: Politics and Culture on the Eastern Fringes of the Roman Empire*. London: Routledge, 2000.

Salles, A. "La Diatribe anti-paulinienne dans 'le Roman pseudo-clémentin' et l'origine des 'Kérygmes de Pierre.'" *Revue Biblique* 64 (1957) 516-51.

– "Simon le Magicien ou Marcion?" *Vigiliae Christianae* 12 (1958) 197-224.

Salles-Dabadie, J. M. A. *Recherches sur Simon le Mage. L'Apophasis megalè*. Cahiers de la Revue Biblique 10. Paris: J. Gabalda, 1969.

Schaeder, H. H. "Bardesanes von Edessa in der Überlieferung der griechischen un der syrischen Kirche." In *Studien zur orientalischen Religionsgeschichte*, ed. Carsten Colpe, 108-61. Darmstadt: Wissenschaftliche Buchgesellschaft, 1968.

Schatzki, Theodore Richard. "Overdue Analysis of Bourdieu's Theory of Practice." *Inquiry* 30 (1987) 113-35.

Schliemann, Adolph. *Die Clementinen nebst den verwandten Schriften und der Ebionitismus*. Hamburg: F. Berthes, 1844.

Schmeling, G., ed. *The Novel in the Ancient World*. Leiden and New York: Brill, 1996.

Schmidt, Carl. *Studien zu den Pseudo-Clementinen*. Leipzig: J. C. Hinrichs, 1929.

Schoeps, Hans Joachim. "Astrologisches im pseudoklementinischen Roman." *Vigiliae Christianae* 5 (1951) 88-100.

– *Jewish Christianity: Factional Disputes in the Early Church.* Translated by Douglas R. A. Hare. Philadelphia: Fortress, 1969.
– *Theologie und Geschichte des Judenchristentums.* Tübingen: Mohr (Siebeck), 1949.
– "Der Ursprung des Bösen und das Problem der Theodizee im pseudoklementinischen Roman." *Recherches de Science Religieuse* 60/61 (1972) 129-41.
Schwartz, E. "Unzeitgemäße Beobachtungen zu den Clementinen." *Zeitschrift für die neutestamentliche Wissenschaft* 31 (1932) 151-99.
Scott, James M. *Geography in Early Judaism and Christianity: The Book of Jubilees.* Society for New Testament Studies Monograph Series 113. Cambridge, UK: Cambridge University Press, 2002.
Segal, Alan F. "Hellenistic Magic: Some Questions of Definition." In *Studies in Gnosticism and Hellenistic Religions presented to Gilles Quispel on the Occasion of his 65ᵗʰ Birthday*, ed. R. van den Broek and M. J. Vermaseren, 349-75. Leiden: Brill, 1981.
Segal, J. B. *Edessa 'The Blessed City'.* Oxford: Clarendon, 1970.
Sellew, Philip. "Thomas Christianity: Scholars in Quest of a Community." In *The Apocryphal Acts of Thomas*, ed. Jan Bremmer, 11-35. Studies on Early Christian Apocrypha 6. Leuven: Peeters, 2001.
Shepardson, Christine C. "In the Service of Orthodoxy: Anti-Jewish Language and Intra-Christian Conflict in the Writings of Ephrem the Syrian." Ph.D. diss., Duke University, 2003.
Simon, M. "Christianisme antique et pensée païenne: rencontres et conflits." *Bulletin de la Faculté des Lettres de Strasbourg* 38 (1960) 309-23.
Siouville, A. *Les homélies Clémentines.* Paris: Rieder, 1933.
Smith, Jonathan Z. "Towards Interpreting Demonic Powers in Hellenistic and Roman Antiquity." In *Aufstieg und Niedergang der römischen Welt* II.16.1, ed. Hildegard Temporini and Wolfgang Haase, 425-39. Berlin and New York: Walter de Gruyter, 1978.
Smith, Rowland. *Julian's Gods: Religion and philosophy in the thought and action of Julian the Apostate.* London and New York: Routledge, 1995.
Smith, Terence V. *Petrine Controversies in Early Christianity: Attitudes towards Peter in Christian Writings of the First Two Centuries.* Wissenschaftliche Untersuchungen zum Neuen Testament 2.15. Tübingen: Mohr (Siebeck), 1985.
Smith, William, and Wace, Henry, eds. *A Dictionary of Christian Biography, Literature, Sects and Doctrines: Being a Continuation of the Dictionary of the Bible*, vol. 1. London: John Murray, 1877.
Snowden, Joe Rodney. "The redactors of the 'Pseudo-Clementines' in the Tripolis Discourses." Th.D. diss., Harvard University, 1990.
Stoetzel, Arnold. "Die Darstellung der ältesten Kirchengeschichte nach den Pseudo-Clementinen." *Vigiliae Christianae* 36 (1982) 24-37.
Strecker, Georg. *Das Judenchristentum in den Pseudoklementinen*, 2d ed., rev. Texte und Untersuchungen zur Geschichte der altchristlichen Literatur 70. Berlin: Akademie, 1981.
Stroumsa, G. "*Paradosis:* Traditions ésotériques dans le christianisme des premiers siècles." *Apocrypha* 2 (1991) 133-53.
Talbert, Charles H. "Biographies of Philosophers and Rulers as Instruments of Religious Propaganda in Mediterranean Antiquity." In *Principat*, ed. Wolfang Haase, 1620-51. *Aufstieg und Niedergang der römischen Welt: Geschichte und Kultur Roms im Spiegel der neueren Forschung*, vol. 2.16, ed. Hildegard Temporini and Wolfgang Haase. Berlin and New York: Walter de Gruyter, 1980.

Tardieu, M. "Une diatribe antignostique dans l'interpolation eunomienne des *Recognitiones*." In *Alexandrina: Hellénisme, judaïsme et christianisme à Alexandrie: Mélanges offerts au P. Claude Mondésert*, 325-37. Paris: Éditions du Cerf, 1987.

Tatum, James, ed. *The Search for the Ancient Novel*. Baltimore and London: Johns Hopkins, 1994.

Taylor, Joan E. "The Phenomenon of Early Jewish-Christianity: Reality or Scholarly Invention?" *Vigiliae Christianae* 44 (1990) 313-34.

Taylor, Miriam. *Anti-Judaism and Early Christian Identity: A Critique of the Scholarly Consensus*. New York: Brill, 1995.

Townsend, John T. "Ancient Education in the Time of the Early Roman Empire." In *The Catacombs and the Colosseum: The Roman Empire as the Setting of Primitive Christianity*, ed. Stephen Benko and John J. O'Rourke, 139-63. Valley Forge, PA: Judson Press, 1971.

– "The Date of Luke-Acts." In *Luke-Acts: New Perspectives from the Society of Biblical Literature Seminar*, ed. Charles H. Talbert, 47-62. New York: Crossroad, 1984.

– "Education (Greco-Roman)." In *The Anchor Bible Dictionary*, vol. 2, ed. David Noel Freedman, 312-17.

Trenkner, Sophie. *The Greek Novella in the Classical Period*. Cambridge: Cambridge University Press, 1958.

Turcan, R. "Littérature astrologique et astrologie littéraire dans l'Antiquité classique." *Latomus* 27 (1968) 392-405.

Tuzlak, A. "The Magician and the Heretic: The Case of Simon Magus." In *Magic and Ritual in the Ancient World*, ed. P. Mirecki and M. Meyer, 416-26. Leiden: Brill, 2002.

Uhlhorn, Gerhard. *Die Homilien und Recognitionen des Clemens Romanus nach ihrem Ursprung und Inhalt dargestellt*. Göttingen: Dieterische Buchhandlung, 1854.

Ullmann, W. "Some Remarks on the Significance of the *Epistola Clementis* in the Pseudo-Clementines." In *Studia Patristica* 4: *Papers presented to the Third International Conference on Patristic Studies held at Christ Church, Oxford, 1959*, ed. F. L. Cross, 330-37. Texte und Untersuchungen zur Geschichte der altchristlichen Literatur 79. Berlin: Akademie-Verlag, 1961.

van Amersfoort, J. "Traces of an Alexandrian Orphic Theogony in the Pseudo-Clementines." In *Studies in Gnosticism and Hellenistic Religions presented to Gilles Quispel on the Occasion of his 65ᵗʰ Birthday*, ed. R. van den Broek and M. J. Vermaseren, 13-30. Leiden: Brill, 1981.

van den Hoek, Annewies. "Techniques of Quotation in Clement of Alexandria: A View of Ancient Literary Working Methods." *Vigiliae Christianae* 50 (1996) 223-43.

van der Horst, Pieter W. *Japheth in the Tents of Shem: Studies on Jewish Hellenism in Antiquity*. Leuven: Peeters, 2002.

van Nes, Hendrik Marius. *Het Nieuwe Testament in de Clementinen*. Amsterdam: de Roever Kröber-Bakels, 1887.

van Voorst, Robert E. *The Ascents of James: History and Theology of a Jewish-Christian Community*. Society of Biblical Literature Dissertation Series 112. Atlanta: Scholars, 1989.

Vanhoye, A. *L'Apôtre Paul: Personnalité, Style et Conception du Ministère*. Leuven: Leuven University Press/Uitgeverij Peeters, 1986.

Vickers, Brian. *In Defence of Rhetoric*. New York: Oxford University Press, 1988.

Vielberg, Meinolf. *Klemens in den pseudoklementinischen Rekognitionen. Studien zur literarischen Form des spätantiken Romans*. Texte und Untersuchungen zur Geschichte der altchristlichen Literatur 145. Berlin: Akademie Verlag, 2000.

von Campenhausen, Hans. *Ecclesiastical Authority and Spiritual Power in the Church of the First Three Centuries.* Translated by J. A. Baker. Peabody, MA: Hendrickson, 1997.

von Harnack, Adolf. *Geschichte der altchristlichen Literatur bis Eusebius,* vol. 2.2. Leipzig: J. C. Hinrichs, 1958.

– *History of Dogma.* 7 volumes. Translated from the third German edition by Neil Buchanan. New York: Dover Publications, 1961.

– *Marcion: The Gospel of the Alien God.* Translated by John E. Steely and Lyle D. Bierma. Durham, NC: The Labyrinth Press, 1990.

– *Die Lehre der zwölf Apostel nebst Untersuchungen zur ältesten Geschichte der Kirchenverfassung und des Kirchenrechts.* Texte und Untersuchungen zur Geschichte der altchristlichen Literatur 2.1-2. Leipzig: J. C. Hinrichs, 1884.

Wagner, M. M. *Rufinus, The Translator. A Study of his Theory and his Practice as illustrated in his Version of the Apologetica of St. Gregory Nazianzen.* Patristic Studies 73. Washington: The Catholic University of America, 1945.

Wagner, Walter H. *After the Apostles: Christianity in the Second Century.* Minneapolis: Fortress, 1994.

Waitz, Hans. *Die Pseudoklementinen Homilien und Rekognitionen: Eine Quellenkritische Untersuchung.* Leipzig: J. Hinrichs, 1904.

– "Die Pseudoklementinen und ihre Quellenschriften." *Zeitschrift für die neutestamentliche Wissenschaft* 28 (1929) 241-72.

Weber, Max. *From Max Weber: Essays in Sociology.* Edited by H. H. Gerth and C. Wright Mills. New York: Oxford, 1946.

Wedderburn, A. J. M. "The 'Apostolic Decree': Tradition and Redaction." *Novum Testamentum* 35.4 (1993) 362-89.

Wehnert, Jürgen. "Abriss der Entstehungsgeschichte des pseudoklementinischen Romans." *Apocrypha* 3 (1992) 211-35.

– "Literarkritik und Sprachanalyse: Kritische Anmerkungen zum gegenwärtigen Stand der Pseudoklementinen-Forschung." *Zeitschrift für die neutestamentliche Wissenschaft* 74 (1983) 268-301.

– "Petrus *versus* Paulus in den pseudoklementinischen Homilien 17." In *Christians as a Religious Minority in a Multicultural City: Modes of Interaction and Identity Formation in Early Imperial Rome. Studies on the Basis of a Seminar at the Second Conference of the European Association for Biblical Studies (EABS) from July 8-12, 2001, in Rome,* ed. Jürgen Zangenberg and Michael Labahn, 175-85. Journal for the Study of the New Testament Supplement Series 243. London and New York: T & T Clark, 2004.

Wendland, P. *Philos Schrift über die Vorsehung: Ein Beitrag zur Geschichte der nacharistotelischen Philosophie.* Berlin: R. Gaertners Verlagsbuchhandlung, 1892.

Wilken, Robert L. "Collegia, Philosophical Schools, and Theology." In *The Catacombs and the Colosseum: The Roman Empire as the Setting of Primitive Christianity,* ed. Stephen Benko and John J. O'Rourke, 268-91. Valley Forge, PA: Judson Press, 1971.

– *John Chrysostom and the Jews: Rhetoric and Reality in the Late 4th Century.* Berkeley: University of California Press, 1983.

Williams, Rowan. *Arius: Heresy and Tradition.* Rev. ed. Grand Rapids, MI: Eerdmans, 2001.

Wilson, R. McL. "Simon, Dositheus and the Dead Sea Scrolls." *Zeitschrift für Religions und Geistesgeschichte* 9 (1957) 21-30.

Wright, William, and McLean, Norman, eds. *A Short History of Syriac Literature.* London: Black, 1894.

–, and McLean, Norman, eds. *Catalogue of Syriac Manuscripts in the British Museum.* 3 volumes. London: Gilbert and Rivington, 1870.

Index of Ancient Sources

1. Old Testament

2. New Testament

3. Jewish Pseudepigrapha, Philo, Josephus, and Rabbinical Writings

de Dec.		Sibylline Oracles	
74	157	3.218–28	95

4. Pseudo-Clementines

Pseudo-Clementines
Recognitions

1	98	1.36.1–1.39.3	207
1.1.4–5	69	1.36–39	203
1.2.3	58	1.38.3	61
1.3.1	43, 58	1.41.1	61
1.3.1, 3	46	1.43.3	4, 175
1.3.1–5	145	1.44.1	175
1.7.14	53, 54	1.44.5	141
1.7.3	4, 158	1.60.5	156
1.9.7	47	1.62.2–7	52
1.12.6–7	158	1.63.1	52
1.14.5	56	1.64.1–2	207
1.16.1–2	140	1.66.1	175
1.16.2	160	1.66.5	175
1.16.2–4	145	1.68.2	175
1.17.2	160	1.72.5–6, 7	176
1.17.2–3	176	2.1.6	162
1.17.6	159	2.2.5	159
1.17.7	47, 54, 55	2.5.4	39
1.18.2	159	2.6.8	61
1.18.5	145	2.7.1	39
1.21.4	61	2.7.1–2	145
1.22.4	163	2.8.3	145
1.22.6	162	2.28.1	167
1.23.2	163	2.33.3–5	154, 162, 166
1.23.3	162	2.33.6–8	155
1.23.5–6	172	2.34.6	166
1.25.10	162	2.36.4–5	56
1.25.2	51, 173	2.45.7	138
1.25.4–5	56	2.45.7–8	112
1.26.1–2	161	2.51.5	140
1.26.3	70	2.55.1	150
1.26.3, 5	163	2.67.2	55
1.27–71	4, 21, 70, 96,	3.2–11	17, 205
175, 177, 180, 203		3.16.7	172
1.28.1–2	95	3.18.2	172
1.29.4	60	3.18.3	151
1.32.3	4, 60, 95, 105	3.31.1	159
1.33–71	151	3.32.2	159
1.34.4	138	3.32.4	171

5. Other Early Christian Writings

6. Classical and Other Ancient Writings

Index of Modern Authors

Index of Subjects and Key Terms

Wissenschaftliche Untersuchungen zum Neuen Testament
Alphabetical Index of the First and Second Series

Böhlig, Alexander: Gnosis und Synkretismus. Volume 1 1989. *Volume 47* – Volume 2 1989. *Volume 48.*

Böhm, Martina: Samarien und die Samaritai bei Lukas. 1999. *Volume II/111.*

Böttrich, Christfried: Weltweisheit – Menschheitsethik – Urkult. 1992. *Volume II/50.*

Bolyki, János: Jesu Tischgemeinschaften. 1997. *Volume II/96.*

Bosman, Philip: Conscience in Philo and Paul. 2003. *Volume II/166.*

Bovon, François: Studies in Early Christianity. 2003. *Volume 161.*

Brocke, Christoph vom: Thessaloniki – Stadt des Kassander und Gemeinde des Paulus. 2001. *Volume II/125.*

Brunson, Andrew: Psalm 118 in the Gospel of John. 2003. *Volume II/158.*

Büchli, Jörg: Der Poimandres – ein paganisiertes Evangelium. 1987. *Volume II/27.*

Bühner, Jan A.: Der Gesandte und sein Weg im 4. Evangelium. 1977. *Volume II/2.*

Burchard, Christoph: Untersuchungen zu Joseph und Aseneth. 1965. *Volume 8.*

– Studien zur Theologie, Sprache und Umwelt des Neuen Testaments. Ed. by D. Sänger. 1998. *Volume 107.*

Burnett, Richard: Karl Barth's Theological Exegesis. 2001. *Volume II/145.*

Byron, John: Slavery Metaphors in Early Judaism and Pauline Christianity. 2003. *Volume II/162.*

Byrskog, Samuel: Story as History – History as Story. 2000. *Volume 123.*

Cancik, Hubert (Ed.): Markus-Philologie. 1984. *Volume 33.*

Capes, David B.: Old Testament Yaweh Texts in Paul's Christology. 1992. *Volume II/47.*

Caragounis, Chrys C.: The Development of Greek and the New Testament. 2004. *Volume 167.*

– The Son of Man. 1986. *Volume 38.*

– see *Fridrichsen, Anton.*

Carleton Paget, James: The Epistle of Barnabas. 1994. *Volume II/64.*

Carson, D.A., O'Brien, Peter T. and *Mark Seifrid* (Ed.): Justification and Variegated Nomism.
Volume 1: The Complexities of Second Temple Judaism. 2001. *Volume II/140.*
Volume 2: The Paradoxes of Paul. 2004. *Volume II/181.*

Ciampa, Roy E.: The Presence and Function of Scripture in Galatians 1 and 2. 1998. *Volume II/102.*

Classen, Carl Joachim: Rhetorical Criticsm of the New Testament. 2000. *Volume 128.*

Colpe, Carsten: Iranier – Aramäer – Hebräer – Hellenen. 2003. *Volume 154.*

Crump, David: Jesus the Intercessor. 1992. *Volume II/49.*

Dahl, Nils Alstrup: Studies in Ephesians. 2000. *Volume 131.*

Deines, Roland: Die Gerechtigkeit der Tora im Reich des Messias. 2004. *Volume 177.*

– Jüdische Steingefäße und pharisäische Frömmigkeit. 1993. *Volume II/52.*

– Die Pharisäer. 1997. *Volume 101.*

Deines, Roland and *Karl-Wilhelm Niebuhr* (Ed.): Philo und das Neue Testament. 2004. *Volume 172.*

Dettwiler, Andreas and *Jean Zumstein* (Ed.): Kreuzestheologie im Neuen Testament. 2002. *Volume 151.*

Dickson, John P.: Mission-Commitment in Ancient Judaism and in the Pauline Communities. 2003. *Volume II/159.*

Dietzfelbinger, Christian: Der Abschied des Kommenden. 1997. *Volume 95.*

Dimitrov, Ivan Z., James D.G. Dunn, Ulrich Luz and *Karl-Wilhelm Niebuhr* (Ed.): Das Alte Testament als christliche Bibel in orthodoxer und westlicher Sicht. 2004. *Volume 174.*

Dobbeler, Axel von: Glaube als Teilhabe. 1987. *Volume II/22.*

Dryden, J. de Waal: Theology and Ethics in 1 Peter. 2006. *Volume II/209.*

Du Toit, David S.: Theios Anthropos. 1997. *Volume II/91.*

Dübbers, Michael: Christologie und Existenz im Kolosserbrief. 2005. *Volume II/191.*

Dunn, James D.G.: The New Perspective on Paul. 2005. *Volume 185.*

Dunn, James D.G. (Ed.): Jews and Christians. 1992. *Volume 66.*

– Paul and the Mosaic Law. 1996. *Volume 89.*

– see *Dimitrov, Ivan Z.*

–, *Hans Klein, Ulrich Luz* and *Vasile Mihoc* (Ed.): Auslegung der Bibel in orthodoxer und westlicher Perspektive. 2000. *Volume 130.*

Ebel, Eva: Die Attraktivität früher christlicher Gemeinden. 2004. *Volume II/178.*

Ebertz, Michael N.: Das Charisma des Gekreuzigten. 1987. *Volume 45.*

Eckstein, Hans-Joachim: Der Begriff Syneidesis bei Paulus. 1983. *Volume II/10.*

– Verheißung und Gesetz. 1996. *Volume 86.*

Ego, Beate: Im Himmel wie auf Erden. 1989. *Volume II/34.*

Ego, Beate, Armin Lange and *Peter Pilhofer* (Ed.): Gemeinde ohne Tempel – Community without Temple. 1999. *Volume 118.*

– and *Helmut Merkel* (Ed.): Religiöses Lernen in der biblischen, frühjüdischen und früh-christlichen Überlieferung. 2005. *Volume 180.*

Eisen, Ute E.: see *Paulsen, Henning.*

Elledge, C.D.: Life after Death in Early Judaism. 2006. *Volume II/208.*

Ellis, E. Earle: Prophecy and Hermeneutic in Early Christianity. 1978. *Volume 18.*

Heiligenthal, Roman: Werke als Zeichen. 1983. *Volume II/9.*

Hellholm, D.: see *Hartman, Lars.*

Hemer, Colin J.: The Book of Acts in the Setting of Hellenistic History. 1989. *Volume 49.*

Hengel, Martin: Judentum und Hellenismus. 1969, ³1988. *Volume 10.*

– Die johanneische Frage. 1993. *Volume 67.*

– Judaica et Hellenistica. Kleine Schriften I. 1996. *Volume 90.*

– Judaica, Hellenistica et Christiana. Kleine Schriften II. 1999. *Volume 109.*

– Paulus und Jakobus. Kleine Schriften III. 2002. *Volume 141.*

– and *Anna Maria Schwemer:* Paulus zwischen Damaskus und Antiochien. 1998. *Volume 108.*

– Der messianische Anspruch Jesu und die Anfänge der Christologie. 2001. *Volume 138.*

Hengel, Martin and *Ulrich Heckel* (Ed.): Paulus und das antike Judentum. 1991. *Volume 58.*

– and *Hermut Löhr* (Ed.): Schriftauslegung im antiken Judentum und im Urchristentum. 1994. *Volume 73.*

– and *Anna Maria Schwemer* (Ed.): Königsherrschaft Gottes und himm-lischer Kult. 1991. *Volume 55.*

– Die Septuaginta. 1994. *Volume 72.*

–, *Siegfried Mittmann* and *Anna Maria Schwemer* (Ed.): La Cité de Dieu / Die Stadt Gottes. 2000. *Volume 129.*

Herrenbrück, Fritz: Jesus und die Zöllner. 1990. *Volume II/41.*

Herzer, Jens: Paulus oder Petrus? 1998. *Volume 103.*

Hill, Charles E.: From the Lost Teaching of Polycarp. 2005. *Volume 186.*

Hoegen-Rohls, Christina: Der nachösterliche Johannes. 1996. *Volume II/84.*

Hoffmann, Matthias Reinhard: The Destroyer and the Lamb. 2005. *Volume II/203.*

Hofius, Otfried: Katapausis. 1970. *Volume 11.*

– Der Vorhang vor dem Thron Gottes. 1972. *Volume 14.*

– Der Christushymnus Philipper 2,6-11. 1976, ²1991. *Volume 17.*

– Paulusstudien. 1989, ²1994. *Volume 51.*

– Neutestamentliche Studien. 2000. *Volume 132.*

– Paulusstudien II. 2002. *Volume 143.*

– and *Hans-Christian Kammler:* Johannesstudien. 1996. *Volume 88.*

Holtz, Traugott: Geschichte und Theologie des Urchristentums. 1991. *Volume 57.*

Hommel, Hildebrecht: Sebasmata. Volume 1 1983. *Volume 31* – Volume 2 1984. *Volume 32.*

Horbury, William: Herodian Judaism and New Testament Study. 2006. *Volume 193.*

Horst, Pieter W. van der: Jews and Christians in Their Graeco-Roman Context. 2006. *Volume 196.*

Hvalvik, Reidar: The Struggle for Scripture and Covenant. 1996. *Volume II/82.*

Jauhiainen, Marko: The Use of Zechariah in Revelation. 2005. *Volume II/199.*

Johns, Loren L.: The Lamb Christology of the Apocalypse of John. 2003. *Volume II/167.*

Joubert, Stephan: Paul as Benefactor. 2000. *Volume II/124.*

Jungbauer, Harry: „Ehre Vater und Mutter". 2002. *Volume II/146.*

Kähler, Christoph: Jesu Gleichnisse als Poesie und Therapie. 1995. *Volume 78.*

Kamlah, Ehrhard: Die Form der katalogischen Paränese im Neuen Testament. 1964. *Volume 7.*

Kammler, Hans-Christian: Christologie und Eschatologie. 2000. *Volume 126.*

– Kreuz und Weisheit. 2003. *Volume 159.*

– see *Hofius, Otfried.*

Kelhoffer, James A.: The Diet of John the Baptist. 2005. *Volume 176.*

– Miracle and Mission. 1999. *Volume II/112.*

Kelley, Nicole: Knowledge and Religious Authority in the Pseudo-Clementines. 2006. *Volume II/213.*

Kieffer, René and *Jan Bergman (Ed.):* La Main de Dieu / Die Hand Gottes. 1997. *Volume 94.*

Kim, Seyoon: The Origin of Paul's Gospel. 1981, ²1984. *Volume II/4.*

– Paul and the New Perspective. 2002. *Volume 140.*

– "The 'Son of Man'" as the Son of God. 1983. *Volume 30.*

Klauck, Hans-Josef: Religion und Gesellschaft im frühen Christentum. 2003. *Volume 152.*

Klein, Hans: see *Dunn, James D.G.*

Kleinknecht, Karl Th.: Der leidende Gerechtfertigte. 1984, ²1988. *Volume II/13.*

Klinghardt, Matthias: Gesetz und Volk Gottes. 1988. *Volume II/32.*

Kloppenborg, John S.: The Tenants in the Vineyard. 2006. *Volume 195.*

Koch, Michael: Drachenkampf und Sonnenfrau. 2004. *Volume II/184.*

Koch, Stefan: Rechtliche Regelung von Konflikten im frühen Christentum. 2004. *Volume II/174.*

Köhler, Wolf-Dietrich: Rezeption des Matthäusevangeliums in der Zeit vor Irenäus. 1987. *Volume II/24.*

Köhn, Andreas: Der Neutestamentler Ernst Lohmeyer. 2004. *Volume II/180.*

Kooten, George H. van: Cosmic Christology in Paul and the Pauline School. 2003. *Volume II/171.*

Korn, Manfred: Die Geschichte Jesu in veränderter Zeit. 1993. *Volume II/51.*

Koskenniemi, Erkki: Apollonios von Tyana in der neutestamentlichen Exegese. 1994. *Volume II/61.*

– The Old Testament Miracle-Workers in Early Judaism. 2005. *Volume II/206.*

Kraus, Thomas J.: Sprache, Stil und historischer Ort des zweiten Petrusbriefes. 2001. *Volume II/136.*

Kraus, Wolfgang: Das Volk Gottes. 1996. *Volume 85.*

Kraus, Wolfgang and *Karl-Wilhelm Niebuhr* (Ed.): Frühjudentum und Neues Testament im Horizont Biblischer Theologie. 2003. *Volume 162.*

– see *Walter, Nikolaus.*

Kreplin, Matthias: Das Selbstverständnis Jesu. 2001. *Volume II/141.*

Kuhn, Karl G.: Achtzehngebet und Vaterunser und der Reim. 1950. *Volume 1.*

Kvalbein, Hans: see *Ådna, Jostein.*

Kwon, Yon-Gyong: Eschatology in Galatians. 2004. *Volume II/183.*

Laansma, Jon: I Will Give You Rest. 1997. *Volume II/98.*

Labahn, Michael: Offenbarung in Zeichen und Wort. 2000. *Volume II/117.*

Lambers-Petry, Doris: see *Tomson, Peter J.*

Lange, Armin: see *Ego, Beate.*

Lampe, Peter: Die stadtrömischen Christen in den ersten beiden Jahrhunderten. 1987, [2]1989. *Volume II/18.*

Landmesser, Christof: Wahrheit als Grundbegriff neutestamentlicher Wissenschaft. 1999. *Volume 113.*

– Jüngerberufung und Zuwendung zu Gott. 2000. *Volume 133.*

Lau, Andrew: Manifest in Flesh. 1996. *Volume II/86.*

Lawrence, Louise: An Ethnography of the Gospel of Matthew. 2003. *Volume II/165.*

Lee, Aquila H.I.: From Messiah to Preexistent Son. 2005. *Volume II/192.*

Lee, Pilchan: The New Jerusalem in the Book of Relevation. 2000. *Volume II/129.*

Lichtenberger, Hermann: Das Ich Adams und das Ich der Menschheit. 2004. *Volume 164.*

– see *Avemarie, Friedrich.*

Lierman, John: The New Testament Moses. 2004. *Volume II/173.*

Lieu, Samuel N.C.: Manichaeism in the Later Roman Empire and Medieval China. [2]1992. *Volume 63.*

Lindgård, Fredrik: Paul's Line of Thought in 2 Corinthians 4:16-5:10. 2004. *Volume II/189.*

Loader, William R.G.: Jesus' Attitude Towards the Law. 1997. *Volume II/97.*

Löhr, Gebhard: Verherrlichung Gottes durch Philosophie. 1997. *Volume 97.*

Löhr, Hermut: Studien zum frühchristlichen und frühjüdischen Gebet. 2003. *Volume 160.*

– see *Hengel, Martin.*

Löhr, Winrich Alfried: Basilides und seine Schule. 1995. *Volume 83.*

Luomanen, Petri: Entering the Kingdom of Heaven. 1998. *Volume II/101.*

Luz, Ulrich: see *Dunn, James D.G.*

Mackay, Ian D.: John's Raltionship with Mark. 2004. *Volume II/182.*

Maier, Gerhard: Mensch und freier Wille. 1971. *Volume 12.*

– Die Johannesoffenbarung und die Kirche. 1981. *Volume 25.*

Markschies, Christoph: Valentinus Gnosticus? 1992. *Volume 65.*

Marshall, Peter: Enmity in Corinth: Social Conventions in Paul's Relations with the Corinthians. 1987. *Volume II/23.*

Mayer, Annemarie: Sprache der Einheit im Epheserbrief und in der Ökumene. 2002. *Volume II/150.*

Mayordomo, Moisés: Argumentiert Paulus logisch? 2005. *Volume 188.*

McDonough, Sean M.: YHWH at Patmos: Rev. 1:4 in its Hellenistic and Early Jewish Setting. 1999. *Volume II/107.*

McDowell, Markus: Prayers of Jewish Women. 2006. *Volume II/211.*

McGlynn, Moyna: Divine Judgement and Divine Benevolence in the Book of Wisdom. 2001. *Volume II/139.*

Meade, David G.: Pseudonymity and Canon. 1986. *Volume 39.*

Meadors, Edward P.: Jesus the Messianic Herald of Salvation. 1995. *Volume II/72.*

Meißner, Stefan: Die Heimholung des Ketzers. 1996. *Volume II/87.*

Mell, Ulrich: Die „anderen" Winzer. 1994. *Volume 77.*

Mengel, Berthold: Studien zum Philipperbrief. 1982. *Volume II/8.*

Merkel, Helmut: Die Widersprüche zwischen den Evangelien. 1971. *Volume 13.*

– see *Ego, Beate.*

Merklein, Helmut: Studien zu Jesus und Paulus. Volume 1 1987. *Volume 43.* – Volume 2 1998. *Volume 105.*

Metzdorf, Christina: Die Tempelaktion Jesu. 2003. *Volume II/168.*

Metzler, Karin: Der griechische Begriff des Verzeihens. 1991. *Volume II/44.*

Metzner, Rainer: Die Rezeption des Matthäusevangeliums im 1. Petrusbrief. 1995. *Volume II/74.*

– Das Verständnis der Sünde im Johannesevangelium. 2000. *Volume 122.*

Mihoc, Vasile: see *Dunn, James D.G.*

Mineshige, Kiyoshi: Besitzverzicht und Almosen bei Lukas. 2003. *Volume II/163.*

Mittmann, Siegfried: see *Hengel, Martin.*

Mittmann-Richert, Ulrike: Magnifikat und Benediktus. *1996. Volume II/90.*
Mournet, Terence C.: Oral Tradition and Literary Dependency. 2005. *Volume II/195.*
Mußner, Franz: Jesus von Nazareth im Umfeld Israels und der Urkirche. Ed. von M. Theobald. 1998. *Volume 111.*
Mutschler, Bernhard: Das Corpus Johanneum bei Irenäus von Lyon. 2005. *Volume 189.*
Niebuhr, Karl-Wilhelm: Gesetz und Paränese. 1987. *Volume II/28.*
– Heidenapostel aus Israel. 1992. *Volume 62.*
– see *Deines, Roland*
– see *Dimitrov, Ivan Z.*
– see *Kraus, Wolfgang*
Nielsen, Anders E.: "Until it is Fullfilled". 2000. *Volume II/126.*
Nissen, Andreas: Gott und der Nächste im antiken Judentum. 1974. *Volume 15.*
Noack, Christian: Gottesbewußtsein. 2000. *Volume II/116.*
Noormann, Rolf: Irenäus als Paulusinterpret. 1994. *Volume II/66.*
Novakovic, Lidija: Messiah, the Healer of the Sick. 2003. *Volume II/170.*
Obermann, Andreas: Die christologische Erfüllung der Schrift im Johannesevangelium. 1996. *Volume II/83.*
Öhler, Markus: Barnabas. 2003. *Volume 156.*
– see *Becker, Michael*
Okure, Teresa: The Johannine Approach to Mission. 1988. *Volume II/31.*
Onuki, Takashi: Heil und Erlösung. 2004. *Volume 165.*
Oropeza, B. J.: Paul and Apostasy. 2000. *Volume II/115.*
Ostmeyer, Karl-Heinrich: Kommunikation mit Gott und Christus. 2006. *Volume 197.*
– Taufe und Typos. 2000. *Volume II/118.*
Paulsen, Henning: Studien zur Literatur und Geschichte des frühen Christentums. Ed. von Ute E. Eisen. 1997. *Volume 99.*
Pao, David W.: Acts and the Isaianic New Exodus. 2000. *Volume II/130.*
Park, Eung Chun: The Mission Discourse in Matthew's Interpretation. 1995. *Volume II/81.*
Park, Joseph S.: Conceptions of Afterlife in Jewish Insriptions. 2000. *Volume II/121.*
Pate, C. Marvin: The Reverse of the Curse. 2000. *Volume II/114.*
Peres, Imre: Griechische Grabinschriften und neutestamentliche Eschatologie. 2003. *Volume 157.*
Philip, Finny: The Origins of Pauline Pneumatology. 2005. *Volume II/194.*
Philonenko, Marc (Ed.): Le Trône de Dieu. 1993. *Volume 69.*
Pilhofer, Peter: Presbyteron Kreitton. 1990. *Volume II/39.*

– Philippi. Volume 1 1995. *Volume 87.* – Volume 2 2000. *Volume 119.*
– Die frühen Christen und ihre Welt. 2002. *Volume 145.*
– see *Becker, Eve-Marie.*
– see *Ego, Beate.*
Pitre, Brant: Jesus, the Tribulation, and the End of the Exile. 2005. *Volume II/204.*
Plümacher, Eckhard: Geschichte und Geschichten. 2004. *Volume 170.*
Pöhlmann, Wolfgang: Der Verlorene Sohn und das Haus. 1993. *Volume 68.*
Pokorný, Petr and *Josef B. Souèek:* Bibelauslegung als Theologie. 1997. *Volume 100.*
Pokorný, Petr and *Jan Roskovec* (Ed.): Philosophical Hermeneutics and Biblical Exegesis. 2002. *Volume 153.*
Popkes, Enno Edzard: Die Theologie der Liebe Gottes in den johanneischen Schriften. 2005. *Volume II/197.*
Porter, Stanley E.: The Paul of Acts. 1999. *Volume 115.*
Prieur, Alexander: Die Verkündigung der Gottesherrschaft. 1996. *Volume II/89.*
Probst, Hermann: Paulus und der Brief. 1991. *Volume II/45.*
Räisänen, Heikki: Paul and the Law. 1983, ²1987. *Volume 29.*
Rehkopf, Friedrich: Die lukanische Sonderquelle. 1959. *Volume 5.*
Rein, Matthias: Die Heilung des Blindgeborenen (Joh 9). 1995. *Volume II/73.*
Reinmuth, Eckart: Pseudo-Philo und Lukas. 1994. *Volume 74.*
Reiser, Marius: Syntax und Stil des Markusevangeliums. 1984. *Volume II/11.*
Rhodes, James N.: The Epistle of Barnabas and the Deuteronomic Tradition. 2004. *Volume II/188.*
Richards, E. Randolph: The Secretary in the Letters of Paul. 1991. *Volume II/42.*
Riesner, Rainer: Jesus als Lehrer. 1981, ³1988. *Volume II/7.*
– Die Frühzeit des Apostels Paulus. 1994. *Volume 71.*
Rissi, Mathias: Die Theologie des Hebräerbriefs. 1987. *Volume 41.*
Roskovec, Jan: see *Pokorný, Petr.*
Röhser, Günter: Metaphorik und Personifikation der Sünde. 1987. *Volume II/25.*
Rose, Christian: Die Wolke der Zeugen. 1994. *Volume II/60.*
Rothschild, Clare K.: Baptist Traditions and Q. 2005. *Volume 190.*
– Luke Acts and the Rhetoric of History. 2004. *Volume II/175.*
Rüegger, Hans-Ulrich: Verstehen, was Markus erzählt. 2002. *Volume II/155.*
Rüger, Hans Peter: Die Weisheitsschrift aus der Kairoer Geniza. 1991. *Volume 53.*

Sänger, Dieter: Antikes Judentum und die My-
sterien. 1980. *Volume II/5.*
– Die Verkündigung des Gekreuzigten und
Israel. 1994. *Volume 75.*
– see *Burchard, Christoph*
Salier, Willis Hedley: The Rhetorical Impact of
the Se-meia in the Gospel of John. 2004.
Volume II/186.
Salzmann, Jorg Christian: Lehren und Er-
mahnen. 1994. *Volume II/59.*
Sandnes, Karl Olav: Paul – One of the
Prophets? 1991. *Volume II/43.*
Sato, Migaku: Q und Prophetie. 1988.
Volume II/29.
Schäfer, Ruth: Paulus bis zum Apostelkonzil.
2004. *Volume II/179.*
Schaper, Joachim: Eschatology in the Greek
Psalter. 1995. *Volume II/76.*
Schimanowski, Gottfried: Die himmlische Li-
turgie in der Apokalypse des Johannes.
2002. *Volume II/154.*
– Weisheit und Messias. 1985. *Volume II/17.*
Schlichting, Günter: Ein jüdisches Leben Jesu.
1982. *Volume 24.*
Schnabel, Eckhard J.: Law and Wisdom from
Ben Sira to Paul. 1985. *Volume II/16.*
Schnelle, Udo: see *Frey, Jörg.*
Schröter, Jens: see *Frey, Jörg.*
Schutter, William L.: Hermeneutic and Com-
position in I Peter. 1989. *Volume II/30.*
Schwartz, Daniel R.: Studies in the Jewish
Background of Christianity. 1992.
Volume 60.
Schwemer, Anna Maria: see *Hengel, Martin*
Scott, Ian W.: Implicit Epistemology in the
Letters of Paul. 2005. *Volume II/205.*
Scott, James M.: Adoption as Sons of God.
1992. *Volume II/48.*
– Paul and the Nations. 1995. *Volume 84.*
Shum, Shiu-Lun: Paul's Use of Isaiah in Ro-
mans. 2002. *Volume II/156.*
Siegert, Folker: Drei hellenistisch-jüdische
Predigten. Teil I 1980. *Volume 20* – Teil II
1992. *Volume 61.*
– Nag-Hammadi-Register. 1982. *Volume 26.*
– Argumentation bei Paulus. 1985. *Volume 34.*
– Philon von Alexandrien. 1988. *Volume 46.*
Simon, Marcel: Le christianisme antique
et son contexte religieux I/II. 1981.
Volume 23.
Snodgrass, Klyne: The Parable of the Wicked
Tenants. 1983. *Volume 27.*
Söding, Thomas: Das Wort vom Kreuz. 1997.
Volume 93.
– see *Thüsing, Wilhelm.*
Sommer, Urs: Die Passionsgeschichte des
Markusevangeliums. 1993. *Volume II/58.*
Souček, Josef B.: see *Pokorný, Petr.*
Spangenberg, Volker: Herrlichkeit des Neuen
Bundes. 1993. *Volume II/55.*

Spanje, T.E. van: Inconsistency in Paul?
1999. *Volume II/110.*
Speyer, Wolfgang: Frühes Christentum im an-
tiken Strahlungsfeld. Volume I: 1989.
Volume 50.
– Volume II: 1999. *Volume 116.*
Stadelmann, Helge: Ben Sira als Schriftge-
lehrter. 1980. *Volume II/6.*
Stenschke, Christoph W.: Luke's Portrait of
Gentiles Prior to Their Coming to Faith.
Volume II/108.
Sterck-Degueldre, Jean-Pierre: Eine Frau na-
mens Lydia. 2004. *Volume II/176.*
Stettler, Christian: Der Kolosserhymnus.
2000. *Volume II/131.*
Stettler, Hanna: Die Christologie der Pastoral-
briefe. 1998. *Volume II/105.*
Stökl Ben Ezra, Daniel: The Impact of Yom
Kippur on Early Christianity. 2003.
Volume 163.
Strobel, August: Die Stunde der Wahrheit.
1980. *Volume 21.*
Stroumsa, Guy G.: Barbarian Philosophy.
1999. *Volume 112.*
Stuckenbruck, Loren T.: Angel Veneration and
Christology. 1995. *Volume II/70.*
Stuhlmacher, Peter (Ed.): Das Evangelium und
die Evangelien. 1983. *Volume 28.*
– Biblische Theologie und Evangelium.
2002. *Volume 146.*
Sung, Chong-Hyon: Vergebung der Sünden.
1993. *Volume II/57.*
Tajra, Harry W.: The Trial of St. Paul. 1989.
Volume II/35.
– The Martyrdom of St.Paul. 1994.
Volume II/67.
Theißen, Gerd: Studien zur Soziologie des Ur-
christentums. 1979, ³1989. *Volume 19.*
Theobald, Michael: Studien zum Römerbrief.
2001. *Volume 136.*
Theobald, Michael: see *Mußner, Franz.*
Thornton, Claus-Jürgen: Der Zeuge des Zeu-
gen. 1991. *Volume 56.*
Thüsing, Wilhelm: Studien zur neutestamentli-
chen Theologie. Ed. von Thomas Söding.
1995. *Volume 82.*
Thurén, Lauri: Derhethorizing Paul. 2000.
Volume 124.
Tolmie, D. Francois: Persuading the Galatians.
2005. *Volume II/190.*
Tomson, Peter J. and *Doris Lambers-Petry*
(Ed.): The Image of the Judaeo-Christians
in Ancient Jewish and Christian Literature.
2003. *Volume 158.*
Trebilco, Paul: The Early Christians in Ephesus
from Paul to Ignatius. 2004. *Volume 166.*
Treloar, Geoffrey R.: Lightfoot the Historian.
1998. *Volume II/103.*
Tsuji, Manabu: Glaube zwischen Vollkommen-
heit und Verweltlichung. 1997. *Volume II/93.*

Sänger, Dieter: Antikes Judentum und die My-sterien. 1980. *Volume II/5.*
– Die Verkündigung des Gekreuzigten und Israel. 1994. *Volume 75.*
– see *Burchard, Christoph*
Salier, Willis Hedley: The Rhetorical Impact of the Se-meia in the Gospel of John. 2004. *Volume II/186.*
Salzmann, Jorg Christian: Lehren und Er-mahnen. 1994. *Volume II/59.*
Sandnes, Karl Olav: Paul – One of the Prophets? 1991. *Volume II/43.*
Sato, Migaku: Q und Prophetie. 1988. *Volume II/29.*
Schäfer, Ruth: Paulus bis zum Apostelkonzil. 2004. *Volume II/179.*
Schaper, Joachim: Eschatology in the Greek Psalter. 1995. *Volume II/76.*
Schimanowski, Gottfried: Die himmlische Li-turgie in der Apokalypse des Johannes. 2002. *Volume II/154.*
– Weisheit und Messias. 1985. *Volume II/17.*
Schlichting, Günter: Ein jüdisches Leben Jesu. 1982. *Volume 24.*
Schnabel, Eckhard J.: Law and Wisdom from Ben Sira to Paul. 1985. *Volume II/16.*
Schnelle, Udo: see *Frey, Jörg.*
Schröter, Jens: see *Frey, Jörg.*
Schutter, William L.: Hermeneutic and Com-position in I Peter. 1989. *Volume II/30.*
Schwartz, Daniel R.: Studies in the Jewish Background of Christianity. 1992. *Volume 60.*
Schwemer, Anna Maria: see *Hengel, Martin*
Scott, Ian W.: Implicit Epistemology in the Letters of Paul. 2005. *Volume II/205.*
Scott, James M.: Adoption as Sons of God. 1992. *Volume II/48.*
– Paul and the Nations. 1995. *Volume 84.*
Shum, Shiu-Lun: Paul's Use of Isaiah in Ro-mans. 2002. *Volume II/156.*
Siegert, Folker: Drei hellenistisch-jüdische Predigten. Teil I 1980. *Volume 20* – Teil II 1992. *Volume 61.*
– Nag-Hammadi-Register. 1982. *Volume 26.*
– Argumentation bei Paulus. 1985. *Volume 34.*
– Philon von Alexandrien. 1988. *Volume 46.*
Simon, Marcel: Le christianisme antique et son contexte religieux I/II. 1981. *Volume 23.*
Snodgrass, Klyne: The Parable of the Wicked Tenants. 1983. *Volume 27.*
Söding, Thomas: Das Wort vom Kreuz. 1997. *Volume 93.*
– see *Thüsing, Wilhelm.*
Sommer, Urs: Die Passionsgeschichte des Markusevangeliums. 1993. *Volume II/58.*
Souèek, Josef B.: see *Pokorný, Petr.*
Spangenberg, Volker: Herrlichkeit des Neuen Bundes. 1993. *Volume II/55.*

Spanje, T.E. van: Inconsistency in Paul? 1999. *Volume II/110.*
Speyer, Wolfgang: Frühes Christentum im an-tiken Strahlungsfeld. Volume I: 1989. *Volume 50.*
– Volume II: 1999. *Volume 116.*
Stadelmann, Helge: Ben Sira als Schriftge-lehrter. 1980. *Volume II/6.*
Stenschke, Christoph W.: Luke's Portrait of Gentiles Prior to Their Coming to Faith. *Volume II/108.*
Sterck-Degueldre, Jean-Pierre: Eine Frau na-mens Lydia. 2004. *Volume II/176.*
Stettler, Christian: Der Kolosserhymnus. 2000. *Volume II/131.*
Stettler, Hanna: Die Christologie der Pastoral-briefe. 1998. *Volume II/105.*
Stökl Ben Ezra, Daniel: The Impact of Yom Kippur on Early Christianity. 2003. *Volume 163.*
Strobel, August: Die Stunde der Wahrheit. 1980. *Volume 21.*
Stroumsa, Guy G.: Barbarian Philosophy. 1999. *Volume 112.*
Stuckenbruck, Loren T.: Angel Veneration and Christology. 1995. *Volume II/70.*
Stuhlmacher, Peter (Ed.): Das Evangelium und die Evangelien. 1983. *Volume 28.*
– Biblische Theologie und Evangelium. 2002. *Volume 146.*
Sung, Chong-Hyon: Vergebung der Sünden. 1993. *Volume II/57.*
Tajra, Harry W.: The Trial of St. Paul. 1989. *Volume II/35.*
– The Martyrdom of St.Paul. 1994. *Volume II/67.*
Theißen, Gerd: Studien zur Soziologie des Ur-christentums. 1979, ³1989. *Volume 19.*
Theobald, Michael: Studien zum Römerbrief. 2001. *Volume 136.*
Theobald, Michael: see *Mußner, Franz.*
Thornton, Claus-Jürgen: Der Zeuge des Zeu-gen. 1991. *Volume 56.*
Thüsing, Wilhelm: Studien zur neutestamentli-chen Theologie. Ed. von Thomas Söding. 1995. *Volume 82.*
Thurén, Lauri: Derhethorizing Paul. 2000. *Volume 124.*
Tolmie, D. Francois: Persuading the Galatians. 2005. *Volume II/190.*
Tomson, Peter J. and *Doris Lambers-Petry* (Ed.): The Image of the Judaeo-Christians in Ancient Jewish and Christian Literature. 2003. *Volume 158.*
Trebilco, Paul: The Early Christians in Ephesus from Paul to Ignatius. 2004. *Volume 166.*
Treloar, Geoffrey R.: Lightfoot the Historian. 1998. *Volume II/103.*
Tsuji, Manabu: Glaube zwischen Vollkommen-heit und Verweltlichung. 1997. *Volume II/93.*

Twelftree, Graham H.: Jesus the Exorcist. 1993. *Volume II/54.*

Urban, Christina: Das Menschenbild nach dem Johannesevangelium. 2001. *Volume II/137.*

Visotzky, Burton L.: Fathers of the World. 1995. *Volume 80.*

Vollenweider, Samuel: Horizonte neutestamentlicher Christologie. 2002. *Volume 144.*

Vos, Johan S.: Die Kunst der Argumentation bei Paulus. 2002. *Volume 149.*

Wagener, Ulrike: Die Ordnung des „Hauses Gottes". 1994. *Volume II/65.*

Wahlen, Clinton: Jesus and the Impurity of Spirits in the Synoptic Gospels. 2004. *Volume II/185.*

Walker, Donald D.: Paul's Offer of Leniency (2 Cor 10:1). 2002. *Volume II/152.*

Walter, Nikolaus: Praeparatio Evangelica. Ed. von Wolfgang Kraus und Florian Wilk. 1997. *Volume 98.*

Wander, Bernd: Gottesfürchtige und Sympathisanten. 1998. *Volume 104.*

Watts, Rikki: Isaiah's New Exodus and Mark. 1997. *Volume II/88.*

Wedderburn, A.J.M.: Baptism and Resurrection. 1987. *Volume 44.*

Wegner, Uwe: Der Hauptmann von Kafarnaum. 1985. *Volume II/14.*

Weissenrieder, Annette: Images of Illness in the Gospel of Luke. 2003. Volume II/164.

–, *Friederike Wendt* and *Petra von Gemünden* (Ed.): Picturing the New Testament. 2005. *Volume II/193.*

Welck, Christian: Erzählte ‚Zeichen'. 1994. *Volume II/69.*

Wendt, Friederike (Ed.): see *Weissenrieder, Annette.*

Wiarda, Timothy: Peter in the Gospels. 2000. *Volume II/127.*

Wifstrand, Albert: Epochs and Styles. 2005. *Volume 179.*

Wilk, Florian: see *Walter, Nikolaus.*

Williams, Catrin H.: I am He. 2000. *Volume II/113.*

Wilson, Walter T.: Love without Pretense. 1991. *Volume II/46.*

Wischmeyer, Oda: Von Ben Sira zu Paulus. 2004. *Volume 173.*

Wisdom, Jeffrey: Blessing for the Nations and the Curse of the Law. 2001. *Volume II/133.*

Wold, Benjamin G.: Women, Men, and Angels. 2005. *Volume II/2001.*

Wright, Archie T.: The Origin of Evil Spirits. 2005. *Volume II/198.*

Wucherpfennig, Ansgar: Heracleon Philologus. 2002. *Volume 142.*

Yeung, Maureen: Faith in Jesus and Paul. 2002. *Volume II/147.*

Zimmermann, Alfred E.: Die urchristlichen Lehrer. 1984, ²1988. *Volume II/12.*

Zimmermann, Johannes: Messianische Texte aus Qumran. 1998. *Volume II/104.*

Zimmermann, Ruben: Christologie der Bilder im Johannesevangelium. 2004. *Volume 171.*

– Geschlechtermetaphorik und Gottesverhältnis. 2001. *Volume II/122.*

Zumstein, Jean: see *Dettwiler, Andreas*

Zwiep, Arie W.: Judas and the Choice of Matthias. 2004. *Volume II/187.*

For a complete catalogue please write to the publisher
Mohr Siebeck • P.O. Box 2030 • D–72010 Tübingen/Germany
Up-to-date information on the internet at www.mohr.de